La Porte County
INDIANA

Early Probate Records
1833-1850

Compiled by
Harold Henderson, CG
Mary Leahy Wenzel
& Dorothy Germain Palmer

CLEARFIELD

Printed for Clearfield Company by
Genealogical Publishing Company
Baltimore, Maryland
2015

ISBN 978-0-8063-5733-1

Table of Contents

Introduction . . . 2

La Porte County, Indiana, Probate Order Book A . . . 5

La Porte County, Indiana, Probate Complete Record [Book] A . . . 82

La Porte County, Indiana, Probate "Loose Papers" . . . 197

Index . . . 255

Introduction

Everybody dies. Many have probates. A few leave wills. Therefore, all serious genealogists consult probate records in their research. Probate transmits property from one generation to the next. Its records frequently state relationships and reveal everyday matters found nowhere else.

This book contains information from the earliest probate records for La Porte County, Indiana:

(A) Probate Order Book A, which tracks the daily activities of the probate court as recorded by its clerk. These cases begin in 1833 and end in 1842.

(B) Probate Complete Record [Book] A, which gives full accounts of some of the completed probate cases once they finish, including clerk's copies of some of the material submitted to the court in the process. These cases begin in 1833 and end in 1848.

(C) The first roll of microfilmed "loose papers" or "probate packets" that were submitted to the court during the probate process, including administrator's reports, receipts, bills, inventories, sales, bonds, letters, and more. These are usually original papers with the original signatures. These cases begin in 1836 and end in 1850.

Due to the different nature of these three sources -- order book, complete record book, and loose papers – they are not synchronized with each other. Additional material on continuing cases may be found in Order Book B, Complete Record B, or the second estates microfilm of loose papers in the La Porte County Circuit Court Clerk's office. Also, the three records often overlap, recording some of the same material in some of the same cases. But some probates appear in only one or two of these records and not the other(s). Each source contains information not found elsewhere.

La Porte County also has will books into which clerks copied the original wills presented in court. The county's first will book was abstracted some years ago by Dorothy Rowley. Her book, *La Porte County, Indiana, Abstract of Wills from Book A,* is available in the three major Midwestern genealogy repositories -- the Newberry Library in Chicago, the Allen County Public Library Genealogy Center in Fort Wayne, and the State Historical Society of Wisconsin in Madison --

and in the library of the La Porte County Historical Society. We have not duplicated Rowley's work. But the county apparently did not begin creating these volumes until about 1840, after many of the probate cases recorded in our three sources. We have made note of original wills mentioned or included in our sources.

Our combined index makes it easy for researchers to check on all three sources at once, and the abstracts give a good idea of what may be found in them. However, it is always good practice to consult the original records before drawing genealogical conclusions, especially when those conclusions rest on hard-to-read words or passages.

We have indexed all the names in the order book and complete record, except for judges, clerks, and attorneys serving in those capacities. In the loose papers we have indexed the names of all decedents, heirs, administrators, buyers at the estate sales, those providing security (bail), and those who signed decipherable names. We have also indexed place names other than La Porte County. Unless otherwise stated, all counties mentioned with no state are in Indiana, and all places with no county mentioned are in La Porte County.

Names in **bold type** in the index are either deceased or those petitioning or appearing before the court. We have spelled names as we deciphered them, even when they were inconsistent or possibly inaccurate. Spelling in the early 1800s was not standardized, and in any case many people were illiterate. Alternative readings are given with slashes / in between; questionable readings have a question mark.

Our index is not infallible. Even if it were infallible, readers would still need to check for variant spellings, especially including variants that begin with different letters. We were abstracting and indexing. We *did not* attempt to do the genealogical task of figuring out which similar names referred to the same person and which referred to different people, nor did we add any other information from any other source or from personal knowledge.

Obviously the main use of this book is to learn about the decedents. But this book also points to information about many people who did not die or leave probates during this time. Their presence in the record, their purchases at estate sales, their signatures on court documents, and other items offer clues about their lives and their relatives. They may even provide evidence for a La Porte County residency certificate (http://www.rootsweb.ancestry.com/~inlcigs/categories.htm)!

For those who are puzzled:

* Old legal terms are defined in John Bouvier, *A Law Dictionary Adapted to the Constitution and Laws of the United States*, revised 6th ed. (1856); digital images, *Constitution Society* (http://www.constitution.org/bouv/bouvier.htm : viewed 14 May 2014).

* Land descriptions under the rectangular survey system are briefly explained at the U.S. Department of Interior's Bureau of Land Management website under General Land Office Records, "Rectangular Survey System" (http://www.glorecords.blm.gov/reference/default.aspx#id=05_Appendices|03_Rectangular_Survey_System : viewed 14 May 2014). La Porte County includes congressional townships from 38 North to 33 North, and ranges from 4 West to 1 West, with Michigan Township (T38N R4W) in the northwest corner. (Since the county is not a rectangle, on the east and south some land with these descriptions falls into St. Joseph and Starke counties.) The David Rumsey Map Collection includes an 1876 map of the county including township, range, and section numbers as well as the named civil townships, enabling us to locate land descriptions (http://www.davidrumsey.com/maps790021-22997.html : viewed 14 May 2014).

* The word "note" in this time and place often referred to an IOU or note of indebtedness. In the early days when cash was scarce the creditor might "assign" a note to someone else as a form of payment.

We thank the staff of the La Porte County Clerk's office for their help, forbearance, and giving us space to work. The La Porte County Genealogical Society brought us together, and fellow members helped us learn the ropes of abstracting and indexing. All authors' royalties for this book will be given to the society.

Dorothy Germain Palmer (Probate Order Book A)

Mary Leahy Wenzel (Probate Complete Record [Book] A)

Harold Henderson, CG (Probate "Loose Papers")

La Porte County, Indiana, Probate Order Book A

REEVES, James Madison   **Estate**

Book, Page	POB A: 2-12; 17-18; 31; 32
Court Dates	11 Feb 1833 (Letters of Administration); 13 May 1833, 14 May 1833, 15 May 1833 (Inventory), 12 Aug 1833 (Sale Bill), 10 Feb 1834, 17 Mar 1834, 12 May 1834, 12 Nov 1834; 10 Nov 1835; 11 Nov 1835
Administrator	Martin BAKER
Heirs	Josiah REEVES; Catherine REEVES
Action	Letters of Administration ordered. Citation issued to the Administrator asking him to appear and show why he has not filed an inventory of the personal estate, or declared whether the estate is solvent, and given additional bond. Inventory filed. Martin BAKER appointed guardian of persons and estates of infant heirs, Josiah REEVES and Catherine REEVES, $700 Bond. Not enough money realized in sale of personal property for sustenance and maintenance of infant heirs. Land is sold. Additional Bond $600. Final settlement. Citation issued for guardian to again come to court to render account and provide additional security.
Incidental Names	Jacob MILLER & Joseph LEAMING, Associate Judges, Probate Court; George THOMAS, Clerk of Probate Court; Adam G. POLKE, Sheriff of La Porte County; Benjamin McCARTY, Judge of Probate Court; John WILLS & John DRULINER, Appraisers; Israel RUSH, Justice of the Peace, St. Joseph County, Indiana; L. H. TAYLOR, Clerk of St. Joseph County Circuit Court; David DINWIDDIE, Acting Deputy Sheriff of La Porte County; Ezekiel PROVALT (also Justice of the Peace), Wilson MALONE, Charles MOWLAN (?), Alex BLACKBURN, Gamailel DRULINER, W. BROWN, M. SAILSBURY, Nathan B. NICHOLS, Aaron LUCAS, Levi BROWN, Jesse McLEAN, Personal Property buyers; Hiram RUSH, Clerk; Israel MARKHAM, & Richard HARRIS, Security; David EVANS, Chapel W. BROWN, Charles IVES, Land Appraisers; James HIGHLY & John CISSNE, Security; Arthur McCLURE, Commissioner of Land Sale.
Comments	Letters granted "In Vacation". 1st case in La Porte County Probate Court held at home of George THOMAS, no courthouse having been yet built and Thomas' home being near the center of La Porte County. This case was advertised in the ST. JOSEPH BEACON and appraised in St. Joseph County, Indiana.

MIX, Jay   **Guardianship**

Book, Page	POB A:9-10
Court Dates	17 Mar 1834

Action	Application to Choose Guardian. Hiram TODD appointed Guardian of person and estate.
Incidental Names	A. P. ANDREW, Charles W. CATHCART, Abram W. HARRISON, Security
Comments	Estate value represented to be $600 or $700. Bond set at $2,000.

BLEVIN, Edward — Estate

Book, Page	POB A: 12; 15; 26; 35
Court Dates	13 Sep 1834 (Letters of Administration granted); 11 Nov 1834; 12 May 1835; 9 Feb 1835 (settlement)
Administrator	James BLEVIN, Robert C. BLEVIN
Action	Letters of Administration ordered and granted. Administrators along with James WALKER put up Security Bond. Inventory recorded. Administration settled.
Comments	Letters granted "In Vacation".

BALDWIN, Daniel Jr. — Estate

Book, Page	POB A: 12-13; 15; 239; 358-361
Court Dates	15 Sep 1834 (Will filed); 11 Nov 1834; 13 Nov 1839; 12 Nov 1840
Executor	Joel A. BALDWIN
Heirs	Joel BALDWIN, Reuben BALDWIN, Rhoda BALDWIN, and the children and heirs of Daniel BALDWIN, Jr. (deceased).
Action	Will filed. Executor appointed. Letters of Administration granted. Application for the appointment of a commissioner to convey real estate, William WALDRIFF, complaint. Court accepts that Waldriff had purchased the land prior to Baldwin's death, but, had not yet received title.
Incidental Names	Zenas PRESTON, Daniel MULKS, G. W. BARRIS, Will Witnesses; Preston & John RUPEL, Security. John H. BRADLEY appointed commissioner to execute conveyance of title of property on 2 Nov 1840 for which he is paid $3.
Comments	Publication of complaint in the LA PORTE HERALD ordered since heirs are not residents of Indiana in 1839.

BUNCE, Simon G. — Estate

Book, Page	POB A: 13; 15; 21-22; 23-25; 31; 34-38: 42; 99-100
Court Dates	18 Sep 1834 (will filed); 11 Nov 1834; 11 May 1835 (guardianships and bond); 10 Nov 1835: 9 Feb 1836 (settlement); 10 Feb 1836; 12 May 1836; 14 Feb 1838

Administrator	Clarissa BUNCE, John MALKS
Heirs	Harriet BUNCE, George L. BUNCE, William BUNCE; Lafayette BUNCE
Action	Letters of Administration granted. Administrators' oaths sworn, Clarissa BUNCE and Andrew BURNSIDE appointed guardians of persons and estates of minor children, Harriet BUNCE, George L. BUNCE, and William BUNCE, then enter bond of $1,000. Lot appraised. Lot sold $425. Purchaser, Robert MERRYFIELD, fails to comply with terms. Settlement. Appraisal and advertisement of lot 25. Lot sold, money delivered to guardian. Order of Distribution. Widow relinquished dower.
Incidental Names	Benoni M. NEWKIRK, security; Adam G. POLKE, security; John STOWN (?), William ALLEN, Albert LUCAS, appraisers; John BROWN, security
Comments	Letters granted "In Vacation". On settlement, Clarissa has remarried and is now Clarissa TEEPLE. Upon distribution, the widow is listed as "the guardian of Lafayette BUNCE, the only remaining heir of the said deceased".

AMBROZE, Ezekiel — Estate

Book, Page	POB A:13-14; 16; 26; 43-44
Court Dates	28 Oct 1834 (Will filed); 11 Nov 1834; 12 May 1835; 8 Aug 1836 (settlement)
Executor	Reason BELL
Action	Last Will and Testament filed. Letters Testamentary granted. Executor's oath sworn. Inventory filed. Settlement.
Incidental Names	Isaac MORGAN & Theadore JONES, Witnesses

CHE KAU KETCH — Heirship Petition

Book, Page	POB A: 16
Court Dates	11 Nov 1834
Heirs	MUPUCH (MUSSUCH), father
Action	CheKauKetch, a minor Indian child, died at the age of 7 yrs. His father, MUPUCH, is certified as his only heir-at-law to property granted to the child by the U.S. government in the treaty of 1826.
Incidental Names	John EGBERT made motion before court; Joseph BAY, witness.

WARD, Seth Edmund — Guardianship

Book, Page	POB A: 17
Court Dates	12 Nov 1834

Action	Application to Choose Guardian. John M. SIMON appointed Guardian.
Incidental Names	Seth Edmund WARD is the infant son of Seth WARD; Hass FREEHOLD, Security-$500.

LAFRAMBOISE, St. Antoine   Heirship Petition

Book, Page	POB A: 18
Court Dates	12 Nov 1834
Heirs	Globe LAFRAMBOISE, father
Action	St. Antoine died while still a minor. His father, Globe, is certified as his sole heir-at-law to property granted to the child by the U.S. government in the treaty of 1826.
Incidental Names	William C. HANNAH made motion before court; Prudence FULLER, witness. H. F. JAMES, acting Justice of the Peace, takes Fuller's deposition.

MISHEWAH/ NISWHEWAK   Heirship Petition

Book, Page	POB A: 19
Court Dates	12 Nov 1834
Heirs	NEGONCONE, father
Action	MISHEWAH died while still a minor. Her father, NEGONCONE, is certified as her sole heir-at-law to property granted to the child by the U.S. government in the treaty of 1826.
Incidental Names	Michael BRAND made motion before court; Prudence FULLER and Celicia (?) EMMONS, witnesses.
Comments	NESHEWAH is another spelling listed in Complete Probate Records on pgs. 630-632. Lists Michael BRAND as an Indian.

PARSONS, Solomon   Estate

Book, Page	POB A: 19: 20; 26; 34
Court Dates	26 Jan 1835 (Letters of Administration); 09 Feb 1835; 12 May 1835; 8 Feb 1836
Administrator	Lydia PARSONS, widow
Action	Letters of Administration granted. Oaths sworn. Inventory filed. Final Settlement.
Incidental Names	Rueben RAMBO entered into bond with Lydia.
Comments	Letters granted "In Vacation".

THOMAS, George   **Estate**

Book, Page	POB A: 20-21; 25-26; 46; 97-98; 106; 424
Court Dates	10 Mar 1835 (Letters of Administration), 12 May 1835; 9 Aug 1836; 16 Nov 1836: 13 Feb 1838; 16 May 1838; 14 Aug 1841
Administrator	Andrew BURNSIDE & William HAWKINS
Heirs	Adult Heirs: Elizabeth THOMAS (widow), John HEWS and Eleanor HEWS (his wife), Eleanor THOMAS, Willard BALL and Nancy BALL (his wife), Nancy THOMAS, Charles EGBERT and Mary EGBERT (his wife), Mary THOMAS.
	Infant heirs represented by guardian, Adam G. POLKE: Reynear THOMAS, Ruth Jane THOMAS, Perlina THOMAS, Joel THOMAS
Action	Letters of Administration granted. Administrators' oaths sworn. Inventory filed. Heirs summoned to show cause why real estate should not be sold to cover debts. Widow objects. Order of Sale of Real Estate. Report of Real Estate Sale. Settlement approved.
Incidental Names	Robert L. MORRISON, JP; Andrew BURNSIDE, William HAWKINS, Adam G. POLKE, entered into Bond. Jacob WAGNER bought real estate for $380 on 31 Mar 1838.
Comments	Balance at final settlement was $108.47, to be disposed of agreeably to the statutes after deducting the expense of settlement.

WE SAW WE   **Heirship Petition**

Book, Page	POB A:23
Court Date	12 May 1835
Heirs	SHICK KOG WISH SHE QUA, mother; MIN NAH CHE QUES MO QUA & WA WAS MO QUA, sisters
Action	WE SAW WE was granted a quarter section of land in the Wabash Treaty of 1826. He has since died. His mother and sisters are certified as his Heirs.
Incidental Names	Prudence J. FULLER & Celicia EMMONS, deposed by Henry F. Sams, J.P.
Comments	WE SAW WE was a student at the Cary Mission School from 1823-25. Further mention in Complete Probate Record, p. 632.

DOWNING, Nathaniel R.   **Estate**

Book, Page	POB A: 27-28
Court Dates	27 Jun 1835 (Letters of Administration granted); 10 Aug 1835 (Letters of Administration revoked)
Administrator	Catherine DOWNING, Jonathan D. MIDDLETON

Action	Letters of Administration granted. Bond set. Petition for revocation of letters of administration granted.
Incidental Names	Administrators along with Henry DAVIS enter into bond.
Comments	Letters granted "In Vacation".

ARMSTRONG James   Estate

Book, Page	POB A:28; 29; 36; 51; 54; 60; 62; 74; 78; 86; 88-89; 101-102; 109; 112-113; 257
Court Dates	28 Sep 1835 (Letters of Administration granted); 9 Nov 1835: 10 Feb 1836; 3 Oct 1836 (this proceeding is X'd out); 14 Nov 1836 (Mudge case filed); 13 Feb 1837; 11 May 1837; 14 Aug 1837; 17 Aug 1837; 13 Nov 1837; 14 Feb 1838; 17 May 1838; 14 Aug 1838; 16 Nov 1839
Administrator	Robert MERRYFIELD
Heirs	Thomas K. ARMSTRONG; Robert V. ARMSTRONG; Samuel H. ARMSTRONG; Rebecca I. C. ARMSTRONG; James ARMSTRONG; and the infant heir-at-law, Aaron ARMSTRONG.
Action	Letters of Administration granted. Bond set. Inventory and appraisement filed. Enoch MUDGE files suit against estate for payment of Debt on Five Promissory Notes in the total of $1128.63. Debts settled. Sale bill recorded. Application to sell real estate. Order of Sale of Real estate. Confirmation of sale & order of conveyance. Application for an additional sale of real estate. Confirmation of Sale and Order of Conveyance. Final settlement.
Incidental Names	The administrator along with Abraham W. HARRISON and William C. HANNAH entered into bond. Warren COLE bought ½ lot in Michigan City for $460 on 25 Sep 1837. Isaac HULL and Nathaniel W. GOTT bought a tract of land from the estate for $670.25 on 28 Jul 1838.
Comments	A case involving Enoch MUDGE vs. the administrator involving a note executed by the deceased during his lifetime is X'd out on 3 Oct 1836, filed later. Citation to Floyd County, 15 Jun 1837. Personal estate was insufficient for the payment of debts. 80 additional acres put up for sale to pay debts. On final settlement the administrator has paid out $31.21 more than the amount of assets.

FOSDICK, Timothy   Estate

Book, Page	POB A: 28-29; 30; 66; 80-81; 96-97
Court Dates	21 Oct 1835 (Letters of Administration granted); 9 Nov 1835; 8 May 1837; 15 Aug 1837; 12 Feb 1838
Administrator	Robert S. MORRISON & William CLARK
Action	Letters of Administration granted. Oaths sworn. Bond set. Inventory put on record. Order of Sale of Real estate. Confirmation of Sale and Order of Conveyance.

Incidental Names	Administrators, along with James WHITTEN, security. Aaron STANTON and Robert S. MORRISON, holders of Title bonds for land.
Comments	11 Mar 1837 inventory was filed by "surviving" administrator, William CLARK. Widow relinquished dower. Land sold to James WHITTEN on 25 Oct 1837 for $360.

SWOPE, Wilson — Estate

Book, Page	POB A: 29; 30; 33; 41; 50; 55: 131
Court Dates	7 Nov 1835 (Letters of Administration granted); 9 Nov 1835; 8 Feb 1836; 12 May 1836; 11 Aug 1836; 13 Nov 1838
Administrator	Jonathon LINE
Heirs	Michael SWOPE of Wayne County; Matilda SWOPE, widow
Action	Letters of Administration granted. Bond set. Application to sell real estate. Final Settlement.
Incidental Names	Administrator with Asbury SWOPE, security; HANNAH, attorney
Comments	Personal estate insufficient to pay debts, court asks that land be sold to pay debts. Widow files cause why real estate should not be sold.

BARTHLOLOMEW, Stephen — Estate

Book, Page	POB A: 32; 38; 50; 57; 71; 110; 112
Court Dates	14 Nov 1835 (Letters of Administration granted); 10 Feb 1836; 11 Aug 1836; 17 Nov 1836; 17 May 1838; 14 Aug 1838
Administrator	Jeremiah BARTHOLOMEW
Action	Letters of Administration granted. Bond set. Administrator cited to appear to file inventory and appraisement bill. Possibly issued a warrant through the sheriff of Porter County. Appraisement and sale bill for personal estate filed. Administrator cited to make final settlement. Final settlement.
Incidental Names	Administrator, along with John BEBILES (?), security. $5 received of Judge JOHNSON in final settlement.
Comments	Letters granted "In Vacation". On final settlement, Administrator entitled to a credit of $253. 41 leaving a balance due him of $6.15.

WELCH, William A. — Estate

Book, Page	POB A: 32; 38; 219; 247
Court Dates	11 Jan 1836 (Letters of Administration granted); 10 Feb 1836; 17 Aug 1839; 14 Nov 1839
Administrator	John M. LEMON

Action	Letters of Administration granted. Administrator ordered to appear in court to file inventory and Sale Bill of said Estate and make final settlement. Account filed and approved.
Incidental Names	Robert SALLEVISON (?), security
Comments	Letters granted "In Vacation". Administrator paid $194.29 over and above the amounts of assets.

VANDALSEM, Henry   Estate

Book, Page	POB A: 39-40
Court Dates	10 May 1836 (Will Filed, Letters of Administration granted)
Executrix	Eunice VANDALSEM
Action	Letters of Administration granted
Incidental Names	Levi LUNPAS & Hugh REED, witnesses to the will as sworn to in an affidavit before Horatio MASON, JP from Fayette County, Indiana, and presented to Probate Court of La Porte County.
Comments	The deceased was from St. Joseph County.

SCHULTZ, John   Guardianship

Book, Page	POB A:40-41
Court Dates	11 May 1836 (Application for Guardianship)
Action	Jacob SCHULTZ appointed guardian.
Incidental Names	William WEST, security of $500.
Comments	John SCHULTZ is the minor son of Philip SCHULTZ.

BELKNAP, Charley (Charles)   Estate

Book, Page	POB A: 43; 46; 219
Court Dates	9 Jul 1836 (Letters of Administration granted); 9 Aug 1836; 17 Aug 1839
Administrator	Solomon OVERMEYER
Action	Letters of Administration granted, bond set. Letters confirmed. Administrator ordered to appear in court to file inventory and Sale Bill of said Estate and make final settlement.
Incidental Names	Administrator, along with Adam G. POLKE, entered into bond.
Comments	Letters granted "In Vacation".

KIMBERLY, Zenas   Estate

Book, Page	POB A: 44-45; 54-55; 219; 282; 562-563
Court Dates	8 Aug 1836 (Will Filed, Letters of Administration granted); 14 Nov 1836; 17 Aug 1839; 14 Feb 1840; 11 Aug 1842
Executors	Samuel MILLER & Francis Porterfield HARRISON. George W. KIMBERLY (son) replaced Samuel MILLER on 14 Nov 1836.
Heirs	Isabella KIMBERLY, Mary Ann McLAUGHLIN, Jeremiah KIMBERLY, Lucian P. KIMBERLY
Action	Will filed, Letters of Administration granted. Samuel MILLER resigns as executor, replaced by George W. KIMBERLY. Executors ordered to appear in court to make final settlement. Complaint filed against Executors. They are ordered to appear in court or "be taken as confessed".
Incidental Names	Benjamin WOODARD, witness; Executors with David DINWIDDIE, security. $1027.75 security provided by George W. MILLER.
Comments	Francis P. HARRISON, on 11 Aug 1842, is not a resident of the state. Notice of the pendency of Complain is to be published in the LA PORTE COUNTY WHIG.

ARMSTRONG, Thomas R.   Guardianship
ARMSTRONG, Robert V.
ARMSTRONG, Samuel H.
ARMSTRONG, Rebecca I. C.
ARMSTRONG, James

Book, Page	POB A: 45; 63
Court Dates	9 Aug 1836; 13 Feb 1837
Action	Application to chose a Guardian. Abram W. HARRISON appointed guardian. Revocation of grant of Letters of Guardianship.
Incidental Names	Guardian along with Robert MERRYFIELD and John CLARK enter into bond for $5,000.
Comments	Minor children appear with their mother, Elizabeth ARMSTRONG asking permission to choose a guardian. They are the heirs of James ARMSTRONG, deceased. Guardian appears in court and says that he intends "removing form the County of La Porte and wishes to be released".

THOMAS, Reynear   Guardianship
THOMAS, Ruth Jane
THOMAS, Perlina
THOMAS, Joel

Book, Page	POB A:47
Court Dates	9 Aug 1836

Action	Application to choose Guardian. Adam G. POLKE appointed Guardian.
Incidental Names	Guardian along with Seneca BALL enters into bond for $2,000.
Comments	Minor children appear with their mother, Elizabeth THOMAS, asking permission to choose a guardian. They are they are the heirs of George THOMAS, deceased.

MORRISON, Robert S.   Estate

Book, Page	POB A:48; 446; 504
Court Dates	10 Aug 1836 (Letters of Administration Granted); 12 Nov 1841; 19 Feb 1842
Administrator	Ezekiel MORRISON
Action	Petition to name administrator. Administrator ordered to appear and present final settlement. Final Settlement approved.
Incidental Names	Administrator along with John BROWN, Andrew BURNSIDE & Adam G. POLKE, security $10,000.
Comments	At final settlement the administrator "Respectfully Represents that soon after he took out Letters of administration on said estate, he purchased from his father, who was the only heir of said Estate, all the property and credits belonging to the same, and that he has since settled up and arranged all the business and paid all the debts of said Estate, so far as the same has come to his knowledge".

WELSH, William Alexander   Guardianship

Book, Page	POB A:48-49; 50
Court Dates	11 Aug 1836
Action	Petition to choose guardian. John M. LEMON named guardian. Application for sale of Real Estate on behalf of infant heir.
Incidental Names	Guardian and Thomas D. LEMON entered into bond for $2,000. Additional bond for $2,000 filed.
Comments	Sarah Ann WELCH, widow of William Alexander WELSH and mother of his infant heir, William Alexander WELSH brings petition to court.

EGANS/EAGANS, William   Estate

Book, Page	POB A:51; 55; 62; 282; 393; 403; 430; 445-446; 452; 478
Court Dates	26 Sep 1836 (Letters of Administration granted); 14 Nov 1836; 13 Feb 1837; 13 Feb 1841; 12 May 1841; 9 Nov 1841; 12 Nov 1841; 16 Feb 1842
Administrator	Jared CHAPMAN & John HEFNER

Action	Letters of Administration granted. Letters of Administration and appointment of Administrators confirmed. Inventory filed. Administrators notified to appear "and make final settlement" of the estate. Administrators again notified to appear to "make final settlement of said estate'. Administrators sued by Samuel EGANS/EAGANS. Plaintiff awarded $92 in damages. Administrators ordered to appear in court and give report. Partial settlement of account. Administrator Jared CHAPMAN cited to appear before Court to make final settlement of Estate. Sums of $22 and $349.78 credited to account of Administrators. Continued.
Incidental Names	Letters granted "In Vacation". Administrators, along with John BATILES, security.
Comments	See Samuel EGANS/EAGANS.

GILLISPIE, Hugh   Estate

Book, Page	POB A: 52: 55; 219
Court Dates	03 Oct 1836 (Letters of Administration granted); 14 Nov 1836; 17 Aug 1939
Administrators	Harriet GILLISPIE & Jabez R. WELLS
Action	Letters of Administration granted. Letters of Administration and appointment of Administrators confirmed. Administrators ordered to appear in court and file the inventory and Sale Bill of said estate and make final settlement.
Incidental Names	Samuel MILLER, Robert STEWART, and administrators, security
Comments	Letters granted "In Vacation".

TUBBS, Hiram   Guardianship

Book, Page	POB A:52
Court Dates	14 Nov 1836
Action	Application to chose a Guardian; Oliver PORTER appointed Guardian
Incidental Names	Applicant is minor son of Lemuel (Samuel?) TUBBS. Guardian, along with Abram W. HARRISON entered into bond with security of $500.

SMITH, John   Estate

Book, Page	POB A: 58; 66: 107; 345; 446; 612
Court Dates	23 Dec 1836 (Letters of Administration Granted); 13 Feb 1837; 8 May 1837; 16 May 1838; 15 Aug 1840; 12 Nov 1841; 19 Nov 1842
Administrator	Adam G. POLKE

Heirs	Rhoda SMITH, Minor heirs: Lester SMITH, Edwina SMITH, Samuel SMITH, Orion SMITH, Olson SMITH.
Action	Letters of Administration Granted. Letters confirmed. Inventory filed. Application for Sale of Real Estate. Continuance. Administrator ordered to appear in court to present final settlement. Adult heir defaults. John B. NILES, appointed Guardian ad Litem to minor heirs. Personal estate insufficient to pay debts. Land to be sold.
Incidental Names	Administrator entered into bond with David B. FREEMAN. Burcholl SPARBUCK, security on sale of real estate ($300). John HUNT.
Comments	Letters granted "In Vacation". Widow and heirs called to show cause why real estate should not be sold to pay debts of estate. Citation issued on heirs in Fayette County.

JUSTICE, Elizabeth   Guardianship

Book, Page	POB A: 59
Court Dates	13 Feb 1837
Action	Application to appoint Guardian of Person and Estate.
Incidental Names	James B. STEVENS appointed Guardian. He entered into bond of $1500 with Daniel BROWN.
Comments	Elizabeth is the infant daughter of William JUSTICE, late of Hancock County, Indiana.

BAY, Elizabeth   Guardianship

Book, Page	POB A: 61; 70-71; 82; 405
Court Dates	13 Feb 1837; 16 Aug 1837; 12 May 1841
Action	Application for appointment of a Guardian; Letter of Guardianship issued; Application to sell real estate. Appointment of Commissioner for sale of real estate. Petition to sell real estate. Security files application to be discharged of responsibility.
Incidental Names	Joseph BAY appointed guardian of estate of his infant daughter. John CISSNE, security $3,000. John WILLS, commissioner. James F. SMITH, Gabriel DRULLINGER, and James WILLS purchasers of land. James WILLS also later listed as security for Guardian along with Joseph W. LYKINS.
Comments	Township Thirty-Eight, Range One West. Joseph BAY has moved out of state and his Guardianship Security wish to be discharged from their responsibilities. Joseph is relieved from his duties as Guardian and ordered to appear in court to render an account of his guardianship. Elizabeth is listed as Joseph's infant heir.

CATOR, William H.   Estate

Book, Page	POB A: 64; 72; 92; 93; 100-101; 107-108; 450; 462; 518
Court Dates	13 Mar 1837 (Letters of Administration Granted); 10 May 1837; 15 Nov 1837; 16 Nov 1837; 14 Feb 1838; 16 May 1838; 12 Nov 1841; 14 Feb 1842; 9 May 1842
Administrator	Jacob DRUMM/DROM
Heirs	Jerimiah VAN NOCKER and his wife, Betsey VAN NOCKER, Calvin CATOR, Julia CATOR, Sally Maria CATOR.
Action	Letters of administration granted. Confirmation of grant of letters. Application for the sale of real estate. Notification of heirs ordered to appear in the Michigan City GAZETTE. Order of Sale of Real Estate. Confirmation of sale of real estate and order of conveyance. Administrator cited to appear before Court to make final settlement of Estate. Administrator asks for continuance. Granted. Administrator files affidavit for continuance. Granted.
Incidental Names	David DINWIDDIE, security.
Comments	Letters granted "In Vacation". Widow and heirs to be summoned to show cause, if any, why real estate should not be sold to pay outstanding debts against estate. The heirs listed are not residents of Indiana on 16 Nov 1837. Administrator buys real estate on 31 Mar 1838 for $1,492.50.

WOODARD, James   Estate

Book, Page	POB A: 64; 72
Court Dates	16 Mar 1837 (Letters of Administration Granted); 10 May 1837
Administrator	Margaret WOODARD (widow)
Action	Letters of administration granted. Confirmation of letters of administration.
Incidental Names	Senicus FOSTER, security
Comments	Letters granted "In Vacation".

JACKSON, Edmund   Estate

Book, Page	POB A: 65; 73; 190
Court Dates	30 Mar 1837 (Letters of Administration Granted); 10 May 1837; 14 May 1839
Administrator	Abigail JACKSON (widow) and John DRULLINER/ DRULLINGER/ DRULINER
Action	Letters of administration granted. Confirmation of letters of administration. Accounting produced. Additional account on settlement.
Incidental Names	John WILLS and Asher WHITE, security

Comments	Letters granted "In Vacation". Balance in final accounting $528.05, disposed of according to law. Administrators find an additional $184.74 for disbursement.

SOSWA · Heirship Petition

Book, Page	POB A: 66-67
Court Dates	9 May 1837
Heirs	ACHEMUKQUEI (brother) and SHESKO (sister)
Action	SOSWA died a minor at the age of 16. His brother and sister are declared his only heirs-at-law to receive property granted to SOSWA in the treaty of 1826.
Incidental Names	John WILLS, lawyer; Joseph BAY and Joseph W. LYKINS, witnesses.
Comments	The Indians named are members of the Pottawatomie tribe.

BURCH, Amanda · Guardianship

Book, Page	POB A: 67; 68; 69; 70; 85-86
Court Dates	9 May 1837; 17 Aug 1837
Action	Application for guardianship of person and estates of minor children. Application for sale of property. Appointment of Commissioner and terms for sale of property. Appraisal of property.
Incidental Names	Hetty BURCH, Washington BURCH, Perry BURCH, Lucy BURCH, William BURCH & Dewitt BURCH, minor children of Peter BURCH, deceased. Charles McCLURE and Abraham FRAVEL, Joseph W. LYKINS, James WELLS, A. M. MIRREN, appraisers. Daniel D. RUTHBRIN, appraiser and commissioner.
Comments	Amanda BURCH is the widow of Peter BURCH. Appraisal was signed 14 Feb 1837. Land was sold and money disbursed to Amanda, as guardian of children.

CLARK, Wilson B. · Estate

Book, Page	POB A: 75; 83; 105
Court Dates	7 July 1837 (Letters of Administration granted); 16 Aug 1837; 15 May 1838
Administrator	Elizabeth CLARK (widow)
Action	Letters of Administration granted; Confirmation of grant of letters; Settlement
Incidental Names	Charles MORROW (?), security
Comments	Letters granted "In Vacation". Remainder of $65.25 disposed of according to laws.

EAGANS/EGANS, Samuel   **Guardianship**

Book, Page	POB A: 76; 403; 515
Court Dates	14 Aug 1837; 12 May 1841; 9 May 1842
Action	Application to choose guardian, letters of guardianship issued. Guardian authorized to pay all moneys received by him as guardian and discharge of Guardians bond since Samuel is now of full age. Full settlement made and receipt given by Samuel to his guardian. Guardian discharged.
Incidental Names	John B. NILES appointed guardian. Robert MERRYFIELD, John HEFNER, & Adam G. POLKE, security $1200.
Comments	Samuel is the infant son of James EAGANS, late of Franklin County deceased. He reaches age of 21 by the May 1841 proceeding.

MUNGER, Gaius W.   **Guardianship**

Book, Page	POB A: 77; 84-85
Court Dates	14 Aug 1837; 17 Aug 1837
Action	Application for the appointment of a guardian. Letters of Guardianship issued. Application to sell real estate.
Incidental Names	Gaius MUNGER appointed guardian of his infant son. Charles McCLURE, security $1200. Horace B. HIBBARD & John W. COLE, appraisers.

FOSDICK, John Alfred   **Guardianship**
FOSDICK, James Arthur
FOSDICK, Mary Francis

Book, Page	POB A: 78
Court Dates	14 Aug 1837
Action	Application to choose a guardian. Letters of guardianship issued.
Incidental Names	William CLARK appointed guardian. Aaron STANTON, security $600.
Comments	Represented by Martha A. FOSDICK, their mother. Infant heirs of Timothy FOSDICK.

FOSDICK, Martha A.   **Petition for Dower**

Book, Page	POB A: 80
Court Dates	15 Aug 1837
Action	Martha A. FOSDICK, widow of Timothy FOSDICK relinquishes "her right and claim to dower" for "the use and benefit of the heirs".

THORTON, Austin   Guardianship
THORNTON, Sarah Jane
THORNTON, Louisa
THORNTON, Wesley C.
THORNTON, Elizabeth
THORNTON, Amanda

Book, Page	POB A: 81-82
Court Dates	15 Aug 1837
Action	Application to choose a guardian. Letters of guardianship issued.
Incidental Names	Elizabeth THORNTON, mother. Samuel ROBINSON appointed guardian. Abram W. HARRISON and Thomas ROBINSON, security $2400.
Comments	Infant heirs of William C. THORNTON, deceased.

PEASE, Enos   Estate

Book, Page	POB A: 87; 89-90; 150; 163-164; 202; 211-212: 240; 310; 446; 507; 536; 567-569; 579-580
Court Dates	30 Sep 1837 (Letters of Administration Granted); 14 Nov 1837; 16 Nov 1838; 12 Feb 1839; 17 May 1839; 14 Aug 1839; 14 Nov 1839; 14 May 1840; 12 Nov 1841; 19 Feb 1842; 12 May 1842; 11 Aug 1842; 14 Nov 1842
Administrator	Asa C. PEASE and Nathan B. NICHOLS
Heirs	Lucinda Ann PEASE, David H. PEASE (infant heirs), Isabella PEASE (widow), Alvln R. PEASE, Enos A. PEASE, Milton SATTERLEE & Artemisia R. SATTERLEE (formerly PEASE), Dennis STOW & Nancy A. STOW (formerly PEASE), Buenos A. PEASE, Orson SATTERLEE & Susan W. SATTERLEE (formerly PEASE), Asa C. PEASE
Action	Letters of administration granted. Confirmation of grant of letters of administration. Application to sell real estate. Order of Sale of Real Estate. Confirmation of Sale and Order of Conveyance. Further application to sell real estate. Application to sell real estate. Report of sale of real estate and order of confirmation. Nathan B. NICHOLS, appointed commissioner of sale of land. Administrator ordered to appear in court and make final settlement of estate. Administrator not prepared, cause continued. Heirs to be notified to show cause why land should not be sold to satisfy debts of estate. On Application of the sale of Real Estate. William ANDREW appointed Guardian Ad Litem of minor heirs, Lucinda and David. Adult heirs did not answer summons and are in default. Personal Estate is insufficient to pay debts. Administrators to proceed to sell real estate to cover debts. On application for the Sale of Real estate. One tract was sold; the other was not due to being encumbered by a mortgage for more than the tract's value.
Incidental Names	Abraham FRAVEL, security. Thomas N. SMITH bought a tract of land from the estate.

| Comments | Letters granted "In Vacation". Alvin, Enos, Artimisa and Nancy are nonresidents. Administrator ordered to advertise sale of real estate in the LA PORTE COUNTY WHIG. Real estate to be offered for sale on 20 March 1839. On 17 May 1839 real estate has been paid for except that owed by the School Commissioners, which would be paid after deed is conveyed. On 14 Aug 1839 Isabella, Alvin, Orson & Susan, Milton & Artemisia, Dennis & Nancy, and Enos are not residents of Indiana. Order to be again published in LA PORTE COUNTY WHIG. Buenos ordered to appear with other heirs on 2nd Monday of November to show cause why real estate should not be sold for the discharge of debts of the estate. |

FARMER, Emerson — Estate

Book, Page	POB A: 87; 90; 148; 493-494
Court Dates	6 Nov 1837 (Letters of Administration Granted); 14 Nov 1837; 15 Nov 1838; 18 Feb 1842
Administrator	Nancy Ann FARMER (widow), Letters of Administration revoked. George SAWIN, appointed.
Action	Letters of administration granted. Confirmation of Grant of Letters. Administrator ordered to appear during next term to file inventory, appraisment and sale bill. Revocation of Letters of Administration).
Incidental Names	Henry DAVIS, security; Richard B HEWS ($500)
Comments	Letters granted "In Vacation". As of 18 Feb 1842, Nancy had failed to act as administrator, remarried to William BAILEY and moved out of the county.

DAVIS, Nathaniel — Estate

Book, Page	POB A: 91
Court Dates	15 Nov 1837
Administrator	John C. DAVIS
Action	Application to be appointed Administrator granted.
Incidental Names	Henry FREDRICKSON, security $500.

DAVIS, Elizabeth Jane — Guardianship

Book, Page	POB A: 91-92
Court Dates	15 Nov 1837
Action	Application for the appointment of Guardian. Henry FREDRICKSON appointed guardian of the estate of Elizabeth.
Incidental Names	John Davis, her next friend. Thomas H. PHILIPS, security $300.
Comments	Elizabeth is the infant daughter of Nathaniel DAVIS.

BECKNER, John   **Estate**

Book, Page	POB A: 95; 98; 282: 304
Court Dates	In Vacation between November 1837 and February 1838 Term (Letters of Administration Granted); 13 Feb 1838; 14 Feb 184013 May 1840
Administrator	Elizabeth BECKNER (widow) and George S. STOVER
Action	Letters of Administration Granted. Confirmation of Grant of Letters. Administrators notified to appear in court to make final settlement. Final settlement.
Incidental Names	Jacob MILLER, security.
Comments	Balance of estate at settlement is $883.93.

WRIGHT, Alexander H.   **Estate**

Book, Page	POB A: 95; 99; 207: 276-277; 297; 299; 330-331; 353; 383-384; 505-506
Court Dates	5 Feb 1838 (Letters of Administration Granted); 13 Feb 1838; 12 August 1839; 12 Feb 1840; 11 May 1840; 11 Aug 1840; 10 Nov 1840; 10 Feb 1841; 19 Feb 1842
Administrator	Alonson W. ENOS
Heirs	Newell WRIGHT
Action	Letters of Administration Granted. Confirmation of Letters of Administration. Inventory and appraisement filed. Application to sell real estate. Application to Settle estate as Insolvent. Application for order to sell real estate. Application to sell real estate. More time granted on order to sell real estate. Report of Sale of Real Estate. Settlement of Estate.
Incidental Names	David SPRAGUE, Security
Comments	Newell WRIGHT is not a resident of Indiana on 12 Feb 1840. Estate is insolvent. "Property, both real and personal is insufficient to pay debts and demands outstanding against it". Newell does not respond to summons by publication. Land ordered to be sold to highest bidder following publication of sale. On final settlement, David SPRAGUE allowed $193.15, which is allowed and then denied. The administrator allowed credits of $376.12 and $478.81.

FOSTER, Seneca   **Estate**

Book, Page	POB A: 102; 103; 127; 174-75; 187; 201; 232-234; 285-287; 315-316; 336-340; 392
Court Dates	9 Mar 1838 (Letters of Administration Granted); 14 May 1838; 12 Nov 1838; 14 Feb 1839; 13 May 1839; 16 May 1839; 13 Nov 1839; 15 Feb 1840; 15 May 1840; 13 Aug 1840; 12 Feb 1841

Administrator	Perlina/Paulina FOSTER (widow) and Joseph ORR
Heirs	Melinda/Belinda S. FOSTER HARPER and Archibald HARPER, (husband and wife) Alanzo L. FOSTER, Laura L. FOSTER, Alonzo S. FOSTER, Harriet N. FOSTER, Amanda H. FOSTER, Narcissa H. FOSTER, Sophronia H. FOSTER.
Action	Letters of Administration Granted. Letters of Administration Confirmed. Application to sell real estate. Order to sell real estate. Assumpset. Andrew MELVILLE & John MELVILLE, JR. sue for and are awarded $15.66 plus costs for debt against estate. Sale of real estate approved. Application to sell real estate. Report of Sale of Real estate and order of Confirmation. Settlement of Estate. Report of Deed of Conveyance acknowledged in court on 11 Aug 1840. On Final Settlement
Incidental Names	Daniel BROWN, security; John B. NILES, guardian of the estates of infant heirs and commissioner for sale of property. Henry ORR of La Porte County bought the 33 acres for $396.
Comments	Heirs are summoned to show cause why real estate should not be sold to pay debts. Administrators must expose 33 acres for sale on 1 April 1839, to be advertised prior in the LA PORTE COUNTY WHIG. Real estate sold to Joseph ORR for $444. Since heirs had not appeared in court, purchaser petitions court to withdraw purchase and get his money back rather than have an unclear title. So ordered. Heirs-at-law and Archibald HARPER, husband of Belinda HARPER, again ordered to appear in court to show cause why real estate should not be sold to pay debts of estate. Heirs do not appear. Real estate again published for sale. Land is sold and sale is confirmed. Balance of estate is $90.24 to be disposed of agreeably to law after expenses of administrator are deducted. 33 acres land description. On final settlement, Joseph ORR has $23.55 left and Mrs. FOSTER has $37.13 left for a total of $60.68 to be divided equally between them, $30.34 to each for their services.

DUKES, Ephraim	**Estate**
Book, Page	POB A: 102; 103; 446; 550
Court Dates	12 Apr 1838 (Letters of Administration Granted); 14 May 1838; 12 Nov 1841; 8 Aug 1842
Administrator	James WARNOCK
Action	Letters of Administration Granted. Letters of Administration Confirmed. Administrator ordered to appear in court and make final settlement of estate. Administrator files "an exhibit of the condition of said estate and not being prepared to make final settlement this cause is continued".
Incidental Names	Lemuel ROBINSON, security

BURCH, Amanda   Guardianship

Book, Page	POB A: 104-105
Court Dates	15 May 1838
Action	Settlement
Incidental Names	Guardian of infant heirs of Peter BURCH.
Comments	Settlement Account approved.

WINCHELL, James   Guardianship

Book, Page	POB A: 111-112
Court Dates	14 Aug 1838
Action	Application to Choose a Guardian; letters of guardianship issued.
Incidental Names	David WINCHELL chosen Guardian. Owens A. OWEN, security.
Comments	Applicant is the infant son of John WINCHELL, deceased.

MASON, Howard   Estate

Book, Page	POB A: 114; 132; 220; 225; 282; 304; 447; 465; 524-525; 573-574
Court Dates	31 Aug 1838 (Letters of Administration Granted); 14 Nov 1838; 17 Aug 1839; 23 Oct 1839; 14 Feb 1840; 13 May 1840; 12 Nov 1841; 14 Feb 1842; 10 May 1842; 12 Aug 1842
Administrator	William CLARK
Heirs	Sidney MASON, widow; Elwood MASON, Elizabeth MASON, Howard MASON, Alice MASON
Action	Letters of administration granted. Confirmation of Grant of letters. Administrator ordered to appear in court and file the inventory and Sale Bill of said Estate. Inventory and appraisal of personal property and Sale Bill filed. Administrator notified to appear in court to make final settlement of estate. Administrator asks longer time to make final settlement. Administrator ordered to appear in court and make final settlement of estate. Administrator granted continuance. Petition to sell real Estate. Inventory filed. On Petition to sell Real Estate. John H. BRADLEY, Esqr. Appointed Guardian Ad Litem of minor heirs, Elwood, Elizabeth, Howard, &Alice. Widow, Sydney, defaults. Real estate ordered to be sold.
Incidental Names	Stephen HOLLOWAY, security. William H. BRADLEY, security ($1,000).
Comments	Letters granted "In Vacation". Heirs to be "cited to be and appear before this Court…to show cause if any they can, why the said real Estate shall not be sold and made assets for the payment of said debts". Personal estate insufficient to pay debts of estate.

ROBINSON, Joseph   Estate

Book, Page	POB A: 115; 132; 282; 300; 447; 469
Court Dates	12 Sep 1838 (Letters of Administration Granted); 14 Nov 1838; 14 Feb 1840; 11 May 1840; 12 Nov 1841; 15 Nov 1842
Administrator	Lemuel/ Samuel ROBINSON
Action	Letters of administration granted. Confirmation of Grant of Letters. Administrator notified to appear in court to make final settlement of estate. Administrator ordered to appear in court to make final settlement. Administrator unprepared to make final settlement, case continued.
Incidental Names	Thomas ROBINSON, security
Comments	Letters granted "In Vacation".

BRADLEY, Bartholomew   Estate

Book, Page	POB A: 115; 133; 177; 283; 314; 328; 362; 380; 447; 474; 522; 533-34; 536-537; 558; 578; 586-589
Court Dates	1 Oct 1838 (Letters of Administration Granted); 14 Nov 1838; 14 Feb 1839; 14 Feb 1840; 15 May 1840; 10 Aug 1840; 12 Nov 1840; 9 Feb 1841; 12 Nov 1841; 15 Feb 1842; 10 May 1842; 12 May 1842; 10 Aug 1842; 14 Nov 1842; 16 Nov 1842
Administrator	Sidney S. BRADLEY, followed by Sutton VAN PELT.
Heirs	Lydia S (?), BRADLEY, George W. BRADLEY, Joseph E. BRADLEY, Sidney S. BRADLEY, William C. BRADLEY, Erasmus D. BRADLEY, Julia H. BRADLEY
Action	Lydia S. BRADLEY (widow) renounced as administrator. Letters of Administration granted to her son, Sidney BRADLEY. Confirmation of Grant of Letters. Petition for permission to sell part of the personal estate at private sale. Petition granted. Administrator notified to appear in court to make final settlement of estate. Administrator asks for more time to make final settlement. Granted. More time asked for by Administrator. On Settlement of the estate. Accounting produced, continued to next Term. On settlement of said estate. Judgment on warrant of attorney, James BRADLEY. Administrator ordered to appear in court to make final settlement of estate. Lewis BLODGET vs. Administrator. Continued. Attachment issued against the administrator for contempt "in failing to appear at the last Term...and make final settlement" and contempt. "Excused on hearing cause." Court rules in favor of Lewis BLODGET by default for the amount of $54.13. Noah NEWELL, agent for a creditor, files and an affidavit "of the insolvency of the security in the official bond" of the Administrator. Administrator asked to file additional bond. He fails to do so and is relieved of the position of Administrator. New Administrator sworn in. Application to sell Real Estate. Aulden TUCKER proves that he is owed $2.50. Application to sell real estate. Adult heirs do not appear.

Incidental Names	Russell HARVEY (?), security. Nicholas McCARTY and James C. HOWELL bring suit for $42.47. Noah NEWELL, security for second Administrator ($1000). John M CLARKAM appointed Guardian ad Litem for Julia, Joseph and William (they are under 21 yrs. old). Noah NEWELL, additional security ($1200).
Comments	Letters granted "In Vacation". Administrator has $100.59 over and above the final accounting. Administrator says the estate is justly indebted to plaintiffs for $42.47 plus $10.62 damages plus costs. Heirs to be notified by citation and publication to appear in court to say why land "should not be sold and made assets for the payment of the debts of said estate". Lydia, George, Joseph and William are non-residents of the state on 16 Nov 1842. Land in Elkhart County to be offered for sale at courthouse door in Town of Goshen.

HIBBARD, Horace B.   Estate

Book, Page	POB A: 116; 133; 195-196; 268-270; 314; 325; 354; 355; 357; 398-399; 433-437; 452-454; 473; 523-524; 544-546; 578-579
Court Dates	6 Oct 1838 (Letters of Administration Granted); 14 Nov 1838; 15 May 1839; 11 Feb 1840; 15 May 1840; 10 Aug 1840; 11 Nov 1840; 11 May 1841; 10 Nov 1841; 12 Nov 1841; 15 Feb 1842; 10 May 1842; 8 Aug 1842; 14 Nov 1842
Administrator	William WRIGHT and Ezra TYLER
Heirs	Annis S. HIBBARD, later SOVINE (widow), Abram/Abraham SOVINE, Marian HIBBARD, John W. HIBBARD, & Daniel W. HIBBARD (minor heirs), Corrintha DINGMAN nee HIBBARD by William DINGMAN, her guardian (husband and wife)
Action	Letters of Administration granted. Confirmation of Grant of Letters. Application to sell real estate. At his request, William WRIGHT discharged and released from duties as administrator. Application to sell real estate. Inventory and appraisal of real estate filed. Heirs summoned to show cause why real estate should not be sold to pay debts. Application to sell real estate. Application to sell real estate, continued. On complaint of Insolvency. Debt, Joseph DAVIS vs. Administrator of Estate. Application to sell real estate for widow's dower. Application for the appointment of Commissioner to convey Real estate. For specific performance of contract for sale of Land. Application to sell real estate continued with description of real estate to be sold. Report of sale of real estate. Proceeds from sale to be used to pay debts of Estate. Petition to sell real Estate. Application to sell Reversionary Interest of Widow's Dower. James BRADLEY is appointed Guardian ad litem of Marion, John W. and Daniel W., minor heirs. On application to sell real estate. The price bid by Abram SOVREEN/SOVEEN is adjudged "unreasonably low". Land must be reexposed for sale.
Incidental Names	Ezra TYLER appeared with administrator to verify the death of Horace HIBBARD. Richard B. HEWS, security. John C. CARTER, files Bill of Complaint. John B. NILES, appointed Guardian ad litem to infant heirs,

Marion, John and Daniel. He was also appointed Commissioner to execute a deed of conveyance of contested land. Some property to be sold was purchased from J. W. WILLIAMSON

Comments   Letters granted "In Vacation". HIBBARD died, intestate, on 15 Sep 1838 with an estate of less than $1000. 54 acres in Township #37 in Range 4 W put up for sale to pay debts. William requests his discharge as administrator due to unnecessary expense of two administrators. He puts up additional security for Ezra to continue as sole administrator. Personal Estate is insufficient to pay debts. Creditors are to be notified by publication in the LA PORTE COUNTY WHIG of the necessity of filing their claims against the estate. Joseph DAVIS awarded $660.63 plus costs and charges. Receipt for said amount filed 28 Nov 1844. By May term in 1841 Aunis has remarried to Abram SOVINE and is listed as Aunis SOVINE, Corrintha and William DINGMAN are not residents of the state, and, only Ezra TYLER is listed as administrator. During his lifetime the deceased executed his title bond to Charles COOPER for land. The title was then assigned to John C. CARTER, the complainant. The deceased died before a deed to the land was issued. Court orders deed to be executed to complainant. Complainant to recover costs. Non-resident heirs to be notified by publication, resident heirs by citation, "to show cause, if any they can, why the said real Estate shall not be sold and made assets for the payment of said debts." Heirs fail to appear.

JOHNSON, Joseph   Estate

Book, Page   POB A: 116; 133-134; 357; 468; 520-521

Court Dates   12 Oct 1838 (Letters of Administration Granted); 14 Nov 1838; 12 Nov 1840; 15 Feb 1842; 9 May 1842

Administrator   John DENHAM and Joel BUTLER

Action   Letters of Administration granted. Confirmation of Grant of Letters. Sale Bill of personal estate filed. Administrators unprepared to make final settlement, case continued. On Settlement. Elizabeth, widow, returns $188.78 for distribution.

Incidental Names   Benjamin BUTTERWORTH, security

Comments   Letters granted "In Vacation". Various sums credited to administrators before remainder of $295.65 is distributed.

DINWIDDIE, David   Estate

Book, Page   POB A: 117; 134; 207-208; 216; 237; 253-254; 301-302; 389-390; 444; 476-477; 495-500; 540; 574; 581-583; 599; 600-607

Court Dates   13 Oct 1838 (Letters of Administration Granted); 14 Nov 1838; 13 Aug 1839; 16 Aug 1839; 13 Nov 1839; 16 Nov 1839; 12 May 1840; 11 Feb 1841; 11 Nov 1841; 15 Feb 1842; 18 Feb 1842; 12 May 1842; 12 Aug 1842; 15 Nov 1842; 19 Nov 1842; 18 Nov 1842

Administrator	Amzi CLARK and James C. HOWELL.
Heirs	Mary DINWIDDIE (widow), John DINWIDDIE, Margaret Jane DINWIDDIE, David DINWIDDIE, Jr., Francis W. DINWIDDIE, and Marietta DINWIDDIE (infant heirs), Matthew L. WALKER and Eleanor H. WALKER (non-resident heirs)
Action	Letters of Administration granted. Confirmation of Grant of Letters. Petition to settle said estate as insolvent. Application for the sale of real estate. Widow and heirs summoned to show cause why real estate should not be sold for discharge of debt. Application to settle the estate as insolvent. Order to publish sale of property except what is set aside for the widow's dower. Report of sale of real estate and confirmation. Report of sale and confirmation and order of conveyance. Application to re-expose land to sale. Report of the re-sale of part of the Real Estate. Commissioner ordered to execute deed of Conveyance. Description of all prior proceedings. Administrator cited to appear in Court to make final settlement. Application to sell real estate. Heirs to be summoned to show cause why real estate should not be sold "and made assets for the payment of the debts of said estate". On application to sell real estate. John B. NILES appointed Guardian Ad Litem for minor heirs. Adult heirs do not appear. More land to be sold. Land sale approved and administrators to execute & deliver a "good and sufficient deed of conveyance for said land" to Abner BAILEY, of La Porte County. Final account. "And said administrators prove to the satisfaction of the court that they have used reasonable & due diligence in collecting the credits of said estate." Creditors listed. It seems that anything left is to be deposited with the Clerk's office for future claims and the Estate was settled.
Incidental Names	Abner BAILEY and Griffin TREADWAY, security. John B. NILES, commissioners.
Comments	Letters granted "In Vacation". The estate is insolvent. Court orders that creditors be notified by publication in the LA PORTE COUNTY WHIG so they can file claims. Indiana non-resident heirs notified by publication in LA PORTE COUNTY WHIG to appear in court. "A portion of the real estate of the said deceased heretofore sold by them as administrators...was held by title bonds and by Michigan Road Certificats". Sale set aside. Land re-exposed for sale. Two tracts of land sold to pay debts of estate were sold to the administrators, all transactions restated for clarity.

BEATTEE/BEATY, William   Estate

Book, Page	POB A: 117; 134; 220; 230; 447; 465
Court Dates	15 Oct 1838 (Letters of Administration Granted); Confirmation of Grant of Letters. 17 Aug 1839; 12 Oct 1839; 12 Nov 1841; 14 Feb 1842
Administrator	Thomas E. STANTON
Action	Letters of Administration granted. Administrator ordered to appear in court to file inventory and Sale Bill of said Estate. Sale Bill filed. Administrator

ordered to appear in court to make final settlement of estate. Administrator presents accounting and asks for $17.59 in expenses. Estate is closed, administrator discharged.

Incidental Names	Michael W. FALL, security
Comments	Letters granted "In Vacation".

SMITH, Hezekiah — Estate

Book, Page	POB A: 118; 135; 220; 283; 448; 614
Court Dates	15 Oct 1838 (Letters of Administration Granted); 14 Nov 1838; 17 Aug 1839; 14 Feb 1840; 12 Nov 1841; 19 Nov 1842
Administrator	Obadiah SMITH
Action	Letters of Administration granted. Confirmation of Grant of Letters. Administrator ordered to appear in court to file inventory and Sale Bill of said Estate. Administrator notified to appear in court to make final settlement of estate. Administrator again ordered to appear in court to make final settlement of estate. Administrator, again, cited to appear in court to make final settlement.
Incidental Names	John W. COLE, security
Comments	Letters granted "In Vacation".

SPRAGUE, David — Estate

Book, Page	POB A: 118; 135; 190-191; 212; 216; 245-246; 272-275; 295-297; 324; 343; 352; 378-379; 387-388; 509
Court Dates	17 Oct 1838 (Letters of Administration Granted); 14 Nov 1838; 14 May 1839; 14 Aug 1839; 16 Aug 1839; 14 Nov 1839; 11 Feb 1840; 11 May 1840; 10 Aug 1840; 14 Aug 1840; 10 Nov 1840; 9 Feb 1841; 10 Feb 1841; 19 Feb 1842
Administrator	Jabez R. WELLS and James W. SPRAGUE
Heirs	Polly SPRAGUE (widow), Sarah ARVILLE nee SPRAGUE (wife of Caleb N. ARVILLE), Sudan SPRAGUE, Henry B. SPRAGUE, John SPRAGUE, William SPRAGUE, Edward SPRAGUE, Thomas SPRAGUE
Action	Letters of Administration granted. Confirmation of Grant of Letters. Application to sell real estate. Revocation of the granting of Letters of administration. Application to sell real estate continued. Application for order of sale of real estate. Order to sell real estate and notify the lien holders of sale by publication. Complaint of Insolvency, unknown claimants notified by publication. Application for order of sale. Application to settle said estate as insolvent. Report of Sale of Real estate, continued. Application to sell additional real estate, said order issued. Report of Sale of Real Estate and Order of Confirmation. Cause continued. Report of Sale of

Real Estate. Report of Sale of Real Estate and Order of confirmation. Cause "certified up to the Circuit Court of said county."

Incidental Names	John JOHNSON and Thomas I. FIELD; Sutton VANPELT appointed guardian ad litem of heirs; Richard BURLEIGH, William SMALL, Henry V. DISBRO and Levi COOK, non-Indiana resident lien holders; James P. PENDILE, the Delphi Insurance Company, the Buffalo and Mississippi Rail Road Company, Joseph H. HACKLEY, survivor of Hackley & Chenney, Robert STEWART, et al and Samuel LINEN/SINEREN, additional lien holders summoned.
Comments	Letters granted "In Vacation". Heirs seem to be non-residents of Indiana. Publication of notice of sale put in LA PORTE COUNTY WHIG. Administrator James W. SPRAGUE left the state and could not perform his duties. His Letters were revoked. Inventory and appraisal of the real estate filed in prior May term was lost or mislaid and had to be refiled in Nov. On 15th of Jan 1839 property was exposed for sale. Only 40 acres sold-to Aaron T. STANTON at private sale for $400. Lienholders failed to appear and defaulted. Creditors notified by publication to file claims. No heirs or lienholders appeared.

HOSMER, Robert — Estate

Book, Page	POB A: 119; 135-136; 283; 302
Court Dates	17 Oct 1838 (Letters of Administration Granted); 14 Nov 1838; 14 Feb 1840; 12 May 1840
Administrator	Nancy HOSMER and Jackson HOSMER
Action	Letters of Administration granted. Confirmation of Grant of Letters. Administrator notified to appear in court to make final settlement of the estate. Estate settlement.
Incidental Names	Joseph DAVIS, security
Comments	Letters granted "In Vacation". Personal estate $2425. No debts. Distributed among heirs after widows portion is deducted.

KEWLEY, John — Estate

Book, Page	POB A: 119; 136; 252
Court Dates	20 Oct 1838 (Letters of Administration Granted); 14 Nov 1838; 15 Nov 1839;
Administrator	John KEWLEY and Thomas KEWLEY
Action	Letters of Administration granted. Confirmation of Grant of Letters. Account filed.
Incidental Names	William SHIMMIN, Andrew BURNSIDE, and Adam G. POLKE, security.

Comments	Letters granted "In Vacation". Administrator has balance of $692 at final accounting, which is ordered to be dispersed of "agreeably to law".

McCLANAHAN, James — Estate

Book, Page	POB A: 120; 136: 189-190; 217-218; 243; 267-268; 289: 307; 332; 346; 352
Court Dates	22 Oct 1838 (Letters of Administration Granted); 14 Nov 1838; 14 May 1839; 17 Aug 1839; 14 Nov 1839; 11 Feb 1840; 15 Feb 1840; 14 May 1840; 12 Aug 1840; 15 Aug 1840; 10 Nov 1840
Administrator	John HOBSON and Benjamin CRUMPACKER
Heirs	Belinda B. McCLANIHAN, Harriet H. McCLANIHAN, James E. McCLANIHAN, Joseph McCLANIHAN and Emily McCLANIHAN, infant heirs-at-law.
Action	Letters of Administration granted. Confirmation of Grant of Letters. Application to sell real estate vs. Heirs of deceased. Order to sell land. Application for further time to sell real estate. Report of Sale of Real estate & order of conveyance. Set aside due to illegality in not notifying the heirs of the sale. Sale of real estate nullified. Application to sell real estate. Order for sale of real estate. Notice of sale to be published. Report of Sale of Real estate and order of confirmation. Settlement of Estate. Receipt for settlement amount. Administrators discharged.
Incidental Names	Griffin TREADWAY, security. John HOBSON and Griffin TREADWAY, guardian of heirs.
Comments	Letters granted "In vacation". Heirs and their Guardian, as well as John HOBSON, holder of lien, summoned to appear in Court in the next August term to show cause why real estate should not be sold for payment of debt. $450 due and unpaid on land purchased prior to decedent's death. Publication for sale of land in LA PORTE COUNTY WHIG. Heirs failed to appear. Land is sold. At settlement there remained $248.26. It was disposed of agreeably to law. Guardian of heirs files receipt for that amount on behalf of the heirs.

WYATT, Joseph — Estate

Book, Page	POB A: 120; 137; 139; 231; 232; 287-288; 299; 324-325; 340-342; 349-350; 393; 399-401; 408; 413; 421; 422; 424; 429-430; 456; 466; 501; 505; 534-535; 539-540; 581
Court Dates	23 Oct 1838 (Letters of Administration Granted); 14 Nov 1838; 13 Nov 1839; 15 Feb 1840; 11 May 1840; 13 Aug 1840; 13 Aug 1840: 9 Nov 1840; 13 Feb 1841; 11 May 181; 13 May 1841; 11 Aug 1841; 14 Aug 1841; 9 Nov 1841; 13 Nov 1841; 14 Feb 1842; 18 Feb 1842; 19 Feb 1842: 12 May 1842; 15 Nov 1842
Administrator	Ezekiel MORRISON

Heirs	Isaac WYATT, Thomas WYATT, James WYATT, all children and only kin.
Action	Letters of Administration granted. Confirmation of Grant of Letters. Petition to Sell part of personal estate at private sale granted. Estate sues Heirs and Creditors. Heirs ordered to appear and show cause why real estate should not be sold for payment of debts. Two heirs, Isaac and Thomas, have not been served. James was served, but not 30 days before the February Term. Cause continued. Application to Settle since estate is insolvent. Thomas Wyatt not found. Cause continued. Application to sell real estate. Guardian-Ad-Litem for under age heirs appointed to serve during the "pendency of this suit". Application for sale of real estate to pay debts. Report of Sale of Real estate and order of Confirmation. Remaining real estate still to be sold. Report of Sale and order of Confirmation. Application to sell additional real estate discovered since last term of court. Noah NEWELL vs. Administrator, case filed and continued. Abram/Abraham W. HARRISON vs. Administrator, case filed, jury waived, court, having heard the widow, will render verdict next Term. Court finds for the Plaintiff the sum of $1789.50 in Damages plus costs. Administrator asks for continuance on sale of land. Schedules filed. "said Joseph WYATT deceased was indebted in his lifetime to said Noah NEWELL in the sum of Twelve hundred thirty Six Dollars & Eighty Two cents." The court rules that that debt plus damages and costs be paid by the administrator from the "good & chattels of said " deceased. Application for sale of real estate in Marshall Co. Sale annulled, bid by A. S. WHEELER too low. Harrison vs. Administrator, Assumpsit, continued. Claim to collect on note from 30 Jun 1836 by Eliza ASPENWALL. Claim allowed, $200 plus ten percent interest. Application for sale of real estate. Abraham HARRISON files suit against estate. Neither party can agree on damages. The court suggests a jury trial. Both parties decline. Plaintiff is assessed $62.84, to be recovered from the defendant plus the costs. William HAGENBUCH vs. estate. Plaintiff claims the estate owes him $6,999.65 plus interest for goods and merchandise purchased by Wyatt during his lifetime. Court agrees and he is awarded $8,343.56. Administrator proves his account against estate for the sum of $30.
Incidental Names	Sutton VANPELT and Hiram WHEELER, security; William E. HANNAH appointed Guardian-Ad-Litem for children as they are under 21 years of age. William HAGENBUCH is insolvent. The purchase from estate of Lot 46 in town of La Porte set aside for failure of payment. John BONER buys section of Michigan Road lands in Marshall County.
Comments	Letters granted "In Vacation". There are insufficient funds in the estate to pay debts. Notification of this fact to be published in the LA PORTE COUNTY WHIG for six weeks. Creditors must file the existence and extent of their claims. Heirs summoned to appear in court to show cause why estate property should not be sold to pay debts. Sheriff of Union County served the citation on James WYATT, Sheriff of Carroll County served the citation on Thomas WYATT, and same officer served citation on Isaac WYATT. There is mention of a Sheriff of Grange county, also. Description of several 80-acre tracts in LaPorte and St. Joseph counties, lots in the city of LaPorte. Publication of sale to be made in South Bend and LaPorte

County. Remaining 80 acres in Marshall County and lot in city of La Porte still to be advertised and sold. Acreage sale approved, Lot sale not approved, to be republished in LA PORTE COUNTY WHIG. Accounts collected, $1288.12; accounts considered non-collectible, $547.22; accounts not collected, but considered good, $529.32; debts considered doubtful, $2021.13; preferred claims and certain expenses of administration, $1937.37.

BAILEY, John	**Estate**
Book, Page	POB A: 121; 137; 226; 283; 325: 575; 580-581
Court Dates	25 Oct 1838 (Letters of Administration Granted); 14 Nov 1838; 23 Oct 1839; 14 Feb 1840; 10 Aug 1840; 12 Aug 1842; 14 Nov 1842
Administrator	Benjamin T. BRYANT
Action	Letters of Administration granted. Confirmation of Grant of Letters. Additional inventory of personal property filed. Administrator notified to appear in court to make final settlement. Settlement of said estate. Administrator cited to appear before Court "on the first day of the next term thereof, to Show & Report to the Court, what disposition has been made of the balance of said Estate, remaining in their hands on settlement of said Estate." On Settlement.
Incidental Names	Josiah BRYANT, security
Comments	Letters granted "In Vacation". Balance on hand at settlement is $237.26. Balance to be disposed agreeably to law. Administrator charges $230.26 to himself and $284.18.

PLATT, Jeremiah	**Estate**
Book, Page	POB A: 121; 137-138; 283; 448; 469; 529
Court Dates	25 Oct 1838 (Letters of Administration Granted); 14 Nov 1838; 14 Feb 1840; 12 Nov 1841; 15 Feb 1842; 10 May 1842
Administrator	Joseph WINCH
Action	Letters of Administration granted. Confirmation of Grant of Letters. Administrator notified to appear in court to make final settlement. Administrator again ordered to appear in court to make final settlement. Administrator unprepared to make final settlement, case continued. Continued, again.
Incidental Names	James M. SCOTT, security
Comments	Letters granted "In Vacation".

ALLEN, Reuben   **Estate**

Book, Page   POB A: 122; 138; 196; 218; 220; 227; 256; 270; 329-330; 379384-385; 509; 609

Court Dates   27 Oct 1838 (Letters of Administration Granted); 14 Nov 1838; 15 May 1839; 17 Aug 1839; 11 Nov 1839; 16 Nov 1839; 11 Feb 1840; 11 Aug 1840; 9 Feb 1841; 19 Feb 1842; 19 Nov 1842

Administrator   Mark ALLEN

Heirs   Jane ALLEN (widow), John ALLEN, William H.C. ALLEN, Erasmus ALLEN, Adam ALLEN, Dewitt C. ALLEN, Hebor___ Reuben ALLEN Jr, Elizabeth ALLEN , Jane ALLEN Jr.

Action   Letters of Administration granted. Confirmation of Grant of Letters. Application for sale of real estate, said application continued. Administrator ordered to appear in court and file the Inventory and Sale Bill of said Estate. Inventor and appraisal of personal estate filed, along with sale bill. Order to Sell Real Estate, except for that which has been set aside as dower for widow. Application for further time to sell real estate. Wrong Entry, stricken out. On complaint of Insolvency. Publication to creditors ordered. Settlement (case continued). Application to Settle said Estate as insolvent. Administrator cited to appear before the court to make distribution "of said estate in his hands". Administrator did not appear as ordered. Attachment is issued against him compelling him to appear "on said first day of said next term to make final settlement".

Incidental Names   Jacob HUPP, security; Charles McCLURE, attorney; Richard MORLEY, holder of lien.

Comments   Letters granted "In Vacation". Property, both real and personal, insufficient to pay debts. Balance on hand of $444.73 (case continued).

MILLER, Peter   **Estate**

Book, Page   POB A: 122: 144; 448; 464

Court Dates   27 Oct 1838 (Letters of Administration Granted); 15 Nov 1838; 12 Nov 1841; 14 Feb 1842

Administrator   John MILLER and Saul/Samuel DAWSON

Action   Letters of Administration granted. Confirmation of Grant of letters. Administrator ordered to appear in court to make final settlement of estate. Administrators granted continuance.

Incidental Names   George DAWSON, security

Comments   Letters granted "In Vacation".

GOSSETT, John   **Estate**

Book, Page   POB A: 123; 144; 228; 407; 448

Court Dates	1 Nov 1838 (Letters of Administration Granted); 15 Nov 1838; 11 Nov 1839; 13 May 1841; 12 Nov 1841; 14 Feb 1842
Administrator	Mary GOSSET and Joseph GOSSET
Action	Letters of Administration granted. Confirmation of Grant of Letters. Gideon HAULEY sues the estate for $20 in a jury trial. Administrators ordered by the court to appear at the next Term of court and make final settlement of the Estate. Administrator again ordered to appear at court and make final settlement of estate. Administrators ask for continuance.
Incidental Names	James WEBSTER, security. At the time of the lawsuit Mary GOSSET is Mary ROUSE.
Comments	Letters granted "In Vacation". Judgment from the lawsuit + interest is paid on 20 Jun 1840.

STONER, William — Estate

Book, Page	POB A: 123; 145; 235
Court Dates	3 Nov 1838 (Letters of Administration Granted); 15 Nov 1838; 13 Nov 1839
Administrator	David STONER
Action	Letters of Administration granted. Estate accounts produced by administrator and approved. Administrator discharged.
Incidental Names	Benjamin CRUMPACKER, security
Comments	Letters granted "In Vacation". Administrator paid out $62.82 more than came into his hands as assets of the estate.

COLLINS, Harvey — Estate

Book, Page	POB A: 126; 148; 257:277-278; 311; 346; 356; 390
Court Dates	12 Nov 1838 (Letters of Administration Granted); 16 Nov 1838; 16 Nov 1839; 12 Feb 1840; 14 May 1840; 15 Aug 1840; 11 Nov 1840; 12 Nov 1841
Administrator	Philena COLLINS, widow (renounces). Samuel STEWART and George C. HAVINS (replacements)
Heirs	Philena COLLINS (widow), Amina COLLINS, Harriet COLLINS, Charlotte E. COLLINS, and Albert COLLINS
Action	Renunciation of widow as administrator. Letters of Administration granted. Inventory and appraisement of estate filed. Application to sell real estate to pay debts. Petition to assign dower by Philena BROWN and William BROWN. Continuance. On application to sell real estate for widow's dower, order issued. Report of Sale of real estate and order of Confirmation.
Incidental Names	Amzie CLARK, security

| Comments | Personal estate is insufficient to pay debts of said estate. On 12 Feb 1840 William BROWN and Philena BROWN, late Philena COLLINS, appear to answer by their attorney to "answer to said application". Notice of application of petition to assign dower appeared in the LA PORTE COUNTY WHIG. |

HOPPER, Melinda S.　　　　　　　　　　Guardianship
FOSTER, Alcanzo L.
FOSTER, Laura G.
FOSTER, Alonzo S.
FOSTER, Harriet N.
FOSTER, Amanda H.
FOSTER, Narcissa H.
FOSTER, Sophronia H.

Book, Page	POB A: 127
Court Dates	12 Nov 1838
Action	Application to choose a guardian.
Incidental Names	John B. NILES, guardian; Adam G. POLKE, security ($500)
Comments	Infant heirs of Seneca FOSTER, represented by their mother.

WASSON, Archibald　　　　　　　　　　**Estate**

Book, Page	POB A: 129; 447; 492-493
Court Dates	13 Nov 1838 (Will Filed and Proved); 12 Nov 1841; 18 Feb 1842
Executor	Jehiel WASSON
Action	Will filed, Letters of Administration granted. Administrator ordered to appear in court and make final settlement of estate. On final Settlement.
Incidental Names	Amos CADWALLADER and Jesse WASSON, subscribing witnesses; Amos CADWALLADER, security
Comments	Expenses ($265) and credits ($265) approved for administrator at final settlement.

CLARK, Charles　　　　　　　　　　**Estate**

Book, Page	POB A: 130
Court Dates	13 Nov 1838 (Will filed and Proved)
Executrix	Lucy CLARK
Action	Will filed. Letters of Administration granted.
Incidental Names	Charles McCLURE and Harvey VAN ORDER, subscribing witnesses; Charles McCLURE, security

KIMBERLY, Isabella   **Petition for Dower**

Book, Page	POB A: 131
Court Dates	13 Nov 1838
Action	Application for the appointment of a Guardian. Letters of Guardianship issued to Isabella as guardian of her two infant sons, Jeremiah Sullivan KIMBERLY and Lucian Proctor Busk KIMBERLY.
Incidental Names	David CLOSSER, security ($280).
Comments	The children are the sons of Zenas KIMBERLY, deceased.

BARGER, Samuel   **Estate**

Book, Page	POB A: 138; 175-176-177; 300; 324; 413-414; 430-432; 552-553; 557
Court Dates	14 Nov 1838 (Letters of Administration Granted): 14 Feb 1839; 11 May 1840; 10 Aug 1840; 10 Aug 1841; 9 Nov 1841; 9 Aug 1842; 10 May 1842
Administrator	William ANDREW
Heirs	Christian BARGER
Action	Letters of Administration granted. Elizabeth HARRISON & John L. HARRISON vs. Elijah STANTON and William ANDREW (as administrator). Petition for rescinding contract between the deceased and Thomas D. LEMON for lot in La Porte. Contract cancelled. Application to sell real estate. Application to sell real estate continued. Rescinding of contract between Thorton EWAN and the deceased for purchase of Lot Number 218 in Town of Laporte. Application for the sale of Real estate to pay debts, approved. Report of Sale of Real Estate. Report is approved, sale confirmed. Administrator authorized to issue a deed after the money is received for the tract of land. Complaint of Insolvency.
Incidental Names	Abraham P. ANDREW, security ($700); George SWOPE, Justice of the Peace.
Comments	"Administrator of the goods chattels rights credits monies and effects". $36.92 + costs to be paid to plaintiffs (p. 175) from estate after costs of burial. Christian BARGER, Decatur County, Indiana, summoned to court on second Monday of August show cause why real estate should not be sold. Answers not. Sale of real estate to be published in LA PORTE COUNTY WHIG, ordered 9 Nov 1841. Condition of insolvency to be published in THE LA PORTE COUNTY WHIG (May 1842). Creditors must notify administrator of any claims against the estate.

UTLEY, Sanford   **Estate**

Book, Page	POB A: 139; 162-163; 229; 259-260; 264-265; 298; 318; 344-345; 364; 488-489; 526-527; 549-550

Court Dates	14 Nov 1838 (Will Filed. Letters Testamentary Granted); 11 Feb 1839; 12 Nov 1839; 16 Nov 1839; 10 Feb 1840; 11 May 1840; 16 May 1840; 14 Aug 1840; 13 Nov 1840; 17 Feb 1842; 10 May 1842; 8 Aug 1842
Executor	Jacob MILLER
Heirs	James UTLEY, Pelig UTLEY, Eleazer WILLARD/MILLARD and Almira WILLARD/MILLARD (his wife), Isaac SCUDDER and Julian/Julia SCUDDER (his wife) and George UTLEY, non-resident heirs; Uriah UTLEY, James NICHOLSON and Catherine NICHOLSON (his wife), the former Catherine UTLEY, resident heirs.
Action	Will filed. Letters Testamentary granted. Application for Sale of Real Estate. Uriah UTLEY sues the estate, cause continued. Order for the sale of real estate to pay debts. The highest and best bid of $3.90 per acre was given to Uriah UTLEY on 18 Jan 1840 at public sale. Uriah failed to meet the conditions of the sale. Land remains unsold. Confirmation of sale of real estate. Application for additional sale of real estate, heirs to be summoned to appear to show cause why additional real estate should not be sold to pay debts. Application to sell real estate, said order issued. Report of sale of real estate and orders of confirmation. Application for additional Sale of Real Estate. Application to sell real estate. Report of Sale of Real Estate. Sale confirmed. When money is received, debts of the deceased will be paid and it will be "otherwise administered and disposed of according to the Law" and purchaser will be given a "good and sufficient deed".
Incidental Names	Alonzo HUBBARD and William BODURTHEE, subscribing witnesses; Griffin TREADWAY, security
Comments	Jacob MILLER was "one of the executors appointed by the said testator in his said last Will and testament". The following is crossed out, "Nathan PORTER the other executor also appointed by the said testator in his said last Will and Testament." Some heirs are non-residents of the state of Indiana on 11 Feb 1839. Notice asking them to appear on the second Monday of May to show cause why real estate should not be sold to "discharge debts" was ordered to be published in La Porte County Whig weekly newspaper. Heirs did not appear. Heirs again summoned to show cause why additional Real Estate should not be sold. Heirs defaulted. "And thereupon the Court, after due inspection…do find that the said personal Estate and the real Estate heretofore sold, are insufficient to pay the debts of said Estate" and orders the sale of real Estate mentioned in the inventory.

BAILEY, Mary Elizabeth
BAILEY, Josiah
BAILEY, Simon

Guardianship

Book, Page	POB A: 140
Court Dates	14 Nov 1838
Action	Application to choose a Guardian.

Incidental Names	Josiah BRYANT, grandfather, files petition. He is appointed Guardian. Benjamin G. BRYANT, security.
Comments	Applicants are infant heirs of John BAILEY, deceased.

HURBUT, Richard/ HERBERT, Richard

Estate

Book, Page	POB A: 141; 176; 200; 205; 229; 541; 550
Court Dates	14 Nov 1838 (Letters of Administration Granted); 14 Feb 1839; 12 Aug 1839; 12 Nov 1839; 12 May 1842; 8 Aug 1842
Administrator	Miciah/Micajah JONES
Action	Letters of Administration granted. Replevin-Administrator vs. James HERBERT, cause continued. James HURBUT loses at jury trial, assessed $10 in damages. Administrator cited to appear in Court to make final settlement. Administrator files exhibit of the "condition of said estate" and asks for continuance. Granted.
Incidental Names	Jesse JONES, security.

PERRY, Betsey
CARL, Rachel
EARL, Charlotte
HOWE, Mary Jane
SMITH, Obadiah
MARSH, Catherine

Pension Petition

Book, Page	POB A: 141-144
Court Dates	15 Nov 1838
Action	For Arrearages of Pension due their father, Hezekiah SMITH, deceased, former Revolutionary War veteran.
Incidental Names	Hugh PERRY, intermarried with Betsey SMITH, resides in Newburg, New York; John CARL, intermarried with Rachel SMITH, resides in Tompkins County, New York; Aaron EARL, intermarried with Charlotte SMITH, resides in La Porte County, Indiana; Amos J. HOWE, intermarried with Mary Jane SMITH, resides in La Porte County, Indiana; Harry MARSH, intermarried with Catherine SMITH, resides in La Porte County, Indiana. John H. BRADLEY, attorney. Obadiah SMITH resides in La Porte County, Indiana. Lewis CASS, Secretary of War. J. S. EDWARDS, Commissioner of Pensions.
Comments	The deceased was from New York State. He died in the county of La Porte, Indiana on the 28 Sep 1838 and left no widow to survive him. He was to receive $140 per annum during his natural life for his services as artificer in the Revolutionary War "commencing on the 4th of March 1831 and payable semiannually on the 4th of March and 4th of September in every year." Original certificate lost and reissued in 1834.

McCLANAHAN, Belinda B.   Guardianship
McCLANAHAN, Harriet H.
McCLANAHAN, James E.
McCLANAHAN, Josephus
McCLANAHAN, Emely

Book, Page	POB A: 145-146; 347
Court Dates	15 Nov 1838; 15 Aug 1840
Action	Griffin TREADWAY appointed guardian of persons and estate. Benjamin CRUMPACKER discharged as security.
Incidental Names	Benjamin CRUMPACKER, security ($500). John TREADWAY and Edmund B. WOODSON, security.
Comments	The applicants are infant heirs of James McCLANAHAN, deceased.

ESSLINGER, Ephraim   Guardianship
ESSLINGER, Antwine

Book, Page	POB A: 146
Court Dates	15 Nov 1838
Action	George W. BRADLEY appointed guardian of persons and estate.
Incidental Names	John F. ALLISON, applicant; Martin HOUSEMAN, security ($500)
Comments	Children are infant sons of Andrew ESSLINGER, deceased.

CLARK, Lucy   Guardianship

Book, Page	POB A: 147
Court Dates	15 Nov 1838
Action	Upon applicants petition, John F. SALE is appointed Guardian of person of Lewis P. CLARK, infant son of Charles CLARK, deceased.
Incidental Names	Thomas W. SALE, security ($200)
Comments	Lucy CLARK is the widow of Charles Clark.

MORSE, James   Estate

Book, Page	POB A: 147; 284; 319; 448; 469
Court Dates	15 Nov 1838 (Letters of Administration Granted); 14 Feb 1840; 16 May 1840; 12 Nov 1841; 15 Feb 1842
Administrator	Jared CHAPMAN

Action	Widow, Delia MORSE, requests the appointment of an administrator. Letters of Administration granted. Administrator notified to appear in court to make final settlement of the estate. Application to sell real estate. Administrator ordered to make final settlement of estate. Administrator unprepared to make final settlement, case continued.
Incidental Names	Andrew AVERY, security
Comments	Heirs summoned to show cause why real estate should not be sold for the payment of debts.

BOND, William, Sr.   Estate

Book, Page	POB A: 149; 449
Court Dates	16 Nov 1838 (Will filed, Letters Testamentary Issued); 12 Nov 1841
Executor	Ira BOND
Action	Will Filed. Renunciation as Executor filed by Charlotte BOND and Jesse BOND. Letters Testamentary issued. Executor of Estate cited to appear in Court to make final settlement of Estate.
Incidental Names	Jesse WATSON and Jesse HOUGH, subscribing witnesses; Jehiel WASSON and Elijah STANTON, security ($4,000)

PEASE, Lucinda Ann   Guardianship
PEASE, David H.

Book, Page	POB A: 150-151
Court Dates	16 Nov 1838
Action	Application for Appointment of Guardian
Incidental Names	Asa C. PEASE appointed guardian of persons and estates of infant heirs; Nathan B. NICHOLS, security ($500)
Comments	Applicants are infant heirs of Enos PEASE.

CLARK, George W.   Guardianship

Book, Page	POB A: 151-152; 238; 279-280
Court Dates	17 Nov 1838; 13 Nov 1839; 13 Feb 1840
Action	Application for Appointment of Guardian. Robert MERRYFIELD appointed guardian of person during minority. Guardian is moving out of La Porte County and wished to resign as guardian. His letters of Guardianship are revoked and set aside. Benjamin BEARD appointed guardian in his stead.
Incidental Names	Lucy CLARK (widow of Charles CLARK, deceased). David S. RYCKMAN, security for Benjamin BEARD.

| Comments | George is the infant son of Charles CLARK, deceased. |

WYATT, Isaac

Book, Page	POB A: 152; 420-421
Court Dates	17 Nov 1838; 13 Aug 1841
Action	Appointment of Guardian. Settlement.
Incidental Names	Stephen G. HUNT appointed guardian of estate; Ezekiel MORRISON, security ($1000).
Comments	Applicant is infant son of Joseph WYATT, deceased. On settlement the sum of $109.72 remains. Sum paid out. Guardian discharged.

ASHTON, Sidney
ASHTON, Jerusha
ASHTON, Phebe   Guardianship

Book, Page	POB A: 152-153
Court Dates	17 Nov 1838
Action	Application to Choose Guardian
Incidental Names	Eliahue ASHTON (uncle) appointed guardian of persons; Stephen G. HUNT, security ($300)
Comments	Applicants are infant heirs of Thomas ASHTON, deceased.

WYATT, Thomas
WYATT, James   Guardianship

Book, Page	POB A: 153; 425
Court Dates	17 Nov 1838; 14 Aug 1841
Action	Appointment of Guardian. Settlement of Guardianship. "It appears that there has come into his hand as such Guardian the sum of One hundred and Twenty Three dollars and thirty Two cents and that he has paid out the same for the use of said heirs as such Guardian as appears satisfactory to the court..."
Incidental Names	Azariah WILLIAMS appointed guardian of estates; Ezekiel MORRISON, security.
Comments	Applicants are infant heirs of Joseph WYATT.

COOPER, Ephraim   Estate

| Book, Page | POB A: 154; 166; 284; 324: 575 |

Court Dates	23 Nov 1838 (Letters of Administration Granted); 13 Feb 1839; 14 Feb 1840; 10 Aug 1840; 12 Aug 1842
Administrator	William WALDRIFF
Action	Letters of Administration Granted. Confirmation of Grant of Letters. Administrator notified to appear in court to make final settlement. Settlement of Estate. Administrator cited to appear before Court "on the first day of the next term thereof, to Show & Report to the Court, what disposition has been made of the balance of said estate remaining in his hands on the settlement of said Estate."
Incidental Names	John COOPER, security
Comments	Letters granted "In Vacation". Balance on hand at settlement is $223.98. After deductions for expenses of settlement, balance distributed agreeably to law.

SHARP, Thomas — Estate

Book, Page	POB A: 155; 166-167; 270
Court Dates	23 November 1838 (Letters of Administration Granted); 13 Feb 1839; 11 Feb 1840
Administrator	Elizabeth SHARP (renounces), Joseph McLELLAN
Action	Renunciation filed. Letters of Administration granted. Confirmation of Letters of Administration. Final Account.
Incidental Names	Adam G. POLKE, security
Comments	Letters granted "In Vacation". Administrator has balance of $144.07 at final accounting to be disposed of agreeably to law.

ANDERSON, John — Estate

Book, Page	POB A: 155; 167; 372; 614
Court Dates	24 Nov 1838 (Letters of Administration Granted); 13 Feb 1839; 14 Nov 1840; 19 Nov 1842
Administrator	Jane ANDERSON (renounces), William K. ANDERSON
Heirs	Jane ANDERSON (widow), William H. ANDERSON, Robert T. ANDERSON, Mary Ann ANDERSON, Catherine F. ANDERSON, Margaret T. ANDERSON, and Agnes Jane J. ANDERSON (children of John ANDERSON).
Action	Renunciation filed. Letters of Administration granted. Confirmation of Grant of Letters. Petition for partition of real Estate. Administrator cited to appear in court to make final settlement.
Incidental Names	David ANDERSON, security; Benjamin BUTTERWORTH and Abel LOMAX, commissioners.

| Comments | Letters granted "In Vacation". |

CROOK, James   Estate

Book, Page	POB A: 156; 167
Court Dates	27 Nov 1838 (Letters of Administration Granted); 13 Feb 1839
Administrator	Sylvanus CROOK
Action	Letters of Administration granted. Confirmation of Grant of Letters.
Incidental Names	Jabez R. WELLS, security
Comments	Letters granted "In Vacation".

MAXSON, Lee H. T.   Estate

Book, Page	POB A: 156; 178-179; 425; 487529-531; 556
Court Dates	3 Dec 1838 (Letters of Administration Granted); 15 Feb 1839; 14 Aug 1841; 17 Feb 1842; 11 May 1842; 10 Aug 1842
Administrator	Paul MAXSON (revoked), Oscar H. BARKER
Heirs	Martha MAXON, Martha M. FISK (formerly Martha M. MAXON) and Samuel FISK, her husband. All heirs not residents of Indiana.
Action	Letters of Administration granted. Joseph W. CHAPMAN files petition for Revocation of the Granting of Letters. On Proof of account of Justin BUTTERFIELD and James H. COLLINS vs. Administrator of estate. Plaintiffs awarded $83.46 plus cost. Application for Sale of Real Estate. Additional bond on sale of real estate. Report of Sale of Real Estate. Report approved, sale confirmed. Administrator authorized to receive payment and issue deed.
Incidental Names	Samuel D. VIELE, security. William W. HIGGINS and Jeremiah HITCHCOCK, additional security ($4,033).
Comments	Letters granted "In Vacation". Original Administrator moved out of the State of Indiana and could not fulfill duties. Notice of land sale and need for court appearance to be given to out of state heirs by publication in the MICHIGAN CITY GAZETTE. Personal estate is insufficient to pay debts of estate, certain real estate must be sold to make payment of debts. Publication of sale to be made in the MICHIGAN CITY GAZETTE.

CHENEY, John   Estate

| Book, Page | POB A: 157; 168; 308-309; 324; 366; 407; 449; 475; 517; 558 |
| Court Dates | 10 Dec 1838 (Letters of Administration Granted); 13 Feb 1839; 14 May 1840; 13 Aug 1840; 13 Nov 1840; 13 May 1841; 12 Nov 1841; 15 Feb 1842; 9 May 1842; 10 Aug 1842 |

Administrator	John E. CHENEY
Heirs	Moses G LORD and Lucricia LORD, his wife; John S. MOSSMAN and Rachel MOSSMAN, his wife; Horace SCOTT and Patty M. SCOTT, his wife; Abner T. MATTHEWS and Lucretia MATTHEWS, his wife; Horace CHENEY, Harriett CHENEY, Rachel CHENEY and Malvina CHENEY, infant children of Rufus CHENEY, deceased, son of John CHENEY, deceased.
Action	Letters of Administration granted. Confirmation of Grant of Letters. Application to sell real estate. Inventory and appraisal filed. Complaint of Insolvency. Cause continued. Order of sale of real estate. Administrator ordered to appear at the next Term of Court and make final settlement of Estate. Again ordered to appear. Report of the sale of Real Estate. Sale approved. Administrator asks for continuance. Granted. Cause continued.
Incidental Names	Nathan JOHNSON, security
Comments	Letters granted "In Vacation". Adult heirs notified of the application to sell real estate by publication in MICHIGAN CITY GAZETTE, a weekly publication. Real estate and personal property is insufficient to pay debts of estate. Creditors are notified of insolvency by publication in the MICHIGAN CITY GAZETTE and the LAPORTE COUNTY WHIG and asked to submit claims. Some heirs living in Porter County.

PETRE, Daniel — Estate

Book, Page	POB A: 157-158; 168; 414-415; 575
Court Dates	5 Dec 1838 (Will filed); 15 Dec 1838 (Letters Testamentary Granted): 13 Feb 1839; 11 Aug 1841; 12 Aug 1842
Executor	John PETRE and Daniel J. PETRE, Jr.
Action	Will filed. Letters Testamentary issued. Confirmation of Grant of Letters. Settlement of Estate. Administrators ordered to appear next term to "show & Report to the Court, what disposition has been made of the balance of said Estate, remaining in their hands on settlement of said Estate".
Incidental Names	Saul L. DAWSON, subscribing witness; James C. CUNNINGHAM and Hugh GRAHAM, security.
Comments	Will filed "In Vacation". "The executors were appointed by the said testator in his said last will and testament..." Upon final accounting there is $1201.24. Account approved and "after deducting the expense of the settlement, be disposed of agreeably to the Will of the Deceased."

UNDERWOOD, Benjamin — Estate

Book, Page	POB A: 158; 168-169; 203; 213-214; 381
Court Dates	17 Dec 1838 (Letters of Administration Granted); 13 Feb 1839; 17 May 1839; 15 Aug 1839; 9 Feb 1841

Administrator	Mary Ann UNDERWOOD (renounces), Isaac CORLISS
Heirs	Elbridge Wright UNDERWOOD and Lucy Ann UNDERWOOD
Action	Renunciation filed. Letters of Administration granted. Confirmation of Grant of Letters. Continuation for report of sale of land. Sale of real estate. Settlement of estate.
Incidental Names	Noah NEWELL, security and commissioner.
Comments	Letters granted "In Vacation". Mary Ann UNDERWOOD, guardian of Elbridge W. and Lucy Ann. Michael SINGER and Erastus PAYNE, purchasers of real estate. Administrator transferred "notes in his hands belonging to said estate, to Noah NEWELL, Attorney-in-fact for Mary Ann UNDERWOOD, Guardian of the heirs" of the deceased.

RITTER, Simon	Estate
Book, Page	POB A: 158-159; 169; 220; 284;
Court Dates	19 Jan 1839 (Letters of Administration Granted); 13 Feb 1839; 17 Aug 1839; 14 Feb 1840
Administrator	Pemelia RITTER (renounces), Peter RITTER
Heirs	Elbridge W. UNDERWOOD, Lucy Ann UNDERWOOD
Action	Renunciation filed. Letters of Administration granted. Confirmation of Grant of Letters. Administrator ordered to appear in court and file the Inventory and Sale Bill of said Estate. Administrator notified to appear in court to make final settlement.
Incidental Names	James M. SCOTT, security
Comments	Letters granted "In Vacation".

TONEY, Jesse	Estate
Book, Page	POB A: 159; 169; 189; 317; 335; 369-370; 455; 506; 523; 528; 540; 547-549; 615
Court Dates	31 Jan 1839 (Letters of Administration Granted); 13 Feb 1839; 14 May 1839; 15 May 1840; 13 Aug 1840; 14 Nov 1840; 12 Nov 1841; 19 Feb 1842; 10 May 1842; 12 May 1842; 8 Aug 1842; 19 Nov 1842
Administrator	George BOSSERMAN and Sebert TONEY. Third Administrator, Samuel STEWART.
Heirs	Allen TONEY, infant son of deceased. "Stephen TONEY, Jesse TONEY, Aaron TONEY, Jesse DEARDORFF, Rebecca DEARDORFF and one other name unknown are non residents of the State of Indiana". Allen NEFF, Abraham NEFF, Francis NEFF, Jesse NEFF, John BOSSERMAN and Caroline BOSSERMAN.

Action	Letters of Administration granted. Confirmation of Grant of Letters. Petition filed and granted to sell "few articles of small value" at private sale. Administrator, George BOSSERMAN is cited to appear next term to show cause why he should not give "further and additional Security". Administrators summoned to appear in court to file additional Bond with security or show cause to the contrary. Sebert TONEY removed as administrator for failing to file additional bond. George BOSSERMAN files additional bond. Partial settlement of account. On settlement. Petition to sell real estate. McCASKEY and Sebert TONEY, security for BOSSERMAN file affidavit to be released from their security. BOSSERMAN tenders his resignation and is discharged as Administrator. New Administrator, Samuel STEWART, provided with Letters of Administration. Petition to sell real estate. William ANDREW, Esq appointed Guardian ad litem of Jesse DEARDORFF, Rebecca DEARDORFF, and one other name unknown, Allen NEFF, Abraham NEFF, Frances NEFF, John BOSSERMAN and Caroline BOSSERMAN, minor heirs of the decedent. Report of Sale of Real estate.
Incidental Names	John HOBSON, security (resigned and released); Jacob McCASKEY and Sebert TONEY, security ($7,000). Creditors denied claims against estate, James VAN VALKINBURGH, Sebert TONEY, John B. NILES, and John H. BRADLEY. John J. CRANDALL, security for Stewart ($500). Franklin THORING (?), security. Land sold to Samuel BOOTH of La Porte County. Sale confirmed.
Comments	Letters granted "In Vacation". Sureties, John HOBSON, appears in court to ask Administrator to provide more and additional security. Administrator allowed the sum of $3561.69 in credits and expenditures for administration. Non-resident heirs to be notified by publication in the LA PORTE COUNTY WHIG of the pendency of sale of real estate. Resident heirs to be notified by citation.

HUNT, James — Estate

Book, Page	POB A: 160; 170; 614
Court Dates	7 Feb 1839 (Letters Testamentary Granted); 13 Feb 1839; 19 Nov 1842
Executors	Nancy HUNT, Jasper S. HUNT, and Charles W. HUNT
Action	Will filed. Letters Testamentary granted. Confirmation of Grant of Letters. Administrators cited to appear in court to make final settlement of estate.
Incidental Names	George HUNT, Sr. and Nathan B NICHOLS, subscribing witnesses; George HUNT, Sr., security
Comments	Letters granted "In Vacation". The executrix and executors were "appointed by the said Testator in his said last Will and testament..."

UNDERWOOD, Mary Ann — Guardianship

Book, Page	POB A: 161; 172

Court Dates	11 Feb 1839; 13 Feb 1839
Action	Petition for Guardianship. Application for Sale of real estate.
Incidental Names	Elbridge Wright UNDERWOOD, Lucy Ann UNDERWOOD, infant Heirs of Benjamin UNDERWOOD, deceased; Noah NEWELL, security ($1200). Henry HARDING, Noah NEWELL and Elbridge G. NEWELL, appraisers. Noah NEWELL, commissioner of sale.
Comments	Petitioner was appointed guardian of persons and estates of infant heirs.

BIAS, Garret Guardianship

Book, Page	POB A: 162
Court Dates	11 Feb 1839
Action	Petition for Appointment of Guardian
Incidental Names	Frederick MORSE, infant son of James MORSE, deceased; Matthew LIVINGSTON (?), security ($100)
Comments	Petitioner was issued Letters of Guardianship of person of infant. Sale of property advertised in the La Porte County Whig.

BASTION, Mary Ann Guardianship

Book, Page	POB A: 165
Court Dates	12 Feb 1839
Action	Petition for Appointment of Guardianship
Incidental Names	Maria B. BASTION, infant daughter of Garret V. BASTION; Nathaniel WINCESE (?), security ($400).
Comments	Petitioner is granted guardianship of person and estate of infant.

DEAN, Jonathan M. Guardianship

Book, Page	POB A: 165
Court Dates	12 Feb 1839
Action	Petition for Appointment of Guardianship
Incidental Names	Julia FORT, minor; Oscar H. BARKER, security ($100)
Comments	Julia FORT is a "colored girl" under the age of 14 years. Petitioner is appointed Guardian of her person.

MILLER, Elizabeth Guardianship

Book, Page	POB A: 170-171

Court Dates	13 Feb 1839
Action	Petition for the Appointment of Guardian
Incidental Names	Jacob MILLER, Delila MILLER, Jeremiah MILLER, and Elizabeth Ann MILLER, infant heirs of Peter MILLER, deceased; Polly MILLER, Daniel MILLER, Eve MILLER, and Elijah MILLER, minor heirs of Peter MILLER; James C. CUNNINGHAM, security ($800)
Comments	Letters of Guardianship of persons and estates of infant and minor heirs issued to petitioner.

CUNNINGHAM, Mary Catharine   Guardianship

Book, Page	POB A: 171
Court Dates	13 Feb 1839
Action	Application for the appointment of Guardian. James C. CUNNINGHAM, appointed guardian the estate of his infant daughter, Mary Catherine CUNNINGHAM.
Incidental Names	Elizabeth MILLER, security ($100)

SPAULDING, Timothy   Estate

Book, Page	POB A: 178; 234-235
Court Dates	15 Feb 1839 (Letters of Administration Granted)13 Nov 1839
Administrator	Sylvia SPAULDING (renounces), John B. NILES
Action	Widow relinquishes her right to be administrator. Letters of Administration granted. Inventory, appraisal, and sale bill of personal estate filed.
Incidental Names	Sutton Van Pelt, security

GOULD, Jeremiah   Estate

Book, Page	POB A: 180; 197; 209; 210; 241; 278-279
Court Dates	16 Feb 1839 (Letters of Administration Granted); 16 May 1839; 14 Aug 1839; 14 Nov 1839; 12 Feb 1840
Administrator	John FRANCIS
Heirs	Anna GOULD (widow), Wellen GOULD, Theresa Ann GOULD, Llewellyn GOULD, Aphia GOULD
Action	Letters of Administration Granted. Confirmation of Grant of Letters of Administration. Application for sale of real estate. On complaint of Insolvency. Application to settle said estate as Insolvent. Order of sale of real estate. Report of sale of real estate, and order of Confirmation.
Incidental Names	Oscar A. BARKER, security

| Comments | Letters granted "In Vacation". Heirs are not residents of Indiana on 14 Aug 1839. Notice of sale by publication in LA PORTE COUNTY WHIG. Heirs notified to appear in court on 2nd Monday of November to show cause why real estate should not be sold to discharge debts of the estate. Creditors notified by publication to file claims. Sale ordered and confirmed. |

TULEY, James   Estate

Book, Page	POB A: 180-181; 197; 449; 468; 518-519
Court Dates	13 Feb 1839 (Will filed.) 26 Feb 1839 (Letters of Administration Granted) 16 May 1839; 12 Nov 1841; 15 Feb 1842; 9 May 1842
Administrator	Marsena CLARK
Action	Will filed. Letters of Administration granted. Confirmation of Grant of Letters of Administration. Administrator cited to appear before the Court to make final settlement of Estate. Administrator unprepared to make final settlement, case continued. On Settlement. Approved.
Incidental Names	Archibald MOORMAN & Charles EATON, subscribing witnesses. Charles EATON, security.
Comments	Letters granted "In Vacation". Executor's expenses, $25.86.

RAMBO, Absalom   Estate

Book, Page	POB A: 181; 198; 470
Court Dates	6 Mar 1839 (Will Filed. Letters Testamentary Granted.); 16 May 1839; 15 May 1842
Executrix	Charlotte RAMBO
Action	Will filed and Letters Testamentary granted. Confirmation of Grant of Letters.
Incidental Names	Aaron M. COLLINS and Timothy C. EVERTS, subscribing witnesses. Adonijah RAMBO, security.
Comments	Will filed "In Vacation". "the Executrix appointed by the said Testator in his said last Will and testament..."

GARDNER, Orange   Estate

Book, Page	POB A: 182; 198; 449; 469: 575; 593-594
Court Dates	14 Mar 1839 (Letters of Administration Granted); 16 May 1839; 12 Nov 1841; 15 Feb 1842; 12 Aug 1842; 16 Nov 1842
Administrator	George W. REYNOLDS
Action	Application for appointment of Administration. Letters of Administration granted. Confirmation of Grant of Letters. Administrator cited to appear

before Court to make final settlement of Estate. Administrators unprepared to make final settlement, case continued. Administrator cited to appear before court to make final settlement of estate. On attachment. Administrator must pay $1 and pay the costs of the attachment and that "he stand committed to the custody of the Sherriff until the said fine and costs are paid in replevin".

Incidental Names	Jacob PEER, security. Edman AVERY, security for fines.
Comments	Letters granted "In Vacation".

DAVIS, Henry   Estate

Book, Page	POB A: 182-183; 199; 284; 449; 462; 521
Court Dates	19 Mar 1839 (Letters of Administration Granted); 16 May 1839; 14 Feb 1840; 12 Nov 1841; 14 Feb 1842; 9 May 1842
Administrator	Nancy DAVIS (Renounces), Gustavus A. EVERTS and Handy DAVIS
Action	Renunciation filed. Letters of Administration granted. Confirmation of Grant of Letters. Administrators notified to appear in court to file "inventory and appraisal and Sale Bill of personal property of said estate". Administrators cited to appear before Court to make final settlement of Estate. Administrators ask for continuance. Application for Citation brought by Jeremiah HYSER and other legal heirs against Handy DAVIS, an administrator. Davis required to appear before Court to make final settlement or "show cause to the contrary".
Incidental Names	Sylvanus EVERTS and Leonard CUTLER, security
Comments	Letters granted "In Vacation".

CRUMPACKER, Abram/Abraham   Estate

Book, Page	POB A: 183; 192-193; 199; 205-206; 284; 318; 450; 485
Court Dates	13 Apr 1839 (Letters of Administration Granted); 15 May 1839; 16 May 1839; 12 Aug 1839; 14 Feb 1840; 16 May 1840; 12 Nov 1841; 17 Feb 1842
Administrator	Owen CRUMPACKER
Heirs	John CRUMPACKER, Jacob CRUMPACKER, Peter CRUMPACKER, Joel CRUMPACKER, Polly THOMPSON nee CRUMPACKER
Action	Letters of Administration granted. Application to sell real estate. Confirmation of Grant of Letters of Administration. Application to sell real estate. Order of Sale of Real Estate. Administrator notified to appear in Court to make report of sale of real estate. Report on order of sale of Real estate. Administrator cited to appear before Court to make final settlement of Estate. Administrator unprepared to make settlement of Estate, cause continued.
Incidental Names	William REED, security; Harrison RODIFER, Holder of lien.

Comments	Letters granted "In Vacation". Heirs, Jacob, Peter, Joel and Polly, are non-residents of Indiana. Notice to heirs of application to sell real estate published in the LA PORTE COUNTY WHIG. Personal estate insufficient to cover debts. Offer to sell real estate published in LA PORTE HERALD, prior to 14 Sep 1839. Real estate was not sold for want of bidders, amicably divided among heirs after lienholder and expenses of estate were paid.

WINCHELL, William B.   Estate

Book, Page	POB A: 184; 200; 271; 305; 450; 490-491; 570-572
Court Dates	8 May 1839 (Letters of Administration Granted); 16 May 1839; 11 Feb 1840; 13 May 1840; 12 Nov 1841; 17 Feb 1842; 11 Aug 1842
Administrator	David WINCHELL
Heirs	Sarah WINCHELL (widow), John WINCHELL
Action	Letters of Administration granted. Confirmation of Grant of Letters of Administration. Application to sell real estate. Heirs to be notified by publication of pendency of sale. Publication appeared in the LA PORTE COUNTY WHIG. Widow and heir not having appeared, Administrator is ordered to publish the sale of land to pay debts of the estate. Administrator cited to appear before Court to make final settlement of Estate. On Settlement. Continued to next term to "make sale of the real Estate heretofore ordered-and to make final settlement..." Sale of Real Estate.
Incidental Names	Joseph Catlin, security; William ANDREW, commissioner ($3.00 for services).
Comments	Letters granted "In Vacation". Heirs are not residents of the state of Indiana (Feb 1840). Personal estate insufficient to pay debts. At Settlement Administrator allowed $170.34 for administration plus $299.14 "account of items with which he claims to be credited". Administrator was unable to sell real estate at the appraised value. Since Administrator is the principal creditor of the estate, he is willing to take the real estate at the appraised value ($125) against the debt.

SCOFIELD/SCHOFIELD, Seeley   Estate

Book, Page	POB A: 184; 200; 285; 450; 489-490; 597-598
Court Dates	9 May 1839 (Letters of Administration Granted); 16 May 1839; 14 Feb 1840; 12 Nov 1841; 17 Feb 1842; 17 Nov 1842
Administrator	Stephen NORTON
Action	Letters of Administration granted. Confirmation of Grant of Letters of Administration. Administrator notified to appear in Court to file inventory and sale Bill of Personal Property of estate. Administrator cited to appear before Court to make final settlement. On final settlement. Administrator charged himself the amount of $408.68 and $409.89. Credits allowed.

Incidental Names	David NORTON, security; Preserved WHEELER, $50 claim against estate.
Comments	Letters granted "In Vacation". At Settlement, administrator "charged himself to the amount of three hundred and seventy-eight and twenty-five cents and also an account of items with which the claims to be credited, amounting with aggregate to the sum of $369.89". Claim allowed.

SPRAGUE, Polly — Petition for Dower

Book, Page	POB A: 188-189; 243-244
Court Dates	14 May 1839; 14 Nov 1839
Action	Petition by PRAGUE to assign her just 1/3 as Dower from the heirs of David SPRAGUE. Petition to assign dower. Dower assigned.
Incidental Names	Robert STEWART, Willys PECK, & Oscar A. BARKER, commissioners. Sutton VANPELT appointed guardian ad litem of heirs.
Comments	Polly is the widow of David SPRAGUE. Petition published in MICHIGAN CITY GAZETTE and COMERICAL ADVERTIZER ("a public newspaper printed in Michigan City") for three successive weeks for more than twenty days before first day of present term.

ALLEN, Nathan — Estate

Book, Page	POB A: 191
Court Dates	14 May 1839 (Letters of Administration Granted)
Administrator	Abner S. ALLEN and Andrew L. OSBORN
Action	Letters of Administration granted

GRIFFIN, Seth — Estate

Book, Page	POB A: 193; 223; 240; 416; 594
Court Dates	15 May 1839 (Will filed. Letters Testamentary Granted); 10 Sep 1839; 14 Nov 1839; 12 Aug 1841; 16 Nov 1842
Executor	Hiram GRIFFIN
Action	Will filed. Letters Testamentary granted. Inventory filed. Account for sale of personal estate filed. Settlement of Estate. Administrator files additional security approved "in discharge of the order heretofore taken against him". Cause continued.
Incidental Names	Ebenezer PALMER and Sylvester GRIFFIN, subscribing witnesses; John C. MOUNTS, security ($10,000); Samuel GRIFFIN, additional security ($6,000)
Comments	At final settlement there is a balance of $57.15 to be disposed of "agreeably to the Will of the deceased" after expenses.

HIBBARD, Marian
HIBBARD, John W.
HIBBARD, Daniel W.

Guardianship

Book, Page	POB A: 194
Court Dates	15 May 1839
Action	Petition for appointment of Guardian. Aunis HIBBARD (widow) appointed guardian of person and estates of infant heirs of Horace B. HIBBARD, Marian, John W. and Daniel W. HIBBARD.
Incidental Names	Ezra TYLER co-petition filer; John W. COLE, security ($500)

DINGMAN, Corrintha nee HIBBARD   Guardianship

Book, Page	POB A: 194-195
Court Dates	15 May 1839
Action	Application to choose a Guardian
Incidental Names	William DINGMAN, appointed guardian of person and estate of Corrintha, DINGMAN, minor heir (over 14 years of age) of Horace HIBBARD, deceased. John BROADED, security ($200).

PINNEY, Horace, Sr.

Estate

Book, Page	POB A: 204; 208; 213; 224; 450; 479-480
Court Dates	15 Jul 1839 (Letters of Administration Granted); 13 Aug 1839; 15 Aug 1839; 14 Sep 1839; 12 Nov 1841; 16 Feb 1842
Administrator	Nancy PINNEY and Horace PINNEY, Jr.
Action	Letters of Administration Granted. Inventory and Appraisement filed. Confirmation of Grant of Letters. Sale Bill filed. Administrators cited to appear before Court to make final settlement of Estate. Administrators allowed the $1271.11 ¾ cents credits in account.
Incidental	William EAHART and Phineas SMALL, security
Comments	Letters granted "In Vacation".

BROWN, Manlius
BROWN, Miles
BROWN, James
BROWN, John
BROWN, Virginia
BROWN, America

Guardianship

Book, Page	POB A: 215

Court Dates	16 Aug 1839
Action	Petition for Appointment of Guardian by the father, John BROWN.
Incidental Names	Ezekiel MORRISON, security
Comments	These infant children wish to dispose of four shares of bank stock held in their name in the branch bank at Michigan City of the State Bank of Indiana. Their father is appointed their guardian for that purpose.

ARGABRITE, William   Estate

Book, Page	POB A: 221; 223; 224; 248; 479
Court Date	28 Aug 1839 (Letters of Administration granted); 4 Sep 1839; 24 Oct 1839; 15 Nov 1839; 16 Feb 1842
Administrator	Elizabeth ARGABRITE (widow) renounces. John HEFNER appointed. Inventory filed. Sale Bill filed.
Action	Renunciation accepted. Letters of Administration granted. Confirmation of Grant of Letters. Administrator unprepared to make settlement. Continued.
Incidental Names	John VICORY, John DUDLEY, and Henry HEFNER, security.
Comments	Letters granted "In Vacation".

EWINGS, James   Estate

Book, Page	POB A: 222; 226; 249; 306
Court Date	29 Aug 1839 (Letters of Administration granted); 24 Oct 1839; 15 Nov 1839; 13 May 1840
Administrator	Laura EWINGS (widow) renounces. Loren DAVIS appointed. Confirmation of Grant of Letters.
Heirs	Laura EWING, widow
Action	Renunciation accepted. Letters of Administration granted. Inventory and appraisal of Personal estate filed.
Incidental Names	Sheldon BOOTH, security $200.
Comments	Letters granted "In Vacation". Estate amounted to $69.

HOLLEY, Daniel   Estate

Book, Page	POB A: 222-223; 224; 225; 249; 451; 478
Court Date	16 Sep 1839 (Letters Testamentary granted); 15 Oct 1839; 23 Oct 1839; 15 Nov 1839; 12 Nov 1841; 16 Feb 1842
Executor	Ebenezer PALMER

Action	Letters Testamentary granted "In Vacation". Appraisal of Personal Estate filed. Sale Bill of Personal Estate filed. Confirmation of Grant of Letters. Executor cited to appear before Court to make final settlement. Administrator unprepared to make settlement. Continued.
Incidental Names	Daniel McLEANING, security.
Comments	John GLIME and Ebenezer PALMER, two subscribing witnesses to the Will provide an affidavit that Palmer was named executor in the Will.

LEWIS, Jabez   Estate

Book, Page	POB A: 223; 225; 250; 451; 479
Court Date	18 Sep 1839 (Letters of Administration granted); 17 Oct 1839; 15 Nov 1839; 12 Nov 1841; 16 Feb 1842
Administrator	Joseph B. LEWIS and George G. McCOLLUM
Action	Letters of Administration granted. Inventory and appraisal filed. Confirmation of Grant of Letters. Administrator cited to appear before Court to make final settlement. Administrators unprepared to make settlement. Continued.
Incidental Names	Isaac B. COPLIN, security.
Comments	Letters granted "In Vacation".

McCLINTOCK, Joseph A.   Estate

Book, Page	POB A: 224; 226; 250; 452
Court Dates	25 Sep 1839 (Letters Testamentary Granted); 23 Oct 1839; 15 Nov 1839; 12 Nov 1841
Executor	William CLARK
Action	Letters Testamentary granted. Inventory and appraisal of personal property filed. Confirmation of Grant of Letters. Executor cited to appear before Court to make final settlement.
Incidental Names	Alva MASON & James ROOD, subscribing witnesses; John H. BRADLEY, security
Comments	Letters were granted "In Vacation". Executor was appointed in Will.

LIVINGSTON, Jacob J.   Estate

Book, Page	POB A: 225; 245; 451: 478; 614
Court Dates	16 Oct 1839 (Letters of Administration Granted); 21 Oct 1839; 14 Nov 1839; 12 Nov 1841; 16 Feb 1842; 19 Nov 1842
Administrator	Mary LIVINGSTON

Action	Letters of Administration granted. Inventory and appraisal filed. Confirmation of Grant of Letters. Administrator cited to appear before Court to make final settlement of Estate. Administrator unprepared to make settlement. Continued. Administrator, again, cited to appear to make final settlement.
Incidental Names	Lewis V. BAKER, security
Comments	Letters granted "In Vacation".

MILLER, Samuel — Estate

Book, Page	POB A: 227; 451; 480
Court Dates	11 Nov 1839 (Letters of Administration Granted); 12 Nov 1841; 16 Feb 1842
Administrator	Curtis TRAVIS
Action	Letters of Administration granted. Administrator cited to appear before Court to make final settlement of Estate. $195.76 aggregate amounts allowed to the Administrator as credit "as such administration".

PEARCE, Henry / PEARCE, Phebe — Guardianship

Book, Page	POB A: 235-236
Court Dates	13 Nov 1839
Action	Petition for appointment of Guardian of Estate. Thomas PEARCE appointed.
Incidental Names	William WILSON, security ($2,000)
Comments	Children are legatees of Michael PEARCE, late of Butter County, Ohio.

SCOTT, Samuel Jr. (?) / SCOTT, Martha Jane — Guardianship

Book, Page	POB A: 236
Court Dates	13 Nov 1839
Action	Petition for appoint of Guardian. James M. SCOTT (father) appointed.
Incidental Names	John P. TEEPLE, security ($800)
Comments	The infant children each own "four shares of the Branch Bank at Michigan City of the State Bank of Indiana which they wish to transfer and dispose of." Father appointed "guardian for purpose of making the legal transfer of Bankstock."

ALLEN, Jane   **Petition for Dower**

Book, Page   POB A: 237

Court Dates   13 Nov 1839

Action   Petition to assign dower.

Incidental Names   Charles McCLURE, attorney; Elijah MAYHEW, guardian ad litem of minor
                      heirs; Abner BAILEY, Joseph BLAKE, Arthur McCLURE, disinterested
                      men appointed commissioners to set off said dower.

Comments   Petitioner is the widow and relict of Reuben ALLEN. Minor heirs of the
                      deceased are: John ALLEN, William H. C. ALLEN, Erasmus ALLEN,
                      Adam ALLEN, Dewitt C. ALLEN, Hebra ALLEN, Reuben ALLEN,
                      Elizabeth ALLEN and Jane ALLEN.

WELCH, William A.   **Guardianship**

Book, Page   POB A: 247-248; 333

Court Dates   14 Nov 1839; 13 Aug 1840

Action   Guardianship of William A. WELCH renounced by John M. LEMON. John
                      M. BARCLAY issued letters of Guardianship. Discharge of administrator.

Incidental Names   John M. Lemon, security ($500).

Comments   William is the infant son of William A. WELSH, deceased. His mother, the
                      widow of William A. WELCH, has married John M. BARCLAY, who
                      wishes to be appointed guardian of the person and estate of said infant.
                      Account filed, final settlement made

KEWLEY, William   **Guardianship**

Book, Page   POB A: 251; 537-538

Court Dates   15 Nov 1839; 12 May 1842

Action   Application to chose Guardian by minor under age of 21 yrs. Andrew
                      BURNSIDE appointed guardian. Discharge of guardian and delivery of
                      deed and note.

Incidental Names   Adam G. POLKE, security ($280)

Comments   William is the infant son of John KEWLEY, deceased. William has reached
                      the age of 21 yrs. recently prior to 12 May 1842. Security bond discharged.

KEWLEY, Philip   **Guardianship**
KEWLEY, Jeremiah

Book, Page   POB A: 252; 416-417; 432; 456; 463-464; 467; 502; 537-538; 560

Court Dates   15 Nov 1839; 12 Aug 1841; 9 Nov 1841; 13 Nov 1841; 14 Feb 1842; 19
                      Feb 1842; 12 May 1842; 11 Aug 1842

Action	Application to choose guardian by minor under age of 21 yrs. Adam G. POLKE appointed guardian. Isabella KEWLEY, next friend to minor heirs files petition for accounting by Guardian. Guardian files answer. Continued. Isabella is appointed Guardian of infant heirs. Polke must deliver note provided by Burnside (security) and execute quit claim deed for "said lot of land" mentioned in answer upon Isabella paying his expenses incurred for letters of guardianship, court cost and expenses of recording deed and of executing a new one. Upon completion of this, Polke shall be fully "released and discharged" as guardian which bond was dated 15 Nov 1839. A similar resolution to the guardianship of William KEWLEY seems to have been effected in this court appearance. Isabella appointed Guardian. William, nearly 21 yrs. of age, does not want Isabella as his guardian. At beginning of next term he will be of age, Adam G. POLKE will be discharged as his guardian. Polke will deliver note and deed to Isabella and William at this time and he and Burnside "shall be in full discharge of all liability" on their bond. Bonds and deeds delivered to Isabella. Polke discharged. Burnside discharged. Polke "fully released from all liability theron".
Incidental Names	Andrew BURNSIDE, security ($560). William SHIMERIN, security ($500).
Comments	Philip and Jeremiah are infant sons of John KEWLEY, deceased.

ALLEN, Jane — Petition for Dower

Book, Page	POB A: 255
Court Dates	16 Nov 1839
Action	Petition to assign dower.
Incidental Names	Arthur McCLURE and Joseph BLAKE, commissioners appointed to set aside 1/3 of the estate of Reuben ALLEN as dower for his widow.
Comments	Jane is the widow of Reuben ALLEN

WALBRIDGE, John — Estate

Book, Page	POB A: 260-261; 280; 551: 586
Court Dates	23 Nov 1839 (Will Proved); 3 Dec 1839 (Letters Testamentary Granted); 14 Feb 1840; 8 Aug 1842; 15 Nov 1842
Executor	Theodore CATLIN, as appointed by testator in his will
Action	Letters Testamentary granted. Confirmation of Grant of Letters Testamentary. Executor cited to appear in Court to make final settlement. Executor asks for continuance. Granted. Executor, again, asked for continuance. Granted.
Incidental Names	Joseph CATLIN and Arad S. CATLIN, subscribing witnesses. Arad S. CATLIN and Henry YOUNG, security.

Comments   Will filed "In Vacation".

JOHNSON, Samuel   Estate

Book, Page   POB A: 261; 281; 531

Court Dates   30 Nov 1839 (Letters of Administration Granted); 14 Feb 1840; 11 May 1842

Administrator   Joseph H. BENEDICT and William EAHART

Action   Letters of Administration. Confirmation of Grant of Letters of Administration. On Settlement.

Incidental Names   James McCORD, security.

Comments   Letters granted "In Vacation. Administrators charged themselves "to the amount of $304.00" and also an account of items they claim to be credited amounting "in the aggregate to $233.44."

WAKEFIELD, Jesse   Estate

Book, Page   POB A: 262; 281; 451; 472; 546-547; 583-584; 593

Court Dates   10 Dec 1839 (Letters of Administration granted); 14 Feb 1840; 12 Nov 1841; 15 Feb 1842; 8 Aug 1842; 15 Nov 1842; 16 Nov 1842

Administrator   Christana WAKEFIELD (widow) renounces. James REEVE appointed.

Action   Letters of Administration granted. Confirmation of Grant of Letters of Administration. Administrator cited to appear before Court to make final settlement of Estate. Continuance. Complaint of Insolvency. On application to Settle said estate as insolvent. Adjudged insolvent. On settlement.

Incidental Names   Asaph WEBSTER, security.

Comments   Letters granted "In Vacation". Creditors to be informed by publication in THE LA PORTE COUNTY WHIG that they must notify the administrator of the existence and extent of claims. Administrator charged himself "to the amount of $921.80 being the amount of the sale bill notes and also an account of Items with which he claims to be credited amounting in the aggregate to $793.57 which said exhibits of debtor & creditors...leaving a balance due the estate of $128.23."

HOLLOWAY, Jason   Guardianship
HOLLOWAY, John S.

Book, Page   POB A: 263

Court Dates   10 Feb 1840

Action   Petition to choose a Guardian.

Incidental Names	Stephen HOLLOWAY appointed guardian. John STANTON, security ($800).
Comments	Petitioners seek appointment of Guardian of estate coming to them from their grandfather.

WOODSON, William Thomas   Guardianship

Book, Page	POB A: 290
Court Dates	15 Feb 1840
Action	Application to choose a Guardian
Incidental Names	Edmund B. WOODSON appointed guardian. William C. HANNAH, security ($100).
Comments	Petitioner is the infant son of Joseph WOODSON, deceased.

SHARP, John
SHARP, Nelson
SHARP, Caroline
SHARP, Martha Ann
SHARP, Elizabeth
SHARP, Benjamin
SHARP, Angeline
Guardianship

Book, Page	POB A: 290-291
Court Dates	15 Feb 1840
Action	Application to choose a Guardian
Incidental Names	Elizabeth SHARP appointed Guardian of the person and estate of her infant children. John JACOBUS, security ($100).

MORSE, Mary   Guardianship

Book, Page	POB A: 291
Court Dates	15 Feb 1840
Action	Application to choose a Guardian.
Incidental Names	Asa M. WARREN appointed Guardian of person and estate of applicant. Joseph W. LYKINS, security ($100).
Comments	Applicant is infant daughter of James MORSE, deceased.

SMEDLEY, Adam   Estate

Book, Page	POB A: 292; 319; 541; 558; 614

Court Dates	22 Feb 1840 (Letters of Administration Granted); 16 May 1840; 12 May 1842; 10 Aug 1842; 19 Nov 1842
Administrator	George BENTLEY
Action	Letters of Administration Granted. Administrator cited to appear in Court to make final settlement. Cause continued. Administrator, again, cited to appear and make final settlement.
Incidental Names	John F. HEWS, security.
Comments	Letters granted "In Vacation".

WILLIAMS, David   Estate

Book, Page	POB A: 292; 320; 560-561
Court Dates	22 Feb 1840 (Letters of Administration Granted); 16 May 1840; 11 Aug 1842
Administrator	Rensselaer SHAW
Action	Letters of Administration Granted; Confirmation of Grant of Letters of Administration. On Settlement.
Incidental Names	George W. REYNOLDS, security.
Comments	Letters granted "In Vacation". Administrator "charged himself to the amount of $186.00 being the amount of the sale bill. And also an Account of items with which he claims to be credited, amounting in the aggregate to $206.16". Accounting allowed.

GOODWIN, William B.   Estate

Book, Page	POB A: 293; 320; 417
Court Dates	29 Feb 1840 (Letters of Administration Granted); 16 May 1840; 13 Aug 1841
Administrator	Warren COLE
Action	Letters of Administration granted. Confirmation of Grant of Letters. Settlement of Estate.
Incidental Names	George R. SELKREGG, security.
Comments	Letters granted "In Vacation". At final settlement Administrator has $49.28 more than the "amount of moneys received by him". Account is approved and Administrator is discharged.

McCLURE, Arthur   Estate

Book, Page	POB A: 293; 321; 346

Court Dates	17 Mar 1840 (Letters of Administration Granted); 16 May 1840; 15 Aug 1840
Administrator	Joseph BLAKE
Action	Letters of Administration granted. Confirmation of Grant of Letters. Discharge of Administrator.
Incidental Names	George W. ALLEN, security
Comment	Letters granted "In Vacation". Administrator is moving out of state. Files statement of accounts as far as it has progressed.

BECKNER, John
BECKNER, Jacob
BECKNER, Sarah
BECKNER, Joel
BECKNER, David
BECKNER, William
BECKNER, Abraham

Guardianship

Book, Page	POB A: 303
Court Dates	13 May 1840
Action	Application to choose a guardian. Elizabeth BECKNER, their mother, appointed guardian of persons and estates.
Incidental Names	George BECKNER, security.
Comments	Applicants are heirs of John BECKNER, deceased. John, Jacob and Sarah are over 14 years of age. Joel, David, William and Abraham are under 14 years of age.

PLANK, Asa Rilburn ### Guardianship

Book, Page	POB A: 304
Court Dates	13 May 1840
Action	Application to choose guardian. Shadrach CRANE appointed guardian of person.
Incidental Names	Applicant is represented by his mother, Sally CRANE. Abram TEAGARDEN, security.
Comments	Applicant is infant son of Abraham PLANK, deceased.

GOBLE, Isaac P. ### Estate

Book, Page	POB A: 306; 331; 333; 391-392; 402
Court Dates	13 May 1840 (Letters of Administration Granted); 12 Aug 1840; 13 Aug 1840; 12 Feb 1841; 12 May 1841

Administrator	Daniel LOW
Action	Letters of Administration granted. Sale bill of personal estate of deceased filed. Application to sell real estate. Report of Sale of real estate and Order of Confirmation. Settlement of Estate.
Incidental Names	George AMES, security
Comments	Heirs to be notified to appear and show cause why real estate should not be sold to discharge debts.

TERRELL, Joseph F.   Estate

Book, Page	POB A: 315
Court Dates	15 May 1840 (Letters of Administration Granted)
Administrator	Jesse H. Waldo
Action	Letters of Administration granted
Incidental Names	Willys PECK, security.

DAWSON, George   Estate

Book, Page	POB A: 322; 335; 541; 559
Court Dates	28 May 1840 (Letters Testamentary granted); 13 Aug 1840; 12 May 1842; 10 Aug 1842
Executrix	Mary DAWSON (widow)
Executors	Matthias DAWSON (son) and John WHITEHEAD
Action	Letters Testamentary granted. Confirmation of Grant of Letters. Executrix and Executors cited to appear in Court to make final settlement. Cause continued.
Incidental Names	George HUNT and Joseph DAWSON, security; Jesse COLEMAN and William A. MARTIN, subscribing witnesses to decedent's Will.
Comments	Executrix and Executors were appointed in said Will.

ANDERSON, Margaret T.   Guardianship
ANDERSON, Mary Ann
ANDERSON, Catharine H.
ANDERSON, Agness Jane

Book, Page	POB A: 323
Court Dates	10 Aug 1840
Action	Petition to choose a Guardian. William K. ANDERSON chosen and appointed Guardian of persons and estates of applicants.

| Incidental Names | Jane ANDERSON (mother) appears on behalf of Agness Jane. David ANDERSON, security ($500). |

WALDRIFF, William vs.　　　　　　**Real Estate Conveyance**
BALDWIN, Ival
BALDWIN, Reuben
BALDWIN, Rhoda
Unknown heirs of
BALDWIN, Daniel, Jr.
BALDWIN, Daniel, Sr.

Book, Page	POB A: 325
Court Dates	10 Aug 1840
Action	Application to appoint Commissioner to convey Real estate.
Incidental Names	John H. BRADLEY, appointed Commissioner.
Comments	Plaintiff was sold land by Daniel BALDWIN, Sr. during his lifetime. At Baldwin's death, Baldwin was still seized of this property.

ANDERSON, David vs.　　　　　　**Partition of Real Estate**
ANDERSON, William K.
ANDERSON, Robert T.
ANDERSON, Mary Ann
ANDERSON, Catherine F.
ANDERSON, Margaret T.
ANDERSON, Agness Jane, children of
ANDERSON, Jane, widow of
ANDERSON, John

Book, Page	POB A: 327-328
Court Dates	10 Aug 1840
Action	Petition for Partition of Real Estate
Incidental Names	Benjamin BUTTERWORTH, Elnathan GREGORY, Abel SOMAN, appointed commissioners. William K. ANDERSON appointed guardian of minor children.
Comments	Commissioners to divide land between Plaintiff (1/2 share) and widow and children (1/2 share).

WELSH, William A.　　　　　　**Estate**

Book, Page	POB A: 334
Court Dates	13 Aug 1840 (Letters of Administration Granted)
Administrator	John M. Barclay

Action	Letters of Administration Granted.
Incidental Names	James C. HEWIT, security

CATTRON, Valentine   Estate

Book, Page	POB A: 347; 368; 566; 584-585; 589-592
Court Dates	8 Sep 1840 (Letters of Administration Granted); 14 Nov 1840; 11 Aug 1842; 15 Nov 1842; 16 Nov 1842
Administrator	Hezekiah CATTRON & John A. G. CATTRON
Heirs	Thomas CATTRON, James B. CATTRON, William CATTRON, Samuel CATTRON, Wesley F. CATTRON, Robert MILFORD (Fountain County), Daniel MAINS and Mary, his wife.
Action	Letters of Administration Granted. Confirmation of Grant of letters. Application for the appointment of Commissioners to convey Real estate. Some heirs have been notified to appear. Cause continued until all heirs are notified. Application for the appointment of Commissioner to convey real estate. Adult heirs summoned, did not appear. "Ordered, adjudged and decreed" that Commissioner be appointed and deed to several tracts of land be executed to the "said Robert MILFORD". Petition for Commissioner to convey real estate. Land is conveyed to Robert, his heirs and assigns.
Incidental Names	Joseph H. BENEDICT and George McCORD, security. John B. NILES, Esq. appointed Guardian ad Litem of minor heirs: William, Samuel and Wesley F. James BRADLEY, Esq. appointed Commissioner, paid $3 for his services.
Comments	Letters granted "In Vacation". Robert MILFORD lives in Fountain County, IN on 16 Nov 1842. Valentine had sold the land in Fountain County to Robert, but, died before he delivered the deed.

HUDSON, Elijah P.   Estate

Book, Page	POB A: 348; 365; 368
Court Dates	7 Oct 1840 (Letters of Administration Granted); 13 Nov 1840 (Will filed); 14 Nov 1840
Executor	Pliney HUDSON
Action	Letters of Administration Granted. Confirmation of Grant of Letters.
Incidental Names	Samuel TREAT & P. B. BILL, security. Patrick B. BILL and Reuben TREAT, affidavit for proof of Will.
Comments	Letters granted "In Vacation". Will filed at later date.

MARTIN, Mary   Estate

Book, Page	POB A: 348; 357; 369; 542

Court Dates	30 Oct 1840 (Letters of Administration Granted); 12 Nov 1840; 14 Nov 1840; 12 May 1842
Administrator	Charles MARTIN
Action	Letters of Administration Granted. Inventory and appraisal of personal estate filed. Confirmation of Grant of Letters. Administrator cited to appear in Court to make final settlement.
Incidental Names	Francis LUCAS, security.
Comments	Letters granted "In Vacation".

HOLLOWAY, Amos — Estate

Book, Page	POB A: 354; 613
Court Dates	9 Nov 1840 (Letters of Administration Granted); 19 Nov 1842
Administrator	Stephen HOLLOWAY
Action	Letters of Administration Granted; Administrator ordered to appear to make settlement.
Incidental Names	Elijah STANTON, security.

BOYLES, Sally Ann / CURRY, Mary Eliza — Guardianship

Book, Page	POB A: 362
Court Dates	12 Nov 1840
Action	Application to appoint Guardian
Incidental Names	George PETRO, appointed guardian of persons and estates of each applicant. William TAYLOR, security ($100).
Comments	Sally Ann is infant daughter of Elijah BOYLES, deceased. Mary Eliza is infant daughter of James CURRY, deceased.

AUSTIN, Sans — Estate

Book, Page	POB A: 362-363; 609
Court Dates	12 Nov 1840 (Letters of Administration Granted); 19 Nov 1842
Administrator	Sarah AUSTIN, widow (renounces); Henry TEETER
Action	Widow renounces her position of administratrix. Letters of administration granted to Teeter. Ordered that administrator be cited to appear to make final settlement of estate.
Incidental Names	Jedediah AUSTIN, security.

SUMMERS, Lucian   **Guardianship**

Book, Page	POB A: 365
Court Dates	13 Nov 1840
Action	Application for appointment of Guardian
Incidental Names	Benjamin F. BAIR is appointed Guardian for the person during the minority of applicant. George REMES, security ($100).
Comments	Applicant is the infant son of ? SUMMERS (given name is blank).

TREAT, Theodore   **Estate**

Book, Page	POB A: 374; 387; 608
Court Dates	24 Nov 1840 (Letters of Administration Granted); 10 Nov 1841; 19 Nov 1842
Administrator	Sarah TREAT (renounced), Alonzo D. TREAT
Action	Letters of Administration granted. Confirmation of Grant of Letters. Ordered that administrator be cited to appear to make final settlement of estate.
Incidental Names	Samuel TREAT (security)
Comments	Letters granted "In Vacation".

PINNEY, Mary   **Guardianship**
PINNEY, Lois

Book, Page	POB A: 375
Court Dates	8 Feb 1841
Action	Application for appointment of Guardian
Incidental Names	Phenias SMALL appointed guardian of person and estate of infant, Mary PINNEY. William PINNEY and Horace PINNEY, security.
Comments	Applicant is infant daughter of Horrace PINNEY, deceased.

PINNEY, Lois   **Guardianship**
PINNEY, Mary

Book, Page	POB A: 376
Court Dates	8 Feb 1841
Action	Application for appointment of Guardian
Incidental Names	Horace PINNEY and William PINNEY appointed guardian of person and estate of infant, Lois PINNEY. Phenias SMALL, security ($400).
Comments	Applicant is infant daughter of Horrace PINNEY, deceased.

BROWN, William	Guardianship
BROWN, Hamilton	
BROWN, Daniel	
BROWN, Sarah	
BROWN, Catharine	
BROWN, Elizabeth	
BROWN, Alfred	
BROWN, Rush	
BROWN, Mary	

Book, Page	POB A: 276-277
Court Dates	8 Feb 1841
Action	Catharine BROWN appointed guardian of persons and estates of the infant sons and daughters of John BROWN, deceased, during their minority.
Incidental Names	Samuel GRIFFIN, security ($100).

BROWN, Catharine	**Application to Sell Real Estate**
Book, Page	POA A: 377-378; 382-383; 389
Court Dates	8 Feb 1841; 9 Feb 1841; 11 Feb 1841
Action	Application to sell real estate. Appraisal presented. Application to sell real estate at private Sale. Order issued for private sale of land. Report of sale of Real estate and order of Confirmation.
Incidental Names	Infant heirs of John BROWN: William BROWN, Hamilton BROWN, Daniel BROWN, Sarah BROWN, Catharine BROWN, Elizabeth BROWN, Alfred BROWN, Rush BROWN, Mary BROWN; John HASELTINE, Cornelius, VAN TASSEL, Ingraham GOULD, appointed appraisers. Harry (?) BROWN, heir at Law of John BROWN of lawful age, relinquishes real estate to be sold. Aaron CONKLIN, purchaser of real estate.
Comments	Property appraised at $40.

HIBBARD, Annis S.	**Petition for Dower**
Book, Page	POB A: 386; 401; 442-443
Court Dates	10 Feb 1841; 12 May 1841; 11 Nov 1841
Action	Petition for the assignment of Dower. Commissioners ask for further time. Dower assigned.
Incidental Names	Joseph OSBORN, Orrin WILLIS/WILLYS, Charles W. CATHCART, appointed commissioners.
Comments	Plaintiff is the widow of Horace B.HIBBARD. William C. HANNAH appointed Guardian ad litem for infant heirs, Marion HIBBARD, John W. HIBBARD & Daniel W. HIBBARD.

FOSTER, Thomas J.   Estate

Book, Page	POB A: 395; 396; 608
Court Dates	27 Mar 1841 (Letters of Administration Granted); 10 May 1841; 19 Nov 1842
Administrator	Alexander BLACKBURN
Action	Letters of Administration Granted. Confirmation of grant of letters. Ordered that administrator be cited to appear to make final settlement of estate.
Incidental Names	James C. HOWELL, security
Comments	Letters granted "In Vacation".

CLARK, John W.   Estate

Book, Page	POB A: 396; 397-398; 608
Court Dates	1 May 1841 (Letters of Administration Granted); 18 Nov; 19 Nov 1842
Administrator	Elizabeth CLARK
Action	Letters of Administration Granted. Confirmation of grant of letters. Ordered that administrator be cited to appear to make final settlement of estate.
Incidental Names	David C. McKELLOPS, security
Comments	Letters granted "In Vacation".

SMALLWOOD, Samuel   Estate

Book, Page	POB A: 409; 410; 438-429; 503; 504-505; 611
Court Dates	24 Jun 1841 (Letters of Administration granted); 9 Aug 1841; 10 Nov 1841; 19 Feb 1842; 19 Nov 1842
Administrator	Elizabeth SMALLWOOD (renounces), Henry BELDEN/BELDING
Heirs	Elizabeth SMALLWOOD, Burnet SMALLWOOD, Samuel SMALLWOOD, Elizabeth SMALLWOOD, JR, Sarah Jane SMALLWOOD.
Action	Letters of Administration granted. Confirmation of grant of letters. Petition to sell real estate, inventory and appraisal filed. Heirs summoned to show cause why real estate should not be sold to pay debts. Application to settle said Estate as Insolvent. So ordered. Creditors must file claims before final distribution or "such claims will be postponed, in favor of the more diligent creditors." Application to sell Real Estate. Creditors have been served with summons and heirs in Marshall County notified. Continued. Adult heirs default. John B. NILES appointed Guardian as Litem of minor heirs, Samuel, Elizabeth and Sarah. Personal estate is insufficient to pay debts. Land to be sold.

Incidental Names	Aquilla W. ROGERS, security. Asa OWENS, Owen A. OWENS, William C. HANNAH, & Ezekiel MORRISON, holders of liens. Theodore CATLIN, security.
Comments	Letters granted "in vacation". Real and personal property is insufficient to pay creditors. Notice sent to creditors by way of LA PORTE COUNTY WHIG.

AUSTIN, Sarah — Petition for Dower

Book, Page	POB A: 411; 419-420
Court Dates	10 Aug 1841; 13 Aug 1841
Action	Petition to assign dower and assign Guardian for Harriet AUSTIN, William AUSTIN, and Alexander AUSTIN, infant heirs of Sans AUSTIN. Dower assigned.
Incidental Names	Henry TEETER, uncle of the infant heirs, appointed Guardian. Alexander BLACKBURN, James CATTERLIN, and Benjamin BREWER appointed commissioners to assign dower "the just third part of and in all the lands..." etc.

JACKSON, Sarah Maria — Petition for Dower

Book, Page	POB A: 412; 418-419
Court Dates	10 Aug 1841; 13 Aug 1841
Action	Petition to assign dower. Dower assigned and set off.
Incidental Names	Samuel TREAT, Lawson HOUGH, and William McPATTERSON appointed commissioners to assign dower "the just third part of and in all the lands, tenements and hereditaments..."
Comments	Sarah is the widow of Jesse JACKSON.

ROUSS, Mary late GOSSETT, Mary — Petition for Dower

Book, Page	POB A: 413; 439-440
Court Dates	10 Aug 1841; 10 Nov 1841
Action	Petition to assign dower. Dower assigned.
Incidental Names	James WEBSTER, John BROWN and John P. COBBS appointed as commissioners to assign dower "the just third part of and in all the lands, tenements and hereditaments..."
Comments	Petitioner is the widow of John GOSSETT.

EAGEN, Rebecca   **Estate**

Book, Page	POB A: 423
Court Dates	14 Aug 1841 (Letters of Administration granted)
Administrator	George AMES and West DARLING
Action	Letters of Administration granted.
Incidental Names	Fisher AMES, security.

SCARCE, Samuel   **Estate**

Book, Page	POB A: 426; 441
Court Dates	11 Oct 1841 (Letters of Administration granted); 11 Nov 1841
Administrator	David HARMAN
Action	Letters of Administration granted. Confirmation of Grant of letters.
Incidental Names	John M. CLARKSON, security
Comments	Letters granted "in vacation".

JUSTICE, William   **Estate**

Book, Page	POB A: 427; 441-442
Court Dates	1 Nov 1841 (Letters of Administration granted); 11 Nov 1841
Administrators	Hannah JUSTICE and John HARVEY
Action	Letters of Administration granted. Confirmation of Grant of letters.
Incidental Names	Jonathan LINE and Samuel WEBSTER, security
Comments	Letters granted "in vacation".

FOSTER, Orlander   **Guardianship**
FOSTER, Thomas

Book, Page	POB A: 428-429
Court Dates	8 Nov 1841
Action	Petition to Appoint Guardian brought by Lucetta FOSTER.
Incidental Names	James PADDOCK appointed Guardian; Anson B. WARNER, security ($600).
Comments	Petitioners are the infant children of Thomas FOSTER, deceased.

RITTER, PEMELIA   Petition for Dower

Book, Page	POB A: 454; 466
Court Dates	12 Nov 1841; 14 Feb 1842
Action	Petition to assign Dower. Case discontinued.
Incidental Names	Andrew McCLAIN, William W. TAYLOR, and William CLARK appointed commissioners to assign just third part of Estate to widow.
Comments	Petitioner, Pemelia RITTER, has deceased between time of Petition and 14 Feb 1842 court date.

WESTERVELT, Abraham   Estate

Book, Page	POB A: 457-458; 468
Court Dates	15 Dec 1841 (Letters of Administration Granted); 15 Feb 1842
Administrator	Catherine WESTERVELT, widow, renounces. James WESTERVELT
Action	Letters of Administration granted. Letters of Administration confirmed.
Incidental Names	Benjamin BEARD, security ($1200)
Comments	Letters granted "in vacation".

SMITH, James F.   Estate

Book, Page	POB A: 458-459; 508
Court Dates	3 Jan 1842 (Letters of Administration Granted); 19 Feb 1842
Administrator	Olivia M. SMITH, widow, renounces. Egbert R. DEWITT
Action	Letters of Administration granted. Confirmation of grant of Letters.
Incidental Names	Benjamin DEWITT, security ($1400)
Comments	Letters granted "in vacation".

GRIFFIN, Daniel   Estate

Book, Page	POB A: 459-460; 508; 525; 569
Court Dates	29 Jan 1842 (Letters of Administration Granted); 19 Feb 1842; 10 May 1842; 11 Aug 1842
Administrators	Alethea GRIFFIN, Homer GRIFFIN, Charles TUCKER
Heirs	Henry MONROE and Angeline MONROE, his wife, Homer GRIFFIN, Wellington GRIFFIN, Bartlet WOOD, and Sally Ann WOOD, his wife, Levi GRIFFIN, Augustus GRIFFIN, Edgar GRIFFIN, and Anson GRIFFIN

Action	Letters of Administration granted. Confirmation of grant of Letters. Petition for sale of real Estate, inventory and appraisal of part of real Estate filed. Petition to sell Real Estate.
Incidental Names	Silas TUCKER and Ingraham GOULD, security ($1150)
Comments	Letters granted "in vacation". Heirs "to be cited to be and appear before this Court....to show cause if any they can, why the said real Estate shall not be sold and made assets for the payment of said debts". Since Anson GRIFFIN is not a resident of the state of Indiana, notice of the pendency of application to sell real estate is to be given by publication in the LA PORTE COUNTY WHIG.

STARRET, Alexander — Estate

Book, Page	POB A: 460-461; 509
Court Dates	31 Jan 1842 (Letters of Administration Granted); 19 Feb 1842
Administrators	Theresa STARRET and Joseph STARRET
Action	Letters of Administration granted. Confirmation of grant of Letters.
Incidental Names	Benjamin SHAW, security ($1000)
Comments	Letters granted "in vacation".

RAMBO, Charlotte — Estate

Book, Page	POB A: 470
Court Dates	15 Feb 1842 (Letters Testamentary Granted)
Executor	Smith RAMBO, Timothy C. EVERTS (declined)
Action	Letters Testamentary granted.
Incidental Names	Jeremiah PATRE, subscribing witness; John HALL and Timothy C. EVERTS, security ($1800)
Comments	Executors were named in Will.

HALL, Amos / HALL, Gustavus — Guardianship

Book, Page	POB A: 471; 559
Court Dates	15 Feb 1842; 10 Aug 1842
Action	Application for appointment of Guardian of persons and Estates. Letters of Guardianship issued. Permission to sell wheat belonging to Amos and Gustavus. Granted. Guardian must report sale to Court at next term.
Incidental Names	Joseph B. SELF appointed Guardian. Handy DAVIS, security ($600).

| Comments | Amos and Gustavus are infant (under 14 yrs.) sons of Wesley HALL and heirs of the estate of the late Henry DAVIS. |

DAVIS, Joshua
DAVIS, George Washington
DAVIS, Polly   **Guardianship**

Book, Page	POB A: 471-472
Court Dates	15 Feb 1842
Action	Application for appointment of Guardian of persons and Estates. Letters of Guardianship issued.
Incidental Names	Jeremiah HUYSER appointed Guardian. Daniel SHAW and David MITCHELL, security ($1800).
Comments	Applicants are infant heirs of Henry DAVIS, deceased. Joshua and George Washington are over 14 yrs., but still minors, and able to choose their own Guardian. Polly is under 14 yrs. and Guardian is Court appointed. Same Guardian for all.

CURRIE, Walter
CURRIE, David C.
CURRIE, Andrew H.
CURRIE, Ebenezer
CURRIE, Elizabeth
CURRIE, James A.   **Guardianship**

Book, Page	POB A: 474-475; 481-482; 522
Court Dates	15 Feb 1842; 16 Feb 1842; 10 May 1842
Action	Petitioner John CHALMERS, Guardian of persons and estates of minor heirs at law of George CURRIE, deceased, files application to sell real estate. Appraisers submit appraisement of $801.20. Terms of sale established. Application by Commissioner for further time to sell real estate.
Incidental Names	Peter WHITE, Benjamin BAIRD and Jacob TEETER, appointed appraisers to appraise the widows half of land belonging to petitioners. James CURRIE with guardian, security ($1602.40) and, also, commissioner for sale of property.

DAVIS, Handy   **Partition of Real Estate**
HUYSER, Priscilla, late DAVIS, Priscilla
MIDDLETON, Margaret, late DAVIS, Margaret
DAVIS, John
DAVIS, Henry
DAVIS, James
   Vs.
DAVIS, Joshua
DAVIS, George W.
DAVIS, Polly
HALL, Amos
HALL, Gustavus

Book, Page	POB A: 482-484; 528
Court Dates	16 Feb 1842; 10 May 1842
Action	Petition for Partition of Real Estate between adult heirs, Handy, Priscilla (wife of Jeremiah), Margaret, John, Henry and James and minor heirs, Joshua, George W., Polly, and the children of Eliza HALL, late Eliza DAVIS, deceased, Amos and Gustavus. All are heirs of the late Henry DAVIS, deceased. In addition, a petition was jointly filed by the widow, Nancy DAVIS, for assignment of Dower. Court orders Commissioners to make partition and assign dower by next term (10 May 1842).
Incidental Names	Jeremiah HUYSER is guardian of Amos and Gustavus. Joseph B. SELF is guardian of the minor Davis heirs. John MOORE, JR., Rensselaer SHAW, and David WINCHELL, commissioners for partition of land in both petitions.

MAXON, Paul H.   **Estate**

Book, Page	POB A: 486
Court Dates	17 Feb 1842 (Letters of Administration Granted)
Administrator	Andrew S. OSBORNE
Action	Letters of Administration Granted.
Incidental Names	Joseph W. CHAPMAN, security ($100)

SOMMERS, Amos   **Guardianship**

Book, Page	POB A: 488
Court Dates	17 Feb 1842
Action	Application for Appointment of Guardian. Elisha K. BROWN appointed Guardian of person of minor under age of 14 yrs.
Incidental Names	Ziba BAILEY, security ($50).
Comments	Amos is the son of Isaac SOMMERS, deceased.

ARGABRITE, John H.
ARGABRITE, Samuel S.
ARGABRITE, Sarah A.
ARGABRITE, Eliza J.
ARGABRITE, William J.
ARGABRITE, Mary E.

Guardianship

Book, Page	POB A: 491-492
Court Dates	18 Feb 1842
Action	Application for Appointment of Guardian. John HEFNER appointed Guardian of person and estates of infant children.
	John, being over age 14 is and permitted to choose his own Guardian. He chooses same Guardian as infant children.
Incidental Names	William H. H. WHITEHEAD, security ($3,350)
Comments	Petitioners are children of William ARGABRITE (deceased).

ROUNDY, John

Estate

Book, Page	POB A: 507
Court Dates	19 Feb 1842 (Letters of Administration Granted)
Administration	Joseph W. CHAPMAN
Action	Letters of Administration Granted.
Incidental Names	James FORRESTER, security
Comments	Decedent died intestate.

WOOD, Lovina

Estate

Book, Page	POB A: 510-511; 532
Court Dates	15 Mar 1842 (Letters Testamentary granted). 12 May 1842
Executor	Oscar A. BARKER
Action	Will filed, executor granted letters Testamentary. Confirmation of Grant of Letters (this time listed as Letters of Administration).
Incidental Names	Dewitt STRONG, security ($300)
Comments	Letters Testamentary were granted "in vacation". Will was filed in open court on 14 Aug 1840 by two subscribing witnesses, Andrew S. OSBORN and Abner DEVALLE (?).

BILLS/BILL, Patrick B.   Estate

Book, Page   POB A: 511-512; 532

Court Dates   8 Mar 1842 (Letters of Administration Granted); 12 May 1842

Administratrix   Frances BILL

Action   Letters of Administration Granted. Confirmation of Grant of Letters.

Incidental Names   Ezekiel MORRISON and Samuel BURSON, security ($600)

WHITEHEAD, Hampton B.   Estate

Book, Page   POB A: 512-513; 532-533

Court Dates   6 Apr 1842 (Letters of Administration Granted); 12 May 1842

Administrator   Margaret WHITEHEAD (widow), renounces. William H. H. WHITEHEAD appointed.

Action   Letters of Administration Granted. Confirmation of Grant of Letters.

Incidental Names   Alexander HASTINGS, security ($600)

Comments   Letters granted "in vacation".

HUDSON, Pliny   Estate

Book, Page   POB A: 513-514; 538

Court Dates   13 Apr 1842 (Letters of Administration Granted); 12 May 1842

Administrator   Ezekiel MORRISON

Action   Letters of Administration granted. Confirmation of Grant of Letters.

Incidental Names   Alexander BLACKBURN, Sutton VANPELT, and Hiram WHEELER, security ($10,000).

Comments   Letters of Administration granted "in vacation". The late Pliny HUDSON is from New York State. Creditors file application for appointment of administrator.

PROVOLT, Ezekiel   Estate

Book, Page   POB A: 514; 533

Court Dates   16 Apr 1842 (Letters of Administration Granted); 12 May 1842

Administrator   Eliza Ann PROVOLT, widow (renounces), Alexander BLACKBURN, appointed.

Action   Letters of Administration granted. Confirmation of Grant of Letters.

Incidental Names   John HEFNER, security ($2,000)

Comments   Letters of Administration granted "in vacation.

SCARCE, Elizabeth   **Petition for Dower**

Book, Page   POB A: 516-517

Court Dates   9 May 1842

Action   Petition to Assign Dower. Dower assigned.

Incidental Names   John HARVEY and Ezekiel MORRISON appointed to assign dower; Elam CLARK, surveyor.

Comments   Petitioner is the widow and Relict of Samuel SCARCE.

THORP, Amos   **Guardianship**

Book, Page   POB A: 517-518

Court Dates   9 May 1842

Action   Application for appointment of guardian. Letters of Guardianship issued.

Incidental Names   John F. DECKER, Jr. appointed guardian of person and estate of Applicant. John F. DECKER, security ($2,000).

Comments   Applicant is the 11 yr. old infant son of the Isaac THORP, deceased.

STEVEN/STEPHENS, Samuel   **Estate**

Book, Page   POB A: 519-520; 563-564

Court Dates   9 May 1842 (Letters of Administration Granted); 11 Aug 1842

Administrator   Sophia STEPHENS, widow, renounces. Orrin WILLYS/WYLLIS, appointed.

Heirs   Alfred STEPHENS, Walter STEPHENS, and George STEPHENS, minor heirs.

Action   Letters of Administration granted. Application to sell real Estate. Widow appears in court without citation and makes no objection to the sale of real Estate. William ALLEN appointed guardian ad litem of minor heirs.

Incidental Names   Nicholas W. CLOSSER, security ($300)

Comments   Personal Estate insufficient to pay debts of Estate. Sufficient land to be sold to pay debts.

CATTRON, Samuel   **Guardianship**
CATTRON, Wesley F.

Book, Page   POB A: 535

Court Dates   12 May 1842

Action	Petition to choose Guardian. John A. G. CATTRON, appointed.
Incidental Names	William EAHART and Henry CLYBURN, security ($5100).
Comments	Originally filed on 8 Nov 1841. Parent's name not listed.

HUNT, William H.   Estate

Book, Page	POB A: 542-543; 553
Court Dates	24 May 1842 (Letters Testamentary Granted); 9 Aug 1842
Executrix	Elizabeth HUNT
Executors	Stephen G. HUNT, George S. HUNT
Action	Will filed. Letters Testamentary granted. Confirmation of Letters.
Incidental Names	Alonzo BETTEYES/BETTEYS and Charles W. HUNT, subscribing witnesses to Will. Alonzo BETTYES/BETTEYES and George HUNT, security ($8,000).
Comments	Letters granted "in vacation".

WELLS, Theodore H.   Estate

Book, Page	POB A: 551-552
Court Dates	9 Aug 1842 (Letters of Administration Granted)
Administratrix	Jane A. WELLS
Action	Application for Appointment of Administratrix
Incidental Names	Orrin WYLLIS and Samuel WEED, security ($2000).

SMALLWOOD, Elisabeth/Elizabeth   Petition for Dower

Book, Page	POB A: 561-562; 594-595
Court Dates	11 Aug 1842; 16 Nov 1842
Action	Petition to Assign dower. William ALLEN, Esqr. Appointed guardian ad litem of Samuel SMALLWOOD, (Jr.), Elisabeth SMALLWOOD, Sarah Jane SMALLWOOD, minor heirs of Samuel SMALLWOOD.
Incidental Names	John WILSON, Stephen NORTON, and Joel BUTLER, commissioners to "assign and set over" dower. Dower assigned to petitioner "for and during her natural life".
Comments	Elisabeth is the widow of Samuel SMALLWOOD.

SMITH, Olivia M.   Petition for Dower

Book, Page	POB A: 565; 595-596

Court Dates	11 Aug 1842; 16 Nov 1842
Action	Petition to Assign Dower. James BRADLEY, Esqr. Appointed guardian at litem of Sanford SMITH, Mary Jane SMITH, Olive SMITH, Charles SMITH, James F. SMITH (Jr.), Frances C. SMITH, and Sylvester SMITH, minor heirs of James F. SMITH. Dower assigned to petitioner to be hers "for and during her natural life".
Incidental Names	Andrew AVERY, Richard CRAMMER, and Asa M. WARREN, appointed commissioners to "assign and set over" dower.

McCOLLOM, Pikeland   Estate

Book, Page	POB A: 577; 597
Court Dates	5 Oct 1842 (Letters of Administration Granted); 17 Nov 1942
Administrators	William A. McCOLLOM and Ferdinand DUNHAM
Action	Letters of Administration Granted. Confirmation of grant of letters.
Incidental Names	Benjamin CRUMPACKER, security ($600)
Comments	Letters granted "in vacation".

JACKSON, Jesse   Estate

Book, Page	POB A: 610
Court Dates	19 Nov 1842
Administrators	Grovenor S. ADAMS appointed Administrator in Pulaski County. Adams failed to administer the estate and moved from the state. Sally JACKSON, widow, declined to act as administratrix. Samuel BUNSON is then appointed administrator "de bonis non administrates" of the goods and chattel of the deceased.
Action	Appointment of Administrator.
Incidental Names	Seonarse(?)CLETTIN (?) and Ezeckiel MORRISON, security ($1,000).
Comments	Jesse died in La Porte County. His family resides in La Porte County and has resided there.

La Porte County, Indiana, Probate Complete Record [Book] A

BLIVENS, Edward   Estate

Book & Page	PCR: 2-5
Court Dates	13 Sept 1834, 10 Nov 1834, 18 Nov 1834, 11 May 1834, 8 Feb 1836
Administrator	James & Robert BLIVENS
Action	Letters of Administration granted to James & Robert BLIVENS. Appraisement inventory and sale bill submitted to court. Amount of sale of personal property came to $309.72.
Incidental Names	James WALKER, bond; R.S. MORRISON, J.P.; Jesse F. MILLER, J.P.

AMBROSE, Ezekiel   Estate

Book & Page	PCR: 5-7
Court Dates	28 Oct 1834, 10 Nov 1834, 27 Nov 1834, 8 Aug 1836
Executor	Reason BELL
Action	Will is filed on 10 Nov 1834. Inventory and sale bill of personal property filed and inventory of sale of estate followed. Estate sold for $313.68. Second inventory of personal property was $123.06. Balance reported by Executor of $239.73 and court orders this to be paid to the Treasurer of the state of Indiana.
Incidental Names	Isaac MORGAN, Theodore JONES, commissioners; Elisha NEWHALL, security

BUNCE, Simon G.   Estate

Book & Pg	PCR: 7-12
Court Dates	18 Sept 1834, 27 Sept 1834, 10 Nov 1835, 29 Jan 1836, 8 Feb 1836, 12 Feb 1838
Administrator	John MULKS, Clarissa BUNCE
Heirs	Lafayette BUNCE
Action	Letters of Administration granted by court. Appraisal and inventory of personal estate filed. Sale held on (no day stated) Oct 1834. $527 realized from sale of personal property. Court approves and administrators file for distribution of settlement. Guardian (unnamed) of only heir agrees to $522.04 which was realized after the debts to the estate are paid. $282.66 paid to widow and minor child. $239.30 placed in hands of Guardian for the minor heir.

Incidental Names	Benoni M. NEWKIRK security; John M. LEMON appraiser; Robert S. MORRISON J.P.; Harry BILDEN purchaser of lot
Comment	Clarissa BUNCE became Clarissa TEEPLES by the time of the 8 Feb hearing.

BUSCH, Amanda,   **Guardianship**
Guardian of Hetty BUSCH
Widow of **Peter BUSCH**

Book & Page	PCR: 13-15
Court Dates	9 May 1837, 6 July 1837, 14 Aug 1837, 14 May 1837
Heirs	Hetty, Washington, Perry, Lucy, & William BUSCH
Action	Widow states to court that her husband, the deceased was not in possession of any land. Her attorney requests court to appoint the widow as guardian of Hetty BUSCH, a minor child. Court orders appraisal of 1/3 of LaPorte city lot #4, property of the deceased. Property sold for $69. Court orders amount given to widow and receives account of debts paid by widow/guardian which were the same as the amount of the sale. Guardian discharged of her duties.
Incidental Names	G.H. EVERTS, lawyer; Charles McCLURE, E, RATHBONE. Abraham FRAVEL, appraisers; Admiral BUSCH, purchaser of lot

CLARK, Wilson B.   **Estate**

Book & Page	PCR: 17
Court Dates	1 July 1837, 9 Oct 1837, 14 May 1838
Administrator	Elizabeth CLARK
Action	Letters of Administration granted to widow of Wilson B. CLARK. Inventory of personal property after appraisal is presented to the court. Final account of estate is $554.23 with a balance in hands of Administrator is $65.25.
Incidental Names	Charles MOORMAN, bond; William WALDRUFF, Jacob HICKMAN, appraisers

BARTHOLOMEW, Stephen   **Estate**

Book & Page	PCR: 17-20
Court Dates	14 Nov 1835, 8 Feb 1836, 8 Aug 1836, 14 Nov 1836
Administrator	Jeremiah BARTHOLOMEW
Action	Letters of Administration granted. Administrator failed to appear for hearing on inventory of estate and is cited to appear by court. Final settlement given

to court of $47.26 after a sale is held on 30 Nov 1835. The balance after bills to the estate are paid is $6.15.

Incidental Names	John B. NILES, security; Ashel NEAL, Lewis COMER, Jonathan D. MOULTON, appraisers; George CLINE, J.P; LaPorte Co.; Henry MISER, J.P.; Porter County
Comments	Entry is made that on the 14 May 1838, George CLINE, Justice of the Peace in LaPorte County gave testimony of MISER, stating that Jonathan D. MOULTON, one of the appraisers of the estate moved out of state and is in the west, whereabouts unknown. He also stated that the testimony of this appraiser could be "easily and truthfully" obtained. On the left of this page is the notation "Porter County" and opposite this is entered "Brot Up", (Significance unknown).

SWOPE, Wilson — Estate

Book and Page	PCR: 20-23
Court Dates	7 Nov 1835, 9 Nov 1835, 7 Dec 1835, 8 Feb 1836
Administrator	Jonathan LINE
Heirs	Michael SWOPE, father of deceased, Matilda SWOPE, widow
Action	Wilson SWOPE died intestate. Letters of Administration granted by court. Inventory appraisal and sale bill filed. Sale was held 5 Dec, 1835. Deceased died intestate. Sale of estate was insufficient to pay debts of estate. Deceased owned tract of land (described within) Land valued at $200. Widow requests court to not order sale of land as she has not received her dower of 1/3 of her deceased husband's estate. Widow allowed by law personal property valued at $100. Administrator paid out $1.30 over what came into his hands.
Incidental Names	Asbury SWOPE, security; Robert MERRIFIELD, Christopher A. BALLARD appraisers; Robert S. MORRISON, J.P.; John BROWN, Asbury SWOPE, William C. HANNAH, appraisers of land

STONER, William — Estate

Book & Page	PCR: 24-25
Court Dates	3 Nov 1838, 12 Nov 1838, 11 Nov 1839
Administrator	Benjamin CRUMPACKER
Action	Letters of Administration granted by court. Inventory of personal property of deceased -totals $74.32. Sale of personal of personal property held on 14 Feb 1839 at the home of a neighbor. Administrator is $62.82 over the amount of assets and is discharged from his duties.
Incidental Names	James WEBSTER, T.D.BAILEY, appraisers; James McCLANAHAN, neighbor of deceased

KEWLEY, John   Estate

Book & Page   CPR: 26-28

Court Dates   20 Oct 1838, 11 Nov 1838, 21 Nov 1838, 28 Jan 1839, 11 Nov 1839, 15 Nov 1839

Administrator   John & Thomas KEWLEY

Action   Letters of Administration granted by court. Personal property appraised and valued at $300. Sale held on 22 Nov 1838. $407.98 realized from sale. Widow of deceased, (unnamed) received $315.30. Final settlement presented in court. Administrator had a balance of $6.92 which court ordered disposed of fairly.

Incidental Names   William SHIMMIN, bond; Andrew BONNSIDE, Adam G. POLKE, Orrin NILES, Jacob R.HALL, appraisers; Eden SHOTWELL, note holder; Joseph HAYWARD, J.P.; James RIDGEWAY, sale clerk; A. BURNSIDE, note holder; H.G. POLK note holder; A.B. SHOTWELL, note holder.

SHARP, Thomas   Estate

Book & Page   PCR: 37-40

Court Dates   23 Nov 1838, 5 Dec 1838, 25, Jan 1839, 11 Feb 1839, 10 Feb 1840, 11 Feb 1840

Administrator   Joseph McCLELLAN

Action   Widow renounced her right as Administrator of her deceased husband's estate, signed and witnessed on 22 Nov, 1838 and filed in court. Letters of Administration granted to Joseph McCLELLON. Inventory & appraisal was done on 30 Nov 1838 and then filed in court. This was sworn to by a J.P. On 3 Dec 1838 sale bill is filed. (Inventory within) Final settlement filed. Widow Received $100 worth of personal property, as was her legal right. Balance after debts were paid was $104 and this was ordered disposed of equally by law.

Incidental Names   Elijah MAYHEW, witness; Adam G. POLK, bond; John VANTRY, Lee BENTLY appraisers; E. PALMER, J.P.; Abraham G. STANDIFORD, H.G. STANDIFORD, estate sales clerks

HOSMER, Robert   Estate

Book & Page   CPR: 40-43

Court Dates   17 Oct 1838, 5 Nov 1838, 12 Nov 1838, 13 Nov 1838, 22 Dec 1838, 10 Feb 1840, 11 May 1840

Administrator   Nancy & Jackson HOSMER

Action   Deceased died intestate. Court appoints Nancy & Jackson HOSMER as Administrators. Deceased's personal property appraised and inventoried and filed in court. (Inventory within) Public auction on 3 Dec 1838 at residence of deceased. A second sale was held on 12 May 1840. This sale amounted to $2,425 with no outstanding debts to estate. This money was distributed equally to both heirs/ administrators and they are discharged from their duties.

| Incidental Names | Joseph DAVIS, bond; Elijah BARNS and Joseph DAVIS, appraisers; Ezra TYLER, sale witness; Lemuel ROBINSON, J.P. |

BECKNER, John   **Estate**

Book & Page	CPR: 43-46
Court Dates	(no day given) Jan 1838, 12 Feb 1838, 10 Feb 1840, 11 May 1840, 13 Nov 1840
Administrator	Elizabeth BECKNER, widow, George S. STOVER
Action	Court grants Letters of Administration. Personal property inventory and appraisal submitted. Inventory taken on 25 Jan 1838. Sale held on 11 May 1840. (Inventory within) Final settlement presented totaling $1,119. Balance on hand is $883.93, after deducting expenses of settlement.
Incidental Names	Jacob MILLER, security; David EVANS, Philip FAIL, appraisers; George SWOPE, J.P.

McCLANAHAN, James   **Estate**

Book & Page	CPR: 47-55
Court Dates	20 Oct 1838, 12 Nov 1838, 6 Feb 1839, 13 May 1839
Administrator	John HOBSON, Benjamin CRUMPACKER
Guardian	Griffin TREADWAY
Heirs	Belinda, Everett E., Herbert H., James E., Joseph, and Emily McCLANAHAN, minor children
Action	Deceased died intestate. Letters of Administration granted to HOBSON and CRUMPACKER. Inventory of personal estate, monies, goods, & chattels taken on 10 Nov 1838 by appraisers and submitted to court (description within). Charles McCLURE, attorney for administrator presented report of sale of personal property of estate. $416.93 was realized. Debts of $260.42 are outstanding. Deceased owned ¼ of a property (described within) in LaPorte Co. which was sold to the deceased by John HOBSON for $450. Attorney for Administrator requests that a subpoena be issued to widow and minor children to show why this land should not be sold and requests also an appraisal of the property. This appraisal done on 4 March 1839. Appraisal came to$1,280, and sworn to by a Justice of the Peace on 18 May, 1839. $150 is yet needed to pay debts of the estate. The heirs of the deceased agree to the sale of 1/6 of. property amounting to 160 acres (description within) On 6 Oct Administrator appears in court to state land is

not sold and requests additional time to do so. Court grants request. Land again advertised for sale on 28 Dec 1839. Griffin TREADWAY, Guardian of minor children was the highest bidder. Court refuses to confirm this sale due to the illegality of non notification of the heirs of the estate. Neighbors of the deceased appear in court to testify that the land is worth $4 per acre and that the deceased paid about $1000 for this land sold to him by John HOBSON and that they were told by the deceased that only $540 remained to be paid. HOBSON has a lien on the land which contains 160 acres @$4 per acre which equals $640. HOBSON claims that the bond for the land in question was signed by the deceased, but now is lost and that the land was to go to the heirs and the widow but that there is no widow. Administrator HOBSON requests court to approve sale of land and approve a deed. Court again orders heirs to appear in court. Once again the heirs fail to appear. The land is then ordered sold according to previous agreement. Court informed a sale of real estate was held on 20th. Itemized report of sale of personal property of deceased (description within) which totaled $1.074.68 and held on 13 Aug 1840. A balance of $448.26 remains and was ordered dispersed by the court. (Additional personal property inventory enclosed) Final settlement made by court.

Incidental Names	Griffin TREADWAY, bond; James WEBSTER, T.D. BAILEY, appraisers; Charles McCLURE, attorney; Joel BUTLER, J.P.; Ralph LOOMIS, Edmund WOODEN, neighbors; John BROWN, of land

FOSTER, Seneca	**Estate**
Book & Page	CPR: 55-66
Court Dates	19 March 1838, 28 March 1838, 14 May 1838, 24 May 1838, 12 Nov 1838, 11 Feb 1839, 13 May 1839, 11 Nov 1839, 10 Feb 1840, 11 May 1840, 15 May 1840, 10 Aug 1840, 11 Aug 1840, 8 Feb 1841, 12 Feb 1841
Administrators	Perlina FOSTER, widow, Joseph ORR
Heirs	Melinda S., Alonzo L., Alonzo T., Laura T., Sophrimia H., Narcissa H., and Amanda, N. Foster and daughter Belinda S. HARPER and Archibald HARPER, her husband
Action	Deceased died intestate. Letters of Administration given to Perlina FOSTER and Joseph ORR. Inventory of personal property of deceased filed. Sale held on April 21, 1838. (Description within) Sale of a portion of land, Twp 37, (Description within) containing 33 acres and valued at $464 was sold to Henry ORR on 15 April 1839 for $396. Court is told that $1,846.69 was still owed by the deceased at the time of his death. The amount of personal property of deceased came to $1,382.95. Attorney for the administrator requests court allow the administrator a refund of the purchase price of the lot bought for $464 as the heirs of the deceased did not appear in court to show cause as to why this tract of land should not be sold and requests that a deed be issued to administrator in defect as a result of this. Court orders purchase of land to be set aside and ORR released from his bid on this tract of land. $463.84 is the remaining deficit on the deceased's estate. Heirs are

again ordered to appear in court to approve or reject the sale of this tract of land. Heirs again fail to appear in court. Court orders the sale of the land at public auction. Partial settlement is made, and $90.25 remains. Deed of Conveyance issued to ORR. Court once again orders heirs to appear in court. Court then notified that on 2nd of May, 1840 the sale was made to ORR of land at $12 per acre. Purchase of land was confirmed and a deed issued to ORR. Supplemental final settlement was made to the court. The court then orders $60.68 be equally divided between the two administrators.

Incidental Names	Daniel BROWN, bond; Abel BURLINGAME, Cornelius SMITH, appraisers; Ira SWOPE, J.P.; James WITTEN, clerk of sale; A.G. POLK, appraiser; John B. NILES, attorney; Sutton VANPELT, sheriff, 1840; William ALLEN, sheriff 1841.

JACKSON, Edmund   Estate

Book & Page	PCR: 66-70
Court Dates	6 April 1837, 30 April 1837, 8 May 1837, 10 May 1837, 10 June 1837, 13 May 1839, 14 May 1839, 30 May 1839
Administrator	Abigail JACKSON, John DRUELINER
Action	Letters of Administration granted to Abigail JACKSON and John DRUELINER. Inventory of personal property and appraisal filed. (description within). Sale bill is filed and $1,422. is realized from the sale of personal property. The amount of the sale over the appraisement was $158.03. List of debts paid by administrator totaled $373.50. Sale of personal property on 4 May 1837 left a balance of $528.0 in the hands of the administrator. They stated they paid out a total $373.50 leaving a balance of $528.05. After other debts are paid there remained a balance of $184.74 over and above the amount of assets which came into their hands.
Incidental Names	John WELLS, J.P.; Asher WHITE, bond, & Appraiser, James DRUMMOND, appraiser; James F. SMITH, J.P.; Thomas D. VAIL & George MALBERA, sales clerks; Sutton VANPELT, Sheriff, 1840, William ALLEN, sheriff, 1841
Comment	Administrators stated they charged themselves with the sum of $777.29 for the erection of a house on deceased's real estate. They also received farm rent of $152.25.

GOBLE, Isaac   Estate

Book & Page	PCR: 70-74
Court Dates	13 May 1840, 21 July 1840, 10 Aug 1840, 30 Aug 1840
Administrator	Daniel LOW
Action	Deceased died intestate. Inventory of personal property and appraisal filed in court. Public auction held of personal estate. Court finds proceeds of sale insufficient to pay debts of deceased. Deceased owned real estate appraised

at $300 (no description given). Debts to estate amounted to $230.69, leaving a deficit to estate. Administrator granted permission to sell the real estate of deceased.

Incidental Names	George AMES, bond; Fisher AMES & O.A. BARKER, appraisers; Jacob BIGELOW J.P.; Orren GOULD sale clerk
Comment	Public auction of real estate held at the Farmer's Hotel in Michigan City, Indiana

GOODWIN, William B — Estate

Book & Page	PCR: 74-77
Court Dates	29 Feb 1840, 5 May 1840, 11 May 1841, 9 Aug 1841
Administrator	Warren COLE
Action	William GOODWIN of Michigan City died intestate. Letters of Administration granted and filed 5 May 1840. Inventory of personal property of deceased also filed. Final settlement shows personal estate netted $479.19. Administrator paid out of pocket by $49.28. Court discharges Administrator from his duties.
Incidental Names	George R. SELKREGG, bond; Robert STEWART & Donald B. KINGSBURY, appraisers; J.R. WELLS, G.R. SELKREGG, John WILLARD, H.N. CRANDLE, note holders; Jacob BIGELOW, J.P.

WYATT, Isaac, son of WYATT, Joseph — Guardianship

Book & Page	CPR: 77
Court Dates	12 Nov 1838, 9 Aug 1840
Guardian	Stephen G. HUNT
Action	Court hears guardianship appointment for infant heir Isaac WYATT, son of deceased Joseph WYATT. Stephen G. HUNT appointed guardian. Guardian appeared in court stating he had paid out a total for support of heir that matches money he received, which was $109.72. Guardian discharged by the court.

Wyatt, Thomas & James, infant heirs of WYATT, Joseph — Guardianship

Book & Page	CPR: 78
Court Dates	12 Nov 1838, 9 Aug 1841
Guardian	Azariah WILLIAMS

Action	Letter of guardianship issued to WILLIAMS. Guardian appeared in court and had on hand $123.32 and stated he paid out the same amount for care of heirs and is discharged by the court.
Incidental Names	Ezekiel MORRISON, bond

BEATTIE, William   Estate

Book & Page	CPR: 79
Court Dates	15 Oct 1838, 12 Nov 1838, 12 Aug 1839, 11 Nov 1839, 8 Nov 1841, 14 Feb 1842
Administrator	Thomas E. STANTON
Action	Letters of Administration granted by court. Inventory and sale bill of deceased's estate filed. Sale held on 23 Dec 1839. Proceeds amounted to $17.39, the same amount paid out for debts to the estate. Administrator discharged of his duties by the court.
Incidental Names	Michael W. FALL, bond

PINNEY, Horace   Estate

Book & Page	CPR: 81-84
Court Dates	5 July 1839, 12 Aug 1839, 8 Nov 1840, 4 Feb 1842
Action	Deceased died intestate. Letters of Administration granted. Inventory of personal property of estate presented to court. Public auction of estate held on 13 Sept 1839. Final settlement produced in court. $1,271.12 paid out by Administrators and the same amount was realized from proceeds of the sale of the estate. Administrators discharged by court.
Incidental Names	William EARHART, Phineas SMALL, bond; John SMALL, Jonathan OSBORN, appraisers; Ichabod GAWLEY, William C. BOND, A. BIGELOW, John FISHER, Stephen STRONG, Daniel PINNEY, George SOUTHAN, John ANDERS, Leander WHEELER, note holders, Charles EATON, J.P.; Lewis TODHUNTER, sale clerk

MILLER, Samuel   Estate

Book & Page	CPR: 85-86
Court Dates	11 Nov 1839, 4 Jan 1840, 8 Nov 1841, 14 Feb 1842
Administrator	Curtis TRAVIS
Action	Deceased died intestate. Letters of Administration granted. Personal property inventory filed. Final settlement presented to court. $195.75 realized from sale of personal property of deceased. Proceeds of sale matched those of debts to the estate. Court discharges Administrators.

Incidental Names	Thomas NORRIS, John GARRARD, appraisers; Willard A. PLACE, clerk of sale

WASSON, Archibald   Estate

Book & Page	CPR: 87-88
Court Dates	13 Nov 1838
Executor	Jehiel WASSON
Heirs	Jehiel WASSON, Calvin WASSON, Macamy WASSON, Eliza WASSON MOORE,
Action	Testimony to the signing and witnessing of the will of the deceased entered to the court. Executor of estate appointed by the court. Contents of the will entered. "I, Archibald WASSON, of the county of LaPorte and state of Indiana, being of sound mind and memory do make and publish this my last will and testament in manner and form to whit: First, I allow my just debts to be paid. Second, I allow at my decease to bequeath to Jehiel WASSON my horse and carriage. Thirdly, as I have given to my son Calvin WASSON, Macamy WASSON, and Eliza MOORE their portion or nearly so according to my ability. I allow them one dollar each. Fourthly, it is my will at my decease to bequeath to Anselm WASSON eighty dollars. When collected of notes I held of Macamy WASSON at three different payments for two hundred and fifty dollars. Fifthly, it is my will that my son Jehiel have all that is ever after Anselm getting eighty dollars of the note I hold on Macamy--. Sixthly, the note I hold on my son Calvin for fifteen dollars it is my will that my Executor hand it to him after my decease. It is my will that Jehiel have my trunk (?) and all that belongs to it – Lastly, I appoint Jehiel WASSON my son and Executor this my last will and testament whereof I have hereunto set my hand and seal in the presence of us who were requested to witness the same this 10th mo. 5th (day?) 1838. Amos CADWALLADER, Jesse WASSON witnesses Final settlement presented to court. Executor states the debts and credits match exactly and he is discharged by the court.
Incidental Names	Eliza MOORE, note; J.W. GREEN, counsel; Hiram WHEELER, A. CLARK, Martin BUTIN, coffin

MORRISON, Robert S.   Estate

Book & Page	CPR: 89-90
Court Dates	10 Aug 1836, 8 Nov 1841, 14 Feb 1842, 10 May 1842,
Administrator	Ezekiel MORRISON
Action	MORRISON states that the deceased died intestate on 6 of August 1836 and that his personal property is situated in LaPorte County, that his estate is in an "unsettled state" and that the deceased's brother, Ezekiel MORRISON

was the only relative within the state. Letters of Administration presented to the court.

Final settlement presented to the court with the Administrator stating he has paid all debts and settled all credits of the deceased's estate. (no details given). Court discharges the Administrator.

Incidental Names John BROWN, Andrew BURNSIDE, Adam POLKE, bond

---

EAGANS, Samuel T., son of
EAGENS, James   **Guardianship**

Book & Page CPR: 90

Court Dates 14 Aug 1837

Guardian John R. NILES

Action Samuel T. EAGENS is the minor son of James EAGENS, deceased, who died in Franklin County Indiana. Samuel EAGENS appears in court to choose a Guardian. Samuel T. EAGENS became age 21 by May 21, 1841, and Guardian is authorized by court to pay to Samuel T. EAGENS money received by him as his Guardian.

Full settlement made the following year and Guardian is given a receipt and discharged.

Incidental Names Robert MERRYFIELD, John HEPNER, Adam G. POLKE, bond

---

Samuel T. EAGENS by   **Guardianship**
John B. Niles, his Guardian
and next friend
  vs
Jared CHAPMAN, A. John HEFNER,
Administrators of the estate of
William EAGENS, deceased

Book & Page CPR: 91-92

Court Dates 10 May 1841

Action The suit is described as "amicable". NILES complains that CHAPMAN & HEFNER, Administrators of estate of William EAGENS, deceased, are accused of a plea of "assumpsit", or breach of contract, for that "whereas heretofore to wit;" on the 10 of June, 1837, the deceased William EAGENS was indebted to Samuel T. EAGENS of $1,000 and that they had not paid the sum. The defendants waived the plea of breach of contract and state the money has been paid to Samuel EAGENS and they will show proof. They waive a jury trial and ask the court for its decision. Court orders the defendants to pay $92 in damages. (no information on court's decision of guilt or innocence, but it is assumed they were found guilty if they were ordered to pay damages).

Agreement between the parties in the words of Samuel T. EAGENS): "On the 26 of September 1837, $22.50 was paid to Samuel T. EAGENS by defendants and that he also received a note from Samuel and John McCOMER for $100 with interest paid from Dec 1836. And whereas also said administrators received from the estate of my father which said William EAGENS was Administrator (?) about $200, ¼ of which belongs to me now, I hereby agree to credit and do hereby acknowledge as a credit on said judgment and on said money (?) from my father's estate the whole amount of said judgment of $22.30 with the interest and also the amount of said note. But it is understood that the other heir are to pay on those each their proportion of a fee of $20 (?) retained by (?) SMITTS out of the amount of said note. LaPorte May 12, 1841. S. T. EAGENS. I agree that in case the above payment should prove to be more than the amount, my due after the exact amount rec'd by said administrator and from my father's estate ascertained, I will refund to them such "excep" - Signed S.T. EAGENS.

Comments   There is handwriting at the top of the page that states: "Probate Court, May Term, AD 1842. The following case should have been entered at the May Term, 1841, but being omitted is here inserted."

Also, the deceased's name in this case is now "William EAGENS", but in the previous case of Guardianship for Samuel T. EAGENS, the deceased's name was given as "James EAGENS".

Elizabeth SCARCE widow of
Samuel SCARCE deceased
    vs   **Petition to Assign Dower**
John V.SCARCE, Nancy Ellen
SCARCE, & William SCARCE,
minor heirs of **Samuel SCARCE**, deceased.

Book & Page   CPR: 92-93

Court Dates   14 Feb 1842

Action   Widow's attorney petitions the court that the deceased's widow is entitled to the real estate of her husband in Twp 30 of LaPorte County (description within) which was sold at a sheriff's sale and which the widow of deceased had no knowledge of. Court appoints commissioners to "set over" to widow of the deceased her "first third part of and in all the lands" of her deceased husbands property.

Commissioners present to the court the widow's portion of the land (description within) and court orders this portion to widow to be hers for her natural life. Expenditures to be paid by petitioner.

Incidental Names   Samuel STEWART, property buyer; George W. ALLEN, property buyer; John HARVEY, Philip BOSSERMAN, Ezekiel MORRISON, commissioners

TULEY, James	**Estate**
Book & Page	CPR: 94-96
Court Dates	6 Feb 1839, 13 Feb 1839, 26 Feb 1839, 13 May 1839, 8 Nov 1841, 14 Feb 1842, 9 May 1842
Heirs	Martha TULEY, wife, & sons, Simon Peter, George Milton, Simon Robinson, John, William, Margaret, James, Elizabeth, Josephine, & Julianna
Action	The last will and testament of James TULLEY is filed in court on 13 Feb 1839, and reads as follows:

"I, James TULEY, of Clinton Township, LaPorte County & state of Indiana, do the 24th day of Dec. the year of our lord One thousand Eight Hundred Thirty Seven make & publish this my will and testament hereby working & making void all former or other wills by me at any time heretofore made. First I direct that my body be conducted in a manner corresponding with my estate and situation in life and as to such estate as it has pleased God to entrust one with. I dispose of the same in the following manner to wit. I direct that all my just debts and funeral expenses be paid as soon after my decease as possible out of the first moneys shall come to the hands of my beloved wife, Martha Tuley, from portions of my personal estate. I direct that my said wife Martha Tuley shall have and enjoy the free and separate use of all my estate or Estates both real and personal. One horse only excepted, for and during the term of her natural life or for so long as she may continue and remain a widow and also that my said wife shall of herself have full power to sell or dispose of any portion parts of my said personal estate which she my said wife may think proper. I direct that the one horse as above excepted and being the largest one I have shall immediately at the time of my decease become the property of my son James Tuley. I direct that all my real estate consisting of Eighty acres of land the same lying and being in Clinton township LaPorte County and State of Indiana shall decease at the time of my said wife Martha Tuley's decease, or at the time of her future marriage that which shall first happen. To my three sons Simon Peter, George Milton, and Simon Robinson, share and share alike their heirs and assigns forever. I direct that as soon as convenient after the time of my said wife's decease the residue of any of my personal Estate shall be sold and out of the proceeds of such sale each of my three children, John, William, and Margaret shall receive the sum of One Dollar and that the balance, if any, shall be equally divided among such of my seven children viz(?) James, Simon Peter, George Milton, Simeon Robinson, Elizabeth, Josephine, and Juliann as may survive my said wife Martha Tuley and in the event of all my said personal Estate having been sold or disposed of previous to the time of my said wife's decease or if after my said wife's decease the residue if any of my said personal estate should be sold for the less than the sum of Seven Dollars then I direct that my seven children viz; John William, Margaret, James, Elizabeth, Josephine and Juliann, shall receive the sum of One Dollar each out of my real Estate". Signed: James Tuley.

Witnesses: George STUBLE, Charles EATON, Archibald MOORMAN.

Letters of Administration granted by court. Final settlement made to the court. The debits and claims to the estate equaled the credits.

Incidental Names	Charles EATON, bond
Comments	No last names of the seven children given in will.

BLODGET, Lewis	**Assumpsit**
vs	
Sidney S. BRADLEY,	
admin of the estate of	
Bartholomew BRADLEY, dec'd	
Book & Page	CPR: 96
Court Dates	14 Feb 1842, 9 May 1842
Action	Attorney for Lewis BLODGET requests the court summon Sidney S. BRADLEY the administrator of Bartholomew BRADLEY'S estate to court. The attorney for the plaintiff BLODGET, files a "note of Declaration" that reads:

"For Value Received I promise to pay Lewis BLODGET or bearer thirty nine Dollars and forty seven cents four months from date with the use" signed: MIDDLEBURY (and) Bart BRADLEY February 8, 1836.

The defendant, S.BRADLEY fails to appear in court, and is in default. The court orders S. BRADLEY to pay the sum of $54.13 in damages as well as the costs. |
| Incidental Names | Andrew L. OSBORN, attorney |

HARRISON, Abram W.	**Assumpsit**
vs	
Ezekiel MORRISON,	
administrator of estate of	
Joseph WYATT	
Book & Page	CPR: 97-98
Court Dates	8 Nov 1841, 14 Feb 1842, 9 May 1842
Action	Attorney for HARRISON files declaration in these words; "Abram W. HARRISON, plaintiff in this suit and his own proper person complains of Ezekiel MORRISON administrator of the estate of Joseph WYATT deceased of a plea of assumpsit. For that "wherein heretofore to wit in the lifetime of said WYATT said WYATT assigned to the plaintiff certain promissory notes against one Charles McCLURE & others which it became necessary for said Plaintiff to sue out & prosecute to the insolvency of said McCLURE & others or till such suit should be otherwise disposed of whereas said plaintiff instituted such suit to recover anything by reason of

the insolvency of said makers in which said suit said plaintiff incurred a great amount of Costs of Suit to whit $100, costs which he has been compelled to pay & which ought to be refunded to him.

And whereupon also said WYATT in his lifetime indebted to said plaintiff in the sum of $100 for so much money before that time paid, laid out and refunded to & for the use of the said WYATT & to be paid to said plaintiff on request. Yet neither said WYATT in his lifetime nor said Defendant hath paid the same or any part thereof but so to do have at all times refused to the damages by said plaintiff of $100."

Cause taken under advisement. Plaintiff, Defendant and attorney appear in court. The charges are not defended and remained unanswered and the court decides against the defendant. The damages are not decided and will be left to a jury to decide. MORRISON is assessed damages of $62.84.

HARRISON, Elizabeth & John HARRISON vs Elijah STANTON & William Andrew Administrator of the estate of **Samuel BARGER**, deceased.	**in the Matter of Execution**

Book & Page	CPR: 98
Court Dates	4 Feb 1839
Action	Court hears petition of plaintiff, Elizabeth HARRISON. Defendants also present. Court orders judgment of $36.92 awarded to defendants, Elijah STANTON and William ANDREW. Court also awards costs of $3.76 levied against William ANDREW for the funeral expenses of deceased. Elizabeth and John HARRISON are discharged from liability.
Incidental names	George SWOPE, J.P.

Andrew MELVILLE & Andrew MELVILLE JR vs Paulina FOSTER, Joseph ORR, administrator of the estate of **Seneca FOSTER** dec'd	**Estate**

Book & Page	CPR: 99
Court Dates	13 May 1839
Action	Court finds in support of plaintiff, the MELVILLES and awards the sum of $15.66 with costs of the suit and that the claim of Andrew MELVILLE against said estate the court considers on evidence heard to be just and correct (several spaces after period in this sentence is written the amount of "$1.50").

Macajah JONES, administrator
of the estate of
Richard HERBERT, dec'd
vs   **Replevin**
James HERBERT

Book & Page	CPR: 99-101
Court Dates	11 Feb 1839, 13 May 1839, 12 Aug 1839
Action	Cause continued after court orders pleadings to be filed. Attorney for the administrator, JONES, files his declaration and asks for damages of $200 and states that on Nov 1 1838 the goods and chattels belonging to estate of deceased (description within) were owed to the plaintiff. Attorney for James HERBERT denies any goods were taken from the estate by the defendant. The bedstead that JONES claims was among items stolen was still in possession of the deceased's widow, Mary HERBERT. Cause continued.
	The attorney for HERBERT waives a jury trial. Court orders any goods of deceased in possession of Plaintiff returned. Court awards for the defendant in the sum of $10 damages and costs of the suit.
Incidental Names	John H. BRADLEY, attorney; MERRYFIELD, attorney; John B. NILES attorney

SPRAGUE, Polly   **Petition to Assign Dower**
vs
The heirs of **David SPRAGUE**, dec'd

Book & Page	CPR: 101-105
Court Dates	13 May 1839, 11 Nov 1839
Heirs	James W. Sprague, Sarah Averil, Caleb N. Averil, & wife, Susan Sprague Averill, Henry B. Sprague, John Sprague, William Sprague, Edward Sprague, Thomas Sprague
Action	Petitioner states her husband, the deceased, David Sprague, was in possession of real estate of which she has the right of Dower (Widow's Share) and for which her husband paid the sum of (left blank and no description given) The deceased also owned lots 10, 11, & 12 in Block 38 in Elston Survey of lots 1, 2, 3, & 4 in block 33 (description within) The petitioner requests disinterested commissioners appointed to set aside her widow's Dower, being the first & 3rd part of all estate properties.
	Court appoints a guardian for the minor heirs, except for James W. SPRAGUE who is not a minor. On 13 June, 1839, the appointed commissioners present to the court their findings. (financial description of each lot within), which is filed. Widow Sprague is allotted her portion of these lots description within) by the court. Cost and expenses will be paid by the petitioner.

Incidental Names | WELLS & ENOS, attorneys; James S. CASTLE, publisher; Willys PECK, Oscar A. BARKER, Robert STEWART, commissioners; Sutton VANPELT, Guardian

---

Reuben ALLEN   **Petition to Assign Dower**
vs
The Heirs of **Rueben ALLEN**, deceased

Book & Page | PR: 105-106

Court Dates | 11 Nov 1839, 16 Nov 1839

Heirs | John Allen, William H.C. Allen, Erasmus Allen, Adam Allen, Heber Allen, Reuben Allen, Elizabeth Allen, Jane Allen, Dewitt C. Allen, minor heirs

Action | Court presented widow's petition and appoints commissioners to set off the Dower for petitioner. (description of real estate within) Cause continued. The widow's Dower of ½ of deceased husband's real estate is granted by the court. (description within), 40 acres, more or less, and the costs and expenses are ordered paid by the petitioner.

Incidental Names | Charles McCLURE, attorney; Elijah MAYHEW, Guardian; Abner BAILEY, Joseph BLAKE, Arthur McCLURE, commissioners

---

UTLEY, Uriah   **Assumpsit**
vs
Jacob Miller, Executor of the
last will & Testament of
Sanford UTLEY

Book & Page | CPR: 106-108

Court Dates | 11 Nov 1839, 10 Feb 1840, 16 Nov 1840

Action | All parties came by agreement and a declaration is waived. An amicable suit is entered into and all pleas are also waived, except to the merits of the action. Cause continued.

Petitioner files his claim against the estate. He was the deceased's doctor. His claim amounts to $483.31 (financial description within). The attorney for the defendant, MILLER, files his response stating that the deceased did not promise to pay the claimed monies & should not receive them. The court orders proof of monies owed through witnesses & "viva vocce" examinations.

Court then orders that Utley is owed the amount of $31 and this amount will be limited to that exact amount. Court also orders that UTLEY pay half the costs of the proceedings & the remaining half of the costs be paid out of the estate of Sanford UTLEY.

Incidental Names | Arthur McCLURE, attorney, John W. BRADLEY, attorney

DAVID, Joseph
     vs   **Debt**
Ezra Tyler, Administrator
of the estate of
Horace B. HIBBARD

Book & Page   CPR: 108-110

Court Dates   21 Oct 1840, 9 Nov 1841, 11 Nov 1841

Action   Attorney for Plaintiff files a declaration stating that on 27 Feb 1838 the deceased died and the defendant TYLER, administrator of the estate of HIBBARD withheld $531 from the estate funds. This money was in the form of a promissory note amounting to $115 with interest of 2% payable in 90 days and was given to the defendant by the deceased and who was ordered to pay this note after the estate was settled. Attorney also stated a 2nd promissory note was owed by the deceased, dated 4 March 1837 for $100 at 10 % interest. He stated that the defendant also promised to pay this promissory note. Since then, the defendant has made no attempt to pay these promissory notes. Furthermore, the attorney states the defendant was also indebted to the deceased on 1 May 1839 in the amount of $11.95 for "goods and merchandise, sold and delivered" to the deceased at his request.

      The defendant appears in court and does not deny money was not paid. Court decides in favor of the plaintiff and orders defendant to pay the full amount of notes owed plus damages of $128.68. Court also orders defendant to pay costs of the suit from any monies coming his hands as administrator.

Incidental Names   John BRADLEY, attorney

McCARTY, Nicholas &
James C. HOWELL,
     vs   **Judgment on Warrant of Attorney**
Sidney S. BRADLEY
Administrator, **Bartholomew**
BRADLEY Estate

Book & Page   CPR: 110-111

Court Dates   12 Jan 1840, 8 Feb 1841

Action   Attorney issues declaration for the plaintiffs stating that the defendant, administrator of Bartholomew BRADLEY's estate withheld $42.47 from the estate funds involving a promissory note made by the deceased dated 1 Aug 1838 with 10% interest. The note became due and defendant did not pay the note. Attorney for the plaintiff requests damages of $25. Defendant notifies court that on 13 Jan 1841 he has appointed an attorney to represent him in this charge. Attorney appears in court and states he personally saw the defendant and executor of deceased's estate within one week ago. Court is informed by defendant's attorney that defendant cannot "gainsay or deny" that he owes the amount of the note from the deceased. Court levies $10.62

in damages plus $42.47, money owed and orders it be paid from the estate of the deceased.

Incidental Names   James BRADLEY, attorney

Abram W. HARRISON,   **Assumpsit**
   vs
Ezekiel MORRISON,
Administrator of estate of
Joseph WYATT, deceased

Book & Page   CPR: 112-113

Court Dates   10 May 1841

Action   Plaintiff HARRISON appears in court and complains that the defendant, MORRISON, Administrator of the estate of the deceased and who died intestate, was in possession of a "plea of trespass on the cases of the premises." He further states that the two builders of a steam mill for the deceased signed a bond to pay in 12 months the amount of $1,500 for the deceased's part of the donation in building the steam mill. The bond did not include the lots on which the mill was to be erected. The bond was signed on 22 May 1837. This bond was signed and given to HARRISON on 4 June 1838, HARRISON brought an action of debt against the two men and the bond has not been paid. This action was served on 3 May 1839, and a judgment was rendered by the court against the two builders for the sum owed, plus $85.

Incidental Names   John CLARK, Charles MCCLURE, steam mill builders

Comments   The steam mill built by the two men was described as being at "Indiana City."

Sarah Mariah JACKSON   **Petition to Assign Dower**
   vs
The Heirs of **Jesse JACKSON**, deceased

Book & Page   CPR: 114-115

Court Dates   9 Aug 1841, 12 Aug 1841

Heirs   Zeddok, Ezra, and Elizabeth JACKSON,& other unknown heirs and children of Samuel JACKSON, brother of deceased, Jesse JACKSON

Action   Attorney for Sarah Mariah JACKSON, of Pulaski County files her petition stating that on the 22 Sept 1840 her deceased husband was in possession of certain tracts of land and town lots (description within) in Fulton County. There was also a property within the town of Lexington Scot (?) Co.(?) on which a large brick house stands (description within). The deceased also owned a lot in the city of LaPorte on which the deceased owned a title bond and the purchase money remains due, but the greater proportion of the title bond has been paid. Lot #177, the 2nd lot, also in LaPorte was also held by title bond from W.G. & S.W (?) EWING, and this bond has been fully paid. As the minor heirs of the children of the deceased brother, Samuel JACKSON, were underage and due to "other causes" the widow's Dower could not be assigned without the intervention of the court. The petitioner requests that part of the deceased's property in LaPorte be set aside as her Dower and commissioners be appointed for that purpose. The petitioner also requests that a portion of the properties mentioned in Pulaski Co. also be a part of her Dower as a way of earning rent. Court accepts the commissioner's report and assigns 1/3 of the properties of the estate as the widow's Dower and declares that lot #119, LaPorte, and lot #177 be a part of the Dower. Improvements are to be paid on the lots from the estate and the properties are assigned to Mariah JACKSON and the cost and expenses of such are to be paid by the administrator of the estate.

Incidental Names   David ROBB, bond owner

Sarah AUSTIN, widow of
Sans AUSTIN, deceased   **Petition to Assign Dower**
vs
The Heirs of the said **Sans AUSTIN**

Book & Page	CPR: 116-117
Court Dates	9 Aug 1841, 13 Aug 1841
Heirs	Harriet, William, & Alexander AUSTIN

Action   Widow appears in court and presents her petition stating the deceased owned property in LaPorte County (description within) containing 40 acres and requests the court appoint commissioner to set off a portion of this land as Dower. She also requests the court appoint a Guardian "ad Litem" for the infant heirs of the deceased. Court appoints Henry TEETER, uncle of the heirs as Guardian.

The commissioners present their report to the court stating that a 10 acre portion of the property owned by the deceased be a portion of the widow's Dower. The Guardian of the minor children also is present and no objections to the decision is presented to the court. The court also orders cost and expenses of this action be paid by the petitioner.

Mary ROUSE,
late Mary GOSSETT,   **Petition to Assign Dower**
vs
The heirs of
John GOSSETT, deceased

Book & Page	CPR: 117-119
Court Dates	9 Aug 1841, 8 Nov 1841, 10 Nov 1841
Heirs	Joseph Gossett, William GOSSETT

Action   Attorney presents petition to the court stating the petitioner, ROUSE, was married to the deceased (date left blank) and lived with the deceased until he died in 1838 and that the deceased owned property (description within) in LaPorte County as well as property in Porter County (description within). the widow's portion of her rightful Dower to those properties. The deceased, John GOSSETT, died intestate without leaving any children or heirs, excepting Joseph, who lives in Henry County, In. and William, who lives in Porter County, In., and who have been given legal notice of the widow's application for Dower. Court appoints commissioners.

Commissioners present their findings for the widow's portion of the land (description within). The widow receives 180 acres. Court accepts the report and orders costs to be paid by the defendant.

Incidental names	John HOBBS, John BROWN, James WEBSTER commissioners: M.H. ORTON, attorney
Comments	Widow's portion includes the "Mill Property" and the homestead of the late **John GOSSETT**. Commissioners are "taxed" $9, $6, and $7.50, respective.

Annis D. HIBBARD
vs   **Petition to Assign Dower**
the Heirs of
Horace B. HIBBARD

Book & Page	CPR: 119-121
Court Dates	Feb 1841, 10 May 1841, 8 Nov, 1841,
Heirs	Harrison & John W. HIBBARD
Action	Attorney presents court with widow's petition to right of Dower of deceased husband's property (description within). One property has a balance yet due in the school section (description within). Court appoints commissioners to set off the portion of the widow's Dower after filing Notice of the petition have been given to the heirs for 3 successive weeks. Cause continued. Court appoints a Guardian for the heirs. The commissioners make their report to court of the widow's portion of her Dower. (description within). Widow also given lot #4, and lot #6 (description within) of the School Section. Heirs present in court and no objection is raised as to the Dower assignment, and the court approves the assignment and orders the cost and expenses of this assignment be paid by petitioner.
Incidental Names	Orrin WYLLIS, Charles W. CATHCART, commissioners

David WILLIAMS   **Estate**

Book & Page	CPR: 122-125
Court Dates	22 Feb 1840, 11 May 1840
Administrator	Rensselaer SHAW

| Action | Letters of Administration were filed and granted in vacation for the estate of David WILLIAM who died intestate. Inventory and appraisal of the personal estate of the deceased was also filed (description within). |

John BAILEY	**Estate**
Book & Page	CPR: 125-129
Court Dates	25 Oct 1838, 12 Nov 1838, 14 Nov 1838, 10 Dec 1838, 14 Nov 1839, 10 Feb 1840, 10 Aug 1840, 12 Aug 1842, 14 Nov 1842
Administrator	Benjamin T. BRYANT
Action	BAILEY died intestate and letters of Administration are granted to BRYANT. Inventory and appraisal of personal estate filed (description within). Sale bill of personal estate presented to court totaling $508.66 and signed by the appraisers on 22 Oct 1839. Sale was held on 8 Dec 1838. Final settlement of estate is made to the court and expenditures are deducted as well as additional credits, leaving a balance of $230.26 in the hands of the administrator. Administrator ordered to appear in court in regard disposition of settlement. An account is given to the court by the administrator of a balance of $154.54 due to the minor heirs of estate after deducting expenses and the court discharges the administrator from his duties.
Incidental Names	Josiah BRYANT, bond, James M. RAY, Daniel ROBERTSON, and Benjamin and Josiah BRYANT commissioners; Charles EATON, J.P.

Elizabeth SMALLWOOD, widow of **Samuel SMALLWOOD,** vs The Heirs of **Samuel SMALLWOOD**	**On Assignment of Dower**
Book & Page	CPR: 129-131
Court Dates	8 Aug 1842, 14 Nov 1842
Heirs	Sarah Jane, Samuel & Elizabeth SMALLWOOD
Action	Attorney files petition for Dower and requests commissioners be appointed to set aside widow's portion of her Dower for lands owned by her husband (description within). No heirs appear in court after notice given legally for the action. Guardian appointed for heirs ad litem. The heirs hen appear in court with Guardian and have no objection to the granting of the Dower. Commissioners appear in court to present their findings which contain 8 acres and a portion of land containing also 17 ½ acres (descriptions within). Court approves the assignment of land to the widow and states. That she shall have the properties for the remainder of her life.

Cost and expenses to be paid by the petitioner. |
| Incidental Names | John B. NILES, attorney; William ALLEN, esquire, Guardian; John WILSON, Stephen NORTON, Joel BUTLER, commissioners |

Olivia M. SMITH widow & Relict of
James F. SMITH, deceased,   **Assignment of Dower**
vs
The Heirs of **James F. SMITH**

Book & Page	CPR: 131-132
Court Dates	8 Aug 1842, 14 Nov 1842
Heirs	Sanford, Mary Jane, Olive, Charles, James F., Francis C., and Sylvester SMITH
Action	Attorney for widow presents court with petition for Dower.

The deceased owned real estate (description within) and also a lot in the township of Hudson (description within).and requests commissioners be appointed to survey the real estate. Guardian appointed ad litem for the minor heirs. Minor children appear in court with Guardian. Commissioners appointed. Cause continued.

Commissioners present their findings to court the widow's portion of her husband's property given (description within). Widow also receives lot #13. Heirs make no objection to the assignment of land to the widow. Court awards the widow her portion, free and clear for her lifetime. Cost and expenses to be paid by the petitioner. Costs of the commissioners are taxed respectively, $2, $2, and $!

Incidental Names	Myron H. ORTON, attorney; James BRADLEY, esquire, Guardian

---

Seeley SCOFIELD   **Estate**

Book & Page	CPR: 133-136
Court Dates	May 1839, 13 May 1839, 10 Feb 1840, 8 Nov 1841, 14 Feb 1842, 14 Nov 1842
Administrator	Stephen NORTON
Action	Court orders Administrator to appear in court and present the inventory and sale bill of personal estate of the deceased. Court also orders a final settlement of the estate of the deceased. Administrator filed an "Exhibit of the Affairs of the Estate", plus items charged to himself in the amount of $378.25, as $50. The "Exhibit of Affairs" presented to the court which includes a charge to himself of $405.68 which is the amount of the ___? of the farm and cash received of the said heirs of the estate. He also presents an account of the credits amounting to $407.89, as well as debts to the estate (description within) Court accepts his account and allows a credit to him as the administrator.
Incidental Names	Preserved WHEELER, bill holder; David NORTON, bond

Joseph B. SELF, Guardian of   **Guardianship**
Amos HALL & Gustavas HALL
Heirs of **Henry DAVIS**

Book & Page	136-137
Court Dates	14 Feb 1842, 8 Aug 1842, 18 Nov 1842, 29 Aug 1842
Action	Self is appointed Guardian of the two minors under age of 14, who are sons of Wesley HALL and also heirs of the estate of Henry DAVIS, deceased of LaPorte In. Self later appears in court to state that a small quantity of wheat had come into his hands and that he believes could be sold at a private sale "to good advantage" and he requests the court's permission to sell the wheat which is the property of the two heirs. Self then reports to the court an inventory and bill of sale from the estate of Henry DAVIS held on 27 Aug 1842. 6 & ¼ bushels of wheat sold @ 60cents per bushel, amounting to $4.05, plus the cost of harvesting, threshing, and cleaning and marketing the wheat which came to $1.75, leaving $2.30 against the balance. SELF later appears in court to give a report on items of credit and debit for the guardianship of Amos HALL. (itemized expenses within).
Incidental Names	Handy DAVIS, bond
Comments	Although the two heirs were mentioned earlier in the court reports Amos HALL's name is the only one mentioned as an heir after November 1842. Within the itemized report of expenses there appears, along with the cost of a spelling book, the further costs of "boarding & washing" from 15 Feb to 17 July, and expenses for nursing and then medicines, and a doctor. Then follows the expense for a "shroud", a suit of clothes, the wood for a coffin, and the digging of a grave, leaving the reader to wonder if the heir, Gustavus HALL, might have died.

Jacob J. LIVINGSTON   **Estate**

Book & Page	CPR: 138-140
Court Dates	16 Oct 1839, 21 Oct 1839, 11 Nov 1839, 8 Nov 1841, 14 Feb 1842, 14 Nov 1842, 13 Feb 1843
Administrator	Mary LIVINGSTON
Action	Letters of Administration granted to Mary LIVINGSTON. Whose husband, Jacob died intestate. Inventory and appraisal of personal property given to the court totaling $383.20. Settlement of the estate presented to the court. Sale was held on 25 April, 1842.
	Administrator unprepared to make settlement at appointed time. Cause continued. Administrator informs the court that the sale of the estate brought in $241.83 and presents the credits and costs to the court. Court approves this account.
Incidental Names	Lewis V. BAKER, bond; David C. KELLIPS, appraiser; James ROOD, clerk of sale.

Theodore TREATS — Estate

Book & Page	CPR: 141-142
Court Dates	24 Nov 1840, 8 Feb 1841, 14 Nov 1842, 13 Feb 1843
Administrator	Alonzo D. TREAT
Heirs	Mary TREAT, Alonzo TREAT
Action	Widow, Mary TREAT renounces her right as administrator to her son, Alonzo D. TREAT. Her husband, Theodore TREAT of LaPorte County died intestate. Inventory of personal property presented to court. $240.92 in debts to the estate had been paid in full and the estate was liable for $400 to the 'Sinking Fund" received by a person who mortgaged the real estate of the deceased, and that this will become due in 4 years, and on which the administrator has paid the interest up until 29th of April next. He further stated that he became administrator only to be able to settle any debts to the estate. He added that he hoped to defray expenses this way to the estate and keep the estate together within the family by adopting the role of administrator, and that this was his sole purpose in serving in this capacity.
Incidental Names	Samuel TREAT, bond; no first name MOSSMAN, mortgage holder

ANDERSON, John, — Estate

Book & Page:	CPR: 142-146
Court Dates	24 Nov 1838, 11 Feb 1839, 14 Nov 1842, 13 Feb 1843
Administrator	William K. ANDERSON
Action	Widow Jane ANDERSON renounces her right to be administrator of her husband's estate and wishes her son, William K. ANDERSON be appointed administrator by the court. Motion filed 23 Nov 1838. Deceased was from Pleasant Township and died intestate. Letters of Administration granted and appraisal of the personal estate ordered by the court. (description within) which amounted to $2,335.59. Sale Bill presented to the court (description within) Sale held on 29 Jan 1839. Final settlement presented to the court. Administrator states the balance due to himself is $2,330.00 and the credits amounted to $2,330.93 (description within). Court accepts his account and discharges him of his duties.
Incidental Names	David ANDERSON, bond; Benjamin BUTTERWORTH, appraiser; E/.B. WOODSON, J.P.

WAKEFIELD, Jesse — Estate

Book & Page:	CPR: 147-153
Court Dates	10 Dec 1839, 24 Dec 1839, 10 Feb 1840, 14 Feb 1842, 8 Aug 1842, 14 Nov 1842, 16 Nov 1842, 18 Feb 1843

Administrator	James RIVE
Heirs	Christiana WAKEFIELD, widow
Action	Widow, Christiana WAKEFIELD, renounces her right as administrator and requests that her friend, James RIVE be appointed instead. Court grants her request. Appraisers present their finding of amount of personal property of the estate, as well as the notes owed by the deceased. $384.50 was the value of the personal property and $633.12 was owed in notes. Sale bill filed on 3 Feb 1840 (description within) $248.68 realized from the sale.
	Debts to the estate totaled $500,"or thereabouts". Sale of the estate is insufficient to pay the debts. Court orders publication of notice as to the deceased's estate. Cause continued until further notification is made to enable "more diligent" creditors to come forward. Administrator presents court with sale bill of the estate, which amounted to $921.80, and also presents charges against the estate $793.57, leaving a balance due to the estate of $128.23.
	Further amounts of charges are presented to the court (description within). All claims are then settled against the estate and the administrator is discharged from his duties.
Incidental Names	Asoph WEBSTER, security; Marsena CLARK, Charles EATON, appraisers; Samuel ROBINSON, J.P.; John F. ALLISON, J.P.; John BRADLEY, attorney; Thomas STEWART, affidavit
Comment	Clerk of court notes an entry regarding creditors and debts owed was mistakenly entered at the bottom of Page 151 and the top of page 152. He then enters a corrected "supplemental" account of expenses in this case.

Isabelle KIMBERLY, Guardian,
Mary Ann McGOUGHLIN,
Jeremiah SULLIVAN KIMBERLY,
& Lucien P. KIMBERLY heirs of
ZENAS KIMBERLY
vs   **In Chancery**
Francis HARRISON,
George W. KIMBERLY
& Samuel MILLER

Book & Page	CPR: 154-156
Court Dates	8 Feb 1842, 13 Feb 1843
Executors	Francis P. HARRISON, George W. KIMBERLY
Heirs	George W. KIMBERLY, Jeremiah KIMBERLY, & his daughter, Mary Ann McLAUGHLIN, Cynthia CAMPBELL, Eliza HARRISON, Emily MILLER & Louisa KIMBERLY
Action	Attorney for the Complainants filed a bill of Complaint which stated that in the August of 1842 term the Complainants are the widow and the Guardian of the children of the deceased, Zenas KIMBERLY of LaPorte County who

died intestate on or about the day of A.D. and that the day before the time of his death, the deceased executed a last will and Testament which was duly approved and filed. Attorney also states that the deceased signified he desired his widow gain her Dower, or 1/3 of his property, after payment of his debts. Attorney claims the deceased bequeathed to his son, Lucien, a sum sufficient to acquire a good education in reading, writing, and geography and arithmetic which would enable his son's guardian "to bind him to a storekeeper", and that if he should "not be raised and educated by one George KIMBERLY that his son Jeremiah should be treated in the same manner". The attorney added that the deceased wished that the remainder of his property, after payment of certain legacies, should be equally divided among his children: son, George W. KIMBERLY, Jeremiah KIMBERLY; Lucien P. KIMBERLY, and his daughter, Mary Ann McCLAUGHLIN; Cynthia CAMPBELL, Eliza HARRISON, Emily MILLER, and Louisa KIMBERLY, and deducting certain sums from the share of Louisa's bequest, as specified.

Deceased also appointed his son in law, Samuel MILLER and Francis P. HARRISON executors of His last will and testament. The attorney further stated Samuel declined the appointment and George W.KIMBERLY was appointed in his stead and $4000 was given in security. Attorney claims the executors eventually received $1,491.91 after the estate was settled in the early Spring and Summer of 1837, and they paid out "appropriated according to the law", only a smaller fraction of that amount and used the remainder for their own purposes without paying any of this amount to the widow and heirs. The attorney further states that the executors also made unreasonable charges against the estate for services rendered. George W. KIMBERLY made a charge against the estate in the amount of $257.75 which should not be allowed to him and that the estate is in danger of being lost. Attorney then requests a motion to call the executors as "defendants" in this case and grant relief to the Complainants in the case. Court finds Francis P; HARRISON is not a resident of this state and orders a bill published of the complaint and the charges of the complainants be answered in court.

The executors fail to appear in court for a hearing on the matter. Court orders a hearing and an account of the papers of the estate be given. A Master of Chancery is appointed to examine a full account of the distribution of the deceased's estate.

$655.80 was found to be wrongfully withheld from the estate by the executors as early as 1 Jan 1838 and that interest is due on this amount from that date which comes to $57.40 which makes $818.42 now due from the Executors.

Court confirms these findings and orders the sum of $818.42 be paid to the Complainants and also all court costs paid by defendants. Cause continued. The court allows the Master of Chancery $4 in fees.

Incidental Names   John B. NILES, attorney; Gilbert HATHAWAY, Esquire, Master of Chancery

Truman FOX &
Alexander SUNDELAND,
Partners & Co.   **Debt**
        vs
Ezra Tyler, admin. of estate of
Horace B. HIBBARD, deceased

Book & Page   CPR: 157-161

Court Dates   8 May 1843

Action   Horace B. HIBBARD died intestate. Attorney for the plaintiffs claim
                     TYLER withheld from them the debt of $260 which the deceased owed to
                     the plaintiffs in regard to a case of assumpsit filed and heard in court on 2
                     April 1838 pertaining to a certain John SHERWOOD and in which these
                     plaintiffs were plaintiffs and SHERWOOD was the defendant and to whom
                     SHERWOOD owed $51.94. The court ruled against SHERWOOD but
                     SHERWOOD did not appeal his case to the Circuit Court.

                     On 13 April 1838, Horace HIBBARD gave in writing to the plaintiffs and
                     acknowledged to be held bound to the plaintiffs in the amount of $60. The
                     attorney states that on the 2nd of April the judgment against SHERWOOD
                     for $20.20 plus costs still stands and that since he did not pursue his case in
                     the Circuit Court he is in default, and thus, HIBBARD remained unable to
                     pay the plaintiffs and the debt is still owed since HIBBARD's death.
                     Attorney further claims that the administrator of HIBBARD'S estate still
                     has not paid the money owed to them.

                     The lawyer for the administrator of HIBBARD'S estate denies any wrong
                     doing against the administrator, TYLER.

                     Defendant claims "action mon". The attorney for TYLER states that the 2nd
                     count made by the plaintiffs is not sufficient in law for them to maintain the
                     action against TYLER. The attorney for the plaintiffs restate their claim and
                     state the 3rd count of the charge remains in effect.

                     Both sides restate their claims and charges. The plaintiffs refuse to
                     withdraw their claims and ask for a jury decision.

                     Eventually a request for a jury is waived. Court decides against the
                     defendant, TYLER in the sum of $270.86

Incidental Names   William ANDREWS, attorney for the defendant; James BRADLEY,
                     attorney for the plaintiffs, E.B. WOODSON, J.P.

Joseph WYATT, deceased   **Estate**

Book & Page   161-267

Court Dates   23 Oct 1838, 12 Nov 1838, 23 Nov 1838, 10 Nov 1839, 20 Nov 1839, 10
                     Feb 1840, 24 March 1840,11 May 1840, 10 Aug 1840, 9 Nov 1840, 24 Nov
                     1840, 8 Feb 1841, 10 May 1841, 11 May 1841, 9 Aug 1841, 14 Aug 1841,

8 Nov 1841, 14 Feb 1842, 19 Feb 1842, 8 May 1842, 9 May 1842, 14 Nov 1842, 13 Feb 1843

Administrator	Ezekiel MORRISON
Heirs	James and Thomas ISAAC
Action	Letters of Administration granted to Ezekiel MORRISON and a request to assess personal property such as goods, wares, and merchandise of the deceased which is in a storehouse in the town of LaPorte. It is requested that private sale be held to protect interests of the estate and ensure these would not have to compete with public merchandise. Court grants this request. An inventory of the goods is filed in court (description within). An appraiser is also appointed.

A 16 pg inventory is presented to court appraised at $3,849.63, along with the notes outstanding amounting to $4,339.97.

Administrator appears in court and states "succinctly" that the amount of debts and demands outstanding against the estate have come to his knowledge and that the estate's income is insufficient to pay the same. He states that the debts amount to $10,559.70 over and above the income from the private sale of goods of the deceased. The entire amount of assets of the estate amount to $11,463.27, the sale of personal property came to $2,423.97 and there are debts of $8,088.30. The appraised value of the land of deceased came to $950. He adds that the cost of converting the goods and wares of the estate would be considerable. He hopes that the real estate itself might be saved for the heirs. He asks that the court grant him permission to settle up said estate as insolvent.

The court orders publication of the filing of the complaint in the newspaper in order to allow creditors time to come forward.

Deceased's. property is in St. Joseph County In., containing 90 acres appraised at the sum of blank $100. Second property in same township (36) containing 80 acres appraised at the sum of blank $100. 3rd section in twp 34 contains 80 acres, fourth section in twp 37, 8 acres, 4th section, same twp, 80 acres. Also, lot #46 appraised at $250 in the original plat of the town of LaPorte with dwelling house appraised at $250.

Administrator files further petition on Nov 19 1839 stating that all real estate of the deceased must be sold to pay outstanding debts to the estate and marks the descriptions of each section of real estate as" Exhibit A" Heirs are issued summons to appear in court. Court orders estate settled as insolvent. Citations for heir's appearance returned to court from Union County Indiana marked "not found".

Administrator files sale bill of personal estate of the deceased (there follows a 37 page itemized description of all articles and merchandise sold with approximately 331 buyers names listed).

Administrator and attorney request court appoint a Guardian for the heirs. Their summons to appear in court has now been served in Union County. Heirs appear before court and Guardian states there is no objection to the

Administrator's request to sell the deceased's personal property at public auction. Court also agrees that the real estate (description within) be sold but first notice of sale be published in newspaper.

Administrator later appears in court and gives account of the advertisement of the real estate (description within) and states the sale will be held at a home in New Carlisle on the 31 Oct 1840, between 10 am and 4 pm. He further states that separate tracts of land were offered on a credit of 6 months and these tracts were bid off and bought for $570.40 and paid in full by promissory note. He requests further time to sell the remainder of the lots. Court orders deed be given to purchaser as soon as money is paid and orders also that the administrator be given more time in which to sell the remaining real estate (description within).

Administrator reports to court that on 29 Jan 1841, in Marshall County a sale was held and part of the real estate was sold (description within) for $50. Money was received and certificate given. Lot #46 in LaPorte was also sold for $100_____ but buyer has failed to give security for payment and is considered "insolvent". Court orders sale of this town lot set side and agrees that administrator shall have more time to sell this lot.

Administrator reports to court that another public sale was deed issued for the property.

Administrator files his record of the sale of real estate and inventory of merchandise of deceased. Court then orders remainder of real estate sold.

Administrator again requests additional time to sell. Administrator files a schedule of notes from the estate of undivided half of the property in Marshall County (description within) held at the courthouse in Plymouth Indiana on 30 Aug. which was sold for $17.81. Court annuls sale as price is considered "unreasonably low". Court orders sale held again. Claim made against estate in the amount of $200 and dated 3 June 1836. Administrator reports to the court that the undivided half of land on Michigan Road in Plymouth Indiana has now been sold for 37cents per acre (description within) and amounting to $26.36 and this was the highest bidder for the property. Court approves the sale and a deed is given to purchaser.

Another claim against the estate is made to the court. The claim involves the goods and merchandise left by deceased in the storehouse and now occupied by the claimant. The goods included groceries and merchandise ordered by claimant from Philadelphia to be sold in New York and amounting to $300. Claimant also states the deceased signed a lease for the claimant to use various rooms in this storehouse (description within) for a period of one year for $200. The signed lease presented to the court as well as the merchandise bill amounting to $6,999.65. In total, the claim amounts to $8,343.56. Court approves the claim.

Administrator presents court with his account of notes against estate and credits to himself for sums paid out against estate and also for his services rendered to the estate. This account includes 5 pages (description within with names of note holders, which number 25) Notes amount to $8,451.12.and there are other uncollected notes amounting to $2,759.56.

$5,691.56 still remains to be collected from unpaid notes. Court approves this account.

$12,815.56 in claims are presented by additional creditors to the court. The court then allows a certain percentage on the dollar to these claims. (description and names within).

Court releases administrator from any liability of further notes filed against the estate and approves of his diligence in pursuing payment of all debts against the estate. The note holders will be considered on a "first come, first served" basis.

Administrator presents court with a satisfactory account of the dispersal of estate monies and is discharged by the court.

Incidental Names   Sutton VAN PELT, security; Azariah WILLIAMS, John RHINEHEART, Franklin __?___, appraisers; Noah NEWELL, Charles McCLURE, defendants in suit against estate; John B. NILES, Sutton VAN PELT, appraisers; William C. HANNAH, guardian; J. IVANS, New Carlisle sale site; Abram HARRISON, purchaser of lot; Thomas BENTLY, Marshall Co site of sale; Samuel BURSON, lot buyer; Wm. HAGENBACK, lot buyer; Harvey LUSK, lot buyers, E. B. WOODSON, witness; Anzie L. WHEELER, lot buyer; Eliza ASPENWALL, claimant; Benjamin KROP, John RINEHART, goods purchasers; John B. NILES, lot buyer

Comments   The 37 page itemized sale bill of WYATT'S personal estate might be well worth going through. Only a few of the purchaser's names are repeated. This could prove a valuable resource for those wishing to determine when their LaPorte County ancestor might have resided in LaPorte. The itemized and lengthy list of notes due could also prove a valuable resource for researchers.

Candy DAVIS,
Priscilla HUYSER/HIZER,
Priscilla DAVIS,
Margaret MIDDLETON,
Margaret DAVIS, John DAVIS,
Henry DAVIS, & James DAVIS,
Adult heirs of **Henry DAVIS**, deceased
       vs   **Partition of Real Estate**
Joshua DAVIS, George W. DAVIS,
& Polly DAVIS, and also
Amos COLLAND, Gustavuz HALL,
children of Eliza HALL, deceased late
Eliza DAVIS, all minor heirs
and legal representatives (sic) of the
late **Henry DAVIS**, deceased

Book & Pg: 233-238

Court Dates   1 Feb 1842, 9 May 1842, 14 Aug 1843

Action   Petitioners file their claim with the court stating Henry DAVIS died Feb 1837 leaving themselves, adult heirs, and also minor heirs: Joshua DAVIS, age 17, George W. DAVIS, 15 yrs, and Polly DAVIS, age 11 yrs who the petitioners request be made defendants to this petition and that Eliza HALL, child and heir of Henry DAVIS and wife of Willy DAVIS who died in March 1839, leaving 2 infant children, heirs and legal representatives of Eliza HALL, to wit: Amos HALL, age 6 yrs, and Gustavus HALL, age 4 yrs, who petitioners also ask to be made defendants to this bill. Henry DAVIS, deceased, left Nancy DAVIS his widow, and left real estate and parcels of land. (description within) which are 3 lots in township 36 containing 139 acres. Petitioners state that the town of Kingsbury was laid out and that there are about 120 unsold lots in the plat of this town, (description within) and that another section of land is held by deed by the deceased. Further land is held (description within) and petitioners request the court the land be divided between the heirs and that the court appoint commissioners to the partition of these lands. Court appoints commissioners and orders a dower be appointed to the widow of the deceased.

Widow of the deceased signed an "Article of Agreement" dated 16 Feb 1842 wherein all parties agree that the real estate of deceased be given a first claim to all (further land descriptions within). It was further requested that the north half of the house in which widow DAVIS now uses may be removed north of the boundary from the 70 acres and that Candy DAVIS may occupy the same until removal is made. Candy DAVIS is then to make a deed for the 70 acres to Nancy DAVIS, his mother, for the remainder of her life if she agrees to release all claim to dower and to the remainder of the lands.

Two commissioners appear and report on the partition of real estate of deceased with consideration as to the Dower of the widow and a division of property to the heirs of deceased. (description within). All heirs declined dividing the Kingsbury town plat. Court confirms and accepts the commissioner's report.

Incidental Names	Henry CATTLIN, deed signer; John MOORE Jr., Renselaer SHAW, David WINCHELL, commissioners, Joseph B. SELF, guardian
Comments	Also left undivided was 5 acres of land known as the "Hiram INMAN lot", which was decided "could not be divided without great prejudice to the value of the property."

Ezra Tyler. Administrator of the
estate of
Horace B. HIBBARD,   **Debt & Judgment on Warrant of Atty.**
vs
James A. Wilkinson

Book & Page	CPR: 239-240
Court Dates	13 Nov 1843
Action	Declaration of promissory note to Ezra TYLER and WILKINSON on 31 Dec 1843 filed in court by attorney. Attorney for Administrator files his response, a "Confession of Judgment" for $207, plus $4.58 in damages in

favor of TYLER. He authorizes payment to TYLER, dated 23 Oct 1843. Attorney states WILKINSON is indeed indebted to TYLER for the amount stated. Court then allows payment in full to TYLER.

Incidental Names   James BRADLEY, attorney

Joseph JOHNSON   Estate

Book & Page   240-245

Court Dates   12 Oct 1838, 12 Nov 1838, 9 Nov 1840, 14 Feb 1842, 9 May 1842, 13 Nov 1843

Administrators   John DENHAM/Joel BUTLER

Heirs   Elizabeth JOHNSON, widow

Action   Joseph JOHNSON died intestate. Administrators file inventory and appraisal of person estate on 19 Oct 1838.

Inventory of estate listed at $1,468.92 (description within).

Personal estate sold at public auction and report submitted to court. Auction held on 1 June 1839. Administrators unprepared to make final settlement and cause continued.

Personal estate sale brought in $821.89. Debts to estate paid our and amounted to $822.26 (description within). $295.65 was left in favor of the estate and to be distributed to the heirs. Widow receives $188.78 and this is also to be given to the heirs.

Administrators later produce vouchers in the amount of $53.84 as money remaining after estate settlement and given to court. The court discharges the Administrators of their duties.

Incidental Names   Benjamin BUTLER, bond; Henry BELDEN, Robert P. BLEVIN, appraisers; Theodore CATLIN, J.P.

Richard HERBERT   Estate

Book & Page   PCR: 246-249

Court Dates   14 Nov 1838, 3 Dec 1838, 9 May 1842

Administrator   Micajah JONES

Action   Letters of Administration granted to JONES, of Galena township and filed on 3 Dec 1838. Administrator files personal estate inventory amounting to $301.32 (description within). Sale bill from personal estate with list of purchasers presented to the court (description within). Sale held on 31 Dec 1838. Court orders Administrator to appear in court to present final settlement of estate.

Administrator asks for continuance. Court grants request. Administrator appears and gives court a list of debits and credits. Sale of property brought in $1,741.64 and further account given (description within). Balance due to Administrator is $336.66. Court approves Administrator's account and discharges him from his duties.

Incidental Names   Jesse JONES, bond; Caleb B. DAVIS, Jacob HICKMAN, appraisers; Byron Cadwallader, J.P.

William JENKINS, Mark JENKINS,
Edward JENKINS &
Benjamin GILBREATH
           vs   **In Chancery**
Mark ALLEN, Jacob HUFF
& George W. ALLEN, heirs of
REUBEN ALLEN

Book & Page   PCR: 249-251

Court Dates   11 Feb 1844

Action   Attorney for complainants files bill of complaints on 30 Dec 1843. All three JENKINS are from Baltimore, MD. Benjamin GILBREATH resides in LaPorte County. The Complainants state that on 12 Mar 1833, Reuben ALLEN, deceased made a promissory note to William JENKINS and sons by which he promised to pay them $411.12 in 6 months time. JENKINS endorsed the note to all three JENKINS. The deceased, ALLEN, was also indebted to GILBREATH for $98 in two promissory notes which are also past due. The deceased, ALLEN, was given the promissory notes and the court was also presented these notes in order to settle the estate of ALLEN. ALLEN died intestate on 27 Oct 1838. Mark ALLEN was appointed Administrator of the estate on that date and a security bond was made. The Administrator was ordered by the court to sell real estate of the deceased for payment of debts, and signed a bond for such. The sum of $3000 was realized from the sale of personal estate and $200 from the sale of lands. The attorney claims the debt to the plaintiff has not been paid and the Administrator was "fraudulently" concealing and disposing of the assets from the estate for his own gain and profit. Attorney claims the Administrator has concealed some of the estate assets and endeavored to obtain credit for large sums of money. Attorney further claims that the Administrator negligently sold estate goods to an insolvent individual in the amount of $94.88 without obtaining any security. Administrator also is accused of selling numerous estate articles worth $67 to another purchaser without obtaining security. He is further charged with conspiring to withhold money from the creditors with claims against the estate and refusing to appear in court to answer these claims. The attorney requests the court to order the defendant to appear to answer these charges.

                   ALLEN appears in court but the remainder of the defendants do not and make default. Court finds charges are true and orders plaintiffs awarded $118.82, plus court costs.

Incidental Names   John B. NILES, attorney; Jacob B. HUPP, bond; George W. ALLEN, bond; Arthur MCCLURE, sold goods; David POUND, purchased goods

George THOMAS, Deceased   Estate

Book & Pg   CPR: 251-260

Court Dates   10 March 1835, 8 May 1835, 11 May 1835, 8 Aug 1836, 14 Nov 1836, 13 Nov 1837, 12 Feb 1838

Administrator   Andrew BURNSIDE/William HAWKINS

Heirs   Elizabeth THOMAS, Eleanore THOMAS HEWS, Nancy THOMAS BALL, Charles & Noory THOMAS, late EGBERT, minor heirs Regina, Ruth, Jane, Portia & Joel THOMAS

Action   Letters of Administration filed in vacation and granted to BURNSIDE and HAWKINS on 10 March 1835. Inventory of personal estate filed (description within). The sale bill is presented to the court. Auction was held on 20 April 1835 at the home of the deceased (description within) and realized $134.43. Letters of Administration are confirmed by court. Court affirms former filing to the record which appeared on pages 252 and 253. Administrators appear and state deceased died intestate and that they find the sale of personal estate insufficient to pay debts of the deceased and that deceased owned tracts of land (description within) and request the court call the widow of the deceased, Elizabeth THOMAS, to court as well as John and Eleanore HEWS late Eleanor THOMAS, Willard and Nancy BALL, late Nancy THOMAS, and Charles and Noory EGBERT, late THOMAS, all adult heirs, as well as Adam G. POLK, Guardian of Regina , Ruth, Jane, Portia and Joel THOMAS infant heirs of deceased to show why these tracts of land should not be sold to pay the debts of the estate.

Inventory and appraisal of real estate filed in court (description within) and it was witnessed on 9 Aug 1836. Attorney for the heirs files his objection to the sale of the real estate as the widow of deceased has not had her Dower to the land set aside for her. Attorney asks that the application for selling the land be set aside until this is done. Cause continued.

All parties appear in court and as the Dower for the widow had been filed subsequently before the objection was presented to the court, the Administrators requests the sale of other tracts of land of the deceased first.

Administrators again affirm there are in sufficient funds to pay debts of the estate and request sale of other tract of land containing 40 acres (description within). Heirs will be again summoned to the court. Appraisement of real estate given whose value is $400 (description within) and sworn to on 16 Nov 1837.

Court orders heirs summoned and publication of sale given. Administrators report sale of one parcel of land on 31 March 1838 for $380. Administrators give account of estate debt and credits (description within). They have a balance of $108.47 remaining in their hands. Court advised Andrew

BURNSIDE has "removed" from the state. Court removes him from his office.

Administrator HAWKINS then files his report of the estate and the claims for debts and credits remaining (description within). There remains a balance of $108.47 on hand. Court approves findings and discharges the Administrators.

Incidental Names	Robert S. MORRISON, J.P.; Adam G. POLK, bond; John M. LEMON, John W. WILKINSON, appraisers; William O. ROSS (?), J.P.; William C. HANNAH, clerk of sale; John JESSUP, Isaac SNEED, appraisers; William C. HANNAH, attorney; George J. SWOPE, J.P.; Jacob WAGNER, land purchaser.

Alexander BLACKBURN, Admin.
of the estate of **Ezekiel PROVOLT**
　　　　　vs　　　　　　　　　　　　**In Chancery**
William MAPLES, William SHAY,
Robert SHARP & widow
& heirs of said deceased.

Book & Page	CPR: 261-262
Court Dates	23 Feb 1844
Action	Attorney for complainants states that the deceased Ezekiel PROVOLT, died on 16 Aug 1844, and sold 80 acres of land (description within) to William M. MAPLES for $200 and MAPLES then gave PROVOLT a note for $106 balance due. A written agreement was given to MAPLES that a deed would be forthcoming on 20 Aug 1838. Court given the written agreement. Attorney claims MAPLES paid the balance except for $50 on Aug 1839 and promised PROVOLT he would pay the remainder at a rate of 10% interest. MAPLES then delivered the note called a title bond to William SHARP and Robert SHARP and the attorney claims this note and bond is now their property. He also states that Ezekiel PROVOLT died without having made any provision by will for the conveyance of this land, but left the following persons his heirs, named by his wife, Eliza PROVALT, now his widow, they are: John PROVOLT, William PROVALT, Mary Catherine & Delilah & Maryann PROVOLT, his children, all of whom are "infant" heirs. Attorney states that the SHARPS are ready to pay off the note whenever a deed can be made to them for the land. Attorney requests a subpoena be issued by the court for the aforementioned SHARPS and PROVOLT heirs to be made defendants in this cause and order that the SHARPS pay said money owed for the land.

Attorney appears in court to state that the subpoena to all defendant parties had been served and the court appoints a Guardian for the minor heirs. The Administrator of Ezekiel PROVOLT'S estate files his response to the court stating the heirs, some of whom are of "tender age", were entirely ignorant of this situation, according to the court appointed Guardian. The remainder of the defendants did not appear in court and thus, are in default. The court declares the charge to be true and appoints commissioners to present to the SHARPS a deed to the land in question and orders the balance owed for the land be paid. The Administrator is ordered to pay court costs.

Incidental Names   John B. NILES, attorney; Samuel B. WILLIAMS, Guardian

Christiana LUCAS
        vs   **To Assign Dower**
The Heirs at law; Executors &
Ten(?) Tenants of **Francis LUCAS**, Deceased

Book & Page	CPR: 263-267
Court Dates	12 Feb 1844, 13 Feb 1844, 13 May 1844
Administrators	Daniel CRANE & Joel NOKES
Heirs	Belinda, Abigail, Debra, & Elizabeth Lucas, children of Sarah Wooley, formerly Lucas, Daniel, Aaron, & Francis Lucas, Rhoda McCurdy, formerly Lucas, Mary Warren, formerly Lucas, George Lucas, Chistiana Dill(?), formerly Lucas, Elizabeth, & Samuel Lucas.

Action   Attorney for widow files petition for assignment of her Dower. Deceased, was from Warren County, Ohio, and died on or about 15 Nov 1843. He had left in his possession certain lands for the benefit of grandchildren and heirs at law, and the administrators then published notice of a Demand for Dower to be made out of the following real estate containing 15 lots in townships 36,37 (description within), as well as lot 24 in Michigan City (description within) and attorney now requests court to appoint three commissioners to survey the properties. Attorney for the defendants answers the complaint, saying the widow should not have one of the tracts, from Section 7, township 36, (description within) because this tract was owned by the defendant by letters of patent from the State of Indiana and delivered to him on 6 July 1841. Attorney further states that the "said" widow was never lawfully married to the deceased. The attorney for the widow tells the court that she will not further prosecute for her claim of Dower.

Both attorneys appear in court and enter their arguments again before the court. Court decides no Dower should be assigned to the widow. A Guardian is appointed for the minor heirs. Minor heirs & Guardian then appear in court. Adult heirs do not appear. Default is made and court appoints commissioners to survey the real estate. Commissioners report their findings for assignment of a Dower for the widow. Court approves the assignment to the widow for her lifetime. Petitioners are to pay the court costs and commissioners are allotted their fees.

Incidental Names   Robert L. COBBS, attorney; Henry MEEKER, Andrew MELVILLE, tenants; John B. NILES, attorney; Thomas A. STEWART, Guardian; Asher WHITE, Elam CLARKE, William A. BLAKE, commissioners; William HAWKINS, witness

Comment   There is no mention within this report as to exactly why the widow's Dower was finally allowed to be made after the accusations of the defendant's attorney claiming she was not legally married to the deceased, and after which the widow then stated she would not further prosecute her claim.

Abraham WESTERVELT   Estate

Book & Page	CPR: 267-271
Court Dates	15 Dec 1841, 16 Dec 1841, 14 Feb 1842, 17 Feb 1844, 30 May 1844
Administrator	James WESTERVELT
Heirs	C. WESTERVELT & Edmund WESTERVELT
Action	Deceased died intestate. Widow renounces her right as administrator on 23 Nov 1841. Letters of Administration granted and filed. on 13 Dec 1841. Personal Estate Inventory filed.

Sale bill filed. Sale held on 8 Jan 1841 in Marshall County, Indiana (description within) Sale bill amounted to $356.58.

Administrator presents court with a final account of the estate's debts and credits (description within). Court accepts the account and discharges administrator of his duties.

Incidental Names	Benjamin BEARD, bond; Benjamin BLAND, Jacob DROM, appraisers; Wilson PATTON, note

George BOSSERMAN   **In Chancery**
      vs
Samuel Stewart, Administrator
of the estate of **Jesse TANEY**, deceased

Book & Page	CPR: 271-273
Court Dates	13 May 1844, 18 May 1844
Action	Attorney for complainant files his bill, sometime in 1844 (no specific date given). TANEY died intestate. BOSSERMAN, as administrator of the estate received estate property worth $232.50 on 1 March 1839, and three notes against the real estate in the amount of $50.80 which were used for the purchase of the real estate. The notes were rescinded and given up, so nothing was realized from these notes. After the debts to the estate were paid, the Administrator was still owed $387.25. An account of this was filed on 19 Feb 1842. Samuel STEWART was appointed administrator on 12 May 1842 and the attorney for complainant now requests STEWART be made a defendant. STEWART', attorney claims, only paid out $76.75 which was supposedly due to the claimant and presented to the court the final settlement of the deceased's estate on 14 Feb 1843. The attorney further claims that a "manifest mistake" was made at that time as the complainant should have received $156.70, plus a further sum of $78.95. Attorney also claims a mistake was made by the administrator when totaling the estate inventory and that the claimant had no prior notice of the final settlement. The attorney then requests the court re-evaluate the final settlement of the

deceased and the administrator STEWART, be subpoenaed to appear before the court to answer these charges.

Administrator STEWART appears in court and states the claimant is not entitled to relief as the matter has already been settled. Court finds the charges to be true and orders the complainant be awarded the sum of $88.23 to be levied against the goods and chattels of the deceased's estate. Complainant ordered to pay court costs.

Incidental Names	John HOBSON, note; James BRADLEY, attorney

Elizabeth BECKNER	**Petition for Assignment of Dower**
vs	

The Heirs of **John BECKNER**, Deceased.

Book & Page	CPR: 273-275
Court Dates	13 April 1844, 13 May 1844, 12 Aug 1844
Heirs	Susan, John & Jacob B., Jonathan B., Lydia Ann Stanton BECKNER, adult heirs, & Sarah, Joel B., David B., William G., & Abraham BECKNER, minor heirs
Action	Attorney for widow files her petition. Her husband died on 16 Sept 1837 and held property in township 37, LaPorte County Indiana which contained lots of 80 acres. (description within). Widow Elizabeth BECKNER appointed the minor heir's guardian. Attorney requests commissioners be appointed to survey the real estate of deceased and that the guardian and heirs be subpoenaed to appear in court.
	Court appoints a guardian for the minor heirs. Adult heirs do not appear in court.
	Widow is allotted her 1/3 portion of the deceased's real estate (description within). Court approves the dower assignment. Commissioners each awarded sums of $2.25 for one day and one half of service.
Incidental Names	Samuel E. WILLIAMS, attorney; James BRADLEY, esq., Guardian; John WITTER, Tobias MILLER, John BUSH, commissioners

William ARGABRITE, deceased	**Estate**
Book & Page	CPR: 275-280
Court Dates	27 Aug 1839, 28 Aug 1839, 4 Sept 1839, 24 Oct 1839, 11 Nov 1839, 14 Feb 1842, 13 Nov 1843, 12 Aug 1844
Administrator	John HEFNER
Heirs	Not named
Action	Widow of deceased, Elizabeth ARGABRITE, renounces right as administrator of deceased's estate and her brother Inventory of estate filed (description within). Inventory totaled $1,169.00.

Sale bill of estate filed after an auction on 10 Oct 1839 (description within). Sale totaled $618.89. Court subpoenas administrator to appear in court to make final settlement of estate (description within). Administrator states that the sale fell short of the appraisement of articles by $110/13 and that 2 notes and claims are awards this amount to the infant heirs of deceased. Administrator discharged.

Incidental Names	John VICKORY, John DUDLEY, bond; Henry HEFNER, security; John B. McDONEL, Newlove SAYBORN, commissioners; Reuben MONDAY J.P.; Joseph HEFNER clerk of sale

John SMITH, deceased   Estate

Book & Page	280-288
Court Dates	23 Dec 1836, 14 Feb 1837, 8 May 1837, 14 May 1838, 11 May 1840, 15 May 1840, 10 Aug 1840, 8 Nov 1841, 4 Nov 1843, 12 Feb 1844, 12 Aug 1844
Administrator	Adam G. POLK
Heirs	Rhoda SMITH, widow, Lester & Olive SMITH, minor heirs
Action	Letters of Administration granted in vacation. Court affirms appointment, Administrator presents inventory and appraisal and sale bill of estate. Sale of personal estate held on 21 Jan 1837 (description within). Administrator files report of sale of estate. Deceased died intestate. Administrator declares sale of personal estate insufficient to complete payments on a certain lot in LaPorte County. He claims appraisal of certain real estate amounts to $205 and submits an inventory same (description within). The lot is #165 in town of LaPorte and he requests it be sold for discharge of debts to estate. Court orders widow, heirs and holder of lien to appear in court and the remainder of the report of the real estate of deceased is given (description within). These are 40 acres in township 37, at $50, lot #165, original plat held by title bond, and is $100, and now appraised and valued at $150. The deceased owed at the time of his death $200. There remains a deficit of $436 to the estate. Court orders heirs and lien holder summoned to court to show why property should not be sold so debts to the estate may be made. Cause continued.

Burwell HEMLOCK, security lien holder responds to petition by stating that on the 3 June 1836, he sold to the deceased the lot and house mentioned in petition for $600, and took from deceased several promissory notes in the sum of $200. One note was for $77.85 and due on 25 Dec 1836, the 3rd note was for $100 with 10 % interest, and due on 1 March 1837. A 4th note was for $200 with 10 % interest and due on 1 Mar 1839. These notes amounted to $577.85. He also stated the balance of $600 was paid down on the day of the sale and that the first mentioned note of $200 was assigned to Joseph WYATT as collateral for the payment of $100 which defendant owed WYATT. He further states he will not consent to a sale of the house and lot as it would deprive him of that lien. He will not issue a deed for the property until all purchase money is paid. This answer is dated 22 July 1840 and signed in Union County, Indiana.

Guardian of minor heirs appointed. Widow does not appear in court. Court orders property sold at public auction to the highest bidder (description within of the 40 acres of real estate). Court also ordered publication of sale be made. Administrator reports sale of property in LaPorte for 9 cents, which was the highest bid. He adds he did not have time to advertise and sell the property that was in St. Joseph County and requests more time to do so. Court orders a quit claim be issued for the property in LaPorte and allows administrator more time to sell St. Joseph property. Administrator once again unable to sell St. Joseph property due to "sickness in his family".

Court grants additional time for the sale. Administrator still unable to sell property of deceased, and once again, for "sickness in his family" He appears in court requesting he be allowed to sell part of the real estate (description within). He also requests court approve a private sale of the St. Joseph County property as it would be of greater benefit to the estate. Court approves request.

Administrator then reports sale of property for $50. Court orders deed for property be issued. Administrator makes final report to the court. $336.77 was amount of sale bill. He reports credits to him of $394.68. Court approves his report.

Incidental Names	Oliver SHETLEFF, Jacob HALAS, appraisers; Arthur McCLURE, Calvin R. EVANS, appraisers; John S. HUNT, lien holder; John WILLS, Joseph W. LYKINS, appraiser; John GARGAN, J.P., Union Co.; John B. NILES, guardian; James BRADLEY, house & lot purchaser; John S. HUNT, purchaser of St. Joseph Co property; David B. FREEMAN, bond.

George V. BECKNER
vs   **Partition of Real Estate**
Johnathan B. BECKNER, &
Lydia, Ann BECKNER, his wife,
Susan BECKNER who intermarried
with **John BECKNER**,
Joel B. BECKNER,
David B. BECKNER,
William G. BECKNER &
Abraham BECKNER

Book & Page	CPR: 288-291
Court Dates	13 April 1844, 13 May 1844, 12 Aug 1844
Heirs	Elizabeth BECKNER, minor heir
Action	George G. BECKNER appears in court to state that his father John BECKNER died on or about 16 Sept 1837, and that the deceased owned tracts of land (description within) died intestate. Guardian appointed by

court for the minor heir. Petitioner claims all heirs are "tenants in common" of real estate of deceased and requests partition of same.

Three commissioners appointed by the court to divide the real estate. Petitioner requests the court have heirs appear to show why real estate should not be partitioned.

Heirs agree that 2/3 of the property which is in twp 37, one of which should go to the widow of deceased as her Dower and agree that the remainder of the property be divided (description within) and go to the heirs equally.

Commissioners present their report to the court on division of the real estate and are awarded 75 cents for one half days work.

Incidental Names	S. WILLIAMS, lawyer; James BRADLEY, Guardian; Tobias MILLER, John BUSH, John WITTER, commissioners.
Comment	Notation at end of page for this judgment: "Carried to page 658 – See Plat".

Mary MARTIN, deceased   **Estate**

Book & Page	CPR: 291-294
Court Dates	30 Oct 1840, 12 Nov1840, 30 Nov 1840, 11 Aug 1842, 27 Aug 1842, 12 Aug 1844
Administrator	Charles MARTIN
Action	Letters of Administration granted in vacation. Deceased died intestate in LaPorte County. Administrator appears in court and files inventory and appraisal of personal estate of deceased. On 11 Nov 1840, an appraisal was made (description within).
	Sale bill presented to court amounting to $262.16.
	Final settlement presented to court (description within). Administrator has a remaining balance on hand of $368.29. Court approves the account and orders balance paid to heirs on or before one day of the next term of court.
Incidental Names	Francis LUCAS, Henry WEED, bond; D.C. McKelleps, J.P.; R.C. INMAN, Sales Clerk; Jas. WARNOCK, J.P.
Comments	No heirs are named, only a notation made at end of final settlement: "7 heirs of $35.74 each".

Belinda B.McCLANAHAN,   **Application for the Appointment of Guardianship**
Harriet H. McCLANAHAN,
James E. MCCLANAHAN,
Joseph McCLANAHAN, heirs of
James McCLANAHAN, dec'd

Book & Page	CPR: 295-296
Court Dates	12 Nov 1838, 10 Aug 1840, 12 Aug 1844

Guardian	Griffin TREADWAY
Action	Belinda and Harriet McCLANAHAN appeared in court & chose a Guardian on behalf of the other children who are under the age of 14. They also made application for advice on behalf of the underage heirs. Guardian appointed. A second bond was made after the first bondholder was discharged.
	Guardian files exhibit of affairs. He received $248 and paid out expenses of $246.18 (description of account within). Guardian finally pays into Clerk's hands the amount of $248.28. Court discharges Guardian from his duties.
Incidental Names	Benjamin CRUMPACKER, bond; John TREADWAY, & Edmund B. WOODSON, bond

---

Daniel PETRY, Deceased   **Estate**

Book & Page	CPR: 298-303
Court Dates	15 Dec 1838, 4 Jan 1839, 11 Feb 1839, 19 Feb 1839, 9 Aug 1841, 8 Aug 1842, 11 Nov 1844
Executors	John PETRY, Daniel PETRY
Action	Daniel PETRY's last will and testament was filed in court on 5 Dec 1838. It follows: "I, Daniel PETRY of the county of LaPorte and state of Indiana; being well stricken in years and being infirm in body, but sound in mind and judgment and calling to mind that there is a time appointed for all men to die I now make and declare this to be my last will and testament. Finally, I will my spirit to God that gave it and my body to be buried in a Christian like manner.
	Secondly, I will and bequeath to my wife Eve PETRY one third of all my property so long as she shall live. I give to my heirs all in like manner equal of all left except the smith tools, and one Hundred dollars and bed and bedding and clothing of case (?) she stop till she is of age. And this is till the year Eighteen hundred and Forty Two. And I will that John PETRY and Daniel PETRY shall be the administrators and the executors of estate and if in case any money is lost each heir shall lose equal shares and said Daniel J. PETRY has got one hundred dollars more than his share and there is something paid on it. And John Clark (?) thirty three Dollars of having as much as the rest. And if my wife Eve PETRY does want to go to Union County the said administrator is to move her there. And now in presence of these witnesses I do declare this to be my last will and testament in testimony thereof I now set my hand and seal this the twelfth day of October, One thousand eight hundred and thirty eight. (signed) Daniel PETRY. Attest Lane DAWSON which was only proved by Lane DAWSON subscribing witness thereto by affidavit __?__ annexed in these words to wit---State of Indiana LaPorte County. Be it remembered that on the fifth day of December in year 1838, before me William HAWKINS, clerk, personally came Lane DAWSON, the subscribing witness to the foregoing will who being by me duly sworn solemnly saith that he saw Daniel PETRY sign, seal publish and declare the within and foregoing writing as his last

will and testament and that he believes he was at the time of its execution of sound mind and memory and that he signed his name thereto as witness in the presence of the said testator and at his request.

John PETRY, Daniel J. PETRY granted letters of administration. Inventory of personal estate of deceased presented to court (description within).

Sale bill filed in court (description within). Sale held ? Jan 1839 at residence of deceased.

Executors present their account of deceased's estate. They have in hand $1,201.24 (description of account within). Court orders monies remaining dispersed according to will of deceased.

Supplemental account of affairs of the estate presented to the court. (description within). Executors credited with expenses paid out and balance remaining to be dispersed is $1,261.24. Court discharges executors from their duties.

Incidental Names	James CUNNINGHAM, Hugh GRAHAM, bond; James WEBSTER, Samuel VAN DOLSON, Appraisers; John TYLER, J.P.; John HEFNER, J.P John DUDLEY owed debt to estate.

William BROWN
vs   **In Chancery**
Arenna COLLINS &
Albert COLLINS, heirs at law of
Harvey COLLINS, deceased

Book & Page	CPR: 303-305
Court Dates	4 Oct 1844, 11 Nov 1844, 10 Feb 1845
Heirs	Arenna COLLINS, Harriet COLLINS, Charlotte COLLINS, Albert COLLINS
Action	Attorney for claimants files his bill of complaint and states that on or about the 12th of Nov 1838 letters of administration were granted to Samuel STEWART and George C. HAVINS for the estate of Harvey COLLINS of LaPorte County and that afterwards the personal property of the deceased were insufficient to pay the debts to the estate. On the 16 Nov 1839 the administrator filed in court for the sale of real estate, 96 acres, to be sold from Section 8 (description within) and also that citations were issued and served to the heirs of the deceased. Attorney also states the heirs did not appear in court by guardian or otherwise and thus a default was made against them by the court, which undid their right to the benefit of the sale of any real estate of deceased. He adds that on 12 Feb 1841, the administrators then sold the real estate to him for the sum of $230, being the highest bid made. On the 5 Feb the administrator then reported to the court of the sale and it was confirmed by the court. He adds that since then two of the heirs, Harriet and Charlotte COLLINS have died and the two remaining heirs should be made defendants in this case. He further requests a clear title to the property he purchased and approved by the court.

Summons issued for defendants. Court appoints a guardian for the remaining heirs and the guardian/attorney answers by requesting the minor heirs be dismissed from the suit.

Court orders the judgment of the 11 Nov for sale of the real estate be confirmed and a title to real estate be made and given to the complainant and administrator.

Incidental Names	T.E. WILLIAMS, attorney; Harrison F. HENCHLEY, sheriff; William C. HANNAH, attty

Ira BOND, deceased   **Estate**

Book & Page	CPR: 306-309
Court Dates	19 Sept 1843, 27 Oct 1843, 14 Feb 1845
Heirs	Jahiel WASSON, Jesse BOND, William BOND, Charlotte BOND, John BOND
Administrators	Jesse BOND, Jehiel WASSON
Action	BOND and WASSON applied for letters of administration. Ira BOND died intestate. An inventory of personal estate filed (description within). Sale bill of estate filed. Sale held on 28 Oct 1843 (description within). Administrators present their final account of debits and credits to the estate of deceased. Personal property sold for $263.31. The amount of cash and notes on hand was $306.63 for a total of $569.93. Cash paid out (description within). Administrators left with a balance due them of 69 cents.
Comments	Charlotte BOND'S name appears as receiving cash from the estate, but her relationship to the deceased is not given.
Incidental Names	Elijah STANTON, bond; Stephen HOLLOWAY, appraisers

Samuel SMALLWOOD, dec'd.   **Estate**

Book & Page	CPR: 310-316
Court Dates	26 June 1841, 9 Aug 1841, 8 Nov 1841, 10 Nov 1841, 14 Feb 1842, 13 May 1844, 12 Aug 1844, 12 May 1845
Heirs	Henry BELDON, Elizabeth BENNET SMALLWOOD, Samuel, Elizabeth, & Sarah Jane SMALLWOOD
Administrator	Henry BELDEN
Action	Samuel SMALLWOOD died intestate. His widow, Elizabeth BENNETT SMALLWOOD renounced her right as administrator. BELDEN appointed. BELDON files petition for the sale of personal estate of the deceased.
	Inventory of personal estate filed (description within). Administrator files petition for sale of real estate of deceased. Administrator informs the court that the personal estate of deceased is wholly insufficient to pay the debts to

the estate. The estate amounted to only $61.99. An inventory and appraisal given, which lies in township 35, and contains 35-40 acres (description within) and it is appraised at $50. Administrator presents court with his 'memorial", and declares the personal estate of the deceased amounted to only $61.99 and the real estate appraised at $50 and that the debts to the estate might amount to $400. $286.87 of this amount is in a mortgage held by the owner and which was taken to court for judgment and monies were owed for court costs in the court settlement in the amount of $75. There are also other smaller debts, amounting to $100-$200. Administrator requests the court declare the estate insolvent. Court orders publication of insolvency in the Whig newspaper.

Creditors served summons by the sheriff to appear in court and heirs served summons as well in Marshall County, In. Heirs fail to appear and are declared in default. Court orders sale of real estate of deceased at public auction and 20-day notice to be given of the sale.

Sale held on 11 Feb 1843 but no bids were made on the real estate and further time is granted to sell the real estate.

Administrator appears in court to report the real estate was sold for $12 on 20 April 1844. Court sets aside this sake as purchase price was much less than the appraised value. Real estate is reappraised at $10.80 and administrator again ordered to proceed with the sale of the real estate.

Sale is made of the land in the amount of $12.50 on 8 June 1844. The widow is assigned her Dower portion by the court, files his final report on the estate (description within) and is discharged of his duties by the court.

| Incidental Names | Thomas NORRIS, witness; Aquilla W. REGERSFREE; Ezekiel MORRISON, William C. HANNAH, lien holders; Samuel STEWART, Azariah WILLIAMS, appraisers; Frederick BARLEY, & Owen A. OWENS lien holders; Ezekiel MORRISON, mortgage holder; E.B. WOODSON, Esq, owed court costs in settlement; Theodore CATLIN, bond; John B. NILES guardian ad litem; Jacob P. ANDREWS, bought real estate |

Sanford UTLEY, deceased   **Estate**

Book & Page	CPR: 317-330
Court Dates	12 Sept 1838, 3 Dec 1838, 11 Feb 1839, 11 Nov 1839, 10 Feb 1840, 11 May 1840, 10 Aug 1840, 14 Aug 1840, 9 Nov 1840, 4 Feb 1842, 9 May 1842, 8 Aug 1842, 3 Nov 1843, 12 May 1845
Administrators	Jacob MILLER, Nathan PORTER
Heirs	Catherine UTLEY, James & Peter UTLEY, Almira MILLARD, formerly UTLEY, intermarried with Eleazer MILLARD, Julia Ann, intermarried with Isaac SCUDDER, Uriah & George UTLEY (Peter UTLEY resides in New York, Julia Ann & Almira and husbands live in Michigan and note made that George UTLEY also lives "out of state")

Action	Last will and testament of Sanford UTLEY filed in court on 14 Nov 1830, in these words: "Know all men by the presents (sic) that I Sanford UTLEY of Pleasant Township LaPorte County and State of Indiana being in a sound state of mind and in possession of all my mental faculties do make this my last will and final deposition of all my property in the following manner to wit First. I give and bequeath free from all encumbrances to my lawful wife Catherine UTLEY, the north half of the Northeast quarter of Section Eight in township six West in LaPorte County the same I now live on. Also the South half of the East half of the North East quarter of Section Twenty One in same town and range. And after paying all debts due by my estate the residue to be equally divided among all my legal heirs. N.B. I further reserve and bequeath to my wife the following property to Wit a Bill of Lumber due to me from Davis on a contract made by son Uriah. And also one brown cow and calf and one small pig. I hereby constitute and appoint Jacob MILLER and Nathan PORTER my administrators. Signed Sanford UTLEY. Signed and sealed in the presence of William BODWORTHA(?) Aliza HUBBARD and duly proved by Alonzo HUBBARD and William BODWORTHA(?) the subscribing witness thereto. Dated 19 Sept 1838.

The will was kept in the home of BODWORTHA(?) for safekeeping but his home was totally destroyed by fire.

Administrator presents a property appraisal of estate to court. Appraisal prepared on 16 Nov 1838 (description within).

Administrator files the sale bill of UTLEY'S personal estate in court on 11 Feb 1839 (description within).

Administrator reads UTLEY'S will to court. UTLEY died on 22 Sept 1838 which stated certain lands to his wife Catherine.(description within). He stated the deceased also held 2 town lots in Plainfield Indiana in St. Joseph County and that the personal property of deceased amounted to $156.93 and ¼ of the personal property was sold. There is no other income from the estate except for $2.75 which was from property not appraised. He adds there is $20 in debts owed to estate, but the estate has debt of $726.74, thus, there are insufficient funds to pay the debts of the estate. An appraisal of one of the various tracts of land mentioned in the above (description within). He requests the heirs be summoned to appear in court so that the appraised portion of the land may be sold. Publication appears in the Whig newspaper and summons issued for the heirs to appear.

Sale held on 18 Jan 1840. Land sold for $3.90 per acre, but as the administrator failed to obtain security on the land for sale, the purchase at that price per acre is canceled.

Administrator appears in court to say he has sold the land previously advertised at $3.90 per acre for $5.88 per acre on 25 April 1840. Purchase price was $429.26. The proceeds of the sale are still insufficient to pay the estate debts and the amount of $50 is still needed to discharge the remaining debt. He further states a Widows' Dower is needed for the widow. He requests the sale of the lots in Plainfield, as well as additional land in

LaPorte County in twp 36 (description within). The land is appraised at $10. Heirs again summoned to appear in court.

The Plainfield lots (description within) are approved for sale by the court. Heirs again fail to appear. Administrator reports the remaining land in LaPorte County was sold for $11.20. Debts still remain from the estate of $120-150, but there is one more portion of land remaining from the estate to be sold in twp 36 (description within). Part of this remaining land left to the widow in the will of the deceased (description within). Both portions of land were appraised, one at $576, the other at $15. Heirs again do not appear in court. One section of land sold for $20, the other for $130 (descriptions within).

Attorney for administrator appears in court to present a final accounting of the estate (description within). The debts and credits to the estate amount equally to $860.12.

Administrator discharged by the court.

Incidental Names	P.J. CRANDAL, Daniel STEWART, appraisers; Samuel STEWART, clerk of sale; Curtis TRAVIS, Samuel STEWART, appraisers; Samuel TREAT, property buyer; Samuel STEWART, John GARRARD, appraisers; John H. BRADLEY, attorney; John MILLS, Joseph W. LYKINS, appraisers; William D. JONES, Plainfield property buyer; Uriah UTLEY, property buyer; James D. BEAR, Zeba BAILEY, appraiser; Jacob KERBY(?) land purchaser; Zeba BAILEY, land purchaser
Comments	No mention is made as to why Nathan PORTER, whose name appeared in UTLEY'S will as co- administrator had no further part in the court proceedings.

Aletha GRIFFIN widow of
Daniel GRIFFIN, deceased
vs   **Petition To Assign Dower**
The Heir of **Daniel GRIFFIN**,

Book & Page	CPR: 331-332
Court Dates	10 Feb 1845 13 May 1845
Heirs	Angeline, intermarried with Henry MONROE, Sarah Ann, intermarried with Bartlett WOODS, Homer GRIFFIN, Wellington, Augustus, Edgar, and Anson GRIFFIN
Action	Petitioner's attorney files his petition in behalf of widow.

Deceased, Daniel GRIFFIN, owned real estate (description within) containing 80 acres in Township 38, as well as a portion of land in section 34 (description within) which also contains 80 acres and a mill. Daniel GRIFFIN died in August of 1841. Court appoints guardian for minor heirs who have no objection to the allotment of the Widow's Dower. Court appoints commissioners to survey the properties.

Widow, Aletha GRIFFIN, allotted her portion of land (description within) by the court. Court costs paid by petitioner. The two commissioners are paid $3 each for two days services and two of them receive $1.50 each for 1 day of service.

Incidental Names   Myron H. ORTON, attorney; Samuel E. WILLIAMS, Guardian; George FOSDICK, Lemuel FITCH, James BARNARD, commissioners

John GOSSETT, deceased   **Estate**

Book & Page   CPR: 333-338

Court Dates   1 Nov 1838, 12 Nov 1838, 30 Nov 1838, 11 Nov 1839, 10 May 1841, 8 Nov 1841, 12 May 1845, 11 Aug 1845

Administrators   Mary & Joseph GOSSETT

Action   Letters of administration filed on estate of John GOSSETT of Pleasant Township, who died intestate, were granted. Inventory and appraisal of personal estate was done on Nov 1838 and presented to the court (description within). This was filed on 30 Nov 1838. Additional inventory and appraisal presented to the court (description within). A sale bill is also presented. Sale held on 27 Nov 1838 (description within).

Lawyer for a plaintiff who sued the estate: Gideon HANDLEY vs Mary GOSSETT presents the plaintiff's case to the court. Court finds for the plaintiff with damages of $21. A citation had been issued against Mary GOSSETT, nee ROUSE. An agreement between the parties was reached however.

Mary GOSSETT SHERMAN claims expenses from the estate totaled $979.87 and credits to the estate amounted to the same (description within). Administrators discharged from their duties.

Incidental Names   James WEBSTER, bond; S. McCOLLUM, George DAWSON, appraisers; John NILES, J.P.; Joel BUTLER, J.P.; George S. McCOLLOM, clerk; John J. CRANDALL, agent for the plaintiff; John BRADLEY, counsel for estate

Comments   Mary GOSSETT evidently married twice between 1838 & 1845 (Mary GOSSETT ROUSE SHERMAN). Sale description contains 89 entries and items purchased with names of buyers.

The Heirs of **Silas HALE**,   **Petition for assignment of Dower**

Book & Page: CPR: 338-340

Court Dates   11 Nov 1844, 10 Feb 1845, 12 May 1845

Heirs   Sarah HALE WOOD & Silas WOOD, her husband, Rock Co. WI, John D. HALE, Champlain Co OH, Almira HALE JOHNSON & Isaac JOHNSON, her husband, Rock Co, WI, Mariah HALE STREEKS & husband William STREEKS, LaPorte Co IN, Hester HALE CLOSSER & husband Clark

CLOSSER, Rock Co WI, & William B. HALE, LaPorte IN, Silas F. HALE, Porter Co IN, & Hester Ann HALE, LaPorte, IN

Action	Attorney for widow, Eva HALE petitions court on her behalf for her portion of her Dower. Silas HALE died 3 Aug 1844 and owned land in Township 36 containing 60 acres (description within). and also 40 acres in township 37, and one lot #50 in town of LaPorte (descriptions within). Court orders notification of heirs as to sale of property to be published in newspaper.
	Heirs do not appear in court and make default. Guardian for minor heir, Hester Ann HALE appointed, and she appears in court. Court appoints commissioners to survey properties of the estate. Survey taken on 1 July 1845.
	Widow is allotted her portion of her Dower containing 47 acres (description within).
Incidental Names	John B. NILES, attorney for widow; Andrew L. OSBORN, Guardian; John WILSON, Josiah W. WING, Elam CLARK commissioners; Abraham FRAVEL, Esq, J.P.

Lee H. T. MAXSON, Deceased   **Estate**

Book & Page	CPR: 341-351
Court Dates	11 Feb 1839, 6 March 1839, 14 Feb 1842, 4 May 1842, 9 May 1842, 8 Aug 1842
Administrator	Oscar H. BARKER & Paul MAXSON (later removed)
Heirs	Martha MAXSON, mother, Martha M. MAXSON FISK, & Lemuel FISK, her husband (All reside in Illinois)
Action	Lee H.T. MAXSON of Michigan City IN died intestate on 3 Dec 1838. Attorney states the assignment of Paul MAXSON should be made void as he is not a resident of the state of Indiana. BARKER is appointed Administrator by the clerk of the court "In Vacation" on 16 March 1839.
	Inventory of personal estate filed (description within).
	On 7 Aug 1839 an additional inventory was filed in court (description within). On 15 Sept 1839, Sale bill of estate filed (description within).
	Administrator states that two suits were filed against the estate: They were both from Cook Circuit Court in Illinois. Illinois vs William Montgomery. This suit found in favor of "said MAXON during of his life time and his request" $30 in costs paid in the suit. Administrator states he will pay this as soon as he has the funds. The deceased retained the firm of Butterfield and Collins to prosecute the two suits against a William MONTGOMERY on a promissory note which deceased held as endorsee. One suit was adjudged for damages of $10.50. The second suit was on a note due subsequent to the commencement of the second suit. Judgment awarded of $62.30 in damages. Butterfield and Collins claim nothing has been collected on these suits. They state they have paid the costs on the suits in the sum of $300 and

can produce a court clerk's receipt to prove this. They claim that the estate owes attorney's fees for both suits of $30. Court orders the administrator to pay these costs to the plaintiff out of the Maxson estate proceeds.

Administrator appears in court to state that the estate has insufficient funds for payment of estate debts. He further states that the deceased owned property worth $2,016.15 but also owed notes to certain individuals at the time of his death.

Administrator then appears in court and states the income from the estate amounts to $1,592.52 and debts are $1,606.21 and he has paid out $13.69 more than he has taken in. He requests the court order a sale of some of deceased's real estate to allow payment of outstanding debts to note holders, etc. The administrator states there are further properties owned by deceased which includes town lots and additional land (description within). These properties were appraised at a value of $2,016.30. Court orders notice to be given in Michigan City Gazette so the heirs will be aware of this proposal.

Heirs appear with their attorney in court. No objection made to the sale of the properties. Court orders publication of sale to be made in Michigan City Gazette newspaper. Heirs then appear in court and object to the sale of properties for payment of the debts. Court orders the sale to proceed (description of lots within). Sale held on 13 June 1842 (description of portions of lots & sale prices within). The total amount for the sale of the lots and properties came to $1,242.33.

Administrator appears in court and files his account of debits and credits of the estate (description within). Credits amounted to $3,08.07 and money paid out came to $3015.18. Heir Martha MAXON, the sole heir to the estate and the only remaining creditor of the estate is said to be "desirous" that all the creditors of the estate should be fully paid and waives all claims of her rights to her proportion of the divided land of the estate until all other claims are fully paid. Administrator discharged of his duties by the court.

Incidental Names

Samuel D. VIELE, Joseph W. CHAPMAN, security; Chancey B. BLAIR, & George AMES, appraisers; William W. HIGGINS, J.P; Willys PECK 2nd appraisal: Jacob BIGELOW, J.P.; G.H. EVERTS, attorney for Administrator; T. A. HOWE, J.P.; Alexander H. WRIGHT, note (dec'd;); William TEALL,; H.W. ENOS, note; F. TUTTLE, note; Andrew D. OSBORN, attorney; Jeremiah HITCHCOCK, security; Willis P. WARD, William W. LOW, Patrick GRIFFIN, Jacob MITZKER, lot buyers; Francis THOMPSON, note

Comments

Lots sold are in the Elston Survey, Michigan City, and also Township 37 & 38, Michigan City.

While Martha MAXSON is stated as the sole remaining heir, at the ending of this suit other heirs were mentioned in the beginning of the suit: Martha M. FISH, wife of Lemuel FISH, and mother of deceased, residents of Illinois.

Attorney OSBORN was the attorney in a suit "MAXSON vs James COWDER" in Porter County, as well as a suit "EVERTS & OSBORN vs John WILLS and others" in LaPorte Circuit Court.

Ephraim DUKES — Estate

Book & Page	CPR: 351-355
Court Dates	12 April 1838, 17 Nov 1840, 8 Nov 1841, 10 Aug 1842, 13 May 1844, 10 Nov 1845
Administrator	Samuel WARNOCK

Letters of Administration granted "in vacation" to WARNOCK. Administrator filed inventory and appraisal for the personal property of deceased on 14 April, 1838. Appraisal made (description within). A list of personal property taken by the widow is also given. Witnessed and signed by the court clerk on 17 April, 1838. Court confirms appointment of Administrator. The sale bill of personal property of estate given to the court (description within). Court orders administrator present final settlement of estate at next court session.

Administrator appears in court and presents final settlement (description within). Administrator not prepared to make a complete and final settlement of estate and the cause is continued.

Administrator appears in court and pays into court the sum of $142 for the heirs of the estate.

Final settlement and account of affairs are presented to the court. Items which he has charged himself are $1.794.46 (description within). Court then discharges the administrator.

Incidental Names	Lemuel ROBINSON, bond; Stephen JONES & Isaac HUPP, appraisers; Charles W. CATHCART, clerk of sale
Comments	A notation was made after this entry: "On the ____ of July 1848, a record was filed in court from Putnam County, Greencastle, Indiana, 4 July 1848 for receipt of $40.30 of each of our distributive (sic) of estate of Ephraim DUKES."

It further stated that this released the estate of all liability. Signed by Ephraim D. ESLINGER, Antonie ESLINGER of Putnam County. P. DAGGY, witness.

Benjamin UNDERWOOD — Estate

Book & Page	CPR: 356-360
Court Dates	17 Dec 1838, 10 June 1839, 11 Feb 1839, 13 March 1839, 8 Feb 1841, 10 Nov 1845
Administrator	Isaac CORLISS

Heirs	Maryann UNDERWOOD, widow
Action	Widow renounces her right to be appointed administrator and CORLISS, the widow's friend, appointed I her place. Benjamin UNDERWOOD, of LaPorte County died intestate.
	Administrator files an inventory and appraisal of the personal property of the deceased. (Description within). The total was $1,559.86. Sale bill filed in court. Sale held on 12 Jan, 1839 (description within).
	Administrator presents his final account of the estate to the court (description within). Administrator also presents account of notes outstanding against the estate which are then given to the widow's attorney, totaling $1,133.55 (description with note holder's names within).
	Court presented the final settlement of the estate and proceeds will be dispensed to the heirs by the widow's attorney.
Incidental Names	Noah NEWELL, witness, & bond;& attorney for widow; Joseph DAVIS, Henry HARDING, appraisers; William N. SYKES, witness for sale bill
Comment	Although mention made that proceeds would be distributed to the "heirs" of the estate, the widow was the only heir recorded.

Caleb GERRY, deceased	**Estate**
Book & Page	CPR: 360-362
Court Dates	22 Oct 1845, 24 Oct 1845, 10 Nov 1845, 12 Nov 1845
Administrator	Cynthia A. GERRY, widow
Action	Letters of Administration filed by widow with the court. Caleb GERRY died intestate in LaPorte County on 6 Oct, 1845. Widow, Cynthia GERRY reports deceased owned property worth $150 "or whereabouts".
	Court presented an inventory of the personal estate of deceased which was made on 23 Oct 1845, and amounted to $114.09 (description within). Administrator GERRY reports deceased also rented a home in LaPorte for 6 months, beginning 1 Oct 1845 but had not yet taken possession of it. The deceased was to pay $25 down, but had only paid $11 in advance. The landlord of the home is supposed to be not 'liable to return the advance." Administrator asks for instructions of the Probate court in regard to this. She also claims her $100 allotment from the estate.
	Administrator appears in court to present her final account of the estate of the deceased. Her legal portion of the estate amounts to $114.07. Court discharges her from her duties.
Incidental Names	Daniel NORTON, Burwell SPURLOCK, bond; Daniel BROWN neighbor; James BOWERS landlord

Dudley MILLER, Deceased   **Estate**

Book & Page	CPR: 363-368
Court Dates	11 March 1844, 20 April 1844, 13 May 1844, 11 Nov 1844, 10 Nov 1845
Administrator	Alonzo CLOUGH
Acton	CLOUGH filed Letters of Administration in court for the estate of MILLER, of LaPorte County who died intestate.
	Inventory of personal property of estate filed in court (description within).
	Sale bill of personal property filed in court. Sale held as a public auction on 29 June 1844 (description within). Additional small inventory from sale also presented (description within). Court confirms the account of sale.
	Administrator files the final settlement of estate. He charges himself with $213.25, the amount of the sale bill. He then claims credit for the charges against the estate, amounting to $213.24 (description within). Administrator states he is left with a balance of $36 to be distributed to the heirs of the estate. (Heirs are not named.) Final settlement produced in court and he is discharged by the court.
Incidental Names	Charles PALMER, bond; Abel & Simon BURLINGAME, appraisers; W.D. PARKER, sales clerk.

James BLACK
       vs   **Petition for Partition of Real Estate**
Benjamin F. GRAHAM &
John NEWTON, estate of
Nathaniel BLACK

Book & Page	CPR: 368-370
Court Dates	3 Sept 1844, 1 Nov 1844, 11 Nov 1845
Heirs	Catherine BLACK, mother of deceased Nathaniel BLACK, William T. BLACK, Samuel F.BLACK, John BLACK, brothers of deceased Nathaniel BLACK, all of Augustin County, VA
Action	Attorneys of petitioner, James BLACK, file their petition stating petitioner's brother, Nathaniel BLACK, since deceased, was in possession of several tracts and parcels of land: #17 and #99, within the town of La Porte, as well as lots #5 and #6, also within La Porte. When the petitioner's brother Nathaniel BLACK died, the petitioner also owned lots #77 and #78 in Wilson's First Addition in La Porte. The petitioner then held title to the undivided half of these lots and at the death of his brother they were held in trust and for the benefit of his brother's heirs. Petitioner further states his brother died intestate in Oct of 1838, and on Jan of 1840, Catherine BLACK, mother of Nathaniel died intestate. Then on 31 March 1843, William F. and Samuel, the deceased's brothers conveyed to Benjamin F. GRAHAM of Augustin Co VA all their claim to the real estate.

The petition continues stating that on 20 April, 1843, the deceased's brother, John BLACK conveyed to one John NEWTON of Augustin Co VA., his title and interest in the real estate, thus, GRAHAM and NEWTON are now tenants in common of these parcels of land. The petitioner claims he is now entitled to 5/8, and 2/8 of the said Benjamin GRAHAM'S portion of the lots and that John NEWTON'S portion of the lots should give him his rightful 1/8 of the properties. If the portions of the lots cannot be divided as he claims, then they should be sold and the proceeds divided among the parties according to their respective rights and interests. He requests commissioners be appointed for division and sale of the lots.

Petitioner appears in court and proves to the satisfaction of the court that Benjamin F. GRAHAM and John NEWTON are now residents of this state and notices were given of filing to defendants in this action, but fail to appear. GRAHAM and NEWTON are in default and cause continued. Petitioner appears in court and the cause, having been settled by the parties involved, the cause is dismissed.

Incidental Names	Niles & Osborn, attorneys for petitioner
Comment	Notation made by clerk that the transactions of transfers of properties were recorded in Book "M" of the record of deeds of LaPorte County on pg 505 & 506.

David DINWIDDIE   Estate

Book & Page	CPR: 371-391
Court Dates	13 Oct 1838, 5 Nov 1838, 12 Nov 1838, 4 April 1839, 12 Aug 1839, 16 Aug 1839, 11 Nov 1839, 16 Nov 1839, 8 Feb 1841, 8 Nov 1841, 14 Feb 1842, 18 Feb 1842, 9 May 1842, 8 Aug 1842, 11Nov 1842, 18 Nov 1842, 13 Feb 1843, 9 Feb 1846
Administrators	Amzi CLARK, James C. NEWELL
Heirs	Martha L. WALKER, Elinor H. WALKER, non residents, Mary DINWIDDIE, widow, John, Margaret, Jane, David Jr., Francis, & Henrietta DINWIDDIE
Action	Letters of Administration granted "in vacation" by clerk of court for David DINWIDDIE who died intestate. Inventory and appraisal of personal property of deceased filed in court (description within). Sale bill of personal property of the estate filed in court (description within). Administrators file their petition for the settlement of the estate as insolvent. They state that the amount due the estate, including what the widow selected to remove from the estate and the appraised value of real estate, excluding the widow's Dower meant debts were stilled owed to the estate and there was a negative balance remaining of $553.00. Court approves a delay to allow creditors to come forward and orders publication of notice be advertised in the Whig newspaper of LaPorte County for a period of 6 weeks.

Administrators petition court for sale of real estate of the deceased appraised at $7,507. An inventory of the property is listed. Those in |

township 36 contains 80 acres and valued at $30 per acre; 30 acres held in title bond and valued at $30 per acre; 79 acres held I title bond valued at $20 per acre. In township 37 there are 48 acres valued at $20 per acre; 1/3 of a lot, #236 in town of LaPorte in Old Town Plat, no value given (detailed description within).

Notice of sale ordered given to heirs of estate in order to appear in court and show cause why real estate should not be sold.

Bond filed in court for sale of real estate. No exception has been made to the sale by the heirs. Court orders properties sold at public auction. A Dower is approved for the, widow and publication of notice of sale ordered.

Sale held on 30 March 1840 and all properties sold to the satisfaction of the court (description of properties within). An attorney is appointed as commissioner to oversee the payment of the properties sold. Court also orders the attorney handle transfer of title bonds from Michigan road certificates to purchaser.

Administrators inform court the parcels of real estate they bid on and purchased must now be set aside as it would be seen as improper by the heirs. They request the court that they be designated as "trustees" of the parcels of land, and the land be offered at public auction so as to present no conflict for the heirs of the estate if these parcels were purchased by others. Court orders their purchase of the tracts of land be annulled and to advertise the same at public auction.

Public sale held on 27 Dec 1841. There were no bids on the tracts of land formerly purchased by the Administrators (description within). Court orders further sale of property at public auction after notification is again given to heirs. Heirs appear in court.

Attorney for Administrators awarded $10, & $5 for conveyance of the two deed to the Administrators.

Court order the Administrators to appear at next session to present a final settlement of the estate.

Administrators file an additional inventory of real estate (description within). Appraisers, free holders of Porter County, value these additional tracts of land at $58.14.

Summons delivered to out of state heirs. Court appoints. Guardian for minor heirs. Guardian tells court the minor heirs have no objection to the sale of the real estate. The adult heirs do not appear in court. The proceeds from the sale of the personal estate are insufficient to meet debts owed the estate, court orders further land to be sold at a private sale (description within). Court informed the land was sold for $58.24, which was the appraised value (description within). Administrators present their final settlement of the estate to the court (description within).

Proceeds of sales amounted to $7,042.95. Debts paid to the estate amounted to $2,296.48. Administrators produce $1,513.53, plus $400 owed for their own "time and responsibility". Court approves their account of the to be distributed to the heirs. (description within). Claims against the estate are weighed and measured by the court as a dividend rate of 40 cents and 8 mills on each 100 cents of each claim. Court further orders the sum of $2,487.39 be distributed to the creditors of the estate.

Administrators appear and state all debts to the estate have been paid except (description within). Court orders clerk to hold the remaining funds for disbursement until all the creditors have been paid. Administrator discharged by the court. Court gives a final discharge to one of the Administrators when he produces his vouchers for payment by him of the dividends on the estate due to the heirs and two creditors.

Incidental Names	Abner BAILEY, Griffin TREADWAY, bond; Andrew BURNSIDE, Samuel POTTINGER, appraisers; Michael DECKER, sale clerk; James ANDREWS, Charles HULL, Adam G. POLK, Title Bond holders; William POLK, Road commissioner Title holder; Alexander BLACKBURN, Ezekiel MORRISON, bond; Amzi CLARK, James C. HOWELL, Samuel TREAT, Alexander BLACKBURN, Abner BAILY, land purchasers; I.R. WELLS, witness; Thomas A. STEWART, witness; Seneca BALL, N. NEVILLE, Valparaiso appraisers; William ALLEN, sheriff; John B. NILES, Guardian
Comment	Administrators, CLARK & HOWELL request the court approve the private sale "due to the peculiar state of the money market"

John MIX, deceased	**Estate**
Book & Page	CPR: 391-396
Court Dates	24 July 1844, 14 Aug 1844, 4 Oct 1844, 10 Nov 1845, 9 Feb 1846
Administrator	Rensselaer SHAW
Heirs	Charlotte MIX, widow
Action	Letters of Administration filed "in vacation" with clerk of the court. Deceased died on 13 June 1844 and left no will.
	His personal estate does not exceed the sum of $250 in value. His widow requested SHAW be appointed administrator.
	Inventory of personal property filed (description within). Sale bill of personal property presented to court (description within). Administrator appears in court to present his account of final settlement of the estate. Sale bill amounted to $106.74. He also presents his account of money paid out of the estate amounting to $107.20. Court accepts his account of the final settlement of the estate. Court discharges the Administrator.
Incidental Names	Handy DAVIS, Charles FINN, appraisers; John P. MABEE J.P.; D. SHAW, J.P.; Edward AVERY, clerk of sale,

George DAWSON	**Estate**
Book & Page	CPR: 396-398

Court Dates	28 May 1840, 10 Aug 1840, 9 May 1842, 8 Aug 1842, 10 Nov 1845, 9 Feb 1846
Executrix	Mary DAWSON, wife & Matthias DAWSON, son
Heirs	Matthew, Nancy, Elizabeth, Rachel, & Pamela DAWSON
Action	Last Will and Testament of George DAWSON filed in court, "in vacation". (To Whit): " I, George DAWSON, of the County of LaPorte and State of Indiana being weak in body but of sound mind, knowing it is appointed once for men to die, do make and ordain this my last will and testament. Then principally and first of all, I would commit my soul unto the hand of God who gave it and my body to be decently buried at the discretion of my executors. And as touching such earthly Estate where with it has pleased God to keep me in this life after my just debts are all paid it is my will it be managed and divided in the following manner. Viz.

I give to my beloved wife Mary, complete control and management of all my property both real and personal to enable her to Educate and support my children as well as to use it for her own comfort with full power to sell or otherwise dispose of any of it to enable her with my other executors herein after named to pay of my just debts, clothing my said executors with her as executrix to sell a part of the outlands of necessary with ample powers to Execute good and sufficient Titles. Therefore as myself could do were I yet living and it is moreover my will that my Executrix shall at any time she may deem it necessary to give any and all my children their several shares in any (?) of it (?) always with the advice and consent of my other children, namely, Matthew, Nancy, Elizabeth, Rachel, Pamela(?) receive equal shares of my estate after my widow is amply provided for. And lastly I constitute and appoint my wife Mary Executrix and Matthias DAWSON son, and John WHITEHEAD, Executors of this my last will and Testament. Witness my hand and seal this 29th day of April, 1840." Signature, signed sealed & delivered in presence of Jesse COLEMAN, Wm A. MARTEN, Charles CARMICHAEL, which said Will was duly proved by Jesse COLEMAN and William A. MARTIN, two of the subscribed witnesses thereto."

Court confirms filing of the will and orders appearance of the Executrix. Executors at next term to make final settlement of the estate. Cause continued. Court orders Executrix and Executors to then appear in court and file an inventory of the estate also to file an exhibit of their proceedings.

Matthew and Mary DAWSON the surviving executors appear in court and present their final report.

Widow and Executrix, Mary DAWSON receives all the personal and real estate of the deceased except for one horse which was sold for $50. Claims to the estate followed (description within). Court discharges Executors.

Incidental Names	George HUNT, Joseph DAWSON, bond
Comment	Unknown why the record states that Matthew and Mary DAWSON are the "surviving executors"; there is no further mention of John WHITEHEAD, also appointed administrator, in the court record.

Emerson FARMER	**Estate**

Book & Page   CPR: 399-404

Court Dates   6 Nov 1837, 14 Nov 1837, 12 Nov 1838, 26 Jan 1839, 11 Aug 1840, 14 Feb 1842, 18 Feb 1842, 8 Aug 1842, 11 Nov 1845, 9 Feb 1846

Executor   Nancy Ann FARMER, widow, George LEWIN/ LARWIN

Action   Letters of Administration granted "in vacation" to Nancy Farmer. Court orders appearance of Administrator and to produce a sale bill, inventory and appraisal of estate or to show cause why the same has not been done.

Administrator appears in court and produces a sale bill, inventory and appraisal of estate (description of inventory within). A representative appears on behalf of the heirs of the estate to state that Nancy A. BAILEY, late Nancy Ann FARMER, has failed to make final settlement of the estate and recently remarried William BAILEY and moved from the county. He asks that her appointment as Administrator be revoked, and that George LEWIN/LARWIN of LaPorte County be appointed in her place. Court agrees after hearing testimony bearing on this request.

Newly appointed Administrator presents an inventory and appraisal of the personal property of the estate. (description within). Administrator requests the court approve his selling at a private sale the personal property of the estate. Court approves his request.

Administrator appears in court and files his account of the settlement of the estate. Items from person property sold, with the exception of the blacksmith tools which were left Henry FARMER and a receipt given. Henry FARMER has since moved to Chicago, address unknown, and has the tolls in his possession. Judgment brought against him over this matter. Administrator was told by Chicago authorities that this judgment could be collected. Final settlement made amounting to $34.80 (description within).

Administrator discharged by the court.

Incidental Names   Henry DAVIS, bond; Joseph CATLIN, Henry VAIL, Charles W. HENRY, appraisers; Aquilla W. ROGERS, J.P.; William; Richard B. HEWS, bond; Handy DAVIS, J.P.

Hezekiah SMITH	**Estate**

Book & Page   CPR: 405-406

Court Dates   12 Nov 1838, 12 Aug 1839, 10 Feb 1840, 8 Nov 1841, 14 Nov 1842, 4 Nov 1845, 9 Feb 1846

Administrator   Obadiah SMITH

Action   On 15 Oct, 1838, Letters of Administration were grated "in vacation" to SMITH in regard to the estate of Hezekiah SMITH of LaPorte County who died intestate. Court approves the appointment.

Court orders appearance of Administrator on five separate occasions for settlement of the estate; inventory of estate; final settlement of the estate. Obadiah SMITH finally appears in court and explains that the sole reason he requested Letters of Administration was because there was due to him a small amount of a pension from the U.S. government and he supposed could only be collected by him. This was the only estate left by the deceased. He had since found out the pension could not be collected by him, as the Administrator, but was payable only to the heirs of the estate. He further stated that since then, a greater part of this pension has been paid to the heirs of the estate.

He requests the court discharge him as Administrator as there are no other properties or personal effects left by the deceased and no debts have come due as well. Court orders Administrator pay court costs of all citations issued by the court in this matter and for failing to appear in court or file a separate report on the condition of the estate. He is ordered to pay these costs within 60 days or be in default and an attachment would be issued against him.

Jabez LEWIS	**Estate**
Book & Page	CPR: 407-409
Court Dates	17 Oct 1839, 11 Nov 1839, 8 Nov 1841, 14 Feb 1842, 13 Nov 1843, 12 Feb 1844, 10 Nov 1845, 9 Feb 1846
Administrator	Joseph B. LEWIS, George S. McCOLLUM
Action	Letters of Administration granted "in vacation" to LEWIS and McCOLLUM 18 Sept 1839 for the estate of Jabez LEWIS of LaPorte County who died intestate.
	Inventory and appraisal of personal property filed in court (description within). Granting of Letters of Administration approved by the court. Administrators unprepared to presented final settlement to the court. Cause continued. Cause continued twice more.
	Administrators appear with their exhibit of the final settlement of the estate (description of items within). They also present the items credited to them in the amount of $646.43. Court approves the settlement and discharges the Administrators.
Incidental Names	B. CAPLIN bond; Joel BUTLER, J.P.; James HIGHLEY, appraiser
Comment	No account is given of the date of the sale; total of sale bill; but in the final settlement under: "Cash Paid" an entry states that $492 was paid to Ferdinand DUNHAM, husband of Angelina DUNHAM, late Angelina LEWIS

John W. CLARK	**Estate**
Book & Page	CPR: 410-416

Court Dates	10 May 1841, 22 May 1841, 24 July 1841, 14 Nov 1842, 13 Feb 1843, 12 Feb 1844, 13 May 1844, 12 May 1845, 11 Aug 1845
Administrator	Elizabeth CLARK
Heirs	Jesse CLARK, age 22, John CLARK, age 20, Mary MALOSH CLARK, age 15 ½, husband James MALOSH, William CLARK, age 13, James CLARK age 6, widow, Elizabeth CLARK age 45
Action	On 1 May, 1841, Letters of Administration granted to Elizabeth CLARK. Court confirms the filing.

Inventory and appraisal of estate filed (description within). Sale Bill filed. Sale held at the home of Elizabeth CLARK in New Durham township on 12 June 1841. Sale Bill totaled $144.55 (description within). Court orders final settlement to be made.

Administrator not yet prepared to present final settlement. Cause continued. Administrator files petition for sale of real estate. Administrator presents debts paid out of estate (description within) totaling $173.60. Debts still outstanding are listed (description within). Theses outstanding debts and notes total $322.93. Deceased had filed a bill in Chancery Court before his death against Ephraim DUKES and heirs. This was over a parcel of land in township 36, containing 80 acres, worth $500 (description within). Once the bill was settled in Chancery, the Court ordered a deed be made by the heirs of Ephraim DUKES to the heirs of the deceased.

Administrator requests court order heirs to appear to determine why this property should not be sold. Court orders heirs summoned to court.

Administrator presents an inventory and appraisal of the real estate to be sold (description within). Value determined to be $500. Heir Jess CLARK appears in court and gives consent to sale of real estate. Remaining heirs do not appear and therefore, make default. Guardian of minor heirs is appointed. Court approves sale of real estate and notice of public sale ordered. Court orders Sale held at home of Elizabeth CLARK on 10 Sept 1842 and the real estate should not be sold for less than 2/3 of appraised value.

Administrator appears in court to make report that she sold the real estate for in townships 35 and 36 for $335 (land description within). Administrator appears in court with a final settlement (description within). The total assets to estate amount to $479.55. Court discharges Administrator.

Incidental Names	David C. McKELLIPS, bond; Charles CATHCART, John W. WILKINSON, appraisers; John M. BARCLAY, Guardian; James LIVINGSTON, bought real estate

Phineas SMALL   **Guardianship**
Guardian of Mary PINNEY,
Daughter of Horace **PINNEY**, dec'd

Book & Page	CPR: 417-418

Court Dates	8 Feb 1841, 5 Nov 1845, 9 Nov 1846
Guardian	William ANDREW
Action	ANDREW files his petition for appointment of Guardian for the estate of Mary and Lois PINNEY. He states that Horace PINNEY of LaPorte County died leaving his daughters, Mary and Lois PINNEY as his minor heirs. Phineas SMALL appointed as Guardian by the court and ordered to appear at next court session to file an inventory of the estate of deceased.

Phineas SMALL appears in court and asks to be discharged as Guardian of heirs of the estate. He states he is the husband of Mary SMALL and has received from the estate the sum of $155.69 and that he received of the estate of Nancy PINNEY, wife of Horace PINNEY, after the death of the deceased, the further sum of $47.00, which totals $202.69. Mary PINNEY SMALL is no longer a minor and the Guardian asks he be discharged from that role.

Court agrees with his accounting of the estate and discharges the Guardian.

Incidental Names	Phineas SMALL, bond

Pikeland McCOLLUM   Estate

Book & Page	CPR: 418-421
Court Dates	16 Oct 1842, 10 Nov 1845, 9 Feb 1846
Administrators	William A. McCOLLUM, Ferdinand DUNHAM
Action	Letters of Administration filed in court on 5 Oct, 1842, "in Vacation." Pikeland McCOLLUM, single, resident of LaPorte County, died intestate on or about 5 Sept, 1842, and it was stated that the personal estate of the deceased would not exceed $300 in value and the deceased had no living parents.

Administrators file an inventory and appraisal of the personal estate of deceased on 14 Oct 1842 (description within). Court approves their appointment as administrators.

Court orders administrators to file their sale bill of personal property of deceased and make final settlement.

On 9 Feb, 1846, administrators file the sale bill of the estate (description within). Administrators appear in court and present their exhibit of the final settlement (description within). They show the court that they are the "heirs at law" of the estate and entitled to 1/3 of the estate. They further state they have paid James McCOLLUM his share in the amount of $69.42 after debts were paid. They present a list of credits paid out (description within) amounting to $149.52. Administrators also present a list of uncollected debts for the use of the heirs* of the estate totaling $31.74 (description within). They have also received funds of $80.12, and after paying various creditors the amount of $20.16 remains and will be given to the heirs.

Incidental Names	Benjamin CRUMPACKER, attorney
Comment	*The heirs' names are not listed.

Harvey COLLINS   Estate

Book & Page	CPR: 421-427
Court Dates	12 Nov 1838, 13 Nov 1838, 11 Nov 1839, 10 Feb 1840, 9 Nov 1840, 8 Feb 1841, 13 Nov 1843, 10 Nov 1834, 9 Feb 1846
Administrators	George C. HAVENS, Samuel STEWART
Heirs	Anna COLLINS, Harriet COLLINS, Charlotte COLLINS, Albert COLLINS
Action	Widow Paulina COLLINS relinquishes her right as Administrator of the estate of deceased and requests the court appoint HAVENS and STEWART in her place.

The deceased was from Pleasant Township and died intestate. Court grants Letters of Administration to HAVENS and STEWART.

Inventory of personal estate filed with the court, totaling $483.35. Administrators file the sale bill of personal estate with the court. Sale held on 8 Dec 1838 (description within).

Inventory of deceased's real estate filed showing 96 acres valued at $10 per acre and appraised on 16 Nov 1839 (description within). Administrators claim the personal property of deceased is insufficient to pay debts to the estate. They request that an "exhibit A" be considered as part of the bill showing liabilities of the estate (description within). Another exhibit, "B" shows the available funds to pay creditors that leaves a deficit of $200. They request the sale of the real estate of deceased (description within) and which the court had granted to Administrator George C. HAVENS. They also request the widow and heirs of the deceased be summoned to court to show cause why this real estate should not be sold.

William and Philamena BROWN, late Philomena COLLINS, appear in court with their attorney. The attorney states the widow of Harvey COLLINS has since remarried but requests her Dower from the court. Cause continued.

Heirs fail to appear. Court orders real estate sold at public auction and allowance for the widow's Dower. Court also orders publication of the sale of real estate to appear in the local newspaper.

Administrators file their report of the sale of real estate. The real estate was sold and court orders a deed made purchaser and the Administrators to appear at next session of court.

Administrators appear in court and present final settlement. Sale bill amounted to $664.46 (description within). Court approves their report and discharges the Administrators.

Incidental Names	Amzi CLARK, bond; William BULL, Daniel STEWART, appraisers; E. MAYHEW J.P.; Harvey NORRIS, Daniel STEWART, appraisers; William ANDREWS, attorney; William BROWN, land purchaser

William WALDRIFF
        vs   **Transfer of Property**
Joel BALDWIN, Reuben BALDWIN,
Rhoda BALDWIN & their children
and heirs of Daniel BALDWIN JR. &
heirs at law of **Daniel BALDWIN Sr,**
late of LaPorte County, deceased

Book & Page	CPR: 428-432
Court Dates	11 Nov 1839, 10 Aug 1840, 9 Nov 1840
Action	Attorney W. CLINE appears for the claimant, WALDRIFF, and states that in 1841, on or about the 25th, WALDRIFF purchased real estate from the deceased, Daniel BALDWIN Sr., in township 38 containing 80 acres and the attorney presents a document verifying this to the court, which is dated 25 August 1834 and witnessed by a justice of the peace. This land was purchased for $200 and this document was all that was available at the time. The signed and witnessed document was sent to the proper department of the U.S. Patents & Lands Office and was then sent to the LaPorte County Lands Office District. The deceased died within 2-3 weeks of this issuance. The attorney requests that the heirs of the deceased be made defendants in this matter. He also requests commissioners be appointed to made a deed to this property. Court orders that since the heirs are not residents of the state that they be notified of this matter and that notice also be published at least three months prior to the next court session in the May term.
	Heirs fail to appear in court. Court confirms the transfer of property to Daniel BALDWIN (description within). Court also orders a deed be made to William WALDRIFF and his heirs. Cause continued.
	Defendants in this case, the heirs, fail to appear in court. Court again confirms the decision made earlier and orders William WALDRIFF to pay court costs
Incidental Names	John H. BRADLEY, commissioner; George THOMAS, clerk, William ROSS, J.P.
Comment	Heirs are not named in this cause.

David ANDERSON
       vs   **Partition of Real Estate**
William K. ANDERSON,
Mary Ann ANDERSON,
Catherine ANDERSON,
Margaret L. ANDERSON,
Agnes & Jane I. ANDERSON, Children,
& Jane ANDERSON,
widow of **John ANDERSON**, deceased

Book & Page	CPR: 432-434
Court Dates	10 Aug 1840, 9 Nov 1840
Action	David ANDERSON, brother of deceased John ANDERSON files a petition claiming he was joint owner with the deceased of real estate (description within) in township 37, containing 80 acres, and township 38, containing 320 acres and a lot, north of the school section #16 in township 37 (description within) which was purchased by John BRADLEY, containing 10 acres. The total acreage for all properties is 534 acres. He further claims that on or about Sept of 1838, John ANDERSON died intestate and that the real estate in question was still held in equal undivided parts by him and the petitioner, and that the deceased left to the petitioner to be given to his widow and surviving heirs who continue to occupy and use this real estate. The petitioner requests partition of the real estate and advertisement of this to be published in the local Whig newspaper. He further requests the court appoint commissioners to make division and partition of the real estate. He also requests this division include his equal one half of these properties. Court agrees and appoints a Guardian for the heirs. Commissioners make their report to the court (description of properties divided within). Court approves the partition and assignment of the real estate.
Incidental Names	Benjamin BUTTERWORTH, E. NATHAN, Gregory Abel LOMAX, commissioners; William K. ANDERSON, Guardian

John A. CATTRON,
Ezekiah CATTRON,
Administrators of the estate of
Valentine CATTRON, Deceased
       vs   **Deed & Transfer of Land**
Robert MILFORD,
Thomas CATTTRON,
James B. CATTRON,
Daniel MAINES & Mary, his wife,
William CATTRON,
Samuel CATTRON,
& Wesley F. CATTRON

Book & Page	CPR: 434-438
Court Dates	15 June, 1842, 8 Aug 1842, 14 Nov 1842, 16 Nov 1842

Action	Claimants, through their attorney file a petition claiming the deceased owned real estate in Fountain County, Indiana (description within) in townships 21, & 22, which was subject to sale at Crawfordsville Indiana, which altogether contained 200 acres. This real estate was then sold to MILFORD of Fountain County and the petitioners request the court make MILFORD a defendant in this cause.

Promissory notes were made in lieu of payment for the real estate and were given to the deceased in the amount of $1,000 payable in Dec of 1840 or thereabouts. A deed was then to be given to the purchaser by the deceased, but the deceased died before this was accomplished and there was no will left by the deceased to the complainants who live in Illinois. The daughter of the deceased, Mary, then married Daniel MAINES, and she and her husband live in Lake County, Indiana. William, Samuel, and Wesley CATTRON, who are minors, live in LaPorte County. The petitioners also claim there is still an unpaid balance of $500 with interest remaining on the note for the land and that no deed has been made to the purchaser. Attorney requests commissioners be appointed to assess these tracts of land and that the heirs be summoned to court and an advertisement of this cause be made in the local Whig newspaper.

Court advised that summons were served on all parties in La Porte and Fountain Counties to appear in court for this cause. Cause continued.

Court appoints Guardian for minor heirs. The minor heirs have no objection to the petition. The remaining adult heirs do not appear in court and make default. Court appoints a commissioner to execute a deed to Robert MILFORD for the land described in the petition. A deed was executed and presented to the court awarding the several tracts of land in Fountain County to MILFORD (description within) containing 200 acres. Court approves the deed and the commissioner is to pay the court costs.

Incidental Names	John H. BRADLEY, attorney & commissioner; William ALLEN, sheriff; John BOWMAN, sheriff, Fountain Co.; R. T. FRAZIER, Sheriff; LaPorte County

John E. CARTER
vs   **Property Transfer**
Wm. DINGMAN &
Corintha DINGMAN, his wife;
Marian, John W. & Daniel W. HIBBARD,
heirs at law of **Horace B. HIBBARD**, deceased,
and Abram S. LOVERIN(?), husband of
the said Annis T. LOVERIN;
& Ezra TYLER, Administrator of
the estate of said **Horace HIBBARD**

Book & Page	438-451 *No pages numbered 440-449 in book
Court Dates	10 May 1841, 8 Nov 1841

Action	Attorney for complainants file a bill of complaint stating that Horace B. HIBBARD, in his lifetime, in 1837, sold property in township 37 for $316 (description within) and the deceased was paid $200 down on this property and HIBBARD executed a title bond binding (with penalties), binding himself to convey to the purchaser and his heirs the deed to this property after payment for it. The attorney further states that in Nov of 1835 the purchaser assigned the title bond to the complainant, CARTER, and that Ezra TYLER, the appointed administrator of the deceased's estate was fully paid the remaining money owed on the property - $316. Since then, the title bond to the property has either been lost or mislaid after being given to one Robert MERRYFIELD, esq., an attorney and that MERRYFIELD was to use this title bond in the case of this present complainant against one Charles COOPER in LaPorte Circuit Court. The attorney further states that the deceased HIBBARD died intestate leaving heirs and the complainant wishes them to be made defendants in this bill of complaint. The attorney requests a commissioner be appointed to convey to the complainant the legal title to the property. The married heir, Marian DINGMAN lives out of state and the court orders she be notified of this complaint by publication in the local Whig newspaper. Cause continued.
	Guardian for the minor heirs appear in court. Ezra TYLER, Administrator of HIBBARD'S estate also appears. TYLER states that the balance of the purchase price for the property has been paid. The adult heirs do not appear however, and make default. Court orders a title bond be made by the appointed commissioner.
	Commissioner reports a title deed has been made for the property in township 37 to the complainant and his heirs. Courts awards commissioner $3 for his service an orders that the court costs be paid out of the estate of Horace HIBBARD.
Incidental Names	W. H. ORTON, attorney; Charles COOPER, purchased property; John E. CARTER, commissioner; John B. NILES, Guardian

James EWING, deceased		**Estate**
Book & Page	CPR: 452-453	
Court Dates	11 Nov 1839, 11 May 1840, 13 May 1840	
Administrator	Loren DAVIS	
Action	Laura EWINGS, widow of James EWINGS, renounces her right as administrator in the clerk's office, Aug 29, 1839. Her husband died intestate on 21 Feb 1839. She requests her friend, Loren DAVIS be appointed in her place or any such person the court considers appropriate. Court appoints DAVIS "in vacation" as administrator.	
	On Oct 24, 1839, an entry in the clerk's office showed an appraisal of the estate was made, amounting to $69 (description within). The appraisal was made on Oct 20, 1839 by the administrator. On May 13 1840 a receipt in the	

amount of $69 was signed by the widow, Laura EWING PRATT who had since remarried.

The court approves the Letters of Administration and receipt that is on file and dismisses the administrator.

Incidental Names	Sheldon BOOTH, bond

Phillip KEWLY and Jeremiah KEWLY, sons of **John KEWLEY**, dec'd	**Guardianship**
Book & Page	CPR: 454-458
Court Dates	11 Nov 1839, 9 Aug 1841, 8 Nov 1841
Guardian	Adam G. POLKE
Action	Phillip and Jeremiah KEWLY appear in court with their brother, Thomas KEWLY and request the court appoint them a Guardian. They are the sons of John KEWLY, deceased. They choose POLKE as their Guardian. Court approves the choice.

Phillip and Jeremiah KEWLY appear in court again with their "next friend", Isabelle KEWLEY and state that POLKE, their appointed Guardian has not disposed of the property of the estate in such a way as to be advantageous and to their benefit and that he has made use of the property belonging to them for his own benefit. They ask the court to cite POLKE to appear in court and present an account of the money and property and effects of the estate. Court orders POLKE to appear in court to address these concerns.

The court clerk issues a citation for POLKE'S appearance for Sept 17, 1840. The sheriff reports to the court that he served a summons to POLKE on Sept 25, 1841.

POLKE appears in court and his attorney files a response to the complaint denying all charges and claims that POLKE has never misused any funds and that the only funds coming into POLKE'S hands was a promissory note for $249.94 dated May 15, 1839 with 10% interest which is yet due and unpaid. He further claims that the date the note was issued was the same date POLKE became Guardian and prior to that Thomas KEWLY, the brother, was the administrator and had used estate assets to issue a note for $392, or "thereabouts". Thomas KEWLY then presented a partial estate settlement to the court and was anxious to distribute among the heirs the portion which belonged to them and this was before they collected the note money from the borrower. The attorney also states the administrator had frequently requested POLKE to become Guardian for some of the heirs and POLKE had refused the request many times, then finally consented without any knowledge of the condition of the estate. The attorney requests another Guardian be appointed of the heirs to the estate. He also added that POLKE was told that the note holder would then give to him the note for the sum of $249.94. POLKE then gave the note holder a paid receipt and canceled the original note. He was not aware of a simultaneous action when the court signed the note to the holder. He was also executing a bond and the court ruled the note holder would be allowed time to pay off this note.

This note remains as yet unpaid and he repeats that no other assets have come into POLKE'S hands from the estate and the note holder is totally insolvent and unable to pay off the note. POLKE, his attorney states, is unable to obtain the security of the bond issued in this matter. He did manage to obtain a conveyance of 80 acres of land in Illinois from the note holder, however, to gain assurance of the bond posted by POLKE. Once the land is sold, he continued, the proceeds will be applied upon the note for the benefit of the heirs. POLKE'S attorney requests the court release POLKE as Guardian and that POLKE be allowed to execute a bond and security for trust of the land in Illinois. Cause continued.

Court appoints Isabella KEWLEY as Guardian of the minor heirs and that POLKE execute a quit claim deed for the Illinois land. Court orders that the note from BURNSDIE be delivered to the appointed Guardian and that she be released from liability in the bond as Guardian, dated 13 Nov 1839, and that the Guardian be given the note from BURNSIDE and POLKE also with a date of 15 Nov 1839. It is further ordered that the Guardian be given a receipt for these items.

William KEWLEY, heir, it now appears states he had not requested Isabelle KEWLEY as Guardian. Court orders the entry stricken regarding this Guardianship. Court also orders that Adam POLKE not be required to deliver the note and execute a deed for the land in Illinois until after heir William KEWLEY reaches 21 years of age, which will occur before the next court term. Court orders that at that time POLKE should be entitled to a receipt and a release from Isabelle KEWLEY as a Guardian of remaining heirs, Phillip and Jeremiah KEWLEY, and then William KEWLEY, and that the note and deed then be given to Isabelle KEWLEY with no liability remaining on POLKE'S part.

All parties appear in court and as William KEWLEY is now age 21, and the transfer of the deed and note will be held in the Court Clerk's office and then given to the Guardian after she pays court costs.

Attorney for POLKE appears in court and states that POLKE'S name is not stricken from BURNSIDE'S bond and as the Guardian of the heirs. Court fully releases POLKE from all liability in this case.

Incidental Names   Phillip and Jeremiah KEWLEY, "next friends"; W. ALLEN, sheriff; John B. NILES, witness and attorney

---

Adam SMEADLEY, deceased   **Estate**

Book & Page   CPR: 459-461

Court Dates   24 March 1840, 11 May 1840, 9 May 1842, 8 Aug 1842, 10 Nov 1842, 13 Feb 1843

Administrator   George BENTLEY

Action	On 22 Feb, 1840, Letters of Administration for the estate of SMEADLEY, who died intestate were granted in vacation to BENTLEY by the clerk of the court.
	Administrator presents an inventory of the estate and an appraisal of personal property. Appraisal made on 23 March 1840 (description within). Also mentioned was a coat owned by the deceased, left with a tailor in LaPorte during his lifetime and valued at $8.00* (See "Comments").
	Court confirms appointment of Administrator. Court later orders Administrator to appear to make final settlement of the estate and file a sale bill. Cause continued until the next term of the court.
	Administrator appears in court and files a sale bill of the estate (description within). The home was appraised at $40* (See "Comments").
	The sale bill came to $91.94. He also presents credits and expenses totaling $110.23, which leaves $18.31 in the estate. Court approves his account and he is discharged.
Incidental Names	John F. HEWS, bond; Alfred STANTON, Abraham LANGDON, appraisers
*Comments	As an aside: *the relative worth of a $40 home would equal about $21,300 today, and the relative worth of a tailored coat valued at $8.00 during that same period would be equal to about $233.00 today.*
	("Measuring Worth" website)

Samuel SCARCE, deceased	**Estate**
Book & Page	CPR: 461-464
Court Dates	8 Nov 1841, 14 Aug 1843
Administrator	David HARMON
Action	On 11 Oct 1841, Letters of Administration granted in vacation for the estate of SCARCE, who died intestate.
	Administrator files an inventory of the personal estate (description within). The widow also had selected articles (description within) for her personal use. The sale bill amounted to $52.48 and the sale was held on 5 Nov 1841.
	Administrator files his exhibit of the affairs of the estate. He claims credits in the amount of $52.48, which was the amount of the sale bill and claims expense amounts (description within).
	Samuel STEWART (name enlarged in court docket entry) appears in court and proves to the court that his claim against the estate is valid. Court awards STEWART $131.19. Court awards monetary claims to others who appear.
Incidental Names	Samuel TEEGARDEN, bill; Samuel DURLINGTON, Jacob KEELEY, Magdelein EVERHART, Samuel BURSON, Calvin EVANS, claims

Noah NEWELL   **Estate**

vs

Ezekiel MORRISON,
Administrator of the estate of
Joseph WYATT, deceased

Book & Page	CPR: 465-466
Court Dates	10 May 1841, 9 Aug 1841
Action	NEWELL'S attorney appears in court and files a declaration claiming that MORRISON owes him $50 in the form of a promissory note signed in 1837, as well as the cost of a suit, on this note in LaPorte Circuit Court that was decided in NEWELL'S favor. He also lists other claimants which were part of the suit. The attorney claims MORRISON owes damages amounting to $1,500. The note was signed and dated by the deceased, WYATT, who died in Sept of 1838.
	MORRISON appears and does not deny that the deceased, WYATT, was indebted to the signers of the note in the amount of $1,236.82. Court orders MORRISON to pay this amount, plus damages, to the defendant plus court costs and also orders expenditures to be levied of the "goods and chattels" of the deceased WYATT.
Incidental Names	John B. NILES, attorney; Charles McCLURE, George W. ALLEN, Arthur McCLURE, claimants in suit

Ezra TYLER, Administrator of   **Assumpsit**
the estate of
Horace B. HIBBARD, deceased

vs

Joseph DAVIS

Book & Page	CPR: 466-474
Court Dates	30 Oct 1843, 3 Nov 1843, 8 Nov 1843, 13 Nov 1843, 13 Jan, 1844, 12 Feb 1844, 16 Feb 1844
Action	Attorney for TYLER asks for damages of $400 against DAVIS. A writ was issued by the clerk of the court on 30 Oct 1843 to the sheriff of LaPorte County and given to Joseph DAVIS on 8 Nov 1843.
	On 3 Nov 1843, TYLER'S attorney filed in Probate Court a complaint of trespass against Joseph DAVIS, the defendant in custody, stating that on 2 April 1838, in Center Township, LaPorte County, the partnership of Truman, FOX and Alexander SUNDELAND rendered a judgment in a suit against John SHERWOOD whom FOX and SUNDELAND did business with and the judgment amounted to $51.94, plus costs of $3.90. SHERWOOD wanted to appeal the case. The deceased, HIBBARD, at the request of Joseph DAVIS would give bail and security and then deliver "this act and deed" to the Justice of the Peace to be filed and would later become an appeal bond in the name of FOX and SUNDELAND in the amount of $100 to be paid to them. This was done with the understanding that

SHERWOOD would go ahead with his appeal in circuit court. If his appeal failed, the agreement was null and void. The appeal bond was dated 24 April, 1838, and signed by DAVIS and delivered to the deceased, HIBBARD, on 30 April 1838. As SHERWOOD did not follow through with his appeal to the circuit court, on 1 May 1840, FOX and SUNDELAND recovered judgment in the sum of $51.94, plus $5.19 for damages, plus $5.40, also in damages which then totaled $ 63.53. SHERWOOD is insolvent, with no goods or chattels or property of any kind leaving TYLER, as Administrator of HIBBARD'S estate liable for payment to FOX and SUNDELAND. TYLER has paid $96.03 on this debt and has also had to pay $200 in defense of this action.

TYLER'S attorney further states that on 2 April 1838 another action was brought about by FOX and SUNDELAND against SHERWOOD for $51.94, plus costs of $3.19.

On 1 May 1840, FOX and SUNDELAND recovered a judgment in court from a prior suit against SHERWOOD. SHERWOOD still remains insolvent and TYLER, after the death of HIBBARD was liable to pay the judgment against SHERWOOD.

On 8 May 1843, TYLER was prosecuted in regard to a court judgment brought by FOX and SUNDELAND in the amount of $83.83 and TYLER has since been forced to expend $200 for the defense of these actions. SHERWOOD has refused in any way to attempt to repay any amount of the judgment costs to TYLER. TYLER'S attorney continues that a further judgment of $20 was levied against SHERWOOD, plus costs, and $60 for the appeal bond. SHERWOOD'S failure to pay these caused FOX and SUNDELAND to sue SHERWOOD for $24.72 and costs.

On 8 May TYLER was forced to pay $38 for SHERWOOD'S debts, totaling: $20.20 plus $3.19 in costs, $51.94, plus costs of $3.19, Appeal Bond costs of $60, further debts of $100, plus another $100.

SHERWOOD, has no goods, property etc with which to seize, so TYLER has been forced to pay $400 in defense of these actions against him as Administrator of HIBBARD'S estate.

TYLER presents his Administrator's certificate, dated 6 Oct, 1838 to the court as proof of his role. The defendant claims his innocence to the court, however. A jury is waived and the court decides in favor of DAVIS, the defendant.

TYLER'S attorney submits an appeal of this decision. Court grants the motion for appeal.

Incidental Names   N. CLARKSON, J.P.; H. HINKLEY, sheriff's deputy; Edmund B. WOODSON, J.P.; James BRADLEY, attorney

Enos PEASE, deceased   **Estate**

Book & Page   CPR: 475-484

Court Dates	13 Nov 1837, 24 March 1838, 12 Nov 1838, 11 Feb 1839, 13 May 1839, 12 Aug 1839, 11 Nov 1839, 11 May 1840, 8 Nov 1841, 14 Feb 1842, 9 May 1842, 8 Aug 1842, 14 Nov 1842, 11 May 1846
Administrators	Asa C. PEASE, Nathan B. NICHOLS
Heirs	Enos A. PEASE, Artimisa PEASE SATTERSLEE, Nancy PEASE STOWE, Susan W. SATTERSLEE, Milton SATTERSLEE, Lucinda H. PEASE, David H.PEASE, Buenos A. PEASE, Alvin B. PEASE, Isabella PEASE, widow
Action	On 30 Sept 1837, Letters of Administration were granted "in vacation" to Asa C. PEASE and Nathan B. NICHOLS as Administrators of the estate of Enos PEASE, who died intestate.

Court then confirms the appointment and also approves an appraisal of the personal estate that was filed on 30 Oct 1837 (description within) amounting to $236.62.

A Sale Bill is filed in court. Sale was held on 22 Nov 1837 at the home of the deceased (description within with names of each purchaser). Total purchases amounted to $398.54 (note made by clerk: "Bill is $400.19, or it should be").

Administrators state that the sale of the deceased's personal estate was insufficient for the payment of debts to the estate. They also state that the deceased was the owner of real estate whose value was appraised at $220. They list the debts owed by the deceased in the amount of $582.64, "to CLARK and others." They claim this leaves a deficit of $182.45 to the estate. Administrators request an order for the sale of the real estate. A list of real estate to be sold presented to the court (description within) and is in township 37 in LaPorte County. One parcel contains 20 acres, valued at $220.

Asa C. PEASE is Guardian of the infant heirs of the deceased and the adult heirs are non residents. Court orders advertisement of the real estate to be published in local Whig newspaper and the Administrators appear at the next February court session. Court also orders the Administrators to advertise the sale of the real estate on 20 March, the following month and to give 20 days' notice of the sale.

Administrators report the sale of the real estate to the court. It was sold for $120, as that was the highest bid. Court approves the sale and orders a certificate be issued to the buyer so a deed may be given.

Court informed of further real estate the Administrators wish to sell to pay the debts of the estate. This additional real estate is appraised at $210, but this still leaves a deficit to the estate of $206. Administrators ask the court to be allowed to conduct a private sale of the property, in the belief that this will bring a higher price under these conditions. They present a description of the property which is in township 37 and appraised at $160, plus another lot in the same township valued at $210 (complete descriptions within). Court orders the publication of private sale and the appearance of all parties at next court session.

Court orders sale of property. Administrators appear in court and report the sale of the property went to the highest bidder for $210. Court approves the sale and appoints Administrator PEASE as a commissioner to receive sale monies and issue a deed to the buyer of the property. Court also orders Administrators to appear and next court session.

Administrators not prepared to make a settlement. Cause continued. Administrators state sale of real estate is still insufficient to meet the debts of the estate. They claim that a nonverbal agreement had been made with the heirs to allow Asa PEASE to purchase one of the properties, but no deed has been given PEASE for the property yet and no valid title for the property is available. They request the original assessment and personal inventory be set aside and made void. Court again orders summons for out of state heirs to appear in order to confirm again the sale of the real estate of deceased and appoints a Guardian for the minor heirs.

Heirs do not appear in court and make default to the sale of the property. Court then orders sale of properties at public auction.

Administrators present their report of the sale of properties (description within), one of $45 and state that the other tract of land was not sold (description within) as the mortgage for the land was greater than its value. Court orders a deed be made for the land that was sold.

Administrators present their final settlement of the estate and they state they have charged themselves with $644.30, or the sale of the personal property of the estate. They claim an amount of $757.43 to be credited with. They present the final account of debts and credits amounting to $751.43 (notation made "should be $811.43"). All debts having been paid, they are left with a balance to distributed to the heirs of the estate.

Incidental Names	Fitch BROWN, Solomon ALDRICH, appraisers; Harrison C. DAVIS, sale clerk; Nathan B NICHOLS, J.P.; A. BLACKBURN, James ANDREWS, appraisers; William ALLEN, sheriff, summons; William ANDREWS, Guardian; Thomas N. SMITH, lot buyer; John B. NILES, attorney

Jason HOLLOWAY and John S. HOLLOWAY, grandsons of **John SMITH**, dec'd	**Guardianship & Final Settlement**
Book & Page	CPR: 485-486
Court Dates	11 Feb 1840, 11 May 1840
Action	Jason and John HOLLOWAY file petition for appointment of a Guardian. The HOLLOWAYS are minors and grandsons of deceased **John SMITH** of Wayne County and inheritors of legacies of the deceased amounting to almost $200 each. They need a Guardian in order to receive the legacies from the estate and to be in charge of these legacies for them. They request the court appoint their father, Stephen HOLLOWAY as Guardian. Court approves the appointment.

Guardian presents final settlement to the court (description within). John HOLLOWAY receives $50 and Jason HOLLOWAY receives $100 from the estate. 80 acres of were sold from the estate for $300 and given to Jason, 80 more acres of land was sold for $200 and given to John. John and Jason state they are now 21 yrs of age and agree with the final settlement report. This was signed on 14 May 1846. Court approves final settlement and discharges Stephen HOLLOWAY as Guardian.

Incidental Names   John STANTON; William BROWN land purchasers; W.C. HANNAH, witness

Noah HULBURT, deceased   Estate

Book & Page: CPR: 487-491

Court Dates   8 May 1843, 16 May 1843, 14 Aug 1844, 12 Aug 1844

Administrators   Nancy HULBURT, John F. DECKER Jr.

Heirs   John Wesley HULBERT, age 6, Mary Elizabeth HULBERT, age 4

Action   Nancy HULBERT and John F. DECKER Jr. appear in court to make application for Administrators of the estate of Noah HULBURT, deceased, Center Twp, LaPorte County. The request is granted and filed by the clerk of the court.

An inventory of personal estate also is filed on 16 May 1843 (description within). The personal estate appraised at $253.92 on 8 June 1843.

Sale bill is filed in court (description within) amounting to $154.92 and witnessed on 27 July 1844.

Administrators appear in court and present their report on sale of real estate of deceased.

Administrators appear in court with their attorney and report that the personal property of the deceased amounted to $150.92, of which the Administrators applied to the debts of the estate (description within). The real estate of the deceased in LaPorte County, Township 37 has been secured by a mortgage of $1000 and the income from the sale of personal property is insufficient to meet the debts of the estate (real estate description within). They request the sale of the real estate at either a private or public sale.

Court orders heirs to appear at the November term of court to determine why the real estate should not be sold.

The real estate was sold for $1,920. They also file the inventory and appraisal of the real estate containing 120 acres (description within) and which was appraised at $8 per acre, on 13 Nov 1844. The court appoints a Guardian for the minor heirs. Summons were delivered to the heirs and the court orders a private sale of the real estate for "cash in hand".

Administrators report sale of real estate for $1,037.10. Court approves the sale and orders a deed be made to the purchaser.

Administrators file an exhibit of the affairs of the estate (description within). Expenditures totaled $1,218.25 and the personal estate brought in $1119.02. Court discharges the administrators.

Incidental Names	John DECKER, Bond; Charles TUCKER, Daniel McLEAN, appraisers; Alvin FRAVEL, J.P.; Moses BULLOCK, witness; Samuel HOLLAND, security; J.P. ANDRESS, West DARLING appraisers; Samuel E. WILLIAMS, Guardian; Waterman BUCKS(?) purchased property.

Matthias KEELEY, deceased   **Estate**

Book & Page:	CPR 491-493
Court Dates	12 Aug 1844, 10 Aug 1846
Administrator	Samuel BURSON
Heirs	Levi W. KEELEY
Action	Administrator files Levi KEELEY's renunciation of his right as the Administrator of his father's estate and requests BURSON be appointed. The deceased died intestate and left property and effects in the amount of $700. Levi W. KEELEY is the only heir residing within Indiana. Court appoints BURSON as Administrator.
	Administrator presents the court with exhibit of the estate. Expenditures were $545.92 and he claims credit for the amount (description within). Court approves this account and discharges the Administrator.
Incidental Names	Jacob KEELEY, Bond

Abraham FRAVEL   **Estate**
vs
Egbert R. DEWIT, Administrator
of the estate of **James F. SMITH**

Book & Page	CPR: 493- 495
Court Dates	9 Feb 1846 11 May 1846, 10 Aug 1846
Action	On 20 Jan 1846, attorney for FRAVEL files complaint in Clerk's Office stating DEWIT, the Administrator of SMITH'S estate had failed to pay FRAVEL money owed from the sale of goods and merchandise of the estate of the deceased, SMITH, amounting to $222.40. On 15 Jan 1840 the deceased was indebted to the mercantile firm owned by two men in the amount of $222.40 for certain wares and goods the deceased had ordered. The partners of this firm dissolved their business relationship and transferred the notes, accounts, wares, and merchandise to the remaining owner if he would within 8 days offer sufficient security to be approved by any person of the deceased's choosing.
	The deceased owed a debt of $1,335.87 to one H. WHEELER & Co. of LaPorte for the payment of a judgment in Circuit Court of $590 due from a

CHAPMAN to James WHITTEM, as well as a note of $200 due from CHAPMAN to the State Bank of Indiana in Michigan City, with security provided. The deceased would have this note to pay and CHAPMAN would then pay his former partners what was owed to him. The deceased promised to pay FRAVEL the first amount of $240 when it was requested. On 23 Jan 1840 the deceased stated that if FRAVEL would purchase all the goods and merchandise, monies, notes, and accounts of the remaining partnership between SMITH & CHAPMAN & BIXBY up to the 15th Jan 1840 and assume the payment of certain of the deceased SMITH'S liabilities amounting to $125.87 that the deceased promised to repay FRAVEL. FRAVEL then agreed to this transaction and assumed payment of the deceased's liabilities.

The $220.40 was still owed to FRAVEL although he requested payment frequently until SMITH was deceased.

The Administrator DEWIT, the defendant, also has not paid the money owed from the estate which also now included the amount of $425.

On 22 Jan 1846, the plaintiff filed a writ from the Clerk's Office which was delivered to the Sheriff of LaPorte Co. Defendant DEWIT appears in court and states that James F. SMITH, the deceased, did not agree and promise what was stated by the plaintiff. Cause continued.

Cause continued. once again. Parties appear in court. A jury is waived. Court hears the evidence and decides for the plaintiff, FRAVEL, in the amount of $310.24 and also awards damages and costs to the plaintiff FRAVEL and an amount is levied and expended from the goods and chattels involved in the suit.

Incidental Names	Gilbert HATHAWAY, attorney

Henry A. THOMPSON, dec'd   Estate

Book & Page	CPR: 496-502
Court Dates	12 May 1845, 11 Aug 1845, 10 Nov 1845, 4 Aug 1846
Heirs	Mary Ann THOMPSON, wife, Olive Jane THOMPSON, William Henry THOMPSON
Administrator	William S. PERRY
Action	On 1 April, 1845, Mary THOMPSON filed a petition in court for appointment of an administrator. Her husband Henry A. THOMPSON died intestate on 23 Jan 1845, leaving personal property amounting to around $125. The widow has requested William S. PERRY, a creditor be appointed as administrator. Granting of this appointment by the clerk will be heard by the court at its next sitting.

On 11 April 1845 an inventory of personal property and real estate also filed with the clerk (description within). Widow claims her share of personal property valued at $150.

On 13 May 1845, Administrator files a sale bill with the Clerk's office (description within). Sale held on 10 May 1845.

Administrator claims debts to the estate amount to about $200 and only $17.14 was realized from the sale. He requests the sale of additional real estate of the deceased which is also in township 37 and might be worth $50. He stated the deceased held a bond for the real estate in township 37 and $35 in interest is due on the bond from April of 1844 and it is worth about $50. Court orders real estate sold and the appearance of the heirs in court to show cause why the real estate should not be sold. Cause continued.

Court confirms the earlier appointment of the Administrator and all other filings prior to this session of the court and also orders that summons to appear in court be verified as delivered to the heirs with proper advertisement in the local newspapers. Administrator files an inventory and appraisal of the real estate. Property assessed at $1 per acre.

Widow does not appear in court and makes default. A guardian of the minor heirs is appointed by the court. Court approves order of the sale of real estate for not less than 2/3 of the appraised value. Court also orders the real estate be sold on 10 Sept between the hours of 10 am and 4 pm.

Administrator appears in court and states he has sold the real estate of the deceased. for $1.33 per acre for a total of $53.33 and 1/3 for the 40 acres. Another tract of land was sold also in township 37. He states the public sale was advertised in the local Whig newspaper. He then presents his final settlement (description within). He states that $21.72 in assets remain to be divided among the several creditors. Court accept his account of assets and distributions and discharges the Administrator.

Incidental Names	William B. JUSTINE, security; Martin H. SELKREGG, Charles KELLOGG, appraisers; W. W. HIGGINS, J.P.; Jared BALDWIN, assessor; A.W. AMES, security; Charles PALMER, Jared BALDWIN, Samuel CLENDENEN, note; A. W. ENOS, clerk of sale; Jonathan BURR, bond; Charles PALMER, C.S. ROBERTS, appraisers; S.E. WILLIAMS, clerk of sale; Charles PALMER Jr, Guardian; Charles F. ROBERTS, John BALDWIN, purchased land; MEEKER & BRADLEY, creditors
Comments	First sale was held at the shop of FISHER & AMES & CO. in Michigan City, IN. Second real estate sale held at the Post Office in Michigan City, IN.

James LOONEY, deceased   **Estate**

Book & Page	CPR: 503-505
Court Dates	10 Nov 1845, 9 Nov 1846
Heirs	Abigail LOONEY, widow
Administrator	Lewis WILKINSON

Action	Application for Administration of estate filed in clerk's office by WILKENSON at the request of the widow on Deceased died intestate around March of 1844 and left property and effects worth about $100.

Court approves the appointment of WILKENSON as Administrator.

WILKENSON files an inventory and appraisal of personal estate of deceased on 25 August 1846. The appraisal was done on 23 Dec 1845 (description within) and totaled $37.75. An account of mortgage and bank bills from the estate is filed, except for one account for $9.69 payable in cattle and one note for $50.

Administrator files a final settlement of the estate (description within). Balance in favor of the estate and granted to the widow amounted to $102.44. Disbursements by Administrator amounted to $94.98, leaving a balance to the estate of $7.46. Court approves of the settlement and discharges the Administrator.

Incidental Names	Edwin G. MATHEWS bond; James ROOD, Jacob G. MORGAN appraisers; Thomas ARMSTRONG clerk; John DILKLINGHAM, note

Hampton B. WHITEHEAD — Estate

Book & Page	CPR: 506-509
Court Dates	8 May 1842, 8 May 1843, 11 Aug 1845, 9 Nov 1846, 8 Feb 1847
Heir	Margaret WHITEHEAD, widow
Administrator	William H.H. WHITEHEAD
Action	Application filed with Clerk of Court for renunciation of the widow of her claim to the appointment as Administrator of her husband's estate. Hampton B. WHITEHEAD died intestate on 15 March. She states she is a "friend" of William WHITEHEAD and she requests he be appointed as Administrator. On 5 April 1842 William WHITEHEAD files his application as such in the Clerk's office. He also claims the personal estate of the deceased would not exceed $300.

Court approves appointment at next session of court.

Administrator files an inventory of the personal estate of the deceased (description within). The total inventory included (description within). The total inventory included personal property, acreage at $3 per acre and a lot, #2 at $2.50 per acre and came to $239.75. A sale bill of property is also presented (description within). Sale held 7 May 1842, and income came to $188.21. Administrator had filed his vouchers for cash outlay on 15 May 1845 (description within). Court orders final settlement of the estate to be made at next term of the court.

Administrator presents final account of the estate. He had a balance of $25.14 after the estate debts were paid out (description within). Court approves his final account and discharges the Administrator.

Alexander HASTINGS, bond; John HEFNER J.P.; Isaac D. MARTIN, Jasper S. HUNT appraisers

John DUDLEY, deceased   **Estate**

Book & Page   CPR: 510-515

Court Dates   8 May 1843, 10 Nov 1845, 9 Feb 1846, 11 May 1846, 9 Nov 1846

Action   On 1 March Catherine DUDLEY and Thomas FISHER filed the Last Will and Testament of DUDLEY as follows: appointed as Administrator. All papers related to the estate delivered to him.

On 17 May, 1842, Administrator VANPELT appears in court and presents his report on the sale of real estate of the deceased (description within) which is in township 38, in Elkhart County Indiana. The widow received her Dower for these properties and the dwelling house. by decree of the Elkhart Circuit Court (description within).

Administrator claims proceeds from sale of real estate is insufficient to pay the debts of the estate. He claims the personal estate amounts to $1,597.68. He also states the former Administrator claimed credits of $1,698.72. There are still unsatisfied debts, including a judgment from Circuit Court in favor of a debtor, and this debt was not paid by the former Administrator. He requests the court summon the widow and heirs to appear in court to state why the real estate should not be sold. Court orders publication of sale and the heirs to appear in court.

On 15 Aug 1842, Administrator files with the clerk of the Court that four of the heirs are non residents of the state; and they are Lydia H. BRADLEY, George W. BRADLEY, Joseph E. BRADLEY, and William C. BRADLEY. Debtor appears in court and claims $2.50 is owed him from the estate.

On 16 Nov 1842, Administrator states that summons were served to the heirs and notice of publication of sale was made. Court appoints a Guardian for the minor heirs; Julia, Joseph, and William BRADLEY. Guardian claims no objection to the sale of real estate. Court orders sale of personal property and real estate, and also orders notice of this sale be posted at the Court House on the front door in Goshen, Elkhart, Indiana. Court further orders Administrator to make report to the court on the sale.

Administrator reports he has sold part of the real estate, 55 acres, at 41 cents per acre (description within). He also states he sold another part of the real estate (description within) for 50 cents per acre which amounted to 557 acres. Court affirms these sales.

Administrator states he has received a receipt for $162.37 and expenses of $43. He now has in his hands $119.37. He further states the former Administrator received $2,000 from assets of the estate and he himself has only received credits of $7.00 - $8.00, and that he should be due more than $1,200. He claims the estate surety now insolvent and there are attorney and offices fees that are owed. He presents an account of the estate to the court. Debts owed are $2,242.96, in the judgment made by the Circuit Court,

$1,500 to another creditor, and $36 to yet another creditor from Elkhart County. He will dispute other claims as possibly doubtful in the final settlement.

Court claims estate to be insolvent and orders that notice of such be published within 10 months. Administrators' expenses are itemized (description within). Administrator states he has $74.42 on hand for disbursement. Court approves of his account and discharges the Administrator.

Creditors appear in court on 13 Feb (description within).

Incidental Names   John B. McDONALD & Enoch ARBOGAST, security; John VICORY & Enoch ARBOGAST, appraisers; John MILLER, J.P.; George McCOLLAM, J.P.; Alfred WHALLON Sale clerk; John INGRAM & John HEPNER, appraisers; Saul E. WILLIAMS J.P.

Samuel JOHNSON, deceased   **Estate**

Book & Page   CPR: 516-520

Court Dates   10 Feb 1840, 9 May 1842, 10 Nov 1845, 9 Feb 1846, 11 May 1846, 10 Aug 1846, 8 Feb 1847

Administrator   Joseph BENEDICT & William EAHART

Action   Samuel JOHNSON died intestate. Letters of Administration granted in vacation to EAHART & BENEDICT on 30 Nov 1839 by the clerk.

On 10 Dec 1839, Administrators file an inventory an appraisal of personal property of deceased taken on 9 Dec 1839 with clerk of the court (description within). Appraisal came to $255.74. On 7 Jan 1840, Administrators filed in the clerk's office a sale bill of the personal property. Sale held at the home of the deceased. On 4 Jan 1840 (description within) Personal property sold for $302.40.

Court confirms Letters of Administration and Administrators present to the court their exhibit of the estate and also the debits and credits of the estate (description within). They stated a total of $233.44 was paid out to the court. Court accepts their report.

Court orders appearance of Administrators to make final settlement. Only EAHART appears. BENEDICT is absent. EAHART requests further time to present a final settlement. Cause continued.

Administrator EAHART appears alone and present a final settlement to the court. He states all assets of estate collected except for a judgment on a note due amounting to $34. Amount now owed on that note is $115. He requests more time in order to have full payment on the note. Cause continued.

EAHART files an exhibit of the condition of the estate. This account shows a total of $309.10 cash collected. The Administrator has a balance of $83.17 on hand. As there are no known legal heirs, court orders publication of the estate holdings.

No one appears to make claim on the estate in court and the court orders assets now totaling $71.71 turned over to the Treasurer of the State and orders $6.12 paid in costs. A receipt dated 12 June 1847 is received from the Auditor of the State.

, Incidental Names	James McCORD, bond; & appraiser; Henry CLYBURN, appraiser; Ezra TYLER, J. P; Lewis TODHUNTER, clerk of sale; William BATTERSON note; D. MAGUIRE, Auditor; A.W. MORRIS, witness for State
Comments	Thomas JERNEGAN, Editor & Publisher of the Indiana TOCSIN, a weekly newspaper of general circulation, published in LaPorte, published the proof of notice. Also, a notation made of the # of this estate, #4763 "Estates without heirs"

Timothy SPAULDING   Estate

Book & Page	CPR: 521-523
Court Dates	11 Feb 1839, 11 Nov 1839, 12 Feb 1844, 12 Aug 1844, 11 Nov 1844, 8 Feb 1847
Administrator	John B. NILES
Heirs	Sylvia SPAULDING, widow
Action	Attorney files renunciation of widow to her right as Administrator of her husband's estate. She requests her attorney be appointed in her stead. SPAULDING died intestate. Court grants request.

Administrator files an inventory and appraisal of the estate. Appraisal taken on 28 Feb 1839 (description within) totaling $130. A sale bill is also filed (description within) totaling $111 from the public sale.

These reports are approved by the court.

Administrator files a complaint of insolvency in court. There is no real estate of the deceased to be sold and states that there are debts to the estate that he has not yet explored. He requests the court declares the estate insolvent. Court orders publication of this complaint in local Whig newspaper. All claims to the estate will be postponed for now, and the court orders estate insolvent.

Administrator make a final settlement with the court. Creditors have filed their claims. He states that the one purchase at the sale is all that that is available to creditors and that the note owed to estate is now uncollectible. Court orders Administrator be given the sum of $11 for the note. Court also orders the amount of $100, for the sale purchase at the sale be given to the purchaser, after deducting $7.67 for costs to the clerk of the court, $5.50 for costs in regard to the settlement of the estate. Court also awards $3.00 for advertisement of notice of insolvency. This left $81.43 to be given to the creditors. Court orders receipts given each creditor and also be filed with the clerk. Administrator discharged. Court creditors their portion due (description within).

| Incidental Names | Sutton VAN PELT, bond; E.L.NATHAN, Gregory & Elijah BECKWITH, appraisers; Samuel NILES, clerk of sale; T.L. STEWART, printer; James WHITTEN, J & P. EASLEY, Hiram WHEELER, creditors |

Bartholomew BRADLEY   Estate

Book & Page	CPR: 524-534
Court Dates	12 Nov 1838, 11 Feb 1839, 10 Feb 1840, 11 May 1840, 10 Aug 1840, 9 Nov 1840, 8 Nov 1841, 9 May 1842, 12 May 1842, 8 Aug 1842
Administrator	Sydney S. BRADLEY/Sutton VAN PELT
Heirs	Lydia S. BRADLEY, widow,
Action	On 1 Oct 1838, Sydney S. BRADLEY filed Lydia BRADLEY'S renunciation as Administrator of her husband's estate with the clerk of the court. Bartholomew BRADLEY died intestate on 14 Sept 1838. He claims the "ultimate value" of the estate is $550.

Court grants Letters of Administration made while court was 'in vacation".

Administrator files an inventory of the estate on 24 Oct 1838, totaling $1345.68 (description within).

Attorney for the Administrator files his request with the court for permission to sell part of the personal estate at private sale. Court approves.

Administrator requests additional time to prepare for the sale of personal estate. Court grants his request. Cause continued.

Administrator presents his report on the deceased's estate (description within). Debits amounted to $1698.27. $100.59 was paid out over and above the amount of assets of the estate.

Court orders an attachment against the Administrator for contempt of court failing to appear at the last term of court to make final settlement.

On 12 May 1842, attorney for the creditors of the estate files an affidavit for the creditors in regard to the insolvency of the security bond. Administrator appears in court and an additional bond filed as security. Court revokes the appointment of Sydney BRADLEY as Administrator and appoints instead Sutton VAN PELT as Administrator and that all papers related to the estate be delivered to VAN PELT.

On 17 May 1842, Administrator VAN PELT appears in court and presents his report on the sale of the real estate of the deceased (description within). Real estate in township 38 in Elkhart County. The widow received her Dower in these properties and the dwelling home by decree of Elkhart Circuit Court (description within). Administrator claims proceeds from sale of real estate insufficient to pay the debts of the estate. He claims the personal estate amounted to $1,597.68. He also states that the former Administrator claimed credits of $1,698.27. There are still unsatisfied debts, including a judgment from circuit Court in favor of a debtor. This debt was not paid by the former Administrator. He requests the court summon the widow and heirs to court to state why the real estate should not be sold. Court orders publication of the ale and heirs to appear in court.

On 15 Aug 1842, Administrator VAN PELT files with the clerk of the court that four of the heirs are non residents of this state; Lydia H. BRADLEY, George W. BRADLEY, Joseph E. BRADLEY and William C. BRADLEY.

Debtor appears in court and claims $2.50 is owed him from the estate.

On 16 Nov 1842, Administrator states that summons were served on the heirs and notice of publication of sale was made. Court appoints a Guardian for minor heirs, Julia, Joseph, and William BRADLEY. Guardian claims no objection is made to the sale of the real estate. Court orders sale of personal property and the real estate. Court also orders notice posted of sale on the door of the court house in Goshen, in Elkhart County. Court further orders Administrator to make report to the court on the sale.

Administrator reports he has sold part of the real estate, 55 ½ acres @ 41cents per acre (description within). He also sold part of the real estate (description within) for 50 cents per acre for 557 acres. Court affirms these sales. Administrator states he has received a receipt for $162.37 and expenses of of $43. He now has in his hands $119.37. He further states the former Administrator received $2,000 from assets of the estate and he himself has only received credits of $7 - $8 and he should be due more than $1200.

Administrator claims the estate now insolvent and there are yet attorney and office fees that are owed. He presents an account of the estate to the court. Debts owed are $2,243.96 in the judgment made by the Circuit Court, and $1500 owed to another creditor for $36 from Elkhart County. He will dispute other claims as possibly doubtful in the final settlement.

Court claims estate to be insolvent and orders that notice of such be published and notice of claims against the estate be published within 10 months. Administrator's expenses are itemized (description within) totaling $43.

Administrator appears and makes report of his further expenditures (description within). He has $74.42 on hand for disbursement. Court approves his account and discharges the Administrator.

Creditors appear in court on the 13th of Feb 1847 (description within).

Incidental Names   Joseph BRADLEY, witness to death of deceased; Rysel HARVEY, bond; Pailey D. SHUMWAY, Gad CRANNEY, appraisers; John BRADLEY, attorney; North NEWELL creditor; John B. NILES, attorney; and purchased part of real estate; Noah NEWELL, bond; William C. HANNA, attorney; Elisha NEWELL, Jeremiah CORLYS, George CRAWFORD, Alden TUCKER, creditors; Erasmus BRADLEY, bought part of real estate; John M. CLARKSON, Guardian

Howard MASON, deceased   **Estate**

Book & Page   CPR: 534-542

Court Dates   12 Nov 1838, 12 Aug 1839, 10 Feb 1840, 12 May 1840, 8 Nov 1841, 14
                   Feb 1842, 9 May 1842, 8 Aug 1842, 13 Nov 1843, 13 May 1844, 16 May
                   1844, 9 Feb 1846, 8 Feb 1847

Administrator   William CLARK

Heirs   Sidney MASON widow, Edward MASON, Elizabeth MASON, Howard
                   MASON, Alice MASON, minor children of deceased

                   On 31 Aug, 1838, Letters of Administration were granted in vacation to
                   William CLARK over the estate of MASON of LaPorte County.

                   Court confirms appointment and orders Administrator to Appear at next
                   court session to file an inventory of personal property of the estate.

                   Administrator files inventory with Clerk of Court on 23 Oct 1839
                   (description within). He also files a sale bill (description within). Sale bill
                   totaled $435.90 and was filed on 21 Sept, 1838.

                   Court orders a final settlement of the estate to be made. Administrator
                   requests further time for this. Court grants his request.

                   Administrator files petition for sale of deceased's real estate. He states that
                   there is no guardian for the minor heirs of the estate. The personal estate of
                   deceased amounted to $442.40 and the expenses of the estate stand at
                   $989.43 - $500 with $90 interest. He adds there is a mortgage due of $5,990
                   to the state with a debt of $25. The personal property is insufficient to meet
                   these debts. The deceased had 180 acres in LaPorte County in township 37
                   (description within). The land was appraised at $960. He requests the heirs
                   be ordered to appear in court to show why the land should not be sold at a
                   private sale. Petition filed in clerk's office on 10 May 1842. Court orders
                   the appearance of widow and heirs in court.

                   Court appoints a Guardian for the minor heirs. Widow does not appear in
                   court and makes default. Court then orders sale of real estate at a private
                   sale.

                   Administrator reports he was unable to sell the real estate and requests
                   additional time to do so. Court grants request.

                   Administrator reports the land sold for $1100. Court confirms the sale and
                   orders a deed be made when the balance of the purchase price has been
                   paid.

                   Administrator files an exhibit of affairs of the estate (description within).
                   Court orders $227.39 paid into the court from the balance left after debts
                   were paid and this be given to the widow and heirs. Cause continued.

                   Administrator pays into court, through the clerk, $118.40 left from debts
                   paid to the estate on 21 Feb 1846. He presents his final account of the
                   estate. The balance owed by the purchaser of the real estate has been paid.
                   Court orders a deed be given to the purchaser on 12 Feb 1847.

Court discharges the Administrator and confirms the report on 12 Feb 1847.

Incidental Names   Stephen HOLLOWAY, bond; William ALLEN, clerk of sale; John H. BRADLEY, James BRADLEY, witnesses; John H. BRADLEY, Guardian & Bond; William ALLEN, Sheriff; Taylor BRADLEY purchaser of land; Thomas STEWART voucher; Thomas P. ARMSTRONG court fees

Amos HOLLOWAY Jr.   **Estate**

Book & Page	CPR: 543-546
Court Dates	9 Nov 1840, 14 Nov 1842, 13 Feb 1843, 11 May 1846
Administrator	Stephen HOLLOWAY
Action	Amos HOLLOWAY died intestate. Letters of Administration granted to Stephen HOLLOWAY.

On 8 Dec 1840, Administrator filed an inventory and appraisal of personal property of the estate with the clerk of the court (description within).

On 9 Jan 1841, Administrator filed a sale bill with the clerk of the court (description within) totaling $87.49. Court orders Administrator to make final settlement of the estate. Administrator states he is not prepared yet to make final settlement. Cause continued.

Administrator files his final settlement of estate. Sale note came to $90.55, with interest of $3.38 (description within). Balance due Administrator was $97.28. One debtor is declared insolvent. There are no further debts against the estate. Administrator claims credit for $375.74. There is still a note owed but it is uncollectible. He also gives an account of the uncollectible notes as well as the credit due him in settling the estate's accounts (description within).

Court approves the settlement and discharges the Administrator.

Incidental Names   Elijah STANTON, bond; John STANTON, Jehiel WAYSON, appraisers; Nathan HOLLOWAY, clerk of sale; STANTON & PEARS, Israel WOODWARD, note holders

John CULLIN   **Estate**
infant son of
John CULLIN, deceased

Book & Page	CPR: 547-553
Court Dates	10 Feb 1843, 8 May 1843, 13 Nov 1843, 15 Nov 1843
Guardian	John P. TEEPLES
Heirs	Otelia CULLEN POLKE, widow
Action	Adam G. POLKE appears in court and states that John CULLEN JR. is under 14 years of age. His father, John CULLIN of LaPorte County died intestate. Court appoints John P. TEEPLES as Guardian of the minor heir.

Guardian files petition for the sale of real estate of deceased which was lot #94 in the original plat of LaPorte which is liable to "decay" and it is necessary that the lot be sold for the benefit and support of the minor heir. Court appoints appraisers to assess the value of the real estate. On 14 Feb 1843, an assessment of the value was stated to be $130.

Court orders lot sold at private sale. Lot is sold for $50 on 9 May 1843. Court confirms the sale and orders a deed be made as soon as final payment has been received.

A credit for $65 for boarding and clothing for minor heir was claimed by the Guardian. Court approves claim and grants a deed to the purchaser of the lot. Court orders Guardian and heir to appear at next session of the court.

Guardian presents his exhibit of the estate and states that deceased had further real estate holdings; Lot #1, 2, 3, 46, 47, and 48 in Williams First Addition to the town of LaPorte. These lots were appraised at $175. He also submits a report of money spent (description within) for the support of heir and other miscellaneous charge. Cause continued.

Guardian appears in court and states that three years support, amounting to $150 for the minor heir of deceased has used up the purchase money for the original lot that was sold. He further states that Otelia CULLEN, widow of deceased has intermarried with Adam G. POLKE and is entitled to a Widow's Dower which has never been granted to her. He adds that the infant heir has continued to reside with his mother, Otelia CULLEN, but they wish to move from LaPorte County and wish the additional lots be sold.

Guardian requests a private sale of these lots. Court orders an appraisal of the lots. Court orders sale of the lots which make up one entire block. Appraisers report the lots value to be $167. Filed with clerk of the court on 10 Feb 1847.

On 12 Feb, 1847, Guardian reports to Clerk of Court that the lots have been sold for $177 and paid for in cash, which was the appraised value. On 13 Feb 1847, commissioner and Guardian report to clerk of court that a deed was issued to lot purchaser.

| Incidental Names | Joseph B. SELF, Davison PATTEN, Burwell SPURLOCK, appraisers; Reuben MONDAY, bond; Henry LUSH, purchased lot; Adam G. POLKE, note for lot; William CLEMENT, Samuel HEATH, appraisers; Thomas ARMSTRONG, clerk; Joel BUTLER, bond; David J. OAKS, lot purchaser |

George W. BARNES/BARNS   Estate

Book & Page	CPR: 553-562
Court Dates	12 Aug 1844
Administrator	Hiram WILLCOX, Caleb B. DAVIS

Heirs	Alvira BARNES, wife, Hannah CUNNINGHAM, Olive MARSTEN, daughters, & sons Joseph and Perry BARNES
Action	Hiram WILLCOX files the Last Will and Testament of George W. BARNES in court: "I, George W. BARNS of Galena of LaPorte County, in the State of Indiana, do make and publish this my last will and Testament hereby revoking and making void all former Wills by me at any time heretofore made – First I direct that my body be decently entered and that my funeral be conducted in a manner corresponding with my Estate and situation in Life and as to such Worldly Estate as it has pleased God to entrust me with. I dispose of the same in the following manner to wit. I direct first that all my just debts and funeral expenses be paid as soon after my decease as possible, out of the first moneys that shall come to the hands of my Executors from any portion of my estate real or Personal. I also direct and bequeath to my beloved wife Alvira BARNS during her natural life time so much of my real estate as lies East of the county road leading from my mill to LaPorte described as follows to wit (property description within, in Twp 38) to have and to hold the same with all the appurtenances thereunto belonging or in any way appertaining during her natural life time except two thirds of the profits of my saw mill and privileged thereunto which I bequeath to my two brothers and two sisters Joseph and Perry - Hannah and Olive to share and share alike. I also direct and bequeath absolutely to my beloved wife all my household furniture and all my sheep and hogs two cows-and calves of which she is to make choice also all the Provisions on hand at the time of my decease I also direct and bequeath to my sister Hannah CUNNINGHAM the (description within, township 38), also two horses one two horse wagon (sic) and harness two sleighs and three hundred dollars in money to be paid to her as hereafter described. I also give and bequeath to my brothers Joseph BARNS (description of property within, township 38) and sixty dollars in one year from the time of my decease to be paid to him by Olive MARSTEN my sister as hereafter described. I also bequeath to my sister Olive MARSTEN forty acres of land (description within township 38) and the said Olive is to pay the sum of sixty dollars in one year to my brothers Joseph BARNS and fifty dollars to my sister Hannah in two years from my decease.

I also bequeath to my brothers Perry BARNES all west of the county road on the (description of property in township 38) except the ten acres bequeathed to Olive MARSTEN and for the same said Perry is to pay to my sister Hannah the sum of two hundred and fifty dollars in five annual payments the first payment to be made in one year from my decease – I also bequeath to my sister Hannah and brother Joseph and sister Olive and brother Perry all the benefit issues and profits of my saw mill except one third part which I above bequeath my beloved wife so long as she lives but after her decease the said third of said mill together with said land bequeath to my wife shall be equally divided between the above mentioned brothers and sisters or their heirs to have and share alike and I further declare and direct that she share of my real and personal estate that bequeathed to my said wife shall be in lieu of her Dower if she shall so elect and the remainder of my property – if any after all my debts and charges are paid shall be divided between my wife and brothers and sisters above mentioned and I hereby make and ordain my worthy and esteemed friend Caleb B. DAVIS and Hiram B. WILCOX executors of this my last will and testament. In witness thereof I George BARNES the Testator have hereunto set my hand and seal this 11th day of June in the year of our Lord one thousand eight hundred and forty four Geo. W. BARNES."

On 13 Aug, 1844, NICHOLS and WILSON filed the will with the clerk of the court certifying its veracity.

Executor WILLCOX resigns as Executor on 18 Aug 1844. On 28 Aug 1844 Caleb B. DAVIS files his appointment as sole Executor with Clerk of the Court.

On 20 Sept 1884 DAVIS files an inventory and appraisal of the estate in the County Clerk's Office which amounted to $147.93, and the personal property came to $229.25 (description within).

Court confirms findings and cause is continued. Executor files an estate inventory and appraisal with Clerk of the court on 23 Nov 1844, while court is in vacation, amounting to $319.83 (description within).

On 30 Nov, 1844, Executor files a sale bill for the personal estate of deceased. Sale was a public auction held at the home of the deceased on 12 Oct 1844. (description within).

Sale brought in $343.92. Executor states that as several items bequeathed to heirs and widow were sold he now had on hand $684.09.

Executor claims credit for items amounting to $592.18 (description within). He files notes due and accounts that are uncollectible (description within). Court confirms his report.

On 10 Feb 1844 Executor files his exhibit of miscellaneous notes due (description within) with the Clerk of the Court. Executor also presents claims that he needs credit for (description within). He now has on hand $13.76 Court confirms his report and discharges the Executor.

Incidental Names	Byron CADWALADER, bond; & J.P.; Robert K. SMITH, William WALDRUFF, appraisers; Joseph FULLER, clerk of sale; A. S. OSBORN, witness; Scipha FOSTER, claimant; Thomas D.LEMON, Joseph FULLER, notes; Thomas P. ARMSTRONG, clerk
Comments	Court case pending outcome of estate entitled: "Robert B. SMITH vs Phineas BARNES". Note to will stated that will was "Recorded on pages 11-12-& 13 in the Record of Wills".

William M. OTIS, deceased   **Estate**

Book & Page	CPR: 563-567
Court Dates	10 Nov 1845
Administrator	Isaac CORLEY
Heirs	Claryssa OTIS, widow

Action`

On 22 Sept 1845 Isaac CORLEY files renunciation of the widow, Claryssa OTIS as Administrator of her husband's estate. Renunciation filed with Clerk of the Court. Deceased died on 20 July 1845 in LaPorte County. CORLEY filed Letters of Administration on his own behalf and states that OTIS had property and effects worth $500, more or less. Clerk grants appointment.

On 27 Sept 1845 Administrator files with clerk of Court an Inventory and appraisal of personal estate of deceased (description within) amounting to $636.27. Appraisal done on 28 Sept 1845.

Sale bill filed in court amounting to $399.72 (description within). Administrator also files a petition to sell a quantity of wheat on the property at a private sale on 11 Nov 1845. Court orders the sale and also confirms the appointment of the Administrator by the clerk while court was in vacation. Administrator appears in court to state that a claim has been filed against the estate of $43. Court authorizes payment of claim. Administrator files the final settlement. The wheat was sold for $840.93. He presents an account of a claims against the estate of $853.73 and the sale of the personal estate (description within) which came to $848.14. Court decrees the estate is not fully accounted for and orders Administrator to produce and file his vouchers. Cause continued.

Administrator appears in court and files his vouchers. Court agrees the estate has been fully administrated and the Administrator is discharged.

Incidental Names

Irwin S. JESSUP, security; Martha BAILEY.J.P.; Christian F. YOUNG, Daniel WOOLEY appraisers; Edmund B. WOODSEN, clerk of sale; Benjamin W. MEYERS, claim; HOLBROOK & KING, bought wheat

Giles BROWNELL   Estate

Book & Page   CPR: 567-570

Court Dates   10 Nov 1845, 8 Feb 1847

Administrator   Erastus H. PAYNE

Action

On 20 Oct 1845, PAYNE files his application as Administrator with the clerk of the court. BROWNELL died intestate about 19 Sept 1845 in Coolspring Township LaPorte County, leaving property and assets in the amount of $200 and left no relatives in the county.

Court later confirms the Letters of Administration by clerk of the court while court was "in vacation."

On 9 Feb Administrator filed account of the sale of personal property of the deceased. Sale held on 29 Nov 1845 (description within). Sale amounted to $16.38.

On 25 June 1846, Administrator filed an inventory of the personal estate of deceased containing notes against the estate (description within).

On 29 August 1846 Administrator files a sale bill of the estate with the clerk of the court (description within). Administrator appears in court and a claim is presented to the court and the court authorizes payment of the claim and approves the Administrator's account of $167.30 cash received and he claims he has $194.98, leaving a balance of $18.48. Court discharges Administrator.

Incidental Names	Alexander ROBINSON, bond; Stephen MISE J.P.; Thomas ARMSTRONG, Probate clerk; Benjamin Lambert clerk, Josephine FIELD, sale clerk; Aaron KIDDER, claim

Lewis REDDING
vs   **Partition of Real Estate**
Josiah REDDING, adult,
Sarah REDDING, now Sarah, COWAN,
James COWAN, Jacob FOGLE & wife
Susannah FOGLE, formerly Susannah REDDING,
Alfred & David REDDING, & Aaron V. REDDING,
infant heirs of **John REDDING**

Book & Page	CPR: 571-574
Court Dates	9 Nov 1846, 8 Feb 1847
Heirs	Widow Nancy REDDING, infant heirs, Alfred, David, & Aaron V. REDDING; adult heirs Sarah REDDING, now COWAN, and husband James COWAN, Jacob FOGLE and wife Susannah REDDING FOGLE, and Josiah REDDING
Action	27 Oct 1846, Lewis REDDING files a petition for Partition of Real Estate with the clerk of the court. He is the son of deceased John REDDING who died intestate about 17 Oct 1836. Deceased owned tracts of land in township 37, of 40 acres, and also another 40 acres (description within). His heirs number seven children, and a widow. He states the widow is entitled to a Dower and requests that commissioners be appointed to divide the real estate and that heirs be made defendants to this petition for Partition of the Real Estate, and also that a summons be issued to all parties to appear in court.

Court appoints a Guardian for the minor heirs of the estate. Adult heirs agree the widow is entitled to her Dower from the estate and she is allowed 40 acres (description within) which will also go the minor surviving heirs. Court also allows the balance of the remaining real estate be divided among the adult heirs (description within).

On 10 Feb 1847 the commissioners presented their division of the real estate and it is approved by the court.

Incidental Names	Samuel E. WILLIAMS, Guardian; James C. BARNARD, Ziba PARMER, John MASON, commissioners

Jeremiah PLATT, deceased   **Estate**

Book & Page   CPR: 575-578

Court Dates   12 Nov 1838 10 Feb 1840, 8 Nov 1841, 14 Feb 1842, 9 May 1842, 10 Nov 1845, 9 Feb 1846, 9 Nov 1846, 8 Feb 1847, 10 May 1847

Administrator   Joseph WINCH

Action   On 25 Oct, 1838, Letters of Administration granted to WINCH by clerk of the court during Court Vacation. PLATT died intestate in Michigan City Township. On 6 Nov 1838, WINCH filed an inventory of the personal property of the estate with the Clerk of the Court (description within) amounting to $154.50. Inventory taken on 31 Oct, 1838. Court confirms WINCH'S appointment as Administrator.

On 22 Dec 1838, Administrator files with the clerk of the Probate Court the sale bill of the personal estate which was sold at auction on 15 Dec 1838. (description within) amounting to $35.86.

Court orders Administrator to appear in Court. Administrator once again ordered to appear in Court. Administrator not prepared to make settlement. Cause continued.

Administrator appears in court and requests further time to present estate settlement. Court grants his request. Court orders Administrator to appear in court. Administrator appears in court and presents a settlement of the estate. The amount of the sale bill came to $544.99 with notes collected (description within). Administrator has in hand a balance of $32.00. Court orders vouchers for expenses and credits presented at next court session.

Again court orders appearance of Administrator. Administrator still unprepared to make final settlement. Cause continued.

Administrator pays clerk of court fees and disbursements of the estate. Court discharges Administrator.

Incidental Names   James M. SCOTT, bond , appraiser; Samuel SCOTT, appraiser; William W. HIGGINS, clerk

---

James HUNT, deceased   **Estate**

Book &Page   CPR: 579-581

Court Dates   11 Feb 1839, 14 Nov 1842, 13 Feb 1843, 8 Feb 1847, 10 Nov 1847

Executors   Nancy HUNT, Jasper S. HUNT, Charles W. HUNT

Heirs   Nancy HUNT, widow, Jasper S, Charles W. David M., and Jonathan S. HUNT, sons; Francine, Phoebe, and Polly HUNT, daughters

Action   On 7 Feb 1839, the last will and testament of James HUNT of LaPorte County was filed in the clerk's office while court was "in vacation".

To wit:" I, James HUNT of LaPorte County and state of Indiana being weak in body but of sound mind and memory calling to mind the mortality of my body knowing it is appointed for all men to die do make this my last will and testament viz (sic). Then principally and first of all I would commit my soul to the hand of God who gave it and my body to be decently buried at the discretion of my executors and friends–and as touching such earthly estate wherewith it has pleased God to bless me in this life I devise and dispose of it in the following manner and form-having given to some of my children–their equal Portions namely Francine–Jasper and Charles W. David M. and Jonathan S also have received their Portions of the Real Estate but not their outfit–I leave to my beloved wife Nancy during her life the farm on which I live viz (sic) the W half of NE quarter of section 23 in township 37N in 2 W and the W half of the SE quarter of Section 23 Township and Range aforesaid–and also all the Land I pyseys (sic) in section 9 in Range one W Township afores (sic)-together with all my personal property for her comfortable maintenance and maintenance of the family and for outfits to share of my children who have not had their share of Personal Property–hereby giving to my said wife ample power to act at discretion always keeping in view–that is my will that my children all have equal shares–and in all matters of Interest she will advise with my other executors herein after named–I give to my Daughters Phebe(sic) two hundred Dollars to (be) levied out of Estate by my Executors. I give to my Daughter Polly two Hundred Dollars. Levied as above–I give to my Two youngest sons James and John M. after the death of my wife Nancy all and entire the three lots of land above described jointly and equally to them and their heirs forever I give it–and I hereby enjoin on my Executers to execute good deeds to my youngest sons above named thereafter–And it is moreover my will that if at any time my wife or either of my children become infirm and get into Suffering circumstances that my Executors make provisions for them out of my estate still keeping in view equality among my heirs–And lastly I constitute and appoint my beloved wife Nancy Executor with my sons Jasper S. and Charles M. Executers of this my last will and testament hereby revoking and annulling all former wills by me heretofore made ratifying this and no other to be my last will and testament. In Witness whereof I have hereunto set my hand and seal this 19th day of April 1838" (signed) James HUNT (sig (sic) Sealed and Delivered in presence of George HUNT and N.B. NICHOLS–State of Indiana LaPorte County. Be it remembered that on this 7th day of February AD 1839.

Court confirms appointment of Executors and orders final settlement made at next court session.

Court approves payment by Executors of $200 each to Polly HUNT WAGNER and Phoebe -----, late HUNT by Executors. Cause continued.

Court orders appearance of Executors at next court session to file an Inventory and exhibit of the estate. Jasper HUNT, Executor, requests a continuance. Court grants request. Jasper HUNT again states that the Executors are still unprepared to make settlement of the estate. Court grants another continuance.

Jasper HUNT files vouchers and receipts. No inventory of the "outfits of the personal property" were submitted by the Executors. Court satisfied with the report of the Executors and discharges them.

Incidental Names   George HUNT, bond

Lydia VANDEVANTER   Estate

Book & Page   CPR: 581-585

Court Dates   10 Aug 1846, 10 May 1847

Administrator   Jesse WAYSON

Heirs   Constantine LOMAX, Peter and John VANDEVATER, William and wife Sarah LOMAX, Andrew MOLTER and wife Paterace, Isaac VANDEVETER

Action   Lydia VANDEVANTER died intestate. John F. VANDEVANTER was the late husband of Lydia. LOMAX files for Letters of Administration with the clerk of the court on 1 July 1846.

On 8 Aug 1846, WAYSON files the inventory of the estate with clerk of the court (description within). Court approves Letters of Administrator for WAYSON. Administrator files an account of the affairs of the estate. Amount of inventory was $417.62. An account of an agreement with interest and a note were given to the Court (description within). Credits of administrator are also presented to the court as well as the funeral expenses. A balance of $431.22 remains in the estate. Court approves the settlement and discharges the Administrator.

Peter and John VANDEVANTER relinquish all claims to the estate on 2 Feb 1847 ($100).

William LOMAX and wife Sarah also legal heirs of the estate likewise relinquish claim to the estate on 3 March 1847.

Andrew MOLTER and wife Paterace, also heirs to the estate convey and relinquish rights to the estate on 10 April 1847 and receive $100.

On 14 April 1847, Joseph AMES and Constantine LOMAX received $357.56 as their dividend of the estate.

On 3 April 1847 Isaac VANDEVANTER of Berrien MI received $50 and relinquished his claim to the estate.

Comments   Names were given to the court by Constantine LOMAX. There was no indication in the record of the relationship existing between the LOMAXES and VANDEVANTERS.

Allan W. REYNOLDS, deceased   Estate

Book & Page   CPR: 585-588

Court Dates   9 Nov 1846, 10 May 1847

Administrator	Harriet M. REYNOLDS, widow
Action	On 24 Aug 1846 Harriet M. REYNOLDS, widow of deceased, filed a petition for Letters of Administration with the Clerk of the Court while court was "In Vacation". Allen REYNOLDS died intestate.
	Court confirms her petition and orders an appraisement of the personal estate of deceased.
	On 12 Sept 1846, appraisers file their report with the Clerk of the court (description within). Appraisement amounted to $145.41. Another appraisement was filed with the Clerk of the Court amounting to $16.68 (description within).
	On 24 Nov 1846, Administrator files a sale bill with the Clerk of the Court which included a sale bill for the undivided half of 2/3 of about 20 acres of wheat which was sold for $30.50 and secured by a note.
	Administrator files exhibit of affairs of the estate. Sale bill amounted to $172.47. She claims credit for $173.55 with vouchers (description within). Court approves her account and discharges her as Administrator.
Incidental Names	Ranselaer SHAW, bond; Abiel LATHROP, Pierserved WHEELER, appraisers; R. SHAW, J.P.; David WINCHELL, James G. WINCHELL, appraisers; C.W. BARBER, purchased wheat; Thomas ELLSWORTH clerk of the sale.

James MACADO/MACADOO   Estate

Book & Page	CPR: 588-592
Court Dates	15 Nov 1844, 8 Feb 1847
Administrator	William GOODHUE
Heirs	Nancy C. MACADOO, widow, John & Mary Jane MACADOO, son & daughter
Action	On 15 Feb, 1844, Widow files her renunciation as Administrator in M City in favor of William GOODHEW with the Clerk of the Court. MACADOO died intestate. Court orders Administrator to appear at next court session to present an inventory of the estate and an exhibit of the affairs of the estate. Citation to appear issued on 26 Dec 1846.
	Administrator appears in court and files an exhibit and report on the estate. The deceased was in the mercantile business with Samuel OSBORN, New York City, and the business was in Michigan City. On 24 Jan 1844, OSBORN came into possession of the assets of the business and continued to act until 3 July 1844. An inventory was then taken of the business, notes, bills, and goods and cash on hand was noted. Goods came to $9016,85 (description within).
	Administrator purchased from Osborn the deceased's interest in the business and entered into co-partnership with the widow of the deceased,

and also acted as a Guardian to her son and daughter. Widow's interest in business remained until 3 July 1848.

On 11 Feb 1847, Administrator GOODHUE filed a statement with the clerk of the court that OSBORN agreed to pay the Eastern distribution of the concern, as well as the debts. GOODHUE paid the Western liabilities. GOODHUE transferred to widow MACADOO and her minor children $4,130.76 as their appraised interest in the business with OSBORN. Appraisal made of personal property of deceased (description within). Cause continued.

Administrator presents the exhibit of the estate. Personal property amounted to $109.95. He claims credits of $134.41, leaving a balance on hand of $24.46 (description within). Court approves this account and discharges the Administrator.

Incidental Names   Charles S. GOODHUE, witness; Jonathan BURR, Abram P. ANDREW, bond; Thompson W. FRANCIS, Oscar A. BARKER, appraisers; W.B. GURTINE, J.P.

Daniel JESSUP, deceased   **Estate**

Book & Page   CPR: 592-598

Court Dates   13 Nov 1843, 10 Nov 1845, 9 Feb 1846, 11 May 1846, 9 Aug 1847

Administrator   John and Irwin JESSUP

Heirs   Ann JESSUP, widow of deceased

Action   On 24 Oct, 1843, the widow of the deceased renounces her right as administrator to her two sons, John & Irwin JESSUP. The deceased died on 28 Aug, 1843. The two Administrators file their petition for Letters of Administration. They state that the estate of deceased would probably not exceed $1,200 in a petition to the clerk of the court.

On 28 Oct 1843, Administrators file with the clerk of the court an inventory of the personal estate of deceased taken on 28 Oct 1843.

Court confirms appointment of Administrators and filings made with the clerk of the court.

On 7 Oct 1844, Administrators file a sale bill with the clerk of the court. A public auction of personal property was held on 9 Aug 1844 (description within).

Court cites Administrators to appear at next court session. Administrators file their report of the estate which came to $1,006.82 with a balance remaining to the estate of $592.00. They file their vouchers and credits. Court confirms their findings.

Administrators appear in court and file their claims against the estate of each of $225. Irwin JESSUP also files his claim for the same amount. Administrators appear again in court and present a final settlement of the estate. They present their last report of the estate (description within). Court confirms their report and Administrators are discharged by the court.

Incidental Names	Isaac CORLYS, bond, appraiser, & clerk of sale; David McKELLUPS, appraiser; Joseph HAYWOOD J.P.

Melissa STANTON   Guardianship

Book & Page	CPR: 599-600
Court Dates	10 Nov 1845, 10 May 1847, 9 Aug 1847
Guardian	Stephen HOLLOWAY and John STANTON appear in court and state that Melissa STANTON is insane. Court issues a writ to the Sheriff of LaPorte County for summons of a jury to inquire into the truth of this statement.

On 11 Nov 1845, the sheriff returns to court and states that the jury interviewed Melissa STANTON on this date and found her to be insane and incapable of taking care of herself. Court accepts the jury's verdict and appoints a Guardian for her. Court orders the care of Melissa STANTON be paid out of her estate.

The Guardian, WAYSON, makes his report. Cause continued for settlement.

Guardian appears in court and presents a report on the estate of Melissa STANTON: William TALBOT, cash received of $83; cash from sale of bedding was $21.53. Further claims amounting to $104.53 were also presented (description within). Vouchers and disbursements approved by the court. Guardian is discharged.

Incidental Names	Harrison F. HINKLEY, Sheriff; Jehiel WAYSON, bond; John STANTON, security
Jury Members	Mark ALLEN, E.B. STRONG, Wm. FRYE, E.S. ORGAN, Daniel FRYE, W.M. PATTERSON, Wm. BARKER, S. TIBBITS, John WALTON, James BLACK, Wm. H. CROOK, Wm BROWN

Nathaniel B. DOWNING   Estate

Book & Page	CPR: 601-602
Court Dates	10 Aug 1835
Administrator	Catherine DOWNING, Jonathan MIDDLETON
Action	On 27 June, 1835, Letters of Administration by the clerk of the court while court was 'in vacation".

Administrators file for revocation of the appointment due to a brother of the deceased appearing on the same day from Vermillion County IN and wishing to move the heirs and widow to that county to friends and relatives there. The deceased also had considerable property in Vermillion County IN. The brother also wished to move the goods and chattels (possessions remaining) to Vermillion County to dispose of in that county. The brother and widow settled all debts and demands of the deceased in LaPorte County and the estate being solvent the need for Administrators in LaPorte County is no longer necessary. Court grants the request. Administrators are discharged.

Incidental Names	Henry DAVIS, bond
Comment	"Brother" of the deceased who appeared in court is not named.

James WINCHELL, son of
John WINCHELL, dec'd   **Guardianship**

Book & Page	CPR: 602
Court Dates	13 Aug 1838, 10 Nov 1845, 9 Feb 1846
Guardian	David WINCHELL
Action	James WINCHELL appears in court and petitions to choose his Guardian. James is the son of John WINCHELL of LaPorte County, deceased. James is "about 14". Court grants petition. David WINCHELL is chosen by James as his Guardian and appears in court. Court grants Letters of Guardianship to David WINCHELL. Court orders David WINCHELL to appear at next court session and file an inventory of the estate of his ward.
	Guardian appears in court and reports no assets came into the hands of his ward. His only duty as Guardian was to make a deed of the real estate. James WINCHELL is now of age and no longer requires a Guardian. David WINCHELL is discharged.

Simon RITTER, deceased   **Estate**

Book & Page	CPR: 603-604
Court Dates	11 Feb 1839, 12 Aug 1839, 10 Feb 1840
Administrator	Peter RITTER
Heirs	Widow Pamela RITTER, children John RITTER, Susan RITTER ASHTON, & husband Galitan ASHTON
Action	On 19 Jan 1839, Peter RITTER filed the petition for relinquishment of the widow Pamela RITTER's right as Administrator of her husband's estate. Her husband died intestate. The widow requests Peter RITTER be appointed as Administrator. Petition filed in Michigan City with the clerk of the court.
	LaPorte court confirms the granting of Letters of Administration to Peter RITTER. Court orders Administrator to file the inventory and sale bill of the estate at next term of the court.
	Court again orders RITTER to appear in court to make final settlement of the estate.

On 190 Aug 1840, Administrator files with the clerk of the court a sale bill of the personal property of the deceased. A public auction was held at the home of the deceased on 30 March 1839 (description within) amounting to $158.70.

On 10 Aug 1840, Administrator filed a final settlement of the estate, leaving in the hands of the estate $202.05. As Administrator is an heir, he retains the balance remaining. Two heirs are given $38.50 each (description within).

Incidental Names   James SCOTT, bond; John McCORMICK, clerk; W.W. HIGGINS., J.P.

Timothy FOSDICK	Estate

Book & Page   CPR: 605-610

Court Dates   9 Nov 1835, 14 Aug 1837, 12 Feb 1838, 8 Nov 1847

Administrator   Robert S. MORRISON, William CLARK

Heirs   Martha FOSDICK, widow, John, James & Mary FOSDICK (minor heirs under 14 yrs.)

Action   On 1 Oct 1835, Letters of Administration granted to MORRISON & CLARK by the clerk of the court for the estate of the deceased. Court confirms the appointments.

On 11 March 1837, the "surviving" Administrator, CLARK, files in the clerk's office the appraisal and inventory of estate. Appraisal and inventory taken on 23 Oct 1835 (description within). A sale bill also is filed totaling $101.27 (description within).

Widow appears in court and relinquishes her right to her Dower and land belonging to her husband, and requests that any remaining land, over and above the amount necessary to pay the debts of the estate, go to the use and benefit of the heirs of the estate. Administrator filed petition for the sale of the land on 8 May 1837 which contained 2 lots in LaPorte County of 20 acres each in township 37 (description of land within). He stated that the proceeds from the sale of the personal property of the deceased is insufficient to pay the debts of the estate. He requests the court summon the widow and heirs to appear in court to show why the land should not be sold. Appraisers claim the land could be sold for $600.

CLARK is appointed Guardian of the minor heirs. Court orders sale of the land on 25 Sept 1837 at public sale, after public advertisement is made for 20 days. Administrator reports sale of land for $3 per acre, which totaled $360. Court confirms sale and orders a title bond issued to the purchaser.

Administrator files his exhibit of the estate with debts owed, amounting to $;536.90 and accounts due, totaling $205.94 (description within). Court approves his report and discharges the Administrator on 9 Feb 1848.

Incidental Names   James WHITTEN, bond; Aaron STANTON, John H. BRADLEY, appraisers; G.B. WOODSON, J.P.; James WHITTEN, purchased land; Robert S. MORRISON, Aaron STANTON, title bond

Comments	No mention made of why CLARK is the "Surviving Administrator"

Joseph STRICKLAND   Estate

Book & Page	CPR: 610-614
Court Dates	11 Nov 1844, 10 Feb 1845, 8 Nov 1847
Administrator	Dorick BRINKERHOF
Action	On 23 Aug 1844, BRINKERHOF files Letters of Administration with the clerk of the court for the estate of Joseph STRICKLAND who died intestate in LaPorte County, on or about 17 July 1844 and formerly resided in the state of New York. He has no relatives in Indiana that the Administrator knows of. The deceased left property in "said" county. Property is reportedly worth $150-$200.
	Court confirms Letters of Administration for BRINKERHOF.
	On 14 Nov 1844, Administrator files an inventory and appraisal of the estate taken on 27 Sept 1844 with the clerk of the court (description within). BRINKERHOF then resigns as Administrator. He is ordered to turn over all necessary paper and report of the estate to his successor.
	On 2 Dec 1844, BRINKERHOF hands over all estate reports and papers for his successor, Jacob MILLER, to the clerk of the court. MILLER'S petition as Administrator is also filed.
	Court confirms MILLER'S appointment as Administrator.
	On 13 May 1845, MILLER files an inventory and appraisement of the estate (description within). A sale bill is also filed (description within). A sale bill is also filed (description within). An account of expenditures and notes are also presented to the court. Court approves Administrator's account and is then given a short list of notes outstanding, but uncollectible (description within). Administrator is discharged by the court.
Incidental Names	Samuel GRIFFIN, bond; John WHITTEN, appraiser; James W. TEEPLE, bond
Comment	Judge of the LaPorte Circuit Court, C.W. BROWN, acted as clerk of the estate sale and as appraiser.

Anna EGBERT, widow of
John EGBERT, dec'd, Charles
EGBERT, Wesley EGBERT   **In Chancery**
Alfred EGBERT,
Courtland EGBERT
& Clarissa EGBERT REYNOLDS
& John REYNOLDS

Book & Page	CPR: 616-619
Court Dates	24 July 1846, 8 Feb 1847, 10 May 1847, 8 Nov 1847

Action	William HAWKINS, complainant, represented by his attorneys, files his complaint in the clerk's office. The attorney claims that John EGBERT, of St. Joseph County Indiana, on Jan of 1842 took for himself and his heirs real estate, lot #8, and the south half of lot #9 in the original survey of the town of LaPorte. John EGBERT, anxious to dispose of the properties, entered into agreement with William HAWKINS and Andrew QUINN for the sale to them of the properties for $100. On 21 of Jan 1842, EGBERT legally bound himself to a bond for the properties with the condition that if he did not make payment within 2 years at the interest rate of 10%, the bond and warranty would be void. On the 17 Jan 1844, QUINN sold and assigned HAWKINS his interest and purchase of the bond and wrote on the back of the bond his intentions to reassign his interest in this warranty and bond to HAWKINS. He also requested that the deed be made to HAWKINS. The attorney further states not long after this was done, John EGBERT "departed this life" without conveying to HAWKINS his interest in the bond. John EGBERT is survived by his wife, Anna and five children. The full payment has been made but the widow and heirs have refused to respond by signing off on this bond. The attorney asks the court to order the widow and heirs of John EGBERT to appear in court. Court orders two subpoenas issued to the Sheriff of Marshall County Indiana and St. Joseph County Indiana for the appearance of EGBERT'S widow and heirs in court. Returns of the subpoenas appeared in court on 27 July 1846. The widow and heirs are not to be found in either county. Court orders publication of the complaint in the LaPorte County Whig newspaper for 3 weeks. Cause continued.
	Attorney for HAWKINS asks for a continuance of the publication of notification. Court grants the continuance.
	Court notified that notice was given to Charles, Alfred, and Clarissa EGBERT, and her husband. Cause continued.
	Heirs do not appear in court. Court given information that Charles EGBERT is insane. Court appoints a Guardian of the minor EGBERT heirs, Anna, Wesley, Charles, Alfred, Courtland, and Clarissa EGBERT. Guardian files a bill with the heirs response to the complaint, stating they are ignorant of the matter. Court holds a hearing on the matter and hears Sarah Maria GROOMS. Court finds the complaint to be true and appoints a commissioner to deliver a deed to the properties to the complainant, HAWKINS.
	Commissioner appears in court and makes a report of the deed and on 12 Nov 1847 in open court, the deed is read and then assigned to HAWKINS.
Incidental Names	NILES & OSBORN, attorneys; Joseph EVANS, sheriff; Lot DAY, Junior Deputy Sheriff; Gilbert HATHAWAY, Commissioner, Guardian
Comment	There is no mention made of exactly who the Sarah Maria GROOMS is who testified at the court hearing, and William HAWKINS, the complainant, is the acting clerk of the LaPorte County Court.

Alexander STARRETT   **Estate**

Book & Page   CPR: 619-623

Court Dates   14 Feb 1842

Administrator   Theresa STARRETT, widow, & Joseph STARRETT, brother

Action   On 31 Jan 1842, the widow and brother of the deceased filed Letters of Administration in the Clerk's Office. Alexander STARRETT died intestate. Administrators claim the estate would not exceed $500.

Court confirms the appointment and an inventory and appraisal of the personal property is presented to the court (description within). Inventory taken on 4 Feb 1842. Sale held on 7 May 1842.

Court orders appearance of administrators to present a final settlement of the estate. Joseph STARRETT appears and the Estate Inventory comes to $462.93. Expenditures (description within) amounted to $340.71. STARRETT reports that he delivered $100 to the widow of the deceased from the sale of personal property. The amount of $62, for personal property bought at the sale is still due the estate. He produces vouchers for expenses of $74.36 and pays into court $39.88 for the benefit of the heirs of the estate (description within). Court agrees with his account and discharges the Administrator.

Incidental Names   Benjamin SHAW, bond; Martin HOUSEMAN, Moses MOULTON, appraisers; John F. ALLISON, clerk of sale.

Comment   Sale of the personal property of the estate was held at "Banker's Hall", location unknown.

Ephraim BOICE   **Partition & Assignment of Dower**
        vs
Ann Eliza SHOP,Peter SHOP,
William H. BOICE & John M. BOICE,
& Elizabeth BOICE, widow of
John J. BOICE. dec'd

Book & Page   623-627

Court Dates   8 Nov 1847, 14 Feb 1848

Heirs   William & John BOICE, minor heirs, widow Elizabeth BOICE, Ann Elizabeth SHOP & husband, Peter SHOP, Ephraim BOICE

Action   On 25 Oct 1847, Ephraim BOICE filed a petition for Partition in the clerk's office. His father, John BOICE died intestate in LaPorte County, owning real estate in township 37 (description within). The deceased also left four children, two of which are minors; William and John. Their mother, Elizabeth is entitled to a widow's Dower and he requests the land be partitioned to allow the widow her portion of the land. He also requests the heirs be summoned to court and a Guardian appointed for the minor heirs.

He further requests that the land be divided to give the married daughter a portion. of the property.

Summons reported delivered to all heirs on 26 Oct 1847. Elizabeth and Peter SHOP do not appear in court and make default. Court decrees the land be divided allowing Elizabeth SHOP and her husband's portion set off together with the widow's portion. Court appoints commissioners to divide the land. Commissioners present to court their division of the properties of the deceased. Sixty acres were apportioned to the widow (description within); 13 acres plus 11 acres and another 20 acres to Ephraim BOICE, minor (description within); and William BOICE, a minor, received 26 acres plus 11 acres and another 45 acres (description within). The tracts assigned to Elizabeth SHOP and husband were mistakenly omitted – she received 46 acres (description within).

The court confirms the findings of the commissioners and orders costs for the division of lands be paid by the parties involved.

Incidental Names	M.H. ORTON, attorney; John B. NILES, Guardian; Elam CLARK, Willard A. PLACE, and Samuel TREAT, commissioners
Comments	A diagram of the property sections divided and labeled with the names of each "signee" appears on the last page of the court proceedings (Page 627).

Rebecca WILLIS, widow of
David Pagan, dec'd   **Assignment of Dower**
          vs
Mary E. PAGAN

Book and Page	CPR: 628-629
Court Dates	9 Aug 1847, 8 Nov 1847, 14 Feb 1848
Heirs	Mary Elizabeth PAGAN, minor, widow Rebecca PAGAN WILLIS
Action	Rebecca PAGAN WILLIS. widow of David PAGAN appears in court with her attorney and files her assignment of a Widow's Dower. David PAGAN died "about" the 29th July 1844, leaving a widow and one child, Mary Elizabeth PAGAN, minor. The deceased held 46 acres of land in township 37 (description within). This land also contained a mill, and a section of this property also contained 166 acres. The attorney requests commissioners be appointed to assign the widow her dower. Cause continued.

Summons for minor heir served on 9 Sept 1847. Court appoints a Guardian for the minor heir. The minor heir appears in court. Court appoints commissioners for division of properties and 46 acres allotted to the widow in township 37 (description within). Cause continued

Commissioners appear in court and present their findings. Widow receives her 1/3 of the properties, but the machinery, etc of the mill are excepted. Court approves of the assignment to the widow and the widow pays the cost of the division of property.

Incidental Names	M.K. FARRAND, Esq, attorney; J.S. McDOWELL, Sheriff, and Guardian; Lemuel FITCH, George FOSDICK, & Daniel M. LEAMING, commissioners

Michael BRAND, an Indian
proves heirship
of **NESHEWAH/MISHEWA**   **Heirship of Land**

Book & Page	PCR: 630
Court Dates	10 Nov 1834
Action	To Wit: "On motion of Michael BRAND it is ordered by the court to be certified on the record that from the Deposition taken by H.F. JANES, an acting Justice of the Peace within and for LaPorte County, State of Indiana pursuant to the Statute in such case made and provided it appears to the satisfaction of the court MISHEWAH or NESHEWA an Indian Girl under the age of eighteen years was by the Treaty of 1826 entitled one gr Sec of land - that since the ratification of said treaty said claim was located in LaPorte County, State of Indiana that said MISHEWAH has since died while a minor under the age of eighteen years. That NEGONCONE is the reported father of said MISHEWAH that said NEGONCONE is still living and that he the said NEGONCONE is the sole heir at law of the said MESHEWAH according to the Statute regulating the __?__ of Real Estate in the state of Indiana. Witness George THOMAS. (S PC ? The following is the Deposition - State of Indiana LaPorte County – this day personally appeared before the subscribing Justice of the Peace Celia (sp) Emmons who being by me duly sworn deposeth and saith that she was a "Schollar"(sic) at the Cary Mission and that an Indian Girl named NISHEWA who was also a "schollar' and whose one quarter section of land was reserved at the Treaty of 1826 which said quarter Section of land has since been located agreeable to the Treaty aforesaid the said land being in the County of LaPorte and state of Indiana and further says that the aforesaid NESHEWAH died in her presence and before the said NESHEWAH had arrived to the Statue or age of a Woman and was under the age of eighteen at the time of her death and this defendant further says that NEGONCONE has never been recognized as the father of said Girl and that at the time of the death of the said NESHEWAH there could not have been any other Legitimate heir except that of her father and further this defendant saith not "(signed) Cecelia (sic) EMMONS- Sworn to and subscribed this 9th day of Nov in the year of our Lord 1834 before me H.F. JANES, Justice of the Peace.

See Page 632 for one other Deposition in this case.

Brought from Page 630, "NEGONCOME & MISHEWAH personally appeared before me the undersigned one of the female of lawful age and about one half white and the other of the "Pottowatame"(sic) tribe of the Indian but "am intelegent" (sic) woman having been educated at the Cary Mission speaks the English language. Well who being by me duly sworn agreeable to the Laws of this state and upon her oath declares that |

MISHEWAH to whom it appears was -----? in the Treaty of Eighteen hundred and twenty six as since located agreeable to said Treaty one quarter Section of land lying and being in the county and state of and that the said MIN SHE WAH deceased in her presence and before the said MUSHEWAH was Grown to the size of a woman and that she was under the age of Eighteen years and this defendant further says that NE GON CO ME has ever been recognized the Father of said Girl and that at the time of the decease (sic) of the said MUSHEWAH there could not have been any other legitimate heir except that of her father and further this defendant saith not" (signed) Prudence FULLER -Sworn to and subscribed this 14th day of July in the year of our Lord 1834-H.F. JANES, Justice of the Peace".

Comments   While some Indian names were difficult to decipher, others were not, but the spelling frequently varied within the document.

St. Antonee La frombid &
Globe La frombid/Fromboire   **Heirship of Land**

Book & Page   CPR: 630-631

Court Dates   12 Nov 1834

Action   On motion of William C. HANNAH, Esq. it is ordered to be certified on the record that from the Deposition of Prudence FULLER of Lawful age taken by H.F. JANES an acting Justice of the Peace within & for LaPorte County State of Indiana pursuant to the Statute in such case made and provided it appears to the satisfaction of the Court that St. Antonee (sic) LAFROMBRIA (sic)) was entitled to one gr of Section of land reserved to him by the Treaty of 1826. That since the ratification of said Treaty said claim was Located on the South East gr of Sec .No 1 in Town N 37 North of Range West the same being in LaPorte County State of Indiana that said St. Antonie has since died while a minor under the age of twenty one years. That Globe La FROMBOIRE (sic) is the reputed father of said St. Antonie (sic) that the said Globe is still living and that he is the sole heir at Law of the Said St. Antoine according to the Statute regulating the ---?-of Real Estate in the State of Indiana. Witness George THOMAS C.S. P.C. The following is the Deposition –State of Indiana LaPorte County. This day personally appeared before the Subscribing Justice of the Peace Prudence FULLER who being of lawful age and duly sworn deposeth and saith that she was Scholar (sp) at the Carey (sp) Mission and that she was personally acquainted with ST. Antonie (sic) who was also a Schollar at the Mission aforesaid and that the said St. Antowine (sic) died at the Mission aforesaid and that the St.Antewine (sic) entitled to one quarter section of Land which was reserved to him the said St. Antowine (sic) at the Treaty of 1826 began and held on the Wabash River which Treaty has since been ratified by the President & Senate of the United State – of America and the said St. Antewine (sic) reserve was Located on the South East gr. of Section one Town thirty Seven N of Range two West it being in LaPorte County and State of Indiana and that the said St. Antownie(sic) was under the age of twenty one years at the time of his decease and that Globe LA FROM

BAIG) (sic) and further this defendant saith not (signed) Prudence FULLER Sworn and subscribed before me this 12th day of Nov AD 1834, H.F. JANES Justice of the Peace".

Comments   Notation made after this entry: "See OBA Probate Record". While some spelling of the Indian names were difficult to read, others were not, but their spellings still varied, from case to case.

WESAW WE, Indian   Proof of Heirship & Title to Land

Book & Page   CPR: 631-632

Court Dates   11 May 1838

Action   "On motion of John B. NILES, Esq. It is ordered by the court to be certified on the Record that from the deposition of Prudence FULLER & Celicia EMMONS of Lawful age taken by Henry F. JANES an acting Justice of the Peace within and for LaPorte County State of Indiana Pursuant to the Statute in such case made and provided it appears to the satisfaction of the Court that WE SAW We an Indian Boy was a Schollar (sic) at the Cary Mission School in the years 1823-4-& 5 and that there was a Quarter Section of land reserved to the said WE SAW WE at the Wabash Treaty of 1826. That the said WE SAW WE has since Died. That his father is dead and that SHIK KOG WISH SHE QUA (sic) is the Mother and MIX NA CHE QUAS MO QUA WA (sic) are the sisters of the said deceased WE SAW WE and that they are the only surviving members of the family Attest Wm. HAWKINS Clk (the following is the Deposition) State of Indiana LaPorte County SS. Be it remembered that on the 20th day of February AD 1835–personally appeared before me Henry F. JANES a Justice of the Peace of said County Prudence FULLER and Cilicia EMMONS of Lawful age who being by me duly sworn depose & Say that they were both Schollars (sic) at the Carey Mission School in the years 1828-4 & 5 and that there was also an Indian boy by the name of WE SAW WE at said school at the same time who has since departed this life and to whom a quarter section of land was reserved at the Wabash Treaty of 1826. They further depose and say that (they) have been well acquainted with all the family connections of the said WE SAW WE that his father is dead and that SHIK KOG WISH SHE QUO (sic) the Mother and that MIX MAH CHE QUASMO QUA (sic) and WA WAS MO QUA (sic) are the Sisters of the said deceased WE SAW WE and that they are the only surviving members of the family –And further these deponents (sic) say not" (Signed) Prudence FULLER Cilicia EMMONS Sworn and Subscribed to before me this 20th day of February AD 1835 Henry F. JANES, justice of the Peace".

State of Indiana Sct LaPorte County

"Before me N.B. NICHOLS a Justice of the Peace of the County aforesaid– This day personally came Cilica EMMONS & Prudence FULLER who being by me duly sworn saith that the South East Quarter of Section twelve in Section thirty Seven North of Range two West in the State of Indiana was reserved to WAS SE WE by the Treaty and that they was well acquainted (with) his father at the Carey Mission and of the death of his father WE SA WE died there the above mentioned. Land fell to ME SA KISH QUA WO WAS MOQUA and GUAS MO QUO and ME MO CHE to which we are well acquainted with them all and know them to be the only right owners of heirship to the aforesaid lands WE SAW WE was a scholar at the Cary Mission at the time of the Treaty when the land was donated to him who since has died." Witness our hands & seals this 23rd day of June 1835 (Signed) Prudence FULLER Celicia EMMONS Given under my Justice of the Peace.

Daniel BALDWIN	**Estate**
Book & Page	PCR: 633-634
Court Dates	10 Nov 1834
Action	"Be it remembered that on the fifteenth day of September in the year of our Lord One Thousand Eighteen and thirty Four The last Will and Testament of Daniel BALDWIN was filed in the Clerk's office of said county and duly proved by Zenos PRESTIN Daniel MULKS & Geo W. BARNES three of the subscribing witnesses thereto who being duly sworn upon their oath say that they saw said Daniel BALDWIN sign seal publish and declare said writing as his last will and testament and that they believe he was at the time of its execution of sound mind and memory and that they signed their names thereto in the presence of said testator and at his request–whereupon letters testamentary on the Estate of said BALDWIN was by me granted to Joel A.BALDWIN the Executor by said Testator appointed who was by me duly sworn to the true and faithful discharge and performance of the duties and rusts committed to and required by heirs by law as such Executor and who with Zenos PRESTON in the sum of Eleven Hundred Dollars John RYSEL (?) Security entered into Bond, conditions for the faithful performance of the duties aforesaid according to Law as such case made and provided George THOMAS, clerk which said Will is in the words & figures following to wit: "I Daniel BALDWIN of LaPorte in the state of Indiana do make and publish this my last Will and Testament hereby revoking and making void all former Wills by me at any time heretofore made First I direct that my body be decently intered (sic)–and as to such worldly estate as it has pleased God to entrust me with I dispose of the same in the following manner to wit – I direct first that all my just debts and funeral expenses be paid as soon after my decease if possible out of the first money that shall come to the hands of Executors from any portion of my estate real or personal. I also direct that a fair valuation appraisement be made by three Indiana neighbors of all my said Estate including my household furniture–(except such articles as my daughter Rehda (?) shall claim as being the property of her own Mother deceased) and after being signed with their name that a copy of the same be given by them to each of my executors. I would also except such and all the property which I delivered over to my beloved wife in the State of New York where I left that of my said wife I also direct that my Estate real and personal be equally divided as soon as it can be done share and share alike amongst my seven

children or such of them as their heirs representing them as shall survive me. And this will provide that if either of my children shall desire my real Estate in the county as in Crawford County Pennsylvania state–they shall have it at the appraised as above named–and whatever it shall amount to more than their share they shall have the privilege of eight years to pay it in by paying simple interest yearly-this privilege granted to my sons first beginning with the oldest and if not accepted by either of them my daughters to have the same privilege beginning with the oldest–this same privilege to is granted with my personal Estate with the exception–that my daughter Rhoda shall have the first offer of my household furniture–I also direct that such of my property as shall not be reserved by the privilege above granted shall note) be sold by Executors for its reasonable value for cash or as such credit and the amount thereof secured in such manner as usual in like manner cares to issue the full and punctual payment thereof– And to effectuate this my intention I thereby vest my executor with full power and authority to dispose of my real estate in fee simple or for a term of years or otherwise in as full and ample a manner in every respect as I could myself do if living. And I further declare and direct that the share of my personal estate this bequeathed to my said wife shall be in lieu of her dower–And I further Direct that all notes and obligations now existing Executors by any of my children to me be given up to them without any reference to the selling of my Estate. And they are by this declared null and void and I hereby make and ordain my son in law Simon BURTON & Son Joel A. BALDWIN Executors of this my last will and testament and my son Joel A. BALDWIN to be the Guardian and to and to act as such for any of my children that I shall leave in their minority. In witness thereof I Daniel BALDWIN the testator have hereunto set my hand and seal this twenty fifth day of June in the year of our Lord Eighteen hundred & Thirty four" (signed) Daniel BALDWIN S.S. as his last will and testament in the presence of us who have hereunto subscribed our names as witnessed thereto in the presence of the said testator subscribed our names as witnesses thereto in the presence of the said testator and in the presence of each other (signed) Zenos RESTON Daniel MULKS J W BARNES Sworn to before me this fifteenth day of September AD 1834 George THOMAS Clerk of Probate in the county of LaPorte Indiana–state of Indiana LaPorte county SS " I George THOMAS clerk of the Probate Court of said County do hereby certify that Zenas PRESTON Daniel MULKS & GW BARNES witnesses to the within will being by me duly sworn according to law made oath that they saw Daniel BALDWIN sign Seal publish and declare the– within writing as his last will and testament and they believe he was at the time of its Execution of sound mind and memory And that they signed their names thereto as witnesses in the presence of the said testator and at his request Sworn to before me on the 15th day of September AD 1834 In witness whereof hereunto set my hand" George THOMAS Clerk of the probate Court – S C.

Court confirms granting of letters of testamentary estate of Daniel BALDWIN while court was 'in vacation".

Comments	Clerk also noted that when the court confirmed this will, there was no court house within the county and that the judge and clerk met in the clerk's office.

"Old Cases November Term 1834" noted at bottom.

James Madison REEVE — Estate

Book & Page	CPR: 635-637
Court Dates	11 Feb 1833, 13 May 1833, 15 May 1833, 12 Aug 1833, 10 Nov 1834
Executor	Martin BAKER
Heirs	Catherine REEVES, Josiah REEVES, infant heirs
Action	On 8 Jan 1833, Martin BAKER filed a bond in Clerk's office. The deceased was from St. Joseph County Indiana but died in LaPorte County. BAKER appears in court to present an inventory of the personal estate of the deceased and to state if the estate is solvent or not. The Sheriff is ordered to issue a citation to BAKER to appear.
	BAKER appears in court and pleads that the publication in the St. Joseph Beacon newspaper is "not agreeable to Manuscript" that was filed in the office to be published and an error appears in the Inventory of the Legal Offices and he asks for a correction. Court grants his request.
	BAKER appears in court and files an appraisement of personal property amounting to $186.37 (description within). Baker again appears in court and files the sale bill (description within) as well as a final settlement amounting to $213.33. Court grants BAKER $411 as $574.33 was the amount stated by the commissioners. Administrator stands charged with $213.33 and is credited with $411.13 leaving a balance of $133.20 (description within of debits and credits of the estate).
Incidental Names	Martin BAKER, Guardian; Daniel MURRAY, Nathan B. NICHOLS, bond; Philip FAIL, David GRANT, witnesses to bond; Adam G. POLKE, Sheriff; John WILLS, John DRULESIS, appraisers; Israel H. RUSH, J.P. St. Joseph County; L.M. TAYLOR clerk St. Joseph Court, Ezekiel PROVOLT, J.P., LaPorte Co.
Comments	Court held at home of George THOMAS as there is no court house yet in La Porte County.

Josiah REEVES & Catherine REEVES heirs of James M. REEVES — Estate

Book & Page	CPR: 638-640
Court Dates	12 May 1834, 10 Nov 1834, 12 Nov 1834, 9 Nov 1835, 11 Nov 1835
Guardian	Martin BAKER

Heirs	Josiah & Catherine REEVES
Action	On 10 Feb 1834, BAKER filed a bond and is appointed Guardian of the heirs and the same day he files a petition for Sale of Real Estate of REEVES. The real estate contains 80 acres in township 38 (description within). He states that debts to the estate do not allow enough funds for support of the minor heirs and asks that the real estate be sold for the benefit of the heirs. Court appoints appraisers.

Appraisers make their report. The real estate is worth $300. Court orders commissioners appointed and the publication of sale is to be advertised in public places. There are to be 2 notices in the county of St. Joseph In, and 4 appearing in LaPorte County. Sale ordered to be held on 5 July next in LaPorte and the purchaser of the real estate is to pay ¼ down of sale amount.

Commissioners report sale for land for $360 and sale was held on 3 Aug 1834. A deed will be presented to the purchaser. Guardian presents a sale bill of $213.33. His expenses as Guardian amounted to $361. He has $574.33 on hand. After expenses as administrator and Guardian, there remains a credit of $163.20 due the estate.

BAKER is ordered to appear in court to give an account as Guardian and file additional security. BAKER appears in court and files for additional security as Guardian to the satisfaction of the court.

Incidental Names	Israel MARKHAM, Richard HARRIS, Nathaniel BAKER, bond; David EVANS, Chapel W. BROWN, & Charles IVES, appraisers; Ezekiel PROVOLT, JP;
	James HIGHLY, John CIJISNI, bond; Arthur McCLURE, commissioner; Charles EGBERT, bought real estate; Oren GOULD, bought real estate

---

Jeremiah GOULD, deceased	**Estate**
Book & Page	CPR: 641-644
Court Dates	13 May 1839, 12 Aug 1839, 11 Nov 1839, 10 Feb 1840
Administrator	John FRANCIS
Heirs	Helen GOULD, Theresa Ann GOULD, Llewellyn GOULD, Apria GOULD, and widow Anna C. GOULD
Action	On 16 Feb 1839 Anna C. GOULD, widow of deceased filed her renunciation as Administrator of her husband's estate with the Clerk of the court. Jeremiah GOULD died intestate.

Court confirms appointment of FRANCIS as Administrator files a report for the sale of real estate. There is on personal property from the estate but there is property belonging to the deceased which is lot #8 in block #19 with 60 ft frontage on Pine St and 165 ft frontage on Market St. with the building in Michigan City and appraised at $1,200. Debts to the estate are

$3,014.50. Administrator requests he be allowed to sell the property. Administrator also files an inventory and appraisal of the real estate.

The heirs are not residents of the state. Court orders notice of the filing be given by publication to the heirs in the Whig newspaper.

On 14 Aug 1839, Administrator files a petition for settlement of the estate as insolvent and states that the claims against the estate amount to $3,014.50. He further states that the estate is insolvent and requests he be allowed to notify the creditors of this. Court approves his request.

Court orders a public sale of the real estate, to be held on 4 Jan 1840 and notice of sale advertised in the local newspaper, the Michigan City Gazette. Administrator reports on sale of the real estate (complete description within). The property was sold for $1,082.32. Ingraham GOULD testifies he heard Jeremiah GOULD state Oren GOULD was indebted to Jeremiah for $3000.

Oren GOULD testifies he owes the notes but they were lost or destroyed and they have never been paid.

Incidental Names	Oscar H. BARKER, security; Willys PECK, Sidney BURKE, appraisers; Oren GOULD bought property; T. Tyrell MARTIN, witness; Rodney B. FIELD supplied white coffin for $10
Comments	It was noted that J.C. ELSTON was the original surveyor of the property. This marked the end of the case and no further testimony or court decisions were recorded.

Sans AUSTIN	Estate
Book & Page	CPR: 644-647
Court Dates	14 Nov 1842, 13 Feb 1843, 13 Nov 1843
Administrator	Henry TEETER
Heirs	Sarah AUSTIN
Action	On 12 Nov 1840, Sarah AUSTIN, widow of Sans AUSTIN files her renunciation as Administrator of her husband's estate. She requests her friend, Henry TEETER, be appointed in her place.

On 12 Nov 1840, Administrator files an inventory and appraisal of the estate with the Clerk of the court (description within) Appraisal amounted to $131.47.

On 1 Feb 1841, Administrator files an additional inventory with the Clerk of the court (description within).

On 8 Feb, 1841, Administrator files a sale bill of the personal estate of deceased with the Clerk of the court (description within). He states that the balance due to the widow is $36.23.

Court orders Administrator to appear in court at next court session. Administrator appears in court and states he is not prepared to make a final settlement yet. Cause continued.

Administrator in court and states there are insufficient funds to meet the debts of the estate and after deducting a sum for the widow, he has only $34.23 on hand. Debts against the estate amount to about $30. Expenses owed the Administrator will exceed that amount. He asks the court for notification to the creditors and to declare the estate insolvent. Court orders notification of creditors by publication in the LaPorte County Whig newspaper and declares the estate insolvent. Administrator discharged.

Incidental Names   Jedediah AUSTIN, security; Benjamin BREWER, James CATTERLIN, appraisers; Edwin JORDAN, clerk of sale; John BOWEL, J.P.; Edwin JORDAN, J.P.; Thomas STEWART, affidavit

---

Harriet BUNCE,   **Guardianship**
George L. BUNCE
& William BUNCE
heirs of **Simon G. BUNCE**

Book & Page   CPR: 648-651

Court Dates   11 May 1835, 9 Nov 1835, 8 Feb 1836, 9 May 1836

Guardians   Andrew BURNSIDE, Clarissa BUNCE TEEPLE

Action   BURNSIDE and Clarissa BUNCE TEEPLE petition the court to be appointed Guardians of the minor heirs. Court approves appointment. On the same date, the Guardian files a "memorial" stating that the deceased held an "out Lot" in the Town of LaPorte; Number 25, with valuable improvements and that the real estate is suffering "unavoidable waste and decay". They request the sale of the lot.

On 12 May 1835, appraisers appointed by the court present their report. The lot is valued at $400. Guardians files an additional bond. Commissioners appointed for sale of the lot. Court also orders publication of sale in public places in LaPorte and also that the purchaser give ¼ down in payment. A deed would be issued after final payment.

Guardians report that the sale was held on 25 July and the lot purchased for $425 but the purchaser failed to comply with the terms of the sale.

Guardians appear in court and ask that new appraisers be appointed for the lot. New appraisers present the court their report stating the lot is worth $400. Guardians file additional bond.

On 10 Feb 1836, the Guardians appear in court and the court appoints another commissioner. Again, court orders publication of sale with the same order of payment.

Commissioner makes his report to the court on the sale of the LaPorte lot. Sale held on 2 May 1836. James TEEPLE was the highest bidder and purchased the lot for $326. Court orders purchase monies given to the heirs and a deed issued to the purchaser.

Incidental Names	Adam G. POLKE, security & commissioner; Abraham W. HARRISON, William O. ROSS, appraisers; Robert MERRYFIELD, original lot purchaser; John STOON, Albert LUCAS, William ALLEN, appraisers; John BROWN, bond; Noah NEWELL, commissioner
Comments	Notation made that there is now a return from "delayed cases" to 1844 cases.

Sidney Mason
vs
Elwood Mason,
Elizabeth Mason,
Howard Mason &
Alice Anna Mason
Infant heirs of
Howard MASON, deceased

**Petition for Allowance and Support
& Maintenance of Heirs**

Book & Page	CPR: 651-653
Court Dates	12 Aug 1844
Action	On 18 May 1844, Sidney MASON'S attorney presents her petition to the clerk of the court. Howard MASON died intestate on the 15th of Aug 1838, leaving minor children under the age of 14 as heirs. Letters of Administration were granted to William CLARK and he has taken charge of the assets of the estate. The personal property valued at $441.90 and the real estate of the deceased was sold for $1,100. CLARK filed by request a statement that showed he yet owed the estate $227.39. Clark stated he paid this amount into court. The petition claims there is still due the estate about $250 over and above all debts due the estate. The attorney further states the minor heirs have been in the custody of the petitioner, Sydney MASON, for 5 years and 9 months and no Guardian has been appointed for them. The petitioner has paid, from time to time, certain bills and charges for the infant heirs, as well as room and board and school fees. He adds that the petitioner also has cultivated and cared for the estate of 30 acres at her own expense. He requests that $227.39 be paid her and that $250 be due her in this case. He requests the court order the Administrator to present evidence as to the debts of the estate. A report of petitioner's expenses regarding the heirs is submitted (description within), totaling $611.75.

A Guardian is appointed by the court and presents answers of minor heirs. Court finds that Sydney MASON should be awarded the sum of $238.50 for the cost of boarding, clothing, & schooling of minor heir, Elizabeth MASON. Court also allows a sum of $240.25 for the same cost for minor heir Howard MASON over and above the rent of the land. A further sum of $91.50 was allowed for expenses for heir Alice MASON, making a total of $683.50. Court orders petitioner to pay the costs of the proceedings. |
| Incidental Names | Samuel E. WILLIAMS, Esq., Guardian; Gilbert HATHAWAY, attorney |

George Bosserman   **Partition of Real Estate**
      vs
Stephen Toney, Davison Patten,
Caroline Bosserman, Allen Neff,
Jesse Neff, Abraham Neff,
Frances Neff, Jesse Deardorf,
Rebecca Deardorf & unnamed Deardorf
Estate of **Jesse TONEY**

Book & Page	CPR: 653-657
Court Dates	11 May 1846
Action	On 14 Jan 1846, the attorney for BOSSERMAN states that Jesse TONEY before his death (no date given), owned real estate, among the real estate were lots (description within) which were in township 36, with a dwelling. TONEY left 8 surviving children; 5 sons, 3 daughters: Jesse, Aaron, Sebert, Stephen, Allen, Susan, Frances, & Mary Jane TONEY. The attorney further states that on 22 June 1845, Allen TONEY, one of the sons, has died and was a tenant in common of 1/8 of the lots and on a date (not specified) bargained to sell the lot to Abraham FRAVEL. FRAVEL then, on 22nd of June 1845, sold the 1/8 portion of the lot to BOSSERMAN, the petitioner, which entitled BOSSERMAN to become a tenant of this portion of the lots. Sebert TONEY, one of the sons, in 1843 became bankrupt and his "assignee" in bankruptcy sold to Davison PATTON his 1/8 portion of the lots and PATTON is now also a "tenant" of the lots. Another son, Aaron TONEY, as well as brothers, Jesse and Stephen TONEY are also lot owners. Susan TONEY, a daughter, married Joseph NEFF but she died in 1835, leaving 4 children; 3 sons and 1 daughter; Allen, Jesse, and Abraham NEFF, and daughter Frances NEFF, thus they inherit their mother's 1/8 portion of the lots, to be divided into another 4 portions. Another daughter, Mary TONEY, intermarried with Peter DEARDORF, but she died in 1837, leaving 3 children; one son, Jesse, 1 daughter, Rebecca, and also one child, name unknown, and they are also inheritors of their mother's 1/8 portion of the lots. Frances TONEY, a daughter, married on the 28th Feb, 1838, but also died on 17 March 1842, leaving one daughter, Caroline, to inherit her mother's 1/8 portion of the lots. All surviving grandchildren are under the age of 21. The lots being free and clear of any mortgages or judgments, the attorney asks that the court fairly and impartially have the lots partitioned to each heir. He also requests that a Guardian be appointed for the minor heirs.

On 14 Jan 1846, the same day, Court is informed that Jesse & Aaron TONEY, & Jesse & Rebecca DEARDRUF are nonresidents of the state of Indiana. Attorney states they have been notified by publication of the partition of the lots and subpoenas have been issued for their appearance.

The heirs do not appear in court and make default.

The court considers all the evidence presented and orders the lot shares in township 36 (description within) be apportioned to the heirs according to their inherited shares; 1/8, 1/24, and 1/32, respectively. The petitioner

George BOSSERMAN, and daughter Caroline receive 1/8 shares each; Davison PATTEN receives 1/8 share; The DEARDRUFS receive 1/24 shares; the NEFFS, receive 1/32 shares; Stephen & Jesse TONEY receive 1/8 share. Court then appoints commissioners to appraise the lots for the heirs.

Incidental Names	John B., NILES, attorney;. A.L. OSBORN, Guardian; Glenn CLARK, Samuel STEWART, & Josiah W. WING, commissioners
Comments	Written at bottom of entry, "Carried to Book B, page 1"

La Porte County, Indiana, Probate "Loose Papers"

BUNCE, Simon G.

Location	Estate #6, Microfilm E1 (formerly box 1), first item on roll
Court Dates	January 1836 documents sworn to, 8 February 1836 account
Administrator	John MULKS, Clarissa BUNCE, "since Clarissa TEEPLE"
Signatures	John M. LEMON, Elisha NEWHALL, Jno. MULKS, Clarissa TEEPLE, W. H.? DINWIDDIE, Wm. VAN OSDAL, A. G. POLKE, William N. BALL, A. P. ANDREW, Dr. ST. CLAIR, Wm. HIGGINS, Henry BELDEN
Sale Buyers	October 1834: David DINWIDDIE, Clarissa BUNCE, Jesse MILLER, Daniel F. RATHBORNE, Albert LUCAS, William HIGGINS, Ward BLAKE, Henry P. VAIL, Granville HOLLAND, A. CASIDA, W. BUNCE, W. VANCE [?], J. JESSUP, C. H. BRONSON, John JESSUP, E. H. BROWN, TAILOR, Doctor ORTON
Comments	Dr. ST. CLAIR's bill of 5 August 1835 "for practicing Medicine in her Family up to this date" is headed "Kankakee"

AMBROSE, Ezekiel

Location	Estate #7, Microfilm E1 (formerly box 1), second item on roll
Administrator	Reason BELL, security Elisha NEWHALL $700 bond.
Heir	Mother Joannah AMBROWS
Actions	25 August 1834 (will made), 11 May 1835 (inventory)
Signatures	Ezekiel AMBROSE, John B. TAYLOR, Sherman WILSON, Theodore D. JONES, Sparry HOWARD, Jonathan MORGAN, Joseph REED, Isaac MORGAN, B. SALOR, Ch. W. CATHCART JP, William MORGAN, Jacob COLMAN?, Reason BELL, Elisha NEWHALL
Sale Buyers	29 November 1834: Jacob COLMAN, Reason BELL, Isaac MORGAN, John DAVIS, William MORGAN, John B. TAYLOR, Sperry HOWARD, Benjaman SAILOR, John DAVIS, C. RUSSELL, Russell C. BRATON, Charles CATHCART
Comment	Will: "My whool and in tire Estate after my Moveable property is sold for cash . . . to My Mother Joannah AMBROWS [in] England Cornwall County Red Ruth parish." If not living [words obscured] "My Nearest living Relatives."

THOMAS, George

Location	Estate #10, Microfilm E1 (formerly box 1), third item on roll
Court Dates	1837 petition to sell real estate, 14 February 1844 Pittsburgh claim settled
Administrator	William HAWKINS, Andrew BURNSIDE
Heirs	Widow Elizabeth THOMAS; adult heirs John F. and Elenor ("late Elenor THOMAS") HEWS or HUGHS, Willard N. and Nancy BALL, Charles and Mary EGBURT; and Adam POLKE guardian of "infant heirs" Raymond THOMAS, Ruth Jane THOMAS, and Joel THOMAS.
Actions	Auction 20 April 1835, final payment 13 August 1846
Signatures	Willard N. BALL, William HAWKINS, Andrew BURNSIDE, William ALLEN, Roberts MERRYFIELD, George THOMAS, Charles EGBURT, A. J. POLKE, Isaac SNYDER, Arba HEALD, Elijah STANTON, John M. LEMON, J. W. WILKINSON, John BROWN, George H. SHIPPEE, Stephen HOLLOWAY, E. MORISON, John JESSOP, Nathaniel NILES, John STANTON, James WHITTEN, John HUGHS, J. HOLLAND
Sale Buyers	John F. HUGHS, James JONES, William CAMPBELL, William HAWKINS, Willard BALL, Hiram WHEELER, Nathaniel NILES
Comments	Property described, including "four United States Patents, one State Patent, one Deed from Mathe WILSON, one Deed from Ezekiel MORRISON & wife & the certificate of Charles JONES County agent," in Township 38 North Range 3 West (present-day civil township of Springfield) and Township 37 North Range 2 West (present-day civil township of Kankakee). Lengthy file includes one-page official transcript dated 13 February 1834 from court case in Pittsburgh, Allegheny County, Pennsylvania, involving George THOMAS in 1826 and 1827. Money paid to Mr. LARAMORE ? of Niles 22 August 1838.

SWOPE, Wilson

Location	Estate #15, Microfilm E1 (formerly box 1), fourth item on roll
Court Dates	8 February 1836 inventory, May 1836 dower petition, 7 November 1836 surety.
Administrator	Jonathan LINN
Heirs	Widow Matilda SWOPE, Michael SWOPE "father and heir at law" of Wayne County
Actions	Property described in Township 37 North Range 5 West (Porter County)
Signatures	Matilda SWOPE, Asbury SWOPE (surety $500), Matilda GREGORY (widow), John BROWN, Peter DAY (grave digger)
	Sale Buyer Matilda SWOPE 5 December 1835
Comment	11 August 1836, Matilda SWOPE failed to prove she was the widow.

VANDALSEM, Henry

Location	Estate #18, Microfilm E1 (formerly box 1), fifth item on roll (one page only)
Executor	Eunice VANDALSEM
Action	Surety 10 May 1836 $500 Eunice and Samuel VANDALSEM
Signatures	Nasha VANDALSEM (by mark), Samuel VANDALSEM

CLARK, Wilson B.

Location	Estate #37, Microfilm E1 (formerly box 1), sixth item on roll
Administrator	Elizabeth CLARK, widow
Action	Died 25 August 1836 in Wisconsin Territory "at the house of John a. m," according to Solomon CLARK of Fountain County, Wilson's brother. Letters of administration and bond of $1090 by Charles MORROW obtained 7 July 1837
Signatures	Solomon CLARK, Elizabeth CLARK, Charles MORROW
Comment	Solomon CLARK received $50 for travel "from Fountain County in Indiana to Des Moines in Wisconsin territory a distance of 350 miles and back for the purpose of procuring necessary and important papers and vouchers of the estate."

BEATIE, William

Location	Estate #57, Microfilm E1 (formerly box 1), seventh item on roll
Court Dates	Thomas E. STANTON swore to the account of personal estate 12 November 1839
Administrator	Thomas E. STANTON, letters 15 October 1838 (bond of $100 by Michael FALL)
Signatures	Betsey LINDSLEY, Thomas E. STANTON, Michael W. FALL
Sale Buyers	25 December 1839: T. E. STANTON, John WHITE, Ezekiel BROWN, Josiah REDDING, Louis REDDING, Henry WHITE

HOSMER, Robert

Location	Estate #60, Microfilm E1 (formerly box 1), eighth item on roll
Administrator	Nancy HOSMER, Jackson HOSMER received letters 17 October 1838 (Joseph DAVIS bond $4000)
Heirs	Widow Nancy HOSMER, George HOSMER (relinquishes "all of my rite and title" 22 January 1839), Jackson HOSMER, Austin HOSMER (received their full shares 12 May 1840), Ursula HOSMER, Leonard STARKWEATHER "son in law and heir"

Action	Property appraised 5 November 1838 by Joseph DAVIS and Elijah BARNES
Signatures	Nancy HOSMER, Leonard STARKWEATHER, George HOSMER, Jackson HOSMER, Joseph DAVIS, Elijah BARNES
Sale Buyers	3 December 1838: James CANNON, John W. WILKINSON, Joseph DAVIS, Henry MARSH, James WATSON, Thomas BENTLY, Ezra TYLER [?], Henly CLYBURN, John W. CLARKE, Richard H. WILKINSON, Andrew CHAMBERS, Jackson HOSMER, Alva MASON
Comment	Starkweather's 10 May 1839 receipt for $310 was from "Newderham," probably New Durham Township. Estate value $2434.95.

KEWLEY, John

Location	Estate #61, Microfilm E1 (formerly box 1), ninth item on roll
Administrator	John KEWLEY and Thomas KEWLEY, letters of administration 20 October 1838 (bond of $2500 by William SHIMMIN, Andrew BURNSIDE, and Adam G. POLKE)
Heirs	Widow Isabella KEWLEY (renounced administration 20 October 1838, naming sons John KEWLEY and Thomas KEWLEY)
Action	Appraisal November 1838 by Orrin WYLLYS and Jacob R. HALL
Signatures	William KEWLEY, John KEWLEY, E. S. ORGAN, Thomas KEWLEY, Wm SHIMMIN, A. BURNSIDE, A. G. POLKE, Orrin WYLLYS, Jacob R. HALL, Joseph LOMAX, Jeremiah HISER, James M. STUART?, Ziba BAILEY, Andrew NICKEL?, Wm. L. WILSON, G. ROSE
Sale Buyers	22 November 1838: John KEWLEY, Thomas KEWLEY, James LOOKER, John DUKES, James RIDGWAY

MCCLANAHAN, James

Location	Estate #62, Microfilm E1 (formerly box 1), 10th item on roll
Administrator	John HOBSON and Benjamin CRUMPACKER
Heirs	Belinda B. MCCLANAHAN, Harriet H. MCCLANAHAN, James E. MCCLANAHAN, Joseph MCCLANAHAN, Emily MCCLANAHAN (administrators said James "left no widow" and described them as "infant heirs," that is, "still under the age of twenty one years")
Action	$1,000 bond 22 October 1838; inventory of goods, chattels, monies, and effects 5 November 1838; $2560 bond 28 August 1839
Signatures	John HOBSON, Benjamin CRUMPACKER, Griffin TREADWAY, Joel BUTLER JP, James WEBSTER, T. D. BAILEY, Ralph LOOMIS, Edmund B. WOODSON, Elijah MAYHEW, John J. CRANDAL, E. S. ORGAN, James MCCLANAHAN, John GARRARD, Daniel MEEKER, T.

THWING, John TAYLOR, Ralph LOOMIS, W. G. WALKER, Christopher
C. JOHNSON, G. A. ROSE

Comment   SE quarter of Section 14, Township 36N Range 2W, 160 acres (likely present-day civil township of Pleasant) appraised at $1280

WASSON, Archibald

Location   Estate #72, Microfilm E1 (formerly box 1), 11th item on roll

Heirs   Original will contained bequeathals to Jehiel WASSON, "my son Calvin WASSON Macamy WASSON and Eliza MOORE," and Anselm WASSON, and was dated "10th mo 5th 1838," probably 5 October 1838

Action   Bond $600 made 13 November 1838

Signatures   Jesse WASSON, Amos CADWALLADER, Archibald WASSON, Jehiel WASSON

SHARP, Thomas

Location   Estate #90, Microfilm E1 (formerly box 1), 12th item on roll

Administrator   Joseph MCLELLAN

Signatures   Abraham G. STANDIFORD, Elizabeth SHARP, John VAN MATRE, Geo. BENTLEY, Joseph MCLELLAN, Adam G. POLKE

Sale Buyers   29 December 1838: Elizabeth SHARP, Joseph MCLELLEN [?], John JACOBUS, Isaac ANDRUS, George PETTY

PINNEY, Horace

Location   Estate #118, Microfilm E1 (formerly box 1), 13th item on roll

Administrator   Nancy PINNEY and Horace PINNEY

Action   Bond $2600 15 July 1839

Signatures   Nancy PINNEY (by mark), Horace PINNEY (administrator, not decedent), William EHEART, John SMALL, Jonathan OSBOURN (by mark), Charles EATON JP

Sale Buyers   Held 13 September 1839: Samuel ALYER, David BUR, Horris PINNEY Jnr, Elisha WILLIAMS, Benjamin LONG, Phineas SMALL, O. J. MINOR, Henry WILKINSON, J. N. WILKINSON, John PIGGET, George PETRO, Cyrus HEATON, John DAVIS, Levi PETTY, Daniel CARLILE, James COTTER, Jesse MCCORD, Gideon LONG, Peter TOOLY [?], Jame, Joseph WRIGHT

MERRIAM, Abner

Location	Estate #130, Microfilm E1 (formerly box 1), 14th item on roll
Administrator	Charles MERRIAM
Action	Middlesex County, Massachusetts, probate court record from 16 May 1836, at which Charles MERRIAM of Weston in same county was appointed administrator of estate of Abner W. Merriam late of Lexington in same county, both merchants. Also a suit between Charles MERRIAM and John SHERWOOD, Jeremy HIXSON Jr., and Thomas SNOW. On 5 November 1835 they allegedly pledged to pay Abner $405--the note was accidentally lost or destroyed.

WAKEFIELD, Jesse

Location	Estate #141, Microfilm E1 (formerly box 1), 15th item on roll
Administrator	James REEVE
Heirs	Widow Christiana WAKEFIELD
Action	Bond $2000 10 December 1839
Signatures	James REEVE, Asaph WEBSTER, Christiana WAKEFIELD (by mark), A. BIGELOW, Thomas ROBINSON JP, Jesse WAKEFIELD (Michigan City note 1 September 1839), Solomon W. BRISTOL, Jonathan GLIMPSE?, Wm. A. VINEY, J. H. WALDO, Amzi CLARK, Marsana CLARK, Charles EATON, Samuel ROBINSON JP, Eli BLACK, William M. WILSON, S. BIGELOW, Herbert WILLIAMS, Samuel DRESDEN, G. WOODS, Benjamin T. BRYANT, John F. ALLISON JP
Sale Buyers	18 January 1840: Charles EATON, James REEVE, Amos G. WEBSTER, Eldridge HARDING, Daniel MAHONY, Abraham LOGAN, Simon P. TULY[?], Benjamin Y. BRIANT, William TULY, Andrew RICHARDSON, David PULVER, Inez[?] REEVE, John EATON, Widow WAKEFIELD, A. F. MARSHAL, Henderson NICKLES [?], William PINNY, Samuel WHITNEY, Charles CAMPBELL, Miron SMITH, Likins RICKINSON
Comment	Jesse executed notes in Michigan City (1 September 1839) and in Clinton Township (8 May 1839). Estate apparently insolvent.

HULBERT, Nancy and Noah

Location	Estate #27, Microfilm E1 (formerly box 1), 16th item on roll
Heirs	John and Mary HULBERT, guardian Peter FREESE (bond of $600 6 April 1850)
Signatures	Mary E. HULBERT, John HULBERT (both as of February 1855), Martin GRIFFIN, Moses BULLOCK, J. P. MILLS, Mrs. M. E. REIGHARD, J. D. REIGHARD (last two as of 16 June 1860), Peter FREESE
Comment	Nice copies of La Porte tax bills from 1850s

On 15 June 1860 Peter FREESE stated that the wards were both over 21 and that Mary had "intermarried with one John REIGHARD."

CRANDAL, Nancy

Location	Estate #40, Microfilm E1 (formerly box 1), 17th item on roll
Heirs	Charles C. CRANDAL, Octavia CRANDAL, and Francis T. CRANDAL, "infant heirs of John J. CRANDAL & Nancy CRANDAL deceased"
Action	Guardianship bond of $1600 13 February 1847 for Levi W. KEELEY
Signatures	Levi W. KEELEY, Wm. D. SHUMWAY
Comment	Guardian stated 16 August 1848 that Nancy CRANDAL's will left W half of W half of SE quarter of Section 5, Township 36N Range 2W (probably present-day civil township of Pleasant) to the three; a clock, one small yearling colt, and one atlas to Charles; 4 beds, bedding and linen to Octavia & Francis to be divided "equal between them," and to all three all other personal property after debts paid.

LIVINGSTON, Jacob

Location	Estate #128, Microfilm E1 (formerly box 1), 18th item on roll
Administrator	Mary LIVINGSTON (summoned to give account 27 December 1841)
Action	Bond of $600 16 October 1839 in La Porte
Signatures	Mary LIVINGSTON (by mark), Lewis V. BAKER, David C. PHILLIPS?
Sale Buyers	11 November 1839, probably in "Newderham": Cornelius BRADLEY, John BRAUDED, William DINGMAN, Joseph DAVIS, Henry HARDING, James LIVINGSTON, Edward HILL, Isaac LIVINGSTON, Mary LIVINGSTON, John LIVINGSTON, Marquis NICKERSON, Erastus PAGIN, James ROOD, Myron STEVENS, Henry WARD, Joseph WEBSTER, David WEAD, Virgil WILCOX
Comment	Of Lake County? List of items widow took for dower included 6 volumes of "Clarks Commentary on the Bible," valued at $6

WYATT, Joseph

Location	Estate #63, Microfilm E1 (formerly box 1), 19th item on roll
Administrator	Ezekiel MORRISON
Heirs	Isaac WYATT, Thomas WYATT, James WYATT
Action	Bond $18,000 23 October 1838
	Appraisal of real estate 13 November 1839, including explanation of why the estate was insolvent. Administrator reported 13 February, 14 August, 9 November 1840

Signatures	Ezekiel MORISON, Sutton VANPELT, Hiram WHEELER, William HAGENBUCH, Joseph WYATT, Leonard CUTLER, Charles MCCLURE, George M. ALLEN, Arthur MCCLURE
Comment	72 pages including 12-page store ledger with entries from 4 September through 15 October 1838
	Much land sold, including lot 46 in original town of La Porte, and land in Marshall and St. Joseph counties
	Thomas WYATT heir, summoned regarding sale, "not found in my County" 21 March 1840
	Agreement of sale from William HAGENBUCH to Joseph WYATT "entire stock of dry goods & groceries," also packages en route from Philadelphia, 1 August 1838
	Promissory note 2 September 1837 to Wyatt for $1838 by Charles MCLURE, George M. ALLEN, and Arthur MCCLURE

GOSSETT, John

Location	Estate #68, Microfilm E1 (formerly box 1), 20th item on roll – some items filmed as part of Estate #183, 21st item *
Administrator	Mary GOSSETT (summoned as Mary SHERMAN 16 June 1845), Joseph GOSSETT
Heirs	*Mary ROUSE late Mary GOSSETT petitioned to assign dower in land, commissioners James WEBSTER, John BROWN, and Jno. P. COBBS report 8 November 1841. Mary says John left no will, no children, and his only heirs were his brothers Joseph of Henry County and William of Porter County.
Action	Bond of $1000 1 November 1838
	Inventory 27 November 1838 (pages in two locations)
Signatures	Mary GOSSETT (by mark), Jos. GOSSETT, George S. MCCOLLOM, George DAWSON (by mark), John GOSSETT, G. A. ROSE, John R. RICHARDS, John J. CRANDALL, Thomas HUGHS, James BRADLEY, *James WEBSTER, *John BROWN, and *Jno. P. COBBS
Sale Buyers	George S. MCCOLLUM, Wm. MAPLE, Joel BUTLER, Jacob GATES, J. [?] ATKINS, John PARROTT, Lazares WHITEHEAD, John MIDDLETON, J. C. [?] WILLIAMS, Tobias MILLER, Jonathan DUDLEY, Orlando F. FIFER [?], Benjamin CRUMPACKER, Frances PEEK, E. PARROTT, Fitch BROWN, Wm BERHANS, Robert G. SISNY [CISNE?], Frances PEAK, Andrew SHAW, John WILLS, John DENHAM, William INGRAM, Samuel WEBSTER, Josiah ROOT, William SHERIDAN, Wm. AGANS, Miles WINCHESTER, Silas HALE, Saml DAWSON, Henry MILLER, Alexander BLACKBURN, Alexander HASTINGS, Wm. ARGUBRIGHT, John MIDDLETON, Jabez LOWELL [?], Mary GOSSETT, Ezekiel PREVOLT, Silas HALE, Wm. PERSONS, Elias AYLES

| Comment | "late of Pleasant Township" |

SCARCE, Samuel

Location	Estate #185, Microfilm E1 (formerly box 1), 22nd item on roll
Administrator	David HARMAN, sworn 11 October 1841
Heirs	Widow Elizabeth SCARCE, minor children John N. SCARCE, Nancy Ellen SCARCE, and William SCARCE
Action	Commissioners appointed to set off widow's dower in land, report May term 1842 (map included)
	Bond, John M. CLARKSON security, 11 October 1841
	Inventory October 1841
Signatures	John HARVEY, Ezekiel MORRISON, Peter MILLER (by mark), Samuel SCARCE, J. P. TEEPLE, Stephen HOLLOWAY
Sale Buyers	Held 6 November 1841: Danl. CARPENTER, Richd. HEATH, Saml. STUART?, Jn. WALKER, David HARMAN, Eliz. SCARCE

WESTERVELT, Abraham

Location	Estate #189, Microfilm E1 (formerly box 1), 23rd item on roll
Administrator	James WESTERVELT
Action	Catherine WESTERVELT declined administration 23 November 1841
	Administrator bond 15 December 1841, security Benjamin BEARD/BAIRD
	Inventory 16 December 1841
Signatures	T. A. STEWART, James BLACK, John L. WESTERVELT, Benjamin BEARD, Jacob DRUM/DROM, James WESTERVELT, Catherine WESTERVELT, Abraham WESTERVELT, Abner BAILEY (17 May 1844), Charles MESSENGER
Sale Buyers	Held 8 January 1842: Edmon WESTERVELT, John L. WESTERVELT, Constantine LOMAX, Mrs C. WESTERVELT
Comment	Note from "Branch at Michigan City of the State Bank of Indiana"

BOND, Ira

Location	Estate #239, Microfilm E1 (formerly box 1), 24th item on roll
Administrator	Jesse BOND, Jehiel WASSON; bond $1,000 19 September 1843, Elijah STANTON security
Signatures	Jesse BOND, Jehiel WASSON, Elijah STANTON, Charlotte BOND, Anson BUSHNELL/BURWELL?, James HANNUM, T. A. STEWART, G.

HATHAWAY, John HOUGHTON, Ira BOND, John THOMSON, Stephen HOLLOWAY, Jesse WASSON

Sale Buyers   Held 10 November 1843, sworn to 14 February 1845: Peter COLLENBACH, Jesse BOND, Wm. FAYE, B. CADWALLADER, Wm. CLARK, Wm. FRYE, Jehiel WASSON, E. STANTON, Elam CLARK, Wm. HAGENBUCH, John FINLEY, Harvey THWING/STRONG, J. BROWN, A. HUPP, H. SMITH, Benajah STANTON, FARNSWORTH, DARLINGTON, Stephen HOLLOWAY, James CUTLER, C. VANTASEL, Eber SMITH

MILLER, Dudley

Location   Estate #251, Microfilm E1 (formerly box 1), 25th item on roll

Administrator   Alonzo CLOUGH, bond with Charles PALMER Jr. security $300, 8 March 1844

Action   Sale 29 June 1844

Signatures   Alonzo CLUGH, Charles PALMER Jr. (Michigan City), S. E. WILLIAMS, Simon BURLINGAME, Ethel? BURLINGAME, Robert MEEKER, J. T. ANDREW, Wm. D. PARKER?, W. J. WALKER, Daniel LOW, Daniel MEEKER, T. A. STEWART, Dudley MILLER, Almasa P. MILLER, Elmina? E. CLOUGH

Sale Buyers   Held 29 June 1844: Charles PALMER, Wanton [?] BURLINGAME, Daniel CLOSSEN [?], C. PALMER, Wm. MAXWELL, J. F. ENOS [?], N. GROSS, Simon BURLINGAME, Denton MILLER, Wm. C. WILSON, Moses CLOUGH, C. SMITH, Francis MILLER, Wm. J. PARKER, John DIZARD [?], Michael FORESTER, W. GOSS, George BENTLY, James MILLER, Francis SINGUY

GERRY, Caleb

Location   Estate #302, Microfilm E1 (formerly box 1), 26th item on roll

Court Dates   Bond with Cynthia A. GERRY, Daniel NORTON, Burwell SPURLOCK, $300, 22 October 1845

                        Inventory 23 October 1845

Administrator   Cynthia GERRY

Signatures   Daniel BROWN, Burwell SPURLOCK, Cynthia A. GERRY

Comment   Died 6 October 1845

SMITH, John

Location   Estate #30, Microfilm E1 (formerly box 1), 27th item on roll

Administrator   A. G. POLKE

Heirs	____ SMITH, Oliver SMITH, Olive SMITH, Rhoda SMITH (widow), Lester SMITH, Elmira SMITH, Samuel SMITH
Action	May term 1843, Polke asks probate court for more time to make ordered sale of real estate "in consequence of the sickness of his family." 19 June 1840, summons issued to lien-holder John HUNT of Union County, Indiana
	Bond Adam G. POLKE and David B. FREEMAN, $700, 15 November 1836
Signatures	John MILLS, Joseph W. LYKINS, E. PALMER, L. PEACE, Daniel HOLLEY, (doctor), A. C LARK (Amzi), Daniel MEEKER, Oliver SHURTLEFF, J. HOAR, Jacob R. HALL, Arthur MCCLURE, Calvin R. EVERS, H. BARBOR (Horace), R. B. HILLS, M. H. ORTON, T. A. STEWART (Thomas), Charles SPENCER, Hiram H. HODGE, E. B. WOODSON
Sale Buyers	James BRADLEY, John D. STREET [?], A. G. POLKE, John SMITH, John S. HUNT, S./L. CATTERLIN, Jacob BARRETT, Ezekiel BROWN, Jacob R. HALL, Chadwick SMITH, Abner BARRETT, H. H. HODGES, Hezekiah SMITH, Thomas BENTLY, Lester SMITH, Charles SPENCER, Rhoda SMITH, William C. CHASE, Daniel MEEKER, Obadiah SMITH
Comment	40 acres in Section 27, Township 37 North, Range 1 East (St. Joseph County?); lot no. 165 in original plat of La Porte [may have been 165 Jackson Street]
	Note from John SMITH and John S. HUNT to McCarty & Howell [Hewett?] for $40 9 September 1836

DUKES, Ephraim

Location	Estate #49, Microfilm E1 (formerly box 1), 28th item on the roll
Court Dates	Administrator's bond $3800, 12 April 1838, James WARNOCK and Lemuel ROBINSON
Administrator	James WARNOCK
Heirs	[list with no heading] George MCCOLLUM son in law, Ephraim DUKES Jr., John RAWLEY, Robert DUKES, John DUKES, Elizabeth DUKES daughter, Joseph ROBINSON son in law, _____ ESLINGER grandson, _____ ESLINGER grandson. Per guardian Rolly GOODWIN's statement, they are Ephraim and Antoine.
Signatures	Joseph ROBINSON (by mark), Rolly GOODWIN, A. W. ENOS, Horace COOPER, John M. CLARK (by mark), Ephraim DUKES [Jr.], Edward KENNEDY, D./A. WILKINSON, Sylvanus EVERTS, L. WOODS, Jeremiah PERKINS, John DUKES, Ephraim D. ESLINGER, Antoine C. ESLINGER (by mark), Lemuel ROBINSON, James WARNOCK, Hezekiah ROBERTSON, Ch. W CATHCART, George MCCOLLUM, Elizabeth CLARK, Joseph ROBISON by mark, John BRADLEY [?], Robert DUKES, Ephraim DUKES, Daniel ROBERTSON, Josiah BRIANT (once by mark), Benjamin T. BRIANT

Sale Buyers	Wm. MCCOY, Ed KENNEDY, Ch W CATHCART, H. ELYEA, Geo MCCOLLUM, M. [?] W. CLARK, Jas. M. RAY, Jas. WARNOCK, Wm. DUKES
Comment	List of store purchases from L. WOODS 1837-1838
	Grandsons Ephraim and Antoine residing in Greencastle, Putnam County, 4 July 1848
	John CLARK's bill for caring for Rhoda DUKES in her last illness is dated from "Newdurham"

BAILEY, John

Location	Estate #64, Microfilm E1 (formerly box 1), 29th item on the roll
Court Dates	25 October 1838 administrator's bond $2000 and letters of administration, 22 October 1839 inventory taken
Administrator	Benjamin BRIANT/BRYANT
Heirs	Matilda BAILEY (widow), Matilda CHAPMAN (widow), minor heirs
Actions	Sale of personalty 8 December 1838
Signatures	Benjamin T. BRIANT, Daniel ROBERTSON, Josiah BRIANT (by mark), Charles EATON JP, James M. RAY, Matilda BAILEY, ?? CLARKSON, Isaac WESTON, John H. BRADLEY, Joseph DAVIS, Josiah BRYANT, Lemuel ROBINSON JP, Matilda CHAPMAN, John B. FRAVEL, Geo. SWOPE JP, John BAILEY, Joseph LOMAX, J. M. STUART, Jonas CLARK, Valentine CATTRON
Sale Buyers	George PETRO, Josiah BRIANT, Daniel CARLISLE, King REED, Elisabeth THORNTON, Gury TODHUNTER, Charles CAMPBELL, Peter HINTON, Benjamin BRIANT, Francis SALES, Eli BLACK, Orson PETTEE, Daniel GARNER

COLLINS, Harvey

Location	Estate #70, Microfilm E1 (formerly box 1), 30th item on the roll
Court Dates	Administrators' bond and letters 12 November 1838; 13 December 1839 administrators petition to sell real estate as Collins's personal property was "insufficient to pay his debts"
Administrator	Samuel STEWART, George C. HAVENS
Heirs	Philura COLLINS (widow), later Philura BROWN (remarried prior to 10 February 1846), Arenna COLLINS, Harriet COLLINS, Charlotte C. COLLINS, Albert COLLINS
Action	Real estate sold to William BROWN for $230, 2 January 1841
Signatures	William BROWN (by mark), Daniel HENKER, L. A. STEWART, John R. RICHARDS, Wm. MASON, E. B. WOODSON JP, E. S. ORGAN, Samuel

STEWART, Geo. C. HAVENS, Daniel STEWART, Harvey NORRIS, Jno. M. LEMON Jr.

Sale Buyers | 8 December 1838: Samuel STEWART, Eben MIX, Benjamin CRUMPACKER, Winston WALKER, William D. BULL, George C. HAVENS, George REAMER, Mrs. COLLINS, Hiram GRIFFITH, Henry RICE, Jacob MILLER, Josiah W. WING, Jacob MICASKY

Comment | Collins was "of Pleasant Township"; some receipts as late as 1846

HERBERT, Richard

Location | Estate #78, Microfilm E1 (formerly box 1), 31st item on the roll

Court Dates | Administrator's bond $200 and letters 14 November 1838; inventory 3 December 1838

Administrator | Micajah JONES

Signatures | Richard HERBERT, Micajah JONES, Byron CADWALLADER JP, John H. BRADLEY

Sale Buyers | Samuel HERBERT, Eli JONES, Jesse JONES, Elihu JONES, Micajah JONES, James HERBERT, Charles FRANCES, B. CADWALLADER, Wm. WALDRUPP, John COOPER, E. RYTHES/RYTHER?, G. W. BARNES, Matthew MAYS, E. BISHUP, C. B. DAVIS, Ezra BARNES, James CATERLIN, Samuel HEVESLIN?, James WARNER, Iver MARKS, Caleb C. DAVIS, Jacob HECKMAN, R. MERRYFIELD

Comment | Richard HERBERT's 21 June 1838 note was from "Kankakee"; administrator attempted to replevin property from James HERBERT, in which action witnesses were summoned 1 November 1839: Samuel HERBERT, Hetty WALDRIFF, Joseph LOW?, William BROWN, Wightman GOIT, Matthew PADDOCK, Mathew MAYZE, Mary D. MAYZE, Mary HERBERT, William WALDRIFF, Charles FRANCIS, and Willis G. WRIGHT, Jesse JONES, Elihu JONES, Ansalem JONES, Eli JONES, Elijah BISHOP, Jacob HECKMAN, Ruth BISHOP

ANDERSON, John

Location | Estate #91, Microfilm E1 (formerly box 1), 32nd item on roll

Court Dates | Widow relinquished administration to eldest son William K. ANDERSON 23 November 1838; letters and $4000 administrators bond 24 November 1838

Administrator | William K. ANDERSON

Heirs | Jane ANDERSON (widow)

Signatures | William K. ANDERSON, David ANDERSON, Benjamin BUTTERWORTH, Jane ANDERSON, William C. ANDERSON, John H. BRADLEY, E. S. ORGAN

Sale Buyers	Wm. K. ANDERSON, Westley MORGAN, Nimrod PHILLIPS, James CALLISON Jr., Hiram INMAN, Thomas KIDEL, David ANDERSON, Edwin BOOTHE, Jeremiah ATKINS, Sheldon BOOTHE, Benjamin BUTTERWORTH, James CURRIE, Edwin MOOTHE, Sheldon MOOTHE, J. T. ATKINS, John WALBRIDGE, Edward BOSS, Wm. CALLISON, Warren COLE, Andrew ANDERSON, Eli BLACK, Solomon OVERMIRE, Warren COLE, Jacob DRUM, HOWEL
Comment	"late of Pleasant Township"

MAXSON, George or Lee H. T.

Location	Estate #93, Microfilm E1 (formerly box 1), 33rd item on roll
Administrator	Paul H. MAXSON, bond of $1800 with surety Samuel D. VIELE 3 December 1838. Maxson resigned 3 February 1839 in favor of Oscar A. BARKER (apparently he had "become a non resident" of Indiana); bond of $4,000 secured by John FRANCES and Eliakim ASHTON 16 February 1839; bond of $4,033 secured by William W. HIGGINS and Jeremiah HITCHCOCK 9 May 1842.
Heirs	Paul H. MAXSON
Action	Report of sale of Michigan City real estate 13 June 1842 to William H. GOODHUE, Martha MAXSON, Orrin J. MINOR, William GARDNER, Willys P. WARD, William W. LOW, Patrick GRIFFIN, Jacob METZKER. Inventory 12 March 1839 by Chaney B. BLAIR and George AMES, 12 June 1839 by Willys PECK and George AMES
Signatures	Oscar A. BARKER, Martha MAXSON, A. L. OSBORN, William W. HIGGINS, Jeremiah HITCHCOCK, Paul H. MAXSON, S. D. VIELE, John FRANCES, E. ASHTON, C. B. BLAIR
Sale Buyers	D. STRONG, T. TYRRELL, PULFORD, A. W. ENOS, G. BARNES, Jas. SMITH, Wm. WICKENS
Comment	Chicago attorneys Justin BUTTERFIELD and James H. COLLINS prosecuted two suits on behalf of "Lee H. T. MAXSON" against William MONTGOMERY in 1837-1839, per affidavit 6 August 1841.
	Inventory of personal estate includes a full-page list of medical books.
	Inventory of real estate includes both city lots and quarter sections, total value $2,016.50 as of 16 February 1842.

COLLINS, Harvey

Location	Estate #278, Microfilm E1 (formerly box 1), 34th item on roll
Administrator	Samuel Stewart and George C. Havens, letters 12 November 1838
Heirs	Widow Philura COLLINS who in 1839 married William BROWN; Areuna COLLINS, Albert COLLINS, Harriet COLLINS, Charlotte COLLINS. The

last two died during the probate process, prior to the November 1844 term of court.

Comment   Harvey COLLINS "deceased in the fall of the year 1838." William BROWN and Philura BROWN sued heirs, evidently for Philura's dower rights in some real property, of which there is a sketch map. Albert was served 8 October 1844, Areuna Collins "not found in my county" per La Porte County sheriff but then served 23 November 1844. William C. HANNAH appointed guardian at litem of heirs Areuna and Albert, who were "infants under the age of twenty one years" when they replied to Brown's suit.

CONNER, William

Location   Estates #285 and #291, Microfilm E1 (formerly box 1), 35th item on roll; in addition six additional pages of #285 are the 59th item on roll.

Court Dates   Will filed 11 February 1845

Executrix   Mary CONNER

Heirs   As named in William CONNER's 5 August 1844 will: children George W. CONNER (oldest son), Crawford CONNER, Nancy WEST, John CONNER, Cader CONNER, Angeline LEWIS, William L. CONNER, Calvin CONNER, Martin CONNER (youngest son); grandson William Wesley Conner ROSS, granddaughter Martha Ellen ROSS. Each was bequeathed one dollar, except for Martin, who received a $50 saddle & bridle) and Martha Ellen ("now living with me") who received his 40 acres after widow's decease or remarriage, W half S half SW ¼ Section 12, Township 38N Range 2W (probably present-day civil township of Galena).

Signatures   William CONNER, Alexander BLACKBURN, Martin CONNER, Rebeca CONNER, Cader CONNER

Comment   Numerous summonses etc. regarding a contest of the will, including:

Handwritten note from Cader CONNER saying that he named Nancy WEST's heir incorrectly as Juliann, the name should be Lucy and this needs to be communicated to "wain Co Ia." [i.e., Wayne County, Indiana].

Also a more formal note from plaintiff's attorney Bradley naming the case as Cader CONNER vs. Mary CONNER et al. and requesting that citations be issued to Mary CONNER, Israel LEWIS, Angeline LEWIS, Calvin CONNER, Martin CONNER, and Martha Ellen ROSS in La Porte County; George W. CONNER and Crawford CONNER in Wayne County; William L. CONNER in Randolph County; John CONNER, Mary Jane CARR, and Sarah Ann CARR, "children of Nancy WEST deceased, late Nancy CARR, but Nancy CONNER and all other children of said Nancy," in Henry County; and William W. C. ROSS and Martha Ellen ROSS in Porter County.

Also lengthy fee bill for the case "Cader CONNER objector to Probate of Will of William CONNER vs. Mary CONNER Executor et al."

Also an apparent jury verdict confirming the will.

Also a 13 January 1846 summons to testify on Cader Conner's behalf: James PADDOCK, Daniel SMITH, Christopher L. DAVIS, and Benjamin HICKS.

Also a partial record of 13 February 1846 hearing on the will contest. Cader CONNER complained that the will was not attested according to law, that William was not of sound mind, and that later William "frequently expressed himself dissatisfied therewith, and desired to alter the same."

REYNOLDS, Nathan

Location	Estate #454, Microfilm E1 (formerly box 1), 36th item on roll
Court Dates	Joshua S. MCDOWELL and Benjamin RHODES appraisers 14 November 1850.
	Andrew J. WAIR and Joel BUTLER signed a guardianship bond of $500 15 November 1850 to guarantee Butler's correct discharge of duties as to the sale.
	Burwell SPURLOCK and Joel BUTLER signed a guardianship bond of $50 13 November 1850.
	Guardian BUTLER reported to the Court of Common Pleas that he sold the land to Jonas FINLEY 24 November 1852 for $85.
	Guardian BUTLER reported to the Court of Common Pleas that Ann "left his care" 6 November 1853 and that he was about to "leave this State with his said wards" 21 November 1855.
Heirs	Ann REYNOLDS, George REYNOLDS (12 years), Nancy Matilda REYNOLDS (7 years), "minor heirs" as of 14 November 1850
Signatures	Joel BUTLER (guardian), J. MCDOWELL, B. RHODES, A. J. WAIR, B. SPURLOCK
Comment	Real estate E ½ SE ¼ Section 32 Township 38N Range 3W (present-day civil township of Springfield)

FOSDICK, Timothy

Location	Estate #14, Microfilm E1 (formerly box 1), 37th item on roll
Court Dates	21 October 1835 administrators bond with Robert S. MORRISON, William CLARK, and James WHITTEN for $800
	8 May 1837 administrator filed to sell real estate because personalty was "insufficient for the payment of his debts" – in Section 10, Township 27N Range 3W (possibly an error, as 37 would be in the county), authorized 9 September 1837.
Administrator	William CLARK

Heirs	"Widow, Martha FOSDICK and three children, to Wit John James & Mary FOSDICK, all minors under fourteen years of age"
Action	Inventory taken 23 October 1835
Signatures	Willard N. BALL, Stephen HOLLOWAY, Charles WOOLVERTON, Timothy FOSDICK, Robert S. MORRISON, Albert G. PRESTON, John HUGHES, Martha A. FOSDICK, David HARRISON, Jehiel WASSON, Aaron STANTON, William CLARK, Andrew HARMAN, James WHITTEN, Thomas STANTON, John H. BRADLEY
Sale Buyers	William FOZDICK, John REESTER (KEESTER??), Martin RULEN, John REESTER, John H. BRADLEY, Amos CADWALADER, Ezekiel BROWN, David HARRISON, Aaron STANTON, William CLARK, John STANTON, Stephen HOLLOWAY, Thomas H. MCKEE?, Jehiel WASSON, Elijah KENT, Widow, R. S. MORRISON, John HUGHS

PEASE, Enos

Location	Estate #42, Microfilm E1 (formerly box 1), 38th item on roll
Court Dates	19 December 1837 widow Isabel PEASE relinquished her dower rights in the estate to Asa C. & Buenos A. PEASE.
	15 November 1838 administrators petitioned to sell real estate, 20 acres in Section 9, Township 37N Range 2W and 2 acres in Section 4 (present-day civil township of Kankakee).
	Another inventory of real estate 15 November 1838 named only 20 acres in Section 16.
	Administrators summoned 12 January 1846 to appear in court.
Administrators	Asa C. PEASE, Nathan B. NICHOLS, $1000 bond with Abraham FRAVEL, undated. Bond for $440 with Amzi CLARK 16 November 1838.
Heirs	Alvin R. PEASE, Asa C. PEASE, Enos A. PEASE, Buenos A. PEASE, Nancy A. PEASE, Susan W. PEASE, Artemisia R. PEASE, Lucinda A. PEASE, David PEASE named in March term 1842 report of real estate sale.
	An undated note refers to "Artemisia R. SATTERLEE of Illinois & Nancy A. STOW of Ohio to be notified, & Isabella PEASE widow [illegible word]"
	A 10 December 1838 court notice regarding real estate sale to "Asa C. PEASE & Buenos A. PEASE adult heirs and also to the said Asa C. PEASE guardian of Lucinda Ann PEASE and David H. PEASE infant heirs of Enos PEASE late of said County."
Action	Inventory taken 30 October 1837. William CLARK presented 3 pages of accounts 14 February 1838, purchases and credits of Enos PEASE. Accounts headed "Michigan City Inda." – dry goods, foods, tobacco, etc. between 24 September 1836 and 6 September 1837

Signatures	Nathan B. NICHOLS JP, Asa C. PEASE, Solomon HORNICH, Fitch BROWN, Enos PEASE, Myron IVES, Buenos A. PEASE, Howell HUNTSMAN, T. A. STEWART, J. M. STUART, Isabel PEASE by mark, Betsey LINDSLEY, Ansel WOODWORTH, John TOMLINSON, Jacob HICKMAN, A. BLACKBURN, James ANDREW, Wm. ANDREW, A. CLARK
Sale Buyers	Thos. N. SMITH, Asa C. PEASE, Buenos A. PEAS, E. PROVOLT, C. W. BRANSON, Wm. SUTHERLAND, Miron IVES, H. C. STERNS, Eri W. FAUTS, Nathan B. NICHOLS, Haris? ASTIN?
Comment	On 24 June 1837, when Howell HUNTSMAN recovered a judgment from Hiram ORUM, Enos PEASE stood security for Orum's payment of $66.70
	On 3 December 1838, Betsey LINDSLEY of Michigan City acknowledged receipt for $4 for medical services "rendered by Ab. S. LINDSLEY deceased."

MASON, Howard

Location	Estate #51, Microfilm E1 (formerly box 1), 39th item on roll
Court Dates	Inventory filed 23 October 1839
Administrator	William CLARK; bond with Stephen HOLLOWAY for $800 filed 31 August 1838. Then 12 August 1842 administrator's bond for $1000 with William CLARK and John H. BRADLEY security
Heirs	Sidney MASON widow, Elwood MASON, Elizabeth MASON, Howard MASON, Alice Anna MASON "infant" as of July 1844
Action	Sidney MASON's undated petition stated that Howard MASON died 15 August 1838. The administrator's petition of 10 May 1842 stated that Howard MASON died in 1837. That petition was to sell his property in Township 37N Range 3E (probably present-day civil township of Center).
Signatures	William CLARK, Stephen HOLLOWAY, John H. BRADLEY, James BRADLEY, S. E. WILLIAMS, Benjamin BUTTERWORTH, Robert HILL (see comments), Sidney MASON, D. P. HOLLOWAY, Joseph LOMAX, Howard MASON, Benjamin BROOKS, Aaron STANTON, Jehiel WASSON
Sale Buyers	S. E. CHAPMAN, Wm CLARK, Stephen HOLLOWAY, Byram CADWALLADER, Ingraham GOLD, Israel WOODWARD, Saml. FISHER, Melzah BUCK, Jonathan SMITH, West DARLING, Benjamin BROOKS, John LEWIS, Aaron STANTON, Irwin N. BENTLY, Juach LIMIG??, N. B. NICHOLAS, C. W. BROWN, James JONES, Wm. ALLEN, Willis WRIGHT, Jeheal WASSON, Saml TURNER, Moses LEWIS, George FOSDICK, John HASITHIN?
Comment	Land sold to Taylor BRADLEY prior to 15 May 1844 for $1100, more than it had been appraised for.
	A variety of evidence is available to guesstimate the children's birth dates.

Robert HILL of Richmond, Wayne County, Indiana, reported receiving a note on Howard MASON dated "the 2nd of the ninth month 1834" $20 borrowed from Cornelius RATLIFF.

BRADLEY, Bartholomew

Location	Estate #53, Microfilm E1 (formerly box 1), 40th item on roll
Court Dates	1 October 1838 widow Lydia S. BRADLEY renounced administration in favor of her son Sidney S. BRADLEY
	17 August 1842 court summoned "Sidney S. BRADLEY, William Erasmus BRADLEY, and Julia H. BRADLEY, heirs of Bartholomew BRADLEY late of Laporte County" to respond to petition to sell real estate in November term of court
	1842 Sutton VAN PELT listed real estate: lots in Township 38N Range 5E and Township 38N Range 4E in Elkhart County, including a description of widow's dower set off by Elkhart Circuit Court (85 acres).
Administrator	Sidney S. BRADLEY bond of $1500 with Russell HARVEY 1 October 1838
	Bond of $1200 for Sutton VAN PELT 16 November 1842 with Noah NEWELL
Heirs	Several different listings:
	Widow Lydia S. BRADLEY, heirs Julia H. BRADLEY, Joseph E. BRADLEY, William C. BRADLEY (all three with guardian ad litem John M. CLARKSON).
	The August 1842 newspaper printing of the application to sell real estate named widow Lydia H. BRADLEY, George W. BRADLEY, Joseph E. BRADLEY, and William C. BRADLEY.
	As named in February 1846 suit by Sutton VAN PELT: Lydia A. BRADLEY, George W. BRADLEY, Joseph E. BRADLEY, Sidney S. BRADLEY, William C. BRADLEY, Erasmus D. BRADLEY, Julia H. BRADLEY
Signatures	Joseph E. BRADLEY, Bart BRADLEY (on 21 March 1838 New Durham note), Erastus PAYN, Lydia S. BRADLEY, Joseph E. BRADLEY, J. M. CLARKSON, T. A. STEWART, Sutton VAN PELT, Noah NEWELL, S. S. BRADLEY, Russell HARVEY, Sylvanus EVERTS, S. S. SABIN, James BRADLEY, Jno. B. NILES, W. C. HANNAH, J. MILLIKAN
Comment	Note dated Middlebury February 8th 1836: Bart BRADLEY promised to pay Lewis BLODGET $39.47 in four months.
	Note dated "Chicago July 31 1839": Bart BRADLEY promised to pay S. S. BRADLEY $83.
	Bart BRADLEY paid taxes on land in Lenawee County, Michigan, for 1838

Noah NEWELL swore 10 May 1842 that Sidney S. BRADLEY's security Russell HARVEY "is insolvent or nearly so."

HIBBARD, Horace Bonaparte

Location	Estate #54, Microfilm E1 (formerly box 1), 41st item on roll. Items misfiled as estates #173 and #176, 75th and 76th items on roll, marked here with *.
Administrator	Bond of $2000 6 October 1838, administrators William WRIGHT and Ezra TYLER, with Richard B. HEWS security. Bond in same amount without Hews 11 February 1840, and $3000 13 November 1841.
	Another bond with the same administrators and John W. COLE security for $800, 13 May 1839.
	Another bond with Ezra TYLER and James WARNOCK for $1000 8 August 1842.
	James BRADLEY administrator as of 14 May 1844; swore 13 August 1846; $200 bond with William HAWKINS.
Heirs	Widow Corinthia [probably a mistake, should be Annis, see below] HIBBARD relinquished administration circa 1838.
	Indiana patent of 1840 listed legal heirs Corrintha DINGMAN, Marian HIBBARD, John W. HIBBARD, and Daniel W. HIBBARD.
	Administrator Ezra TYLER reported at an unknown date that "William DINGMAN & Corrintha DINGMAN his wife . . . reside somewhere in the state of Michigan."
	In an 1846 report to the court, administrator Ezra TYLER reported that Hibbard's widow was Annis S. SAREEN [probably SOVEREIGN] whose dower portion was lands in Sections 23 and 26 of Township 36N Range 4W (present-day civil township of New Durham).
	Petition of 13 February 1840 to sell real estate named "Annis S. HIBBARD (widow), William DINGMAN and Corrintha DINGMAN late Corrintha HIBBARD, Marian HIBBARD, John W. HIBBARD, and Daniel W. HIBBARD heirs at law."
	Marian, John W., and Daniel named as "infant heirs" in 12 March 1841 and John BAKER their guardian ad litem. Also widow Annis had married Abraham SOVEREIGN.
	*John W. HIBBARD, Daniel W. HIBBARD, Marion HIBBARD "infant heirs of H. B. HIBBARD decd." by guardian John B. NILES.
Action	Administrators stated Horace HIBBARD died 15 September 1838.
	Unspecified land sold at public vendue for $40 to Abram SARREEN [SOVEREIGN?] 3 October 1842. Court order of 19 August 1842 finding the estate otherwise insolvent, listed three tracts to be sold in Sections 23 and 26 of Township 36N Range 4W (present-day civil township of New Durham).

Inventory taken 18 December 1839.

Signatures — William WRIGHT, Ezra TYLER, R. B. HEWS, Joseph REED, Benjamin FLOOD, James BRADLEY, Horace B. HIBBARD, Jno. B. NILES, Aaron COOLEY, John W. ARMSTRONG, Thomas JERNEGAN, C. H. CATHCART, Omer [?] WYLLIS, Annis S. HIBBARD, John B. FRAVEL, John R. RICHARDS, Annis S. SOVEREIGN, Jacob BRYANT, Harlow WEBSTER, Adam WITENBECK, Horace CROSS, B. SPURLOCK, J. C. HOWELL, Joseph DAVIS, C. S. SAWLEY, Joseph HAYWOOD, Josiah BRYANT (by mark), L. WOODS, Wm. ANDREW, J. A. WILKINSON, A. CLARK, Joseph LOMAX, Stephen F. HOLLOWAY, Elam CLARK, E. B. WOODSON, H. P. HOLBROOK, Isaac CORLISS, Wm. M. BOAST, Alexander NICKERSON, John BROWN, Urian [?] BAILEY, A. CLARK, John H. BRADLEY, Alex NICKERSON, John J. CRANDALL

Sale Buyers — Purchasers of variously described real estate 20 January 1842: Charles HIBBARD, , Richard H. WILKINSON, Nathaniel CASE, Luther CASE, Wm. HAWKINS. Other land sold to James A. WILKINSON 31 December 1842.

Sale 1 November 1838: Joseph REED, Joseph DAVIS, Alexander PERSON, Albert COURIER, Wm. DINGMAN, Joseph DAVIS, John CLOSER, David MCKELLIP, Wm. WRIGHT, Joseph B. REED, James R. BENHAM, Elijah BARNS, Allen LUCK, Abiram SNODGRASS, Silas LOVING, Sterling HOLLIDAY, John W. WILKERSON, Charles COOPER, Obadiah SMITH, Edward WRIGHT, Wm. D. PARKER, Joseph DAVIS, Harry MARSH, Ivry [?] TODHUNTER, Henry FREDERICKSON, Alexander NICKERSON, Widow HIBBARD, Zachariah DROW---, A. G. WEBSTER, James CATTERTON, John BRODDED, Wm. G. HARDING, James TITUS, Samuel TURNER, James CANNON, Harry JONES, Simeon JESSUP, Stephen NOWLAND, Harry MARSH, Charles HIBBARD, Isaac ANDREWS, Abraham BURNER, Jeremiah PERKINS, D. A. STEPHENS, Jacob BRIANT, Alexander STARKET [?], Benjamin BAIRD, Alvah MASON, Virgil WILCOX, John HARRIS, Samuel COX, Daniel JESSUP, Chapen FAREWELL, Chancy COOPER, Harris ORVIS [?], Lewis TODHUNTER

Comment — Two original US land patents, certificates 4104 and 4105, 20 March 1837, giving his full name, to NW quarter of Section 25, Township 36 N, Range 4W (present-day civil township of New Durham).

Three original Indiana land patents to Michigan Road Lands in Section 34 of Township 37N Range 4W (present-day civil township of Coolspring), 12 February 1840, to Andrew BURNSIDE and Horace HIBBARD (heirs). Also 13 September 1842, to lands in Section 26 of Township 36N Range 4W (present-day civil township of New Durham). Also same date for Section 23, assignee Sidney WILLIAMS. Also same date for Section 26, assignee Martin BAKER.

* Court granted petition in Annis S. HIBBARD vs. the heirs of Horace B. HIBBARD deceased, and on 15 February 1841 appointed Joseph OSBORN, Orrin WILLIS, and Charles W. CATHCART, "disinterested men

and not allied to the said parties," to set over to Annis "her just and full third"of several described lands in Township 36N Range 4W (present-day civil township of New Durham) and Township 37 Range 4W (present-day civil township of Coolspring).

Two misfiled items:

"Page" 11 in the filming of Horace HIBBARD Estate No. 54 contains material from the James HUNT estate, #120, 45th item on roll.

"Pages" 12 and 13 in the filming of Horace HIBBARD Estate No. 54 contain material from the Amos HOLLOWAY estate, #163, 48th item on roll.

DINWIDDIE, David

Location	Estate #56, Microfilm E1 (formerly box 1), 42nd item on roll
Administrator	Amzi CLARK and James C. HOWELL; bond of $6000 13 October 1838 with Abner BAILEY and Griffin TREADWAY securities, after the widow renounced administration 12 October 1838. Another bond 16 November 1839 with securities Alexander BLACKBURN and Ezekiel MORRISON.
Heirs	Mary DINWIDDIE (widow), John DINWIDDIE, Margaret June DINWIDDIE, David DINWIDDIE Jr., Frances W. DINWIDDIE, Marietta DINWIDDIE, Mathew S. WALKER, Eleanor H. WALKER
Signatures	A. CLARK, W. R. BOSTWICK, Horace L. THORP, Westell RIDGLEY (of Porter County), John PRICE JP (of Porter County), T. C. SWENEY, Thomas DINWIDDIE, Jno. B. NILES, David BARGER, Mary DILLEY, J. C. HOWELL, Abner BAILEY, Griffin TREADWAY, Mary DINWIDDIE. A. G. POLKE, Charles MCCLURE
Sale Buyers	24 November 1838: Harvey STRONG, George REYMER/REAMER, J. G. ATKINS, M. DILLY, Mrs. DINWIDDIE, Wm WINDLE, John CHAPMAN, Thos DINWIDDIE, Wm DINWIDDIE, Hiram GRIFFITH, Aron STANTON, Alex BLACKBURN, Griffin TREADWAY, R. DOWLING, James BURLINGAME, J. M. CLARKSON, E. OLIVER, J. C. REED, Bankes HALL, John JESSUP, John MOORE, J. CURTIS, J. R. HALL, J. C. HOWELL, J. B. BOSTWICK, Seth WAY, James WALKER, Wm. HAGENBUCH, N. P. BLISS, C. R. EVANS, David POWERS, John HILL, James EWINGS, Saml TREAT, A. LEACH, H. FREDRICKSON, Jacob DRUM, Johnathan SMITH, Andrew MCLEAN, R. B. HEWS, Miles GODFREY, A. HUPP, A. LOMAX, Thos. C. SWENY, J. GOLD, Orrin GOLD, H. GODFREY, Johnathan BURR, N. BARTLIT, L. LOMAX, David TURNER, N. BARTLET Jr., John PRATT, Chappel W. BROWN, Bennet WARREN
Comment	Public notice of application to sell real estate 15 August 1842 published in the La Porte County Whig because the court found that heirs Mathew S. WALKER and Eleanor H. WALKER were not residents of Indiana.

Thousands of dollars were involved, but the administrators petitioned the court that the estate was insolvent. Real estate sold in Township 36N Range 3W (probably present-day civil township of Scipio), and in Township 35N Range 5W (Porter County).

PLATT, Jeremiah

Location	Estate #65, Microfilm E1 (formerly box 1), 43rd item on roll
Administrator	Joseph WINCH, $800 bond made 25 October 1838 with James M. SCOTT security. In note to the probate court Joseph reported that Jeremiah died "on or about" 18 August 1838, and that he had "no family or relation in the county."
Signatures	Eldred PLATT, Phebe SNEDECOR, Richard PLATT, Watts PLATT by mark – all of Hempstead, Queens County, New York as of 6 August 1839 -- John E. SHEPARD, John E. CHENEY, James M. SCOTT, Joseph WINCH, James M. GOLD, James M. SCOTT, Samuel SCOTT
Sale Buyers	15 December 1838: Joseph WINCH, P. SHEPHEARD, Jas. M. SCOTT, E. J. CHENEY, Lemon THOMPSON, A. M. WADDELL, John RITTER
Comment	Letter 19 July 1849 from Eldred PLATT of Hempstead, Queens County, New York, to Thomas P. ARMSTRONG, noting the settlement of "my Brothers affairs" and mentioning his "widowed mother" to whom the $24 would "come very acceptable."

SPAULDING, Timothy

Location	Estate #119, Microfilm E1 (formerly box 1), 44th item on roll
Court Dates	Complaint of insolvency published 19 February 1844
Administrator	John B. NILES
Action	14 February 1839, administrator's bond of $2000 with Sutton VAN PELT
Signatures	Elnathan GREGORY, E. BECKWITH, A. CLARK (Amzi), S. VAN PELT (Sutton), Jno. B. NILES
Comment	Two pages of Spaulding's debts to J. & E. J. EARLY of Kingsbury.

HUNT, James

Location	Estate #120, Microfilm E1 (formerly box 1), 45th item on roll. Item evidently misfiled and filmed as "page" 11 in Horace Hibbard Estate (Estate #54, 41st item on roll) marked *.
Heirs	"Francina Jasper S. and Charles W." named in will, also "David M. and Jonathan S.," wife Nancy, also Phebe, Polly, "my two youngest sons James A. and John M."

* 19 April 1847 letter from the heirs of the estate of James HUNT deceased swore that they had received "our outfit as set fourth in the will" from "Administrators Jasper S. HUNT and Charles W. HUNT." They signed as David M. HUNT, Jonathan S. HUNT, John M. HUNT, Lucy C. HUNT, Aaron FOSTER, Phebe FOSTER, and B. F. WAGNER.

Action   Original will, apparently signed by Hunt, 19 April 1838. Clerk's copy in Complete Record A:579.

Signatures   George HUNT, Nathan B. NICHOLS, James HUNT, Nancy HUNT (by mark), Jasper S. HUNT, Charles W. HUNT

Comment   Property bequeathed in Township 37N Range 2W (present-day civil township of Kankakee).

JOHNSON, Samuel

Location   Estate #140, Microfilm E1 (formerly box 1), 46th item on roll

Court Dates   Administrator's account filed 11 May 1842, additional account 10 August 1846

Administrator   William EAHART, Joseph H. BENEDICT; bond 30 November 1839 with James MCCORD for $400

Heirs   Certificate 12 June 1847, Treasury Department, Auditor's Office, Indianapolis, for "estate without heirs"

Signatures   James MCCORD, Henly CLYBURN, Joseph H. BENEDICT, William EAHART, Thomas JERNEGAN, Ezra TYLER JP, Lewis TODHUNTER, Thomas P. ARMSTRONG, Gilbert HATHAWAY, Henry HARDING

Sale Buyers   James MCCORD, Lewis TODHUNTER, J. L. COLLINS, R. G. MOODY, Ezra TYLER, Leonard WOODS, Joseph LOMAX, Stephen HOLIDAY, James WARNOCK, G. A. EVERETTS, Henry HARDING, Wm. EAHART, Joseph H. BENEDICT, Owen CRUMPACKER, Purdy SMITH, Thomas FARLEY, Henry FREDERICKSON, H. STEPHENS, William HOLLIDAY, Isaac WESTON, H. STEVENS, H. CLYBURN, Richard BOSLEY, Wm D. LABER, Wm. BATTERSON, Walker ROSS, Calvin NAPIER, G. STOLLER, Joseph K. REED, Samuel WHITNEY, Ezra TYLER, Stephen JESSUP, E. C. STEVENS

Comment   "loss on Michigan Money"

CATTRON, Valentine

Location   Estate #160, Microfilm E1 (formerly box 1), 47th item on roll

Court Dates   Executors summoned to court 23 May 1849

Administrator   John A. G. CATTRON, Hezekiah CATTRON letters 8 September 1840 with Joseph H. BENEDICT and George MCCORD for $7000 bond

Heirs	"Eight children" per 1842 court petition: Thomas CATTRON and James B. CATTRON of Illinois; Mary and Daniel MAINE of Lake County, Indiana; Samuel CATTRON, Wm. CATTRON (minor), and Wesley F. CATTRON (minor) of La Porte County; and administrators Hezekiah CATTRON, John A. G. CATTRON. Most signed receipts.
Action	28 September 1840 estate inventory
Signatures	Edwin ALLEN, Hezekiah CATTRON, John A. G. CATTRON, James MCCORD, S. E. WILLIAMS (deputy county treasurer and collector), T. A. STEWART, James B. CATTRON, Joseph H. BENEDICT, George MCCORD, J. HUELKINSON, Jonathan TABER Jr., James BRADLEY, W. PECK, Arba HEALD, B. SPURLOCK, Thomas P. ARMSTRONG, George SANFORD, Sylvanus EVERTS, J. P. ANDREW, James B. CATTRON, Samuel CATTRON, Wm. CATTRON, Wesley F. CATTRON, Daniel MAINE, Mary MAINE (by mark), C. HARREE, John B. FRAVEL, Abram EAHEART, B. F. GREGORY, Robard PATTRICK (by mark), Peter CATRON, Edwin WEST, Jas. WARNOCK, Valentine CATTRON, John K. HENTON?, L. WOODS, W. W. MOORHED, Monor P. HANKS, -- BONESTEEL, Horace? LIGGET, Peter HENTON, George PETERS, James MCKAY, Newton BUSHNELL, Anson GREGG
Sale Buyers	1-2 October 1840 at the residence: Peter BRADLEY, John A. G. CATTRON, Samuel TURNER, Myron STEVENS, D.M.F. CLOSSER, John WEST, James MCCORD, Wm. GARWOOD, John HARRIS, Levi MASSEY, Henry GEIST, Daniel MAIN, James RAY, Wm. KIDD, Daniel MAHONY, Hezekiah CATTRON, Melzai BUCK, James CALLISON, Johnathan OSBURN, Gideon LONG, Wm. MAXWELL, John WARNICK, Samuel PARKINSON, Rodolph BASON, Daniel WOOLEY, Levi PATTER, Wili JONES, Silas LOVING, Minor HANKS, Ward BLAKE, Wm. HALADAY, Wm. TRINKLE, Daniel KNELLINGEN?, Wesley WILKINSON, Nicholas CLOSSER, Henly CLYBURN, Robert WORLY, Thomas SAYLES, John GILMAN, James J. SMITH, Daniel DRULINGER, Isom CAMPBELL, Jesse MCCORD, Mark ALLEN, James COLTER, Wm. D. PARKER, James P. CAIN, John PRATT, Benjamin BEARD, Edward WRIGHT, Jacob DROM, Nimrod PHILLIPS, Wm. D. TABER, Edwin A.WEST, Joseph K. REED, E. J. SIMMONS, John PATTEE, Wm. PETRO, George REED, Sterling HALODAY, Benjamin FLOOD, Adam HAMILTON, Edward EVANS, David REED, Josiah BRIANT, Samuel MAINE, B. REED, Benj. LONG, Orson PATTEE, Wm. LYNN, John EAHEART
Comment	29 June 1842 petition for a commissoners' deed to Robert MILFORD for land that Valentine had executed a title bond for.
	10 May 1836 Valentine purchased lots 20 and 21 of the school section of Township 36N Range 4W (present-day civil township of New Durham) and was paying installments thereafter.
	18 November 1821 Robard PATTRICK note to "Vallinetine Catron" for $65 "in good Land office Money," witnessed by Peter CATRON.

Valentine assigned a note to John R. HENTON 5 March 1833 who then assigned it back on 7 December 1833.

1835-1836 notes from HENDERSON & BAXLEY of Fountain County to Hezekiah CATTRON.

August 1842 petition to court explained the situation of Robert MILFORD of Fountain County and the 200 acres of land in Townships 21 and 22N Range 7W that Valentine owned there, also named heirs.

HOLLOWAY, Amos Jr.

Location	Estate #163, Microfilm E1 (formerly box 1), 48th item on roll. One item misfiled under estate of Horace HIBBARD, # 54, 41st item on roll, marked*.
Administrator	Stephen HOLLOWAY, who made a $300 bond with Elijah STANTON 9 November 1840
	*13 January 1843 summons to "Stephen HOLLOWAY administrator of the estate Amos HOLLOWAY deceased."
Signatures	Stephen HOLLOWAY, Elijah STANTON, Jehiel WASSON, John STANTON, Amos HOLLOWAY, Thos. D. LEMON, Israel WOODORD
Sale Buyers	Held 2 January 1841: Stephen HOLLOWAY, Harding BUCKMAN, William CLARK, M. W. PATTEN, Jesse WASSON, John STANTON

RAMBO, Charlotte

Location	Estate #194, Microfilm E1 (formerly box 1), 49th item on roll
Court Dates	Full amount said to be distributed 7 August 1849
Executor	Smith RAMBO, executor's bond of $1800 with John HALL and Timothy C. EVERTS, 15 February 1842 – her will named Smith as her son and included Everts as "administrator"
Heirs	"My son Isaac Nuton RAMBO" (land in Township 35N Range 3W, present-day civil township of Noble), "my daughter Charlotte E. MOWLAN," "my son Edanijo [Adonijah] RAMBO" ($80 he borrowed in 1839), "my son Smith RAMBO."
Signatures	Smith RAMBO, John HALL, Timothy J. EVERTS, Charlotte RAMBO (by mark), J. P. RAMBO, Charlotte MOWLAN, Adonijah RAMBO
Comment	Original will with bequests 30 December 1840; no copy in will book.

WHITEHEAD, Hampton B.

Location	Estate #207, Microfilm E1 (formerly box 1), 50th item on roll
Administrator	Bond 6 April 1842 of $600 for William H. H. WHITEHEAD to administer, security Alexander HASTINGS

Heirs	Widow Margaret WHITEHEAD
Action	Inventory taken 11 April 1842
Signatures	Margaret WHITEHEAD, William WHITEHEAD, Thos. A. STEWART, R. H. [Richard] DAWSON, Hampton B. WHITEHEAD, John WHITEHEAD, William H. H. WHITEHEAD, Alexander HASTINGS, Jasper S. HUNT, Isaac A. MARTIN
Sale Buyers	John HASTINGS, Wm. A. MARTIN, Isaac N. WHITEHEAD, David HUNT, Lazarus WHITEHEAD, Alexander HASTINGS, Josiah MARTIN, Hiram TUBBS, John WHITEHEAD, Wm. H. H. WHITEHEAD, Isaac MARTIN, Titus PERRY, Richard DAWSON, Martin PERRY, Willard PERRY, William HASTINGS, John HARNESS, Thomas WHITEHEAD
Comment	Receipt for taxes paid in St. Joseph County on property in Township 35, Range 1E (Liberty Township).
	Notes of 16 April 1841 signed by Hampton.

WELLS, Theodore H.

Location	Estate #215, Microfilm E1 (formerly box 1), 51st item on roll
Court Dates	Petition to sell real estate in Township 35N Range 3W (present-day civil township of Noble)
Administrator	Widow Jane A. WELLS, bond of $2,000 with Orrin WYLLIS and Samuel WEED 9 August 1842, bond of $1000 with Samuel M WEED 12 August 1844
Heirs	What appears to be a list of heirs, all born Noble Township except Margaret C. in Brownhelm[?], Lorain, Ohio: Abby W. 28 January 1825, Mary J. 5 July 1826, Louisa A. 20 September 1828, Margaret C. 5 April 1829 [a different mother?!], Alice H. 17 October 1830, Theodore H. 1 December 1833, Lewes D. 21 November 1835, Hariet V. Henrietta 3 June 1837, Charles F. 9 November 1839
	Summons of 16 May 1844 names them as Abby W. WELLS, Mary J. WELLS, Louisa A. WELLS, Margret C. WELLS, Alice H. WELLS, Theodore H. WELLS Jr., Lewis P. WELLS, Harriet WELLS, Henrietta WELLS, and Charles F. WELLS.
Action	Inventory sworn to 7 September 1842
Signatures	Jane A. WELLS, Samuel M. WEED, Orrin WYLLIS, Josiah GROVES, W. G.BUTLER, Anthony DEFRIES, Samuel E. WILLIAMS, Lewis STEVENSON, Joseph MCPHERSON, Reuben CHAPIN, J. P. COBBS, Theodore H. WELLS, W. H. PHILLIPS, Timothy C. EVERTS, Edwin BOOTH, Wyllis A. ROBINSON, Isaac WAY, Ivey[?] H. DUNCAN, W. A. WEBSTER, Jacob GOODRICH, A. P. ANDREW, Sylvanus EVERTS, Jesse M. LOW, Wm. D. HEMENWAY, Benj. F. WALKER, James BRADLEY
Sale Buyers	Held 6 October 1842: Nimrod PHILLIPS, David FINLEY, Wesley MORGAN, T. C. EVERTS, Admiral BURCH, Wm. PRATOR, N. P.

HUGGINS, Jno. ENGLISH, Jacob GOODRICH, G. EVERTS, J. G. MORGAN, Isaac HUTCHINS, Jacob EARLY, Edwin OHARA, Hiram MARKHAM, Jane WELLS, Samuel E. WILLIAMS

Comment   Theodore died 3 March 1842 per his widow's letter to the court 9 March 1842.

The President of the Branch of the State Bank and South Bend presented a claim for $531.25.

On 16 May 1844, Samuel E. WILLIAMS swore that "some of the heirs of Theodore H. WELLS is about to leave the State of Indiana."

Theodore WELLS note in Noble 16 April 1839.

Theodore WELLS note in Michigan City 2 December 1840 with Jesse M. LOW.

MCCOLLUM, Pikeland

Location   Estate #220, Microfilm E1 (formerly box 1), 52nd item on roll

Administrator   Ferdinand DUNHAM, William A. MCCOLLUM, bond of $600 with Benjamin CRUMPACKER 5 October 1842

Action   Inventory and appraisal filed 14 October 1842

Signatures   Frederick MCCOLLUM, George S. MCCOLLUM, Aaron MOSER, Ferdinand DUNHAM, Wm. A. MCCOLLUM, Randall HILLS(?), Reuben WEBSTER, Pikeland MCCOLLUM, James WEBSTER, Joel BUTLER, Joseph JAMES, James WESTERVELT, Daniel MUKES(?)

Sale Buyers   Held 5 November 1842: F. DUNHAM, J. B. LEWIS, Wm. M. MAPLE, Henry RICE, J. W. TAYLOR, John VANDEMARKER

Comment   "Late Justice of the Peace" Joel BUTLER on 25 September 1843 acknowledged receipt of costs from a case "in which Reuben WEBSTER assignee of Pikeland MCCOLLUM was plaintiff and J. & C. REEVE defendants."

George S. MCCOLLUM's receipt is headed "Pleasant Township Laporte Co.," as is that of Joseph JAMES, both 1 February 1846.

HULBERT, Noah

Location   Estate #229, Microfilm E1 (formerly box 1), 53rd item on roll

Court Dates   Petition to sell real estate 21 August 1844

Administrator   John F. DECKER Jr., Nancy HULBERT bond of $400 with John F. DECKER 8 May 1843; then with Lemuel(?) J. HOLLAND for $1920 13 November 1844.

Heirs   John Wesley HULBERT, Mary Elizabeth HULBERT, named in administrator's petition of 21 August 1844.

Signatures	J. P. ANDREW, Wes DARLING, Thos. P. ARMSTRONG, S. E. WILLIAMS, Nancy HULBERT, John F. DECKER, L. J. HOLLAND, D. M. LEAMING, Charles TUCKER, Noah HULBERT, Moses BULLOCK, W. A. PLACE, M. W. PETTON (?), Levi FOGLE, Daniel OVERMYER, A. TEEGARDEN
Sale Buyers	Sale report filed 27 July 1844: C. W. BROWN, Joshua ATWATER, J. F. DECKER, Henry WHITE, Hezekiah BUSSEY, Allen NICKERSON, D. C. M. LEAMING
Comment	Real estate appraised 13 November 1844 was in Township 37, Range 3 (probably present-day civil township of Center)
	S. E. WILLIAMS "Guardian ad litem" of the two heirs
	Noah HULBERT executed a note 19 March 1842 in "Springfield."

MIX, John

Location	Estate #261, Microfilm E1 (formerly box 1), 54th item on roll. The last two pages microfilmed under this estate number 261 appear to belong to estate 301, Giles BROWNELL. One is an inventory headed "Coolspring November 4th 1845," signed by Stephen MIX (JP), Alfred STANTON, and Samuel WESTON. The other (probably the reverse side) is the jacket and affidavit in which administrator Erastus H. PAYNE swore to the inventory 6 November 1845.
Administrator	Rensselaer SHAW, Handy DAVIS, $500 administrators bond 24 July 1844
Action	Inventory taken 22 August 1844
Signatures	Rensselaer SHAW, Handy DAVIS, Charlotte MIX, JOHNSON & STEWART (Whig newspaper office), John P. MABEE (St. Joseph County JP), D. HALSEY (Daniel), D. MANVILLE (Dewitt), Edward AVERY
Sale Buyers	P. WHEELER (COOLY security), Orange/George(?) MIX (R. B. HEWS security), Thomas HALL (Edward AVERY security), VANDOSON, Edward AVERY (VANDOSON security), G. J. HALL (Lewis REYNOLDS security), FARNSWORTH, M. C. ORTON, Wm. D. HARRIS, R. B. HEWS, George WAKEMAN, J. WHITMORE
Comment	On 24 July 1844 R. SHAW reported to the clerk of probate court that John MIX "died on or about the 15th day of June A. D. 1844 in Laporte," leaving no will and an estate not exceeding $250 in value.
	On 9 February 1846 Charlotte MIX and R. SHAW advised probate court that they would assign R. B. HEWS's likely uncollectable debt to the estate's creditors: "if they should succeed in the collection they are welcome to [it]."
	Estate expenses included hiring of teams and travel to "Terricoupie" to "settle up said Estate & Dry good."

KEELEY, Matthias

Location	Estate #265, Microfilm E1 (formerly box 1), 55th item on roll
Administrator	Samuel BENSON made $1500 bond with Jacob KEELEY 24 July 1844
Heirs	Named in administrator's report of August 1846: John KEELEY, Joseph KEELEY, Jas. KIMES, Catharine KIMES, Levi W. KEELEY, Conrad KEELEY, Margaret KEELEY
Action	On 31 May 1844 Levi W. KEELEY relinquished administration of the estate.
Signatures	Saml. BENSON, John KEELEY Jr., Joseph KIMES, Catharine KIMES, John STITELER, Joseph KEELEY, Wm WOLLERTON Jr., Peter KING, Levi W. KEELEY
Comment	As of August 1846, Joseph KIMES was guardian of Conrad KEELEY, and John STITELER was guardian of Margaret KEELEY

STRICKLAND, Joseph

Location	Estate #268, Microfilm E1 (formerly box 1), 56th item on roll
Administrator	$400 bond for Derrick BRINCKERHOFF's administration 23 August 1844. $400 bond for Jacob MILLER's administration 2 December 1844.
Action	Death reported "on or about 17 July 1844."
Signatures	Joseph STRICKLAND, Jacob MILLER, C. W. BROWN, Samuel GRIFFIN, David BRINCKERHOFF, John WITTER, James W. TEEPLE, John HASELTINE, Ralph TETER (by mark), James BRADLEY, John MILLIKAN
Sale Buyers	J. F. DECKER, Edwin GRIFFIN
Comment	Note of the estate's debt to David BRINCKERHOFF is headed "Kankakee Oct 15th 1844."

BARNES, George W.

Location	Estate #271, Microfilm E1 (formerly box 1), 57th item on roll
Administrator	$800 bond for executor Caleb B. DAVIS 28 August 1844. Per will Hiram B. WILCOX was also to be executor.
Heirs	From original will 11 June 1844: Widow Alvira BARNES, brothers Joseph BARNES and Perry BARNES, sisters Hannah CUNNINGHAM and Olive MARSTON.
Signatures	Caleb B. DAVIS, Byron CADWALLADER, Ivory BARNES, Hiram B. WILCOX, Hannah CUNNINGHAM, Aaron FOSTER, Noah MILLER, Robert K. SMITH, William WALDRUFF, Geo. W. BARNES, Nathan B. NICHOLS, Hiram B. WILLCOX, William BIDWELL, W. N. BALL, Noah MILLER, Joseph FULLER, Isaac DADE, John A. FRAZIER, J. W.

WERNER, J. H. FRANCIS, Lewis WEED, David HUDSON, Edwd. D. GRIGG, J. W. WARNER, John MARSTON, Perry BARNES, Matthew MOYES?, E. MORRISON, Wm. TIBBITS, D. D. PEATTELUM?, A. G. BURGER, Ralph TEETER (by mark).

Sale Buyers	Sale record certified 21 November 1844: Wm BIDWELL, Jonathan S. HUNT, Wm. PALMER, Enoch LEWIS, Robert K. SMITH, Elfonzo ELLIOT, John FRAZIER, Lazerus WHITEHEAD, Ivory BARNES, Jon COOPER, David HUDSON, Aaron WARNER, John F. WRIGHT, John GRILL, Kelogg HEAD?, John MASTON, Samuel STEWART, Joseph BARNES, Perry BARNES, Joseph WINCH, Hiram B. WILCOX, Caleb B. DAVIS, Edwin D. GRIGG, Wm. WALDRUFF, Henson P. DAVIS, Isaac B. COPLAND
Comment	Alvira BARNES's receipt for $171.83 of "household and kitchen furniture" done by way of William BIDWELL and dated "Galena May 14th 1846."
	Sylvanus EVERTS bill to George BARNES "for medical service To visit 20 Miles & consultation $10.00 Union Mills May 23 1844."
	Bequeathed land in Township 38 North Range 2 West (probably Galena).
	Two-page listing of debts and how much the estate hoped to collect from each debtor.

MAXWELL, Arthur

Location	Estate #275, Microfilm E1 (formerly box 1), 58th item on roll.
Court Dates	William NILES stated that Arthur MAXWELL died in La Porte County "about the 15th day of June last [1844]."
Administrator	Widow Elizabeth MAXWELL relinquished right to administer; $700 bond 10 October 1844 for William NILES, John MCINTOSH security.
Action	Inventory 5 November 1844.
Signatures	Herbert WILLIAMS, John EATON, William NILES, Elizabeth MAXWELL, Elnathan DAVIS, Arthur MAXWELL, L. WOODS, E. DAVIS, Sylvanus EVERTS, Nelson AKER?, George BIGGART, Jno. BARTHOLOMEW
Sale Buyers	Held 5 November 1844: MCANTUSH (possibly John MCINTOSH), Edward HALL, Darwin PATTERSON, Jess MORMAN, Charles EATON, Chansey NICKERSON, John MAXWELL, Wm. NILES, A. BIGELOW, Wm. MAXWELL, George BIGARD, Samuel BIGARD
Comment	Letter from William NILES to "Mr. ARMSTRONG" dated "Clinton May 8th 1849" (possibly 1847), reporting on his collections and asking to be excused from attending court.

CONNER, William (again)

59th item is six additional pages of estate #285 – see that entry above.

THOMPSON, Henry A.

Location	Estate #292, Microfilm E1 (formerly box 1), 60th item on roll
Administrator	William S. Pray
Signatures	Henry A. THOMPSON, Robert E. TUTTLE, Charles PALMER

LOONEY, James

Location	Estate #297, Microfilm E1 (formerly box 1), 61st item on roll
Administrator	Lewis WILKINSON; $200 bond with him and Edwin G. MATHEWS 26 August 1845
Heirs	Widow (paid 30 November 1846), evidently Abigail SPEIRS
Action	Inventory sworn 23 December 1845
Signatures	James ROOD, Jacob G. MORGAN, Lewis WILKINSON, James L. LOONEY (on note dated 20 November 1844), Abigail SPEIRS, William R. SPEIRS, John MILLIKAN, Abigail LOONEY, John DILLINGHAM?
Comment	Receipt from the clerk of the County Commissioners Court in Will County, Illinois, to James S. LOONEY for $2.49 paid to redeem real estate there 17 November 1843: in Section 36, Township 35 North, Range 11 East, 3rd principal meridian.

OTIS, William M.

Location	Estate #300, Microfilm E1 (formerly box 1), 62nd item on roll
Administrator	Isaac CORLISS, bond 23 September 1845 with Irwin S. JESSUP for $500
Heirs	Widow Clarissa OTIS
Action	Inventory taken 25 September 1845
Signatures	William M. OTIS (note 1 July 1845 in Michigan City), Isaac CORLISS, Jeremiah HUNT, Irwin S. JESSUP, Daniel WOOLLEY, C. [Christian] T. YOUNG, James FORRESTER, Andrew MELVILLE, John S. JESSUP, J. H. PEARSALL, S. D. HALL, Aaron KIDDER, A. H. MATHEWS, Arba HEALD, B. W. MYERS, A. H. ROBINSON, George D. BAKER, Obadiah SMITH, Lester LOOMIS, B. F. DOWNING, Luther CASE, John CLOSSER, George HALL, C. H. DOWNING, A. TEEGARDEN, Isaac WESTON, Orin BANKS, Albert HARTSWELL, James ROOD, Isaac GOODPASTER? (of New Durham, by mark), George PRATTON, Branson PARKER, Robe GRAHAM, E. B. WOODSON
Sale Buyers	Clark MEEKER (security A. MELLVILLE), Branson PARKER (security Wm. D. PARKER), Clark MEEKER (security A. MELLVILLE), Christian YOUNG, Joseph DOWNING (security B. W. MYERS), Joshua DOWNING (security B. F. TREADWAY) Andrew MELLVILLE (crossed

out), Eli BLACK, Aaron KIDDER (security Henry LOOMIS), John JESSOP, Branson PARKER (security Wm. D. PARKER), Elder LELAND, Wm. GARWOOD, Abm SOVEREIGN (security Wm. M. BORST), Wm. M. BORST, C. BRADLEY (security Wm. M. BORST), Jno CLOSSER (security Matthew FORRESTER), Wm BRAYTON (security Alexr. CROME?, Mrs. OTIS, F. MARSHALL, A. MORRIS

Comment   An 8 March 1845 note in Michigan City to CARTER & CARTER identified William M. OTIS as of Scipio Township. In October 1845 "Jernegan & Harris, Proprietor of Indiana Tocsin," receipted the estate for payment for publication.

BROWNELL, Giles

Location   Estate #301, Microfilm E1 (formerly box 1), 63rd item on roll. Two items misfiled and erroneously microfilmed under estate number 261 are marked*.

Administrator   Erastus H. PAYNE, per $400 bond with Alexander H. ROBINSON 20 October 1845.

Action   *Inventory headed "Coolspring November 4th 1845," signed by Stephen MIX (JP), Alfred STANTON, and Samuel WESTON.

*Jacket and affidavit in which administrator Erastus H. PAYNE swore to the inventory 6 November 1845.

Signatures   Erastus H. PAYNE, A. H. ROBINSON, Alfred STANTON, Samuel WESTON, Aaron KIDDER, John MILLIKAN, Eliphalet PATEE (Coolspring Twp.), Elmore PATTEE (Scipio Twp.), A. W. ROBINSON, James ROOD, STEPHEN MIX (JP)

Sale Buyers   18? July 1846: William LOWELL, Erastus H. PAYNE (security Joseph FIELD), Joseph FIELD, C. POTTER?

Also, an administrator's sale at residence of Henry C. PAYNE (Coolspring Twp.) 29 November 1843?!: Franklin CLOSSER (security A. H. ROBINSON), William LERWILL (security Alfred STANTON), Benjamin J. LUMBAR, Orange MIX? (security Stephen MIX?), Eliphalet PATTEE, E. H. PAYNE (security Alonso D. PAYNE), Alfred STANTON (security Wm. LERWILL), Samuel WESTON, Alonso D. PAYNE (security Asa BUNSE), E. ROBINSON (security Franklin CLOSSER)

VANDEVANTER, Lydia

Location   Estate #323, Microfilm E1 (formerly box 1), 64th item on roll

Administrator   Jesse WASSON affirmed (did not swear) to faithfully administer 1 July 1846

Heirs   Constantine LOMAX, "being an heir," petitioned 27 June 1846 for Wasson to administer. William LOMAX and Sarah his wife, Andrew MOTTER and

Patience his wife, possibly Isaac VANDEVANTER (Berrien County, Michigan)

Signatures   Jesse WASSON, Constantine LOMAX, Charles VAIL, Jehiel WASSON, Joseph G. AMES, John MILLIKAN, Peter M. VANDEVANTER, John T. VANDEVANTER, William LOMAX, Sarah LOMAX, Isaac VANDEVANTER

REYNOLDS, Allen W.

Location   Estate #325, Microfilm E1 (formerly box 1), 65th item on roll

Administrator   Harriet Maria REYNOLDS, widow, petitioned to administer 24 August 1846; $300 bond with "Ransalaer" SHAW made that date

Heirs   Harriet Maria REYNOLDS, widow

Signatures   Harriet M. REYNOLDS, R. SHAW, Thomas JERNEGAN, William S. WESTON, Thos. ELLSWORTH, David WINCHELL, James G. WINCHELL, Abiel LATHROP, Preserved WHEELER

THOM, John

Location   Estate #327, Microfilm E1 (formerly box 1), 66th item on roll

Administrator   Richard ETHERINGTON made bond of $600 with Ira C. NYE 28 October 1846

Heirs   Elizabeth ETHERINGTON (Richard's wife), Grace THOM, Eliza PARTRIDGE (Richard their guardian)

Signatures   Bradley HUDSON, Richard ETHERINGTON, Ira C. NYE, Wm. WALDRUFF

Sale Buyers   At the dwelling of Richard ETHERINGTON in Galena Township, 21 November 1846: Richard ETHERINGTON, Scipha FOSTER, William WALDRUFF, Ira C. NYE, Solomon L. PALMER, Edward FORD, Ambrose BLANY, Jonathan S. HUNT, Charles FRANCIS, Roswell LEWIS, John FRAZIER, Bradley HUDSON, Zebulin COLLINS, John BREWER

Comment   Etherington billed the estate $40.65 for "expenses and time in going to the State of New York to collect note against Richard BENDALL."

DOWNING, Nathaniel B.

Location   Estate #12, Microfilm E1 (formerly box 1), 67th item on roll

Administrator   Katharine DOWNING and Jonathan D. MIDDLETON made bond of $1000 with Henry DAVIS 27 June 1835.

Signatures   Katharine DOWNING (by mark), Jonathan D. MIDDLETON, Henry DAVIS (by mark)

Comment	MIDDLETON's petition to the court refers to DOWNING as "of Virginia," which is crossed out, and then of "Laborte County Ind." and states that he died 27 June 1835. "And on the same day A Brother of the said Decd arrived From Vermillion County Ind. and wishing to remove the widow and minor heirs of the said decd to the afforesaid county of Vermillion to their Friend and Relatives and Also representing that the said Decd was Possesed of Considerable of Property in the afforesaid County of Vermillion and Judging that it would be more Advantageous to the Estate to remove the goods & chattles of said decd to the said county of Vermillion to be Desposed of According to Law . . . and having settled all Debts Dues and Demands Against said Estate."

EGANS, William

Location	Estate #26, Microfilm E1 (formerly box 1), 68th item on roll. Three pages belonging to the following file, William BOND, estate no. 83, were mistakenly filmed at the end of this estate, and then filmed again under 83.
Administrator	John HEFNER, Jared CHAPMAN: Bond with them and John B. NILES for $2000 made 26 September 1836. Another bond with Matilda Egans and Wm. M. MAPLE made 1 October 1836, Elizabeth VICORY witnessing.
Heirs	Widow Matilda EGANS waived administration 27 September 1836 in statement to court. In 1849 statement, HEFNER names "three of the heirs of James EGANS" as Samuel EGANS, Jared CHAPMAN, and William TYNER.
Action	Sale bill states William died 27 October 1836; inventory sworn to 29 September 1826
Signatures	John HEFNER, Matilda EGANS (by mark), Samuel VAN DALSEM, Jared CHAPMAN, William TYNER, S. T. EGANS, Jno. B. NILES, John WHITEHEAD, John WILLS JP, Elizabeth VICORY, Wm. M. MAPLE, John B. FRAVEL, John HEATON?, Willis COX, Nancy MOWERY?, James TONE, William WEST, Jacob PICKLE (by mark), Thomas POWELL (by mark), John BOWELL, Daniel CROSS, Charles EGBERT, Robert STANFIELD
Sale Buyers	Jared CHAPMAN, John HEFNER, Willis COX, Jacob PALLION, Garret BIAS, Wm. M. MAPLE, T. LEAMING, Ingraham GOULD, Jacob PICKLE, Samuel VAN DALSEM, Joseph RICHEY, Andrew PICKLE, Wm. EGANS, Wm. M. MAPLE, Wm. MCLANE, Miles WINCHESTER, Jesse COLLAM, Benjamin GILBRETH, William ARGERBRIGHT, Ezekiel PROVAULT, Samuel SCARCE, Joseph STARRET, Joseph CHAPMAN
Comment	William EGANS deceased is named as guardian of the minor heirs of James EGANS deceased, "Hudson Feb 11th 1839." Nancy MOWERY? made depositions from Fayette County 5 July 1837 and from Franklin County 27 June 1837 where she was identified as Nancy EAGANS widow of James EAGANS. Bonds $600 with Andrew PICKLE, Jarred CHAPMAN, and John HEFNER 25 September 1839, for renting undescribed farmland, and the same parties for $500 1 October 1836 for undescribed farmland.

BOND, William

Location   Estate #83, Microfilm E1 (formerly box 1), 69th item on roll

Administrator   Executors Charlotte BOND, Jesse BOND, Ira BOND.

Bond of $5000 on 16 November 1838 for Ira BOND to execute, co-signed by Jehiel WASSON and Elijah STANTON.

Undated memorial to court from Jehiel WASSON stating that Ira BOND died before completing administration.

Bond of $400 on 17 November 1843 Jehiel WASSON and Elijah STANTON to administer.

Heirs   Bond's will of "the twelfth of the fifth month" 1838 provided for the sale of "my half of the sawmill and half the land belonging to it" and "the lot of land in section one by David HARMONS." To his wife, her choice of 2 cows, 2 feather beds and furniture, one case of drawers, one pot, one dutch oven, two buckets, "all of our puter, one tee pot six china plates & one set of tee cups and sasors and two chairs and all of her wareing clothes and every thing about the house that is cold hern" for her and her heirs. Other household furniture during her widowhood, to be divided among children if she remarried. To son-in-law Calvin WASSON $100. To son Jesse BOND "ten acres of land in the southeast corner of the lot in the fourteenth section," described, plus half of the apple nursery. To son William BOND $10. To son John BOND $100. To son Ira BOND 140 acres in Section 36, "the north part of the tract I now live on," also 70 acres in section 14, and 40 acres in Section 25 "joining the lake in southwest corner of section." Also the farming tools, a one-horse wagon, a 2-horse wagon and mare, and half the apple nursery. Ira was to take "good care" of his mother. To son-in-law Jehiel WASSON 20 acres "the south side of his plantation to go to the state road (described). To son-in-law Elijah STANTON 20 acres of land "north of his cabben to the meeting house ground." To all his children equally the proceeds of selling 80 acres of the south part of "the track of land where I now live," namely Marah WASSON, Lydia WASSON, Jesse BOND, Charlotte STANTON, William BOND, and John BOND – except Ira who already had his share. Also specified what to do with livestock and crops.

Action   Will proved in court 13 November 1838. Charlotte BOND and Jesse BOND renounce their executorships in Ira's favor 14 November 1838.

Signatures   William BOND, Jesse WASSON, Jesse HOUGH, Jehiel WASSON, James ANDREW, Aaron STANTON, Martin W. RUTON, Arthur MCCLURE, Jesse JACKSON, A. TEEGARDEN, R. MERRYFIELD, Joseph PETERS, James BRADLEY, Calvin WASSON, John BOND, Jesse BOND, William CLARK, Elijah STANTON, Ira BOND, Samuel TREAT, John STANTON, Stephen HOLLOWAY, A. WILLIAMS, Charlotte BOND, Lydia BOND

Sale Buyers	The record is extremely faint – most names illegible. Joshua CANADEY, David TURNER, Elijah STANTON, Edward STANTON, James TEEPLE, Hiram JONES, Daniel RATHBONE.
Comment	William BOND note of indebtedness signed 6 October 1835.
	A. TEEGARDEN's medical bill records four visits and medicines in June and July 1838, and a final visit 13 September 1838.
	John BOND affidavit of 10 August 1844 refers to "William BOND of the state of Missouri."
	A list describes land BOND owned in Townships 37 and 38, Range 3 (present- day civil townships of Springfield and Center).

COOPER, Ephraim

Location	Estate #89 Microfilm E1 (formerly box 1), 70th item on roll
Administrator	William WALDRUFF. $600 bond dated 23 November 1838 signed by him and John COOPER.
Signatures	Matthew MAYES, B. SPURLOCK, Henry HILYAR, Mary HILYAR, Charles FRANCIS (Galena), Henry SPERRY, Mahetibel WALDRUFF, Jacob HECKMAN, Geo. W. BARNES, C. B. DAVIS, Mary COOPER
Sale Buyers	C. B. DAVIS, Lewis MEAD, G. W. BARNES, Kellog SHED, H. C. DAVIS, James WILSON, Cyphus FOSTER, Henry SPERRY, James CATERLIN, Willis WRIGHT, Richard HUDSON, Birum CADWALADER, Samuel HERBERT, Mary COOPER, W. GOIT, C. FRANCES, D. HARMON, Perry DUNKIN, Matthew MAYS, Joseph STANTON, D. C. BRICKET, Urasmus SHED, John BARINER/PARINER
Comment	Filed in court 17 February 1849 and signed: "William WALDRUFF Administrator of Ephraim COOPER decd asks to be discharged from his said trust as such Administrator as he expects to remove from this state."

GOULD, Jeremiah

Location	Estate #105 Microfilm E1 (formerly box 1), 71st item on roll
Administrator	John FRANCIS. Bond of $200 signed by him and Oscar A. BARKER 16 February 1839. Bond of $2,000 signed by him and Oren GOULD 14 November 1839.
Heirs	Widow Anna C. GOULD, who renounced administration 11 September 1838.
Action	Administrator petitioned for sale of real estate 14 August 1839. He found "no personal property of any description," and one parcel of real estate, a house and lot on Pine Street in Michigan City appraised by Willis PECK and Udney BURKE at $1200, and debts of $3014.50. An affidavit from Ingraham GOULD reported that Jeremiah owed Oren some $3000 secured by real estate as of 7 September 1837. Oren swore that he lost the notes.

Signatures   Anna C. GOULD, Oren GOULD, John FRANCIS, Oscar BARKER, Rodney B. NILES, Ingraham GOULD, Willis PECK, Udney BURKE

WINCHELL, William B.

Location	Estate #111 Microfilm E1 (formerly box 1), 72nd item on roll
Administrator	David WINCHELL. Bond of $600 signed by him and Joseph CATLIN 8 May 1839. Bond of $250 signed by him and William SHIMMIN 13 May 1840.
Heirs	Sarah "Sally" WINCHELL, "wife of Wm. Winchell," declined administration in a note dated Pleasant Township and probably 3 May 1839.
Signatures	David WINCHELL, Wm. SHIMMIN, Joseph CATLIN, Sally WINCHELL, Ephraim BARNEY, Sarah WINCHELL (by mark), Ephraim BARNEY
Sale Buyers	15 June 1839: B. WINCHILL, Steven "WINCHILL," Widow WINCHILL, Sarah WINCHILL, J. HAMILTON, P.? TAYLOR, Hiram CATER, Eli MACENTAFFEE, John DAVIS, D. WINCHILL, Amo WINCHILL, J. BARNARD, Abm. G. BURGET, Wm. B. WINCILL (by mark)
Comment	Note signed by mark by "Wm B WINCILL" to John DECKER 28 January 1839, witnessed by Abm. G. BURGET.
	Land owned by Winchell in Township 35 North, Range 2 West (present-day civil township of Union)

HOLLEY, Daniel

Location	Estate #125 Microfilm E1 (formerly box 1), 73rd item on roll
Heirs	Holley's will of 13 June 1839 (not in Will Book A) provided for $40 to daughter Sophronia and named Ebenezer PALMER as executor, witnessed by John GLIME, Brownell BROWN, and E. PALMER. Bond of $1800 signed by E. PALMER and D. McLEAMING 16 September 1839.
Signatures	Daniel HOLLEY, John GLINN, Brownell BROWN, E. PALMER. Robert ALLEN, John GLIME, Simeon FREES
Sale Buyers	Held 10 October 1839: John GLINN, John VAN METRE, John WHITE, E. PALMER, Robert ALLEN, Lemuel FITCH, John F. DECKER, John BUSSEY, John WHITE, Simeon FREECE, Henry JONES, George BUSSEY, Hiram GRIFFIN, A. LANGDON, Isaac WATKINS, Alex MILLER, Thomas PIERCE, John WATSON, John BUSSEY,
Comment	On one note, the deceased's surname was spelled HAWLEY.

HUDSON, Elijah P.

Location Estate #161 Microfilm E1 (formerly box 1), 74th item on roll

Administrator $10,000 bond for Pliny HUDSON administrator, also signed by Patrick B. BILL and Samuel TREAT, 7 October 1840. Petition to court from Gilbert HATHAWAY 24 June 1844 stated that Pliny died 4 February 1841 before the estate was fully administered, and "a considerable amount of assets" remained, leaving the estate in an "unsettled condition." Same-sized bond for Benoni M. NEWKIRK dated 24 June 1844 and co-signed by Jacob MILLER, William D. SHUMWAY, Noah NEWELL, Willard A. PLACE, Joseph S. STEBBINS, and William FRYE. In a note to the court 11 February 1845, NEWKIRK resigned as administrator, "no assets having come into my hands of said estate."

Heirs Will dated 13 July 1840 identified deceased as "of the Town of Arcadia in the County of Wayne and State of New York." He bequeathed everything he had in Noble Township, La Porte County, to "my mother Patty HUDSON wife of Pliny HUDSON of Arcadia," including one undivided half of a tract of land with a "grist & flouring mill" called "Newark Mills," subject to "a certain contract of defeasance executed to John Gray." He nominated his father Pliny as executor. Witnesses Geo. H. MIDDLETON of Arcadia, Saml. E. HUDSON of Palmyra (Wayne County, New York), and Elisha M. Holmes of Philips, Ontario County, New York.

Signatures B. O. NEWKIRK, Pliny HUDSON, Samuel TREAT, P. B. BILL, Jacob MILLER, Wm. D. SHUMWAY, Noah NEWELL, W. A. PLACE, Joseph STEBBINS, William FRYE, Reuben TREAT

Comment A note from Bills & Hudson, dated 21 April 1840 South Bend, promised to pay Timothy C. EVERTS, Nimrod PHILLIPS, and Sylvanus EVERTS $1000.

Patrick B. BILL and Reuben TREAT testified to Elijah P. HUDSON's signature on the will and those of his witnesses, adding that the witnesses were residents of the state of New York, where Elijah died.

HIBBARD, Horace B. (again)

Location Estates #173 and #176, microfilm E1 (formerly box 1), 75th and 76th items on roll, are listed above under estate #54, 51st item on roll.

STARRETT, Alexander

Location Estate #192, microfilm E1 (formerly box 1), 77th item on roll.

Administrator Joseph STARRETT and Therisa STARRETT (widow) signed bond of $1000 with Benjamin SHAW

Signatures Joseph STARRETT, J. M. CHAPMAN, Sylvanus EVERTS, Martin HOUSEMAN (?), Theresa STARRETT (by mark), Benjamin SHAW, Timothy A. EVERTS, WYLLIS & ROBINSON, Samuel STARRETT,

	Edward O'HARRA, Richard SMITH, Moses MOULTON, Banks HALL, Martin HOUSEMAN
Sale Buyers	26 February 1842: Silas LOVEING, Wm. PATTERSON, Right LOVEING, James GREERSON, H. BEAHM, Wm. MCLONE, Alexander MEEREANZ, John CHARLESWOORTH, Henry GEIST, Westley MORGAN, Charles EASTON, Banks HALL, Benjamin SHAW, Joseph STARRETT, Jesse WEST, Nimrod WEST, Arthur JOUIN (?), Barclay UNDERWOOD, Harry MUN, John WEBSTER, David BROWN, Dexter BROWN, Blake RIZER, Chester MESSEN (?) Jr., Joseph LINARD, Nelson AERE, Samuel BURSON, Jeremiah WILLSON, John WILLS, Henderson SICKELL, Wm. C. NELSON, Michael OHARA, Stephen JACKSON, John WILLS, Albert LILLY, Wm. FREELAND
Comment	Died 10 January 1842, according to administrators in court 31 January 1842.

JESSUP, Daniel

Location	First 26 pages microfilmed and properly labeled as estate #240, microfilm E1 (formerly box 1), 78th item on roll.
Administrator	John S. JESSUP and Erwin/Irwin S. JESSUP, sons of the widow Ann JESSUP, who renounced administration 24 October 1843. Bond of $2400 with Isaac CORLISS same date.
Signatures	John S. JESSUP, Erwin S. JESSUP, Ann JESSUP (by mark), Isaac CORLISS, Bailey M. PERKINS, Abiezer M. JESSUP, Samuel WESTON, Sylvanus EVERTS, CLARKE & HOWELL, Nathaniel CASE, Bush BRUNSON, Bailey M. PERKINS, Roswell MILLER, Wm. REED, James CURRY, C. B. BLAIR, Jos R. KING/RING, Daniel WOOLLEY, G. A. ROSE, George W. RICE, Lester LOOMIS, D. G. ROSE, Allerton HARTWELL, George W. BRUNSON, William TAYLOR, Joseph DAVIS, Clark MEEKER (by mark)
Comment	Died 28 August 1843, according to administrators' petition 24 October.
	The three sons claimed $225 apiece from the estate at New Durham 14 May 1846 for "labor done in the life time of Daniel JESSUP (Dec) for the Said Daniel JESSUP after he had arrived at the age of twenty years."
	Nancy BRUNSON received $75 from the estate for 1/3 of the proceeds of a "Nurcery of Apple trees let on shares to the said D. Jessup, in his life time."
	G. A. ROSE billed the estate $15 for medical services "after deducting therefrom certain fruit trees received by me."

NOLAND, Barbara

Location	Last 20 images microfilmed and mislabeled as estate #240, microfilm E1 (formerly box 1), 79th item on roll. Should have been labeled as estate 277.

Administrator	Aquila W. ROGERS and Silas NOLAND signed $600 bond with Stephen Noland 13 November 1844. Aquila W. ROGERS and Jacob FRAVEL signed bond of $600 10 February 1845.
Signatures	Henrietta BROWN (by mark), David BROWN (apparently by mark), F. MCCALLUM, Edward AVERY, Aquila W. ROGERS, Jeremiah HISER, Philip EDINGER, Silas NOLAND, Stephen NOLAND, Jacob PERKINS
Sale Buyers	8 March 1845 (terms: "the highest bidder is the buyer all sums over three dollars nine months credit note and surety will be required"): Nathan BARTLETT, Obediah CHAMBERS, Aquila W. ROGERS, J. P. MILLS, George WINTERS, Jeremiah HISER, Isaac S. EVINS, Philip ETINGER, Arthur ERVIN, E. AVERY, A. LILLY, Thomas WILLETT

ROSS, Solomon

Location	Estate #292, microfilm E1 (formerly box 1), 80th item on roll.
Administrator	James DRUMMOND, William FENLEY, Elizabeth A. ROSS. Along with Jesse H. G. COPLIN, they signed a $17,000 bond 6 June 1868.
Heirs	Widow Elizabeth A. ROSS
Signatures	Elizabeth A. ROSS, Henry E. HUNTLEY, C. G. POWELL, James BRADLEY, Catharine ROSS, William W. FINLEY, James DRUMMOND, Minor NESBIT, Phineas HUNT

MARSHALL, Aaron Foster

Location	Estate #298, microfilm E1 (formerly box 1), 81st item on roll.
Administrator	Marshall S. BIGELOW signed $800 bond with Herbert WILLIAMS 9 February 1845, and $200 27 August 1845.
Heirs	infant heirs" Amelia MARSHALL, Maria MARSHALL, and Henry MARSHALL, guardian ad litem Andrew L. OSBORN
Signatures	Marshall S. BIGELOW, Herbert WILLIAMS, Andrew L. OSBORN, Patrick DORAN
Comment	Marshall S. BIGELOW petitioned court 27 August 1845: "Aaron Foster MARSHALL late of By-Town District of Dalhousie Upper Canada died intestate on or about the 4th day of October AD 1844 and left personal property and effects in said Laporte County . . . also some real estate." Bigelow billed the estate $727 on 10 October for 21 months services in upper Canada, and services rendered to 3 children including sending them to Vermont from Canada.

Two-page inventory of lots and notes totaling $584.24.

WESTCOTT, Zeri C.

Location	Estate #306, microfilm E1 (formerly box 1), 82nd item on roll.
Administrator	Edmond S. GARDNER, James HASKILL made bond of $300 with Philip DAVIS 20 November 1845.
Signatures	Edmond S. GARDNER, James HASKILL, Philip DAVIS (by mark), Horace PINNEY, Joseph Y. WRIGHT
Sale Buyers	Held at GARDNER's residence in Clinton Township, 31 December 1845. He was the only purchaser, and all to be sold were 34.5 bushels of wheat @ 90 cents. T. J. S. HIXON was security.

GRIFFITH, Jacob

Location	Estate #328, microfilm E1 (formerly box 1), 83rd item on roll.
Administrator	Seth WAY and Abram G. BURGER posted bond of $150 on 9 November 1846. BURGER's petition of that date told the court that Griffith had died 29 or 30 August 1846. WAY's petition of that date identified him as a creditor.
Signatures	Seth WAY, Abram G. BURGER, J. B. M. GRIFFITH, Benjamin DEWITT (by mark), W. A. PLACE, D. POTTER, W. N. BALE, Davison PATTEN (POTTER?), M. A. PATTERSON, Thos D. LEMON, W. A. PLACE, Jane E. WILLIAM
Sale Buyers	12 December 1846 at the courthouse: Seth WAY, John LOWE, Alex WOODARD, David DINWIDDIE, Patrick OHANNAN, Peter RICHLEY, Jacob SHULTS, A. G. BURGHER, F. W. SWANEY, Jas. R. HOWELL, Alex MAZE, A. MORTON

EGBERT, John

Location	Estate #330, microfilm E1 (formerly box 1), 84th item on roll.
Heirs	Widow Anna EGBERT and children Charles EGBERT, Wesley EGBERT, Alfred EGBERT, Courtland EGBERT, Clarissa REYNOLDS wife of John REYNOLDS, according to creditor William HAWKINS's letter to the court for the August 1846 term.
Signatures	William HAWKINS, Andrew GWINN, Paul EGBERT, Elisha EGBERT, William EGBERT
Comment	Sheriff served subpoena on "Anney" EGBERT, Wesley EGBERT, and Courtland EGBERT 6 August 1846; others not found, Charles EGBERT reportedly residing in Marshall County. Other defendants elsewhere said to reside in St.Joseph County, as Jacob EGBERT himself apparently did. Marshall County sheriff did not find Charles 27 August 1846. The REYNOLDS were said to live in Berrien County, Michigan.
	Controversy over ownership of two town lots in La Porte.

WILLIAMS, Micajah T.

Location	Estate #336, microfilm E1 (formerly box 1), 85th item on roll.
Administrator	William W. NILES made $1000 bond with John B. NILES 1 March 1847, and later apparently moved to New York City and was replaced by Andrew L. OSBORN, who made bond with William C. HANNAH for $100 on 10 May 1848. OSBORN and John B. NILES made $1000 bond 18 August 1848.
Heirs	According to OSBORN's report to the court 11 May 1848, widow Hannah J. WILLIAMS, age 56; supposed adult children Charles H. WILLIAMS, Granville L. WILLIAMS, Elizabeth W. PERRY and Aaron F. PERRY her husband; and minor children Alfred H. WILLIAMS, Sarah A. WILLIAMS, George F. WILLIAMS, and John E. WILLIAMS, "all of whom are nonresidents of the State of Indiana."
	Proceedings of the Court of Common Pleas, Hamilton County, Ohio, stated that WILLIAMS's will was presented 22 May 1845, leaving everything to Ohio Life Insurance & Trust Company, to be managed for the benefit of his widow and her heirs.
Signatures	Andrew L. OSBORN, Wm. W. NILES, Jno. B. NILES, HAMISON & TALCOTT, W. T. MILLIKAN
Comment	Administrator reported to the court that WILLIAMS was a resident of Hamilton County, Ohio, at the time of his death and letters of administration were there granted 18 June 1845, along with many other difficulties involving the estate.
	Williams owned land in Township 35 Ranges 4, 5, and 6 West (present-day civil township of Clinton and two townships directly west of it in Porter County) as well as lots in Brookville, Franklin County.
	Probate proceedings from Cook County, Illinois, included from 1849.
	Petition from William B. OGDEN (of Chicago?) states that Williams died 21 March 1839 in Hamilton County and owed Ogden $155.43 plus interest.

MOULTON, Moses

Location	Estate #341, microfilm E1 (formerly box 1), 86th item on roll.
Administrator	John CLOSSER; bond with Wm. GOGAN for $600 on 26 July 1847
Heirs	Widow Lydia MOULTON
Action	Personal property appraised 3 August 1847.
Signatures	John CLOSSER, Hervey MUIR(?), Martin HOUSEMAN, Edward OHARA, James MOTT, G. C. ROGERS, Nelson AKER, L. STEVENSON, Richard GOLDSMITH (by mark), William OHARA, Cornelius CALKINS, Moses MOULTON, Jeremiah PERKINS, Isaac CORTES, W. & J. MILLIKAN, Jacob ANDREWS

Sale Buyers	John TAWAN(?), Daniel PANGBURN, Jacob ANDREWS, John CLOSSER, L. W. LOCKWOOD, B. SHAW, BLAIN Esqr., Michael OHARROW, Jacob H. MANN, J. PERKINS, J. HALL, Mr. LANGBURN, Tho. STEPHENSON, Harvey MUN, Hiram BLACKMUN
Comment	Noble Township

CHAPMAN, John

Location	Estate #345, microfilm E1 (formerly box 1), 87th item on roll
Administrator	Joseph CHAPMAN, brother, petitioned the court to administer 23 August 1847, estimating the state at $5000. Bond of $10,000 with William CLEMENT and Charles LADD. Asked to be dismissed 13 November 1849.
Heirs	Two children, Henry Clay CHAPMAN and Francis Marion CHAPMAN
Signatures	Joseph CHAPMAN, John CHAPMAN, William CLEMENT, Charles LADD, Samuel DARLINGTON, Frederick GEER, Thomas ATKINS, Isaiah ATKINS, Wm. L. WILSON, Litheland GILLESPIE, Ferris PIERCE, Wm. CLEMON, Gabriel DROLLINGER, Edward KIRTON (by mark), William HAGENBUCH, A. CLARK, F. ROBERTS, Jehiel WASSON, James M. ALLEN, Henry LUSK, Isaac V. BOND, E. S. PENWELL, S. S. MCCORMICK, Joseph KENNEDY, W. S. CLEMENT
Comment	Real estate in Township 35 North Range 2 West and Township 36 North Range 3 West (probably present-day civil township of Union).
	Chapman signed a note as late as 14 June 1847.

BOICE, John J.

Location	Estate #170, microfilm E1 (formerly box 1), 88th item on roll
Heirs	Partition suit involving Elizabeth BOICE, widow; Ephraim BOICE, plaintiff; Ann Eliza SHOP, Peter SHOP, Wm. H. BOICE, John M. BOICE. William and John later identified as minor heirs; guardian ad litem John B. NILES as of November 1847 term of court. Ephraim BOICE told court his father John died 6 August 1847.
Signatures	W. A. PLACE, Elam CLARK, Samuel PRETT[?]
Comment	Land in Township 37N Range 2W (probably present-day civil township of Kankakee). Hand-drawn map shows lands in three sections as partitioned.

ROSS, William

Location	Estate #376, microfilm E1 (formerly box 1), 89th item on roll
Administrator	Zechariah WAXHAM. A $520 bond with him and Samuel NEVINS 11 April 1849. William ALSOP and William EDWARDS relinquished to him 18 May 1849.

Signatures	A. A. REYNOLDS, Zechariah WAXHAM, William ALSOP, William EDWARDS, Richard A. LONGSHORE, Dorothy ALSOP (signed Kingsbury 18 May 1849), D. SHAW, Frederick CHAPMAN, Charles HENSON
Comment	Ross's "will by word of mouth" heard 26 March 1849, reduced to writing 11 April, had William ALSOP settling up and paying debts, and all the rest to Dorothy ALSOP, "to and for her own sole use absolutely."

PAGAN, David

Location	Estate #395, microfilm E1 (formerly box 1), 90th item on roll
Administrator	Nathan HOLLOWAY. Bond of $400 with Thomas E. STANTON 26 August 1844. Bond of $600 with Jehiel WASSON 10 August 1847.
Heirs	Mary Elizabeth PAGAN "infant" (who apparently had two guardians ad litem), Jackson WILLIS, Rebecca WILLIS "his wife late Rebecca PAGAN," the widow
Action	Inventory taken 28 August 1844.
Signatures	Stephen HOLLOWAY, Thomas E. STANTON, Nathan HOLLOWAY, D. MCLEAMING, Lemuel FITCH, James E. WILLIAMS, Joseph WILLIS (by mark), Rebecca WILLIS (by mark), W. N. BALL, Rebecca PAGIN, Rebecca PAGIN (by mark), David PAGIN, W. C. HANNAH, Carter CURTIS
Comment	Land in Township 37N Range 3W (probably present-day civil townships of Springfield and Center), including a parcel "conveyed to said David Pagan by Joseph Pagan with a mill situated thereon."
	Rebecca WILLIS petitioned the probate court stating that David PAGAN died "about the 29th day of July 1844 leaving your petitioner his widow and one child to wit Mary Elizabeth."
	Rebecca signed a statement in August 1844 stating that she had remarried. A later petition identified her husband as Jackson WILLIS.

ALLEN, Reuben

Location	Estate #66, microfilm E1 (formerly box 1), 91st item on roll
Administrator	Mark ALLEN – bond of $1200 with Jacob HUPP 27 October 1838, bond of $1300 with George W. ALLEN 13 November 1839
Action	Administrator's final report and petition to be released 13 November 1851
Signatures	Sylvanus EVERTS, Ball H. PENCE, Mark ALLEN, A. R. TREAT, John B. FRAVEL, Henry BEAHM, Joseph STARRET, G. W. ALLEN, Jacob HUPP, Reuben ALLEN, Jacob EARLY, John BROWN, A. H. ROBINSON, Joseph HAYWOOD JP, S. VAN PELT, Ward BLAKE, R. MUNDAY, Edward OHARRA, James THOMPSON, William HAGENBUCH, Solomon ROSS, Benjamin GILBREATH, Richard WORRELL, Philip HART, J. [Jeremiah]

PERKINS, Barclay UNDERWOOD, Israel UNDERWOOD, John UNDERWOOD, John F. ALLISON, John KOONTZ, James THOMPSON

Sale Buyers   10 November 1838: John KOONTZ, Joseph STARRETT, J.PERKINS, William PRATT, Silas LOVING, George W. ALLEN, H. BEHM, Michael O'HARRA, S. EVERTS, Alexander CAMPBELL, Mark ALLEN, A. STARRETT, Peter TULY [JULY?], Wright LOVING, David POWERS, John PRATT, William PRATT, David POWERS, Arthur MCCLURE, Edward O'HARRA, John DECKER, John HARRISON, Washington MCCLANE, James CALLISON.

Comment   Deceased signed a note dated 17 November 1837.

Administrator petitioned to sell real estate in Township 35N Range 3W (present-day civil township of Noble), noting that the deceased left "a wife & nine Children," widow Jane, children John, William H. C., Erasmus, Adam, Dewitt C., Heber, Reuben, Elizabeth, Jane.

Complaint to the court from Benjamin GILBREATH of La Porte and from William JENKINS and sons Mark JENKINS and Edward JENKINS of Baltimore, Maryland, regarding $410.12 owed through a note of 12 March 1833. The two-page complaint may be incomplete and is hard to read.

CLARK, Charles

Location   Estate #73, microfilm E1 (formerly box 1), 92nd item on roll

Administrator   Lucy TEETER executor of Charles's will, petitions to close the estate 12 May 1850; bond with Charles McClure for $200 13 November 1838.

Heirs   Widow Lucy TEETER, formerly Lucy CLARK; George CLARK, Wesley CLARK, George CLARK "the youngest" who would be 21 on 13 June 1849, Ezra CLARK, Lewis CLARK.

Signatures   Lucy TEETER, Jacob TEETER (by mark), Jno. FRAVEL, T. D. BAILEY, William CLARK, C. W. CLARK, Ezra C. CLARK, Lewis P. CLARK, G. W. CLARK, Robert MERRYFIELD, Charles MCCLURE, Charles CLARK, Charles MCCLURE, Harvey VAN ORDE

Comment   1838 survey and map of adjoining properties of Charles CLARK and Esqr WILLIS of Door Village

M. C. [??] CLARK signs receipt for $78 bequeathed to him in the will of "my late father Charles CLARK decd.," approved by his guardian Benjamin BEARD

Original will of Charles CLARK 24 March 1838, proved in court 13 November 1838

CRUMPACKER, Abram

Location	Estate #110, microfilm E1 (formerly box 1), 93rd item on roll
Administrator	Owen CRUMPACKER, bond with William REED for $200 on 13 April 1839, bond with John CRUMPACKER $900 on 12 August 1839.
Signatures	Owen CRUMPACKER, William REED, John CRUMPACKER, Daniel MEEKER, B. W. TUTTLE, RATHBUN
Comment	Real estate sold: west half of lot 83 in the original town of La Porte.
	Owen CRUMPACKER to court: Abraham died "some time in the year AD 1838, . . . leaving no heirs except Brothers & Sister," namely John CRUMPACKER, Jacob CRUMPACKER, Peter CRUMPACKER, Joel CRUMPACKER, and Polly THOMPSON late Polly CRUMPACKER

TERRELL, Joseph

Location	Estate #155, microfilm E1 (formerly box 1), 94th item on roll
Administrator	Jesse H. WALDO; bond with Willys PECK for $100, 15 May 1840
Signatures	Jesse H. WALDO, Willys PECK, D. E. GARNSEY, Fisher AMES

EAGER, Rebecca

Location	Estate #184, microfilm E1 (formerly box 1), 95th item on roll
Administrator	George AMES and West DARLING were on bond with Fisher AMES for $2500 12 August 1841 (last digit uncertain); George AMES and Thomas. W. DARLING gave account and asked to be dismissed 15 February 1850.
Heirs	Ames BURR, Sarah JUSTICE
Signatures	George AMES, West DARLING, Ames BURR (of Massachusetts), Fisher AMES, J. P. ANDREW, E. E. ANDREW late Elise EAGER, Ames BURR, Mary EAGER, William EAGER, Mary EAGER, Horace BURR, George A. BURR, W. A. PLACE, Jonas BURR
Comment	28 June 1849 power of attorney from heir Ames BURR of Worthington, Hampshire County, Massachusetts, to Horace BURR of Michigan City, in order to settle the estate of Rebecca EAGER of Michigan City.

JUSTICE, William

Location	Estate #186, microfilm E1 (formerly box 1), 96th item on roll. This file also includes one receipt from the estate of Joseph WHEATON. The final 21 ½ pages mislabeled "186" belong to the estate of E. W. (Ebenezer) ALLEN, which in fact is no. 263.
Administrator	John HARVEY and Hannah JUSTICE; bond of $4000 dated 1 November 1841 involving Jonathan LINE and Samuel WEBSTER as well

Heirs	Hannah JUSTICE, widow; Eliza YOUNG m. R. B. YOUNG, Henry C. JUSTICE, Sarah Ann JUSTICE, Joanna JUSTICE, Patrick C. JUSTICE, Lorenzo JUSTICE; John D. STEWART was guardian of the last two. Extensive statement of their credits and liabilities to the estate.
Signatures	E. E. CAMPBELL, John D. STEWART, R. B. YOUNG, Sarah A. JUSTICE, Joanna JUSTICE, Hannah JUSTICE, Henry C. JUSTICE, John HARVEY, Charles CARMICHAEL, Nathan B. NICHOLS, James WHITTEN, Samuel W. WEBSTER, Jacob HICKMAN, James GALBREATH, C. W. BROWN, W. L. F. TALBOT, Andy L. OSBORN, Lewis PAGAN, Jonathan LINE
Sale Buyers	Held 25 November 1841 "at the late dwelling house of the said deceased": N. B. NICHOLS, Isaac HUNT, John BUSH, Henry JUSTICE, Abraham BIRCHIM, John SUTHERLAND, Wm. JEFFERS, John HARVEY, Isaac MARTIN, Charles HUNT, Joshua ALDRICH, Erbin PRESTON, Wesley COOLEY, Hiram DEES [?], Mixon DEES [same surname as Hiram], Hannah JUSTICE, Belzar BUCK, Richard ETHERINGTON
Comment	Property in St. Joseph County, Township 37 Range 1 (present-day civil township of Olive); also in Porter County, Township 36 Range 4; La Porte County Township 37 Range 1 (probably present-day civil township of Wills), T37 R2 (probably present-day civil township of Kankakee), and Township 38 R4 (probably present-day civil township of Hudson).

ALLEN, Ebenezer

Location	Estate #263, misfiled as the last 21 ½ pages of 186, microfilm E1 (formerly box 1), 97th item on roll.
Administrator	John PRATT, Peter BRADLEY, apparently on separate occasions. Bradley's bond with John M. CLARKSON for $360 29 July 1844. John PRATT's bond of 12 May 1845 with Asa NORTHAM for $200.
Signatures	Geo. J. HYMON (?), William J. BUMSTEAD, Peter BRAWLEY (?), Ebenezer W. ALLEN, John PRATT, Peter BRADLEY, Asa NORTHAM
Sale Buyers	A. MARKHAM, J. PERKINS, C. FESSONDEN, B. SHAW, J. PRATT, John HILE, Thomas STEPHENSON, J. POUND, D. B. HILL, Jesse MCLANE
Comment	Administrator PRATT noted that the estate of Joseph WHEATON has a claim against Allen's estate, 13 May 1850.
	Peter BRADLEY informed court of Allen's death 22 July 1844.

CISSNE, John

Location	Estate #276, microfilm E1 (formerly box 1), 98th item on roll
Court Dates	18 November 1849 La Porte issued an attachment against Henry DENSLOW executor of said estate and the St. Joseph County sheriff failed

to return the writ. St. Joseph County coroner ____ TUTTLE served it on the sheriff.

Administrator	Henry DENSLOW of St. Joseph County made $700 bond with Henry BROWN 11 November 1844
Heirs	Widow Jane CISSNE relinquished will and claimed her dower instead 27 November 1844. Children Joseph CISSNE, Robert CISSNE, John CISSNE, Elizabeth BAY, Polly WILLS, and (adopted) Sarah DENSLOW.
Signatures	H. DENSLOW, Henry BROWN, Joseph BAY (Rolling Prairie), Joseph W. LYKINS, Jane CISSNE (by mark), Jonathan CISSNE, Casper FOX, John MILLER JP, J. & G. W. REYNOLDS, Andrew FOSTER (Hudson), John D. STEWART, F. W. HUNT, James MCCOLLUM JP, John CISSNE, Andrew FOSTER, Joseph W. LYKINS
Sale Buyers	Auction 21 December 1844: Joseph CISSNE, Robert CISSNE, Naton WHITEHED, Moses LEWIS, Joseph CISSNE, John CISSNE, Theopolis CASE, H. DENSLOW, Wm. TROBRIDGE, Benjamin SAULSBERY, Weastly CHENEAULT, Timothy HUNT, John DAVIS, Samuel ANDERSON, Henry BROWN, Daniel HALSEY, Wm. IRWIN, Reuben SHOFFLER [?], Cain AUSTIN, John B. CASE, Orvel A. ENOS, Isaac E. HUNT, John WILLSON, Wm PARNELL, Joshua JORDAN.
	Separate list of those who gave notes (in pairs, apparently implying one acting as security for the other): Cain AUSTIN & John CISSNE, Bejmin SALSBERY & Samuel ANDERSON, John CASE & T. CASE, Wm. TROBRIDGE & Edmon LUTHER, D. HALSEY & J. B. WARNE, Samuel ANDERSON & Bej. SALSBERY, John WILLSON & Cain AUSTIN, Wm. IRWIN & Moses LEWIS, Henry BROWN & O. A. ENOS.
Comment	John CISSNE's will of 13 August 1844 (proved 11 November) bequeathed his real estate in Township 37 North Range 1 West [Wills Township] to his three sons Joseph (oldest), Robert (second), and John (youngest), and $40 apiece to daughters Elizabeth BAY and Polly WILLS and adopted daughter Sarah DENSLOW. Widow Jane was to "remain in possession of and occupy my mansion house or Messuage during her life time." Whichever son chose the real estate with the orchard "shall permit the rest of my children to share equally with him in the fruit thereof until such times as they shall have had sufficient time to have fruit from orchards of their own planting."

LEWIS, Moses

Location	Estate #307, microfilm E1 (formerly box 1), 99th item on roll
Administrator	Executors "my Farther John LEWIS & Amos LEWIS." Executors' bond by John LEWIS, Amos LEWIS, and Joel LEWIS for $800 made 12 December 1845.
Heirs	Widow Lucy M.LEWIS, son John William LEWIS, daughters Ellen Mariah LEWIS, Isabella Sutherland LEWIS

Signatures	Moses LEWIS, Caleb B. DAVIS, Wesley M. CHENAULT, Joel LEWIS, John LEWIS, Amos LEWIS, Joel LEWIS, Jesse JONES, John S. BOIES, Daniel LEERY, Elijah JACK, M. H. ORTON, W. N. BALL, A. J. RIDGWAY, Lucy M. LEWIS, Ferdinand ROBERTS, Absalom THORNBURGH
Comment	Moses LEWIS's will of 4 May 1845 (proved 4 December) bequeathed bed and clothing to wife, family Bible to son, $1 each to daughters, and all other personal and real property to be sold and divided among his lawful heirs.

WHEATON, Joseph

Location	Estate #307, microfilm E1 (formerly box 1), 100th item on roll
Administrator	Allida F. J. WHEATON and Jackson WHEATON on 9 June 1846 informed the court that Joseph WHEATON died intestate 1 January 1846. Bond of $900 made same day with Jacob GOODRICH. Jackson WHEATON made final settlement 15 August 1851 as "surviving administrator."
Heirs	Widow Allida J. F. WHEATON
Signatures	Amos B. HILL, Jackson WHEATON, Allida F. J. WHEATON, Jacob GOODRICH, Joseph WHEATON, A. CLARK, Jno. M. LEMON Jr.
Sale Buyers	Martin HOUSEMAN (security Nymrod WEST), Banks HALL (security S. G. HAS), Robert FULTON (security Joseph McPHERSON), Jeremiah PERKINS (security Wright LOVING), Preston CHAMBERS (security Obadiah CHAMBERS), Samuel OHARA (security Benjamin SHAW), John GENT (security Preston CHAMBERS), William STEPHENSON (security Preston CHAMBERS), Samuel HAS (security Banks HALL), Francis TOINE, George BUTT (security John FENNER), Joseph B. WHEATON (security Clinton WHEATON), Clinton WHEATON (security Joseph B. WHEATON)
Comment	Receipts from "county treasurer" in Plymouth to Joseph Wheaton for taxes on property in Township 35 Range 2E (Marshall County)

BOICE, John J.

Location	Estate #346, microfilm E1 (formerly box 1), 101st item on roll
Administrator	Ephraim BOICE, Peter SHOP made $2200 bond with Elias LOWE 26 August 1847
Heirs	Elisabeth BOICE widow in bond of $50 with Peter SHOP and Ephraim Boice 20 September 1847
Signatures	John WITTER, A. J. RIDGWAY, Ephraim BOICE, Peter SHOP, Thos. P. ARMSTRONG, Elisabeth BOICE, William H. BOICE, M. H. ORTON, Elias LOWE, Jacob MILLER, Calista SIMS (the last two witnessing Elisabeth BOICE's relinquishment of administration 17 August 1847).

Sale Buyers	25 September 1847: J. VAN VALKENBURGH, P. SHOP, S. S. MILSPAUGH, M. H. ORTON, John BLAKE, William HAGENBUCH (security M. H. ORTON), Henry WILLETS, Hiram ANDREWS, BUSH, L. CUTLER (security P. SHOP), John BECKER Sen., Moses SHAFT, E. BOICE, John WITTER (security J. F. DECKER), Danl. CARPENTER, O. WARRINER, Robert MILLER (security SHULTZ), P. FAIL, S. DARLINGTON, Wm. BOICE, Ja. JONES, Isaac NORTON, John THOMPSON, Tobias MILLER, C. EVERHART, Joshua RING, Wm. BELL, J. S. MCDANIEL, John THOMPSON Jr., Jesse MATHIS, J. F. DECKER (security WITTER).
Comment	Peter SHOP and Ephraim BOICE petition court 26 August 1847 stating that John J. Boice died "about the 6th day of August AD 1847" leaving widow Elizabeth BOICE.
	A 13 February 1850 receipt for legal services refers to the case of Shop & Boice vs. Hagenbuch & Orton in La Porte Circuit Court.
	Jacob MILLER "affirmed" in an apparent transcript of testimony given in a case of assumpsit in probate court, E. BOICE vs. Peter SHOP, no date given, but based on summons early 1850.

SPRINGER, Henry

Location	Estate #354, microfilm E1 (formerly box 1), 102nd item on roll.
Administrator	Solomon WAGENNER sworn in 30 March 1848, and as Solomon WAGNER made bond with Joseph C. BARKER for $260.
Heirs	Jane WAGENNER, sister (per receipt), Marget WAGENNER mother (per receipt), Sarah INGRAM sister (per receipt).
Signatures	Solomon WAGENNER, Thomas FISHER, A. TEEGARDEN, B. C. BOWELL, W. & J. MILLIKAN, Joseph HOSTETLER, James E. WILLIAMS, Jane WAGENNER, Marget WEGENNER, Sara INGRAM, Joseph C. BARKER.

PATTEE, Levi

Location	Estate #359, microfilm E1 (formerly box 1), 103rd item on roll
Administrator	Milton PALMER and Elmore PATTEE made bond of $600 19 July 1848 for Milton's administering the estate. PALMER and Aaron KIDDER and William M. BORST made bond of $1700 on 15 February 1849.
	Elizabeth PATTEE was not named as widow but she relinquished "my right of administering on the estate" 17 July 1848, and on 14 September 1848 acknowledged receipt of $40.67 "in part pay for my dower."
Heirs	Administrator reported paying $16.43 to Elenore PATTEE heir, Thomas IRWIN (ditto mark), Alexander MCCREERY (ditto mark), Orson PATTEE, and Lewis PATTEE on 12 November 1850.

Letter from court 21 August 1848 regarding sale of real estate sent to "Lewis PATTEE, Elmore PATTEE, Orson PATTEE, Sarah MCCRERA, Alexander MCCRERA, Polly IRWIN, Thomas IRWIN, William P. MILLS, Sidney MILLS, and Mason MILLS heirs of Levi PATTEE."

Signatures   Elmore PATTEE, Catharine LIVINGSTON, Thomas IRVIN (by mark?), Orson PATTEE, P. KING, Mark BAILEY, Alexander MCCREERY, J. C. COLE, Samuel ALLEN, John DOTY, William TAYLOR, Adam WITENBECK, Thomas GALLOWAY, Thos. B. COTE, Alvah MASON, G. D. BAKER, Luis PATTEE, Joseph JACKSON (of Crown Point, Lake County), W. & J. MILLIKAN, Sylvanus EVERTS, Virgil WILCOX, A. P. WELLS, Wm. G. MILLS, Aaron KIDDER, Henry HERROLD, Moody KIMBELL, C. BOOTHE, Jacob PECK, Obadiah SMITH, William GOTT, Charles SPEAR, A. G. STANDIFORD, Jesse MATHIS (of Scipio), Aaron KIDDER, Wm. M. BORST, Levi PATTEE.

Sale Buyers   Held in Scipio Township 12 August 1848, "all sums less than any dollar cash in hand, all sums over one Dollar Nine Months credit with approved security": Lewis PATTEE (Orson PATTEE security), Wm. G. MILLS (Orson PATTEE security), Saml. ALLEN, Tho. B. COLE (Aaron KIDDER security), Moody KIMBELL (Thomas GALLIWAY security), Orson PATTEE (Elmore PATTEE security), Alex MCCREERY (Jacob G. MORGAN security), Adam WHITTENBROCK (Jacob PEER security), Thos GALLIWAY (Moody KIMBELL security), Elmore PATTEE (Orson PATTEE security), Barnard COLE (Avery A. COLE security), Henry MEEKER (Thos. B. COLE security), Eli BLACK (Elmore PATTEE security), Jacob G. MORGAN (Alex MCCREERY security), Thos. H. LASHBAUGH (Horace HEMROD security), Horace HEMROD (T. H. LASHBAUGH security), Ralph THORDON (Saml. COX security), Jacob PEER (A. WHITTINBECK security), John LIVINGSTON, Wm. M. BORST, Thomas IRVING, Joseph DOWNING, John   C. COLE.

Comment   Letter from A. MCKINNEY, received in La Porte 12 December 1850, asking that moneys due be sent to Anson BISSELL in Milan, Erie County, Ohio, and signed by Lyman SCOTT, Mary SCOTT, Anson BISSELL, and Clarissa BISSELL.

Petition by administrator 16 August 1848 to sell real estate in Township 36 North, Range 3 East (probably present-day civil township of Scipio).

Letter of 19 July 1848 referred to "some contention about the right to administer the Estate among the heirs of said deceased" and said Milton PALMER should administer until the probate court comes in session, signed by Alexander MCREERY, Elmore PATTEE, Luis PATTEE, and Orson PATTEE.

MEEKER, Henry

Location   Estate #375, microfilm E1 (formerly box 1), 104th item on roll

Heirs   Anna MEEKER, widow, renounced administration 5 April 1849 and asked that it go to "my friend John W. COLE." Caleb H. DOWNING petitioned the court to appoint an administrator, stating that Henry died intestate on or about 22 March 1849, leaving the widow and seven living children (not named). John W. COLE and David C. MCKILLIPS made $800 bond 6 April 1849.

Signatures	Anna MEEKER (by mark), Milton PALMER, Virgil WILCOX, TEEGARDEN, HEALD, C. (Cornelius) BRADLEY, Clark MEEKER (by mark), Thos. B. COLE, Virgil WILCOX, Henry MEEKER, John LIVINGSTON, A. G. STANDIFORD, J. W. COLE
Sale Buyers	15 May 1849, approved security over $3, cash in hand for purchases less than $3: Joel MARTIN (security D. C. MCKILLIPS) Cornelius BRADLEY (security W. M. BORST), Robert MCCORMICK (security (Henry MCCORMICK), Clark MEEKER (security (A. B. CAMPBELL), Milton PARMER, James FORSTER, Moody KIMBLE (security Clark MEEKER), Abram SOVEREIGN (security W. M. BORST), Virgil WILCOX (security A. MASON), Jno. C. COLE (security M. PARMER), Amos THURBER (security H. THURBER), Erastus PAYNE (security M. PARMER), Vi. WILCOX, William MAXWELL (security B. BEARD), Alexander McCREERY (security Wm. M. BORST), John MEEKER, security C. H. DOWNING), Saml. MOODY, W. M. BORST (security A. JERNIGAN), David MCKELIPS (security A. SOVEREIGN), Jno. LIVINGSTON

MCENTAFEE, John

Location	Estate #373, microfilm E1 (formerly box 1), 105th item on roll
Heirs	Stephen WINCHELL "subscribed & affirmed" 10 March 1849 that John MCENTAFFEE died 19 February 1849 leaving wife Lydia MCENTAFFEE and children Birt MCENTAFFEE, Stephen W. MCENTAFFEE, Augusta MCENTAFFEE, and Ruth MCENTAFFEE.
Signatures	David BARNEY, Robt. WILLIAMSON, Silas W. HOLMES, Stephen WINCHELL.

PERRY, Joseph

Location	Estate #385, microfilm E1 (formerly box 1), 106th item on roll
Administrator	Lucy PERRY made $700 bond with Daniel S. WELLS 18 August 1849.
Heirs	Widow Lucy PERRY
Signatures	Lucy PERRY, Daniel S. WELLS, Samael ELLITHORP, John A. FRAZIER, James A. FERGUSON
Sale Buyers	Held "at his late residence," Saturday 29 September 1849: James WILLIAMS, John A. FRAZIER, Joseph STANTON, Joshuway JUDSON, Joel LEWIS, Daniel ELLITHORP, B. CADWALLADER, Ephram GREEN, Lucy PERRY, Charls CLARKSON, Daniel HERBET, James FINDLY.
Comment	On 18 August 1849, Lucy PERRY told the court that Joseph had died "more than one year since."

BECKNER, Elizabeth

Location	Estate #388, microfilm E1 (formerly box 1), 107th item on roll
Administrator	Jonathan BECKNER and George G. BECKNER, who made $800 bond with John B. BECKNER 29 August 1849, and $1500 14 November 1849.
Heirs	Jonathan BECKNER identified himself as the "oldest surviving heir" of Elizabeth in his petition to the court to be named administrator, stating that she died intestate "on or about the 14th day of August 1849."
Signatures	Jonathan BECKNER, George G. BECKNER, John B. BECKNER, David BECKNER, Joel B. BECKNER, Samuel H. NOFSINGER, Jacob B. BECKNER, William F. STANTON, Benajah S. FAIL, John O. GISH, James C. LORING/LOVING, Miss Susan VAIL, James CROOK, A. J. RIDGWAY, A. TEEGARDEN, John A. GISH,
Sale Buyers	22 September 1849: Jacob BECKNER, Sylvanus JONES, J. B. BECKNER, John BECKNER, Philip FAIL, Benj. FOGLE, John BUSH, G. L. BUNCE, A. S. HARTFORD, Jas. CROOK, G. G. BECKNER, Jacob BECKNER, Jonathan BECKNER, Lewis IRELAND, Joshua ATWATER, James KUSTARDT, J. H. FINLEY, F. COLSSER, D. MCLEMING, Thos. BURGET, H. MUNDAY, E. S. JUDSON, Jas. WILLIAMS, S. L. or A. S. CARPENTER, Jesse MATHIS, Benj. STANTON, James CATTERLIN, E. BARNES, S. L. FERGUSON, E. PRESTON, J. N. WHITEHEAD, David CARPENTER, Ziba BAILEY, Benj. CRUMPACKER, John EWING, Peter SHOP, F. REYNOLDS, Moses STANTON, Oren LAMB, J. P. TEEPLE, P. DRAKE
Comment	Jonathan BECKNER reported on administration at the August 1851 term of court, "his Coadministrator G. G. BECKNER having left the State."

WICKHAM, Marvin S.

Location	Estate #394, microfilm E1 (formerly box 1), 108th item on roll
Heirs	Widow Eliza Ann WICKHAM
Signatures	Wm. W. TRAVIS, W. G. FINLEY, Elisa Ann WICKHAM
Comment	Died 18 May 1849 leaving an estate of about $200.
	By 6 February 1850 Elisa Ann WICKHAM had evidently died, as Henry M. SHAW, guardian of her minor heir John R. WICKHAM, claimed $77.26 "for expences during the said [Shubel 'F. LANE]'s sickness in the State MO at Kirkville in June 1849." See following estate, #395.

LANE, Shubel F.

Location	Estate #395, microfilm El (formerly box 1), 109th item on roll
Administrator	William G. FINLEY, who with Nathan PALMER made bond of $300 on 25 September 1849.
Action	Inventory 24 October 1849 of personal property: one rifle, one coat, one "Clarionett," and one pair of calf boots, totaling $26.50, plus $91.60 owed to the estate by Nathan PALMER.
Signatures	Nathan PALMER, Wm. W. Travis, J. D. PALMER, W. G. FINLEY, Henry M. SHAW, David BARNEY, Emory BARNEY
Comment	On 25 September 1849 Nathan PALMER petitioned the court, saying that Lane "Started some time last Spring for the Gold regions in California that about the 28th June 1849 he died in the State of Missouri on his return from California Expedition that he left some eighty nine dollars . . . & some other personal property . . . that there are Sundry Claimants & Creditors of said estate . . . that his relatives live in the State of New York Ohio Pennsylvania" requesting an administrator.
	David BARNEY of Kirkville, Missouri, submitted claim of $30 for his son Clinton BARNEY's care of Shubel in his last illness June 1849.

STONER, Joel

Location	Estate #396, microfilm El (formerly box 1), 110th item on roll
Administrator	David STONER, who petitioned the probate court 2 October 1849 saying that Joel had died on or about 17 August 1849, "he had no wife or children . . . left surviving several relatives & his mother mostly residing in Montgomery County Indiana . . . his personal estate consists mostly in fruit trees or nursery," perhaps valued $1000-$3000, and asking that the court appoint "some suitable person." He was appointed and with Benjamin CRUMPACKER posted bond of $4000.
Heirs	Mother Barbary STONER, siblings David STONER, Jacob STONER, Catharine STONER now Catharine WINTERS, Daniel STONER, Magdaline STONER now Magdaline WINTERS, Sarah STONER now Sarah HINES, Hannah STONER now Hannah ODELL, Rebecca STONER, Lydia STONER, and Susanna STONER now Susanna LAMAN. After administration $53.07 was left for them.
Signatures	David STONER, Benj. CRUMPACKER, Leonard CUTLER, William F. STANTON, John O. GISH, William HAGENBUCH, Joel STONER, Volney W. BAILEY, Hannah ODELL, John ODELL (by mark), Magdalene WINTER, Rebecca STONER, Lydia STONER, Jacob STONER, Barby STONER (by mark), Susan LAYMAN, Sarah HINES, Catharine WINTER, Saml. E. WILLIAMS, J. P. EARLY, A. TEEGARDEN, Peter HEISER, John L. ARMSTRONG Jr., George H. ANDREWS, W. & J. MILLIKAN, Henry MYERS.

| Sale Buyers | C. H. HIBBARD, Geo. HIBBARD, David STONER, Saml. POTTINGER, Geo. W. GISH, B. CRUMPACKER, J. ATWATER, John ANDREWS, P. BARHARES [?], Hibbard D. ARMSTRONG. |

BOSSERMAN, Philip

Location	Estate #417, microfilm E1 (formerlybox 1), 111th item on roll
Court Dates	Order to sell real estate 14 May 1850
Administrator	John W. BOSSERMAN was named executor by the Register of Perry County, Pennsylvania, 25 January 1849. Philip BOSSERMAN was "late of Newport, Perry County," Pennsylvania. In an undated note, John W. appointed Jacob MCCASKEY of La Porte County his attorney. McCaskey posted $1000 bond with George BOSSERMAN 16 February 1850.
Heirs	The proceeds of the sale of his property were to be distributed among John W. BOSSERMAN, Margaret THOMAS, Elenor EVENT [?], David BOSSERMAN, and Catharine W. MCCASKEY.
Signatures	Jacob G. MCCASKEY, George BOSSERMAN, Geo. SEYMOUR, J. W. BOSSERMAN, Saml. BURSON
Comment	MCCASKEY stated that Philip died 16 January 1849. He owned land in Section 15 of Township 36 North Range 2 West (present-day civil township of Pleasant).

CRALL, Dr. Samuel

Location	Mistakenly labeled Estate #417, microfilm E1 (formerly box 1), 112th item on roll – according to the Estates Index should be Estate #428
Administrator	Mrs. Nancy M. CRALL petitioned the court 28 May 1850 stating that Dr. Samuel CRALL "late of Michigan City Laporte County departed this life about the 9th day of May AD 1850," leaving her (the widow) and two children, one of whom resided with her "& is her only child." She posted bond of $1000 that day with James V. HOPKINS.
Signatures	Mrs. N. M. CRALL, James V. HOPKINS, S. J. SMITH, GOODHUE & BARKER, B. C. POTTER (POTTLE?), Thomas JERNEGAN, Lucy BEESMER, G. C. & C. S. WINSHIP, G. A. ASHTON, J. S. BIGELOW
Comment	17 September 1850 Mrs. CRALL wrote the court inquiring about the decision on an accusation of perjury against her, giving her address as Pulaski, Oswego County, New York. Another document 22 July 1850 gave Richmond, Oswego County.
	List of items purchased from "AMES & HOLLIDAY" (?) by Dr. CRALL between 11 March and 2 May 1850, such as a syringe, blister salve, opium powder. Also a second list of items returned to them.

RICE, Luther

Location	Estate #437, microfilm E1 (formerly box 1), 113th item on roll
Administrator	William W. CLEGHORN, $100 bond with William DAVIS 14 August 1850.
	Joseph W. LYKINS; $2240 bond with Henry BROWN 12 February 1851, $100 bond with Henry BROWN 17 February 1851.
Signatures	William W. CLEGHORN, Joseph W. LYKINS, William DAVIS, Benja. HICKS (JP), Henry BROWN, John VICORY, James BRADLEY, Luther RICE (on note to Victory & Lucy 27 January 1838).
Comment	Property to be sold in Sections 17 and 32, Township 38, Range 1 West (present-day civil township of Hudson).
	Per Cleghorn's petition 14 August 1850: "Luther RICE alias NO-A-QUET, a member of the Pottawatomie nation, died sometimes in the year 1843 in the Indian Country west of the State of Missouri, leaving to survive him Ann S. RICE, alias A-KAT, his widow, and one child William M. RICE, who is now about eighteen years of age, who resides in said Indian country and of whom your petitioner is Guardian; that after the death of said Luther the said Ann S. his widow intermarried with your petitioner and has since died." Claimed estate owed him $370.30 for settling debts, providing for William, and paying taxes on the land.
	John VICORY's petition of 17 February 1851 claimed he was a creditor of the estate, that CLEGHORN lived outside of Indiana and gave no bond for the real estate sale, and asked that Joseph LYKINS be appointed instead, who was RICE's agent in his lifetime.

MCGOGEY, James F.

Location	Estate #441, microfilm E1 (formerly box 1), 114th item on roll
Court Dates	Clerk Thomas P. ARMSTRONG received petition and affidavit from widow Mary MCGOGEY stating that John died about 13 August 1850 leaving her and 7 children, owned no real estate and personal property less than $200, which she claimed under the state law for widows of 1848. He appointed appraisers.
Signatures	John GISH, A. P. ANDREW, Mary T. MCGOGEY

BARNES, Perry

Location	Estate #441, microfilm E1 (formerly box 1), 115th item on roll
Administrator	Hannah BARNES made bond of $700 with Oliver MARSTON 15 October 1850.
Heirs	Widow Hannah BARNES, five children Lydia BARNES, Julia BARNES, William BARNES, Henrietta BARNES, and Adaline BARNES "and two others which . . . have departed this life."

Signatures	Hannah BARNES (by mark), Oliver MARSTON, Joseph WINCH, Joseph H. FRANCIS
Sale Buyers	Held "at the late residence" 16 November 1850: Kellogg SHEAD, William C. CUMMINS, Joseph FULLER, Charles CLARKSON, Charles FRANCIS, John A. FRAZIER, Oliver MARSTON, Joseph WINCH, James WILLIAMS, George GARLAND,
Comment	Oliver MARSTON's 15 October 1850 petition said Perry died about 28 September 1850.

HUDSON, Richard

Location	Estate #452, microfilm E1 (formerly box 1), 116th item on roll
Signatures	Caleb B. DAVIS, Robert H. SMITH, Mariah HUDSON (by mark), David HUDSON
Comment	Affidavit from David HUDSON states Richard died 2 September 1850, leaving no real estate and personal property under $200, and widow Maria HUDSON who would be entitled to the estate under the law of 1848.

#

Index

A

Achemukquei, 18

Adams, Grovenor S., 81

Aere, Nelson, 236

Agans, Wm., 204

A-kat, 253

Aker, Nelson, 227, 239

Aldrich, Joshua, 244
Aldrich, Solomon 155

Allegheny County, Pennsylvania, 218
Allen, Abner S., 53
Allen, Adam, 34, 58, 98, 242
Allen, Dewitt C., 34, 58, 98, 242
Allen, Ebenezer W., 243, 244
Allen, Edwin, 221
Allen, Elizabeth, 34, 58, 98, 242
Allen, Erasmus, 34, 58, 98, 242
Allen, G. W., 241
Allen, George M., 204
Allen, George W., 63, 93, 115, 116, 152, 241, 242
Allen, Heber/Hebor, 34, 98, 242
Allen, Hebra, 58
Allen, James M., 240
Allen, Jane (Jr.), 34, 58, 242
Allen, Jane, 34, 58, 98, 242

Allen, John, 34, 58, 98, 242
Allen, Mark, 34, 115, 178, 221, 241, 242
Allen, Nathan, 53
Allen, Reuben (Jr.), 34, 58, 98
Allen, Reuben, 34, 58, 59, 98, 115, 241
Allen, Robert, 234
Allen, Samuel, 248
Allen, W., 150
Allen, William H. C., 34, 58, 98, 242
Allen, William, 7, 79, 80, 88, 103, 138, 147, 155, 167, 194, 198, 214
Allison, John F., 40, 107, 183, 202, 242

Alsop, Dorothy, 241
Alsop, William, 240, 241

Alyer, Samuel, 201

Ambrose, Ezekiel, 7, 82, 197
Ambrows, Joannah, 197

Ames & Holliday ?, 252
Ames, A.W., 159
Ames, Fisher, 72, 89, 243
Ames, George, 64, 72, 89, 132, 210, 243
Ames, Joseph G., 230

Anders, John, 90
Anderson, Agness Jane, 43, 64, 65, 146
Anderson, Andrew, 210
Anderson, Catharine H./F., 43, 64, 65
Anderson, David, 43, 65,

106, 146, 209, 210
Anderson, John, 43, 65, 106, 146, 209
Anderson, Margaret T., 43, 64, 65
Anderson, Mary Ann, 43, 64, 65
Anderson, Robert T., 43, 65
Anderson, Samuel, 245
Anderson, William C., 209
Anderson, William K., 43, 64, 65, 106, 146, 209
Andress, J. P., 157
Andrew, A. P., 6, 197, 223, 253
Andrew, Abraham P., 37
Andrew, Abram P., 177
Andrew, Elise E., 243
Andrew, J. P., 221, 225, 243
Andrew, J. T., 206
Andrew, James, 214, 232
Andrew, William, 20, 37, 47, 52, 96, 143, 214, 217
Andrews, George H., 251
Andrews, Hiram, 247
Andrews, Isaac, 217
Andrews, Jacob, 239, 240
Andrews, James, 138, 155
Andrews, John, 251
Andrews, William, 109, 145, 155
Andrus, Isaac, 201

Arbogast, Enoch, 162

Argabrite, Eliza J., 77
Argabrite, Elizabeth, 55, 120
Argabrite, John H., 77
Argabrite, Mary E., 77
Argabrite, Samuel S., 77

Argabrite, Sarah A., 77
Argabrite, William, 55,
77, 120, 204, 231 (also
Argerbrite, Argubright)
Argabrite, William J., 77

Armstrong, ____, 227
Armstrong, Aaron, 10
Armstrong, Elizabeth, 13
Armstrong, Hibbard D.,
251
Armstrong, James (heir),
10, 13
Armstrong, James, 10,
13
Armstrong, John H., 217
Armstrong, John L. Jr.,
251
Armstrong, John W., 217
Armstrong, Rebecca I.
C., 10, 13
Armstrong, Robert V.,
10, 13
Armstrong, Samuel H.,
10, 13
Armstrong, Thomas K., 10
Armstrong, Thomas P.,
167, 170, 219, 220, 221,
225, 246,
253
Armstrong, Thomas R.,
13
Armstrong, Thomas, 160,
168, 172

Arville, Caleb N., 29
Arville, Sarah, 29

Ashton, E., 210
Ashton, Eliahue, 42
Ashton, Eliakim, 210
Ashton, G. A., 252
Ashton, Galitan, 179
Ashton, Jerusha, 42
Ashton, Phebe, 42
Ashton, Sidney, 42
Ashton, Susan, 179
Ashton, Thomas, 42

Aspenwall, Eliza, 32, 112

Astin?, Haris?, 214

Atkins, Isaiah, 240
Atkins, J. G., 218
Atkins, J. T., 210
Atkins, J.?, 204
Atkins, Jeremiah, 210
Atkins, Thomas, 240

Atwater, J., 252
Atwater, Joshua, 225, 250

Augustin County, Virginia,
135, 136

Austin, Alexander, 71, 101
Austin, Cain, 245
Austin, Harriet, 71, 101
Austin, Jedediah, 67, 193
Austin, Sans, 67, 71, 101,
192
Austin, Sarah, 67, 71,
101, 192
Austin, William, 71, 101

Avery, Andrew, 41, 81
Avery, E., 237
Avery, Edman, 51
Avery, Edward, 138, 225,
237

Ayles, Elias, 204

B

Bailey, A., 236
Bailey, Abner, 28, 58, 98,
138, 205, 218
Bailey, John, 33, 39, 103,
208, 228
Bailey, Josiah, 38
Bailey, Mark, 248
Bailey, Martha 171
Bailey, Mary Elizabeth,
38
Bailey, Matilda, 208

Bailey, Nancy Ann, 21,
140
Bailey, Simon, 38
Bailey, T. D., 84, 87, 200,
242
Bailey, Urian?, 217
Bailey, Volney W., 251
Bailey, William, 21, 140
Bailey, Zeba/Ziba, 76,
129, 200, 250
Bair, Benjamin F., 68
Baird, Benjamin, 75, 217,
see also Beard

Baker, George D./G. D.,
228, 248
Baker, John, 216
Baker, Lewis V., 57, 105,
203
Baker, Martin, 5, 190,
191, 217
Baker, Nathaniel, 191

Baldwin, Daniel Jr., 6,
65, 145
Baldwin, Daniel Sr., 65,
145
Baldwin, Daniel, 188,
189
Baldwin, Ival, 65
Baldwin, Jared, 159
Baldwin, Joel A., 6, 188,
189
Baldwin, Joel, 6, 145
Baldwin, John, 159
Baldwin, Reuben, 6, 65,
145
Baldwin, Rhoda, 6, 65,
145
Bale, W. N., 238
Ball, Nancy, 9, 116, 198
Ball, Nancy Thomas, 116
Ball, Seneca, 14, 138
Ball, W. N., 226, 241, 246
Ball, Willard N., 198, 213
Ball, Willard, 9, 198
Ball, William N., 197
Ballard, Christopher A.,
84

Baltimore, Maryland, 115, 242

Banks, Orin, 228

Barber, C. W., 176
Barbor, H./Horace, 207
Barclay, John M., 58, 65, 142
Barclay, Mrs. John M., 58
Barger, Christian, 37
Barger, David, 218
Barger, Samuel, 37, 96
Barhares?, P., 252
Bariner/Pariner, John, 233
Barker, Joseph C., 247
Barker, O.A., 89
Barker, Oscar, 234
Barker, Oscar A. 49, 53, 77, 98, 177, 210, 233
Barker, Oscar H., 44, 48, 131, 192
Barker, Wm., 178
Barley, Frederick, 127
Barnard, George, 131
Barnard, J., 234
Barnard, James, 130
Barnard, James C., 172
Barnes, Adaline, 253
Barnes, Alvira, 169, 226, 227
Barnes, E., 250
Barnes, Elijah, 87, 200, 236
Barnes, Ezra, 209
Barnes, G. W., 189, 209, 233
Barnes, G., 210
Barnes, George W., 168, 169, 170, 188, 226, 233
Barnes, George, 170, 227
Barnes, Hannah, 245, 253, 254
Barnes, Henrietta, 253
Barnes, Ivory, 226, 227
Barnes, J. W., 189
Barnes, Joseph, 169, 226, 227
Barnes, Julia, 253

Barnes, Lydia, 253
Barnes, Olive, 245
Barnes, Perry, 169, 226, 227, 253
Barnes, Phineas, 170
Barnes, William, 253
Barney, Clinton, 251
Barney, David, 249, 251
Barney, Emory, 251
Barney, Ephraim, 234
Barrett, Abner, 207
Barrett, Jacob, 207
Barris, G. W., 6
Bartholomew, Jeremiah, 11, 83
Bartholomew, Jno., 227
Bartholomew, Stephen, 11, 83
Bartlet, N. Jr., 218
Bartlett, Nathan, 237
Bartlit, N., 218

Bason, Rodolph, 221
Bastion, Garret V., 48
Bastion, Maria B., 48
Bastion, Mary Ann, 48

Batiles, John, 15
Batterson, William, 163, 220

Bay, Elizabeth, 16, 245
Bay, Joseph, 7, 16, 18, 245

Beahm, H., 236
Beahm, Henry, 241
Bear, James D., 129
Beard, B., 249, *see also Baird*
Beard, Benjamin, 41, 73,119, 205, 221, 242
Beattee/Beaty, William, 28
Beattie, William, 90, 199

Bebiles (?), John, 11

Becker, John Sen., 246
Beckner, Abraham, 63,

120, 122
Beckner, David, 63, 120, 122, 250
Beckner, Elizabeth, 22, 63, 86, 120, 122, 250
Beckner, G. G., 250
Beckner, George G., 122, 250
Beckner, George V., 122
Beckner, George, 63
Beckner, J. B., 250
Beckner, Jacob, 63, 120, 250
Beckner, Joel B., 120, 122, 250
Beckner, Joel, 63
Beckner, John (heir), 63, 120, 122
Beckner, John B., 250
Beckner, John, 22, 63, 86, 120, 122, 250
Beckner, Jonathan, 122, 250
Beckner, Lydia Ann Stanton, 120, 122
Beckner, Sarah, 63, 120
Beckner, Susan, 120, 22
Beckner, William, 63, 120, 122
Beckwith, E., 219
Beckwith, Elijah, 164
Beckwith, Gregory, 164

Beesmer, Lucy, 252

Behm, H., 242

Belden/Beldon/Belding, Henry, 70, 114, 126, 197
Belknap, Charley, 12
Bell, Reason, 7, 82, 197
Bell, Wm., 247

Bendall, Richard, 230
Benedict, Joseph H., 60, 66, 162, 220, 221
Benham, James R., 217
Benson, Samuel, 226
Bentley, George, 62, 150,

151, 201, 206
Bently, Irwin N., 214
Bently, Lee, 85
Bently, Thomas, 112, 200, 207

Berhans, Wm., 204
Berrien County, Michigan, 175, 230, 238

Betteyes/Betteys, Alonzo, 80

Bias, Garret, 48, 231
Bidwell, William, 226, 227

Bigard, George, 227
Bigard, Samuel, 227
Bigelow, A., 90, 202, 227
Bigelow, J. S., 252
Bigelow, Jacob, 89, 132
Bigelow, Marshall S., 237
Bigelow, S., 202
Biggart, George, 227

Bilden, Harry, 83
Bill, Frances, 78
Bill, P. B., 66, 235
Bill/Bills, Patrick B., 66, 78, 235
Bills & Hudson, 235

Birchim, Abraham, 244

Bishop, Elijah, 209
Bishop, Ruth, 209
Bishup, E., 209
Bissell, Anson, 248
Bissell, Clara, 248
Bissell, Clarissa, 248

Black, Catherine, 135
Black, Eli, 202, 208, 210, 229, 248
Black, James, 135, 178, 205
Black, John, 135, 136
Black, Nathaniel, 135

Black, Samuel F., 135
Black, William T., 135
Blackburn, A., 155, 214
Blackburn, Alex, 5, 218
Blackburn, Alexander, 70, 71, 78, 117, 138, 204, 211, 218
Blackmun, Hiram, 240
Blain, ____ Esqr., 240
Blair, C. B., 210, 236
Blair, Chancey B., 132, 210
Blake, John, 247
Blake, Joseph, 58, 59, 63, 98
Blake, Ward, 197, 221, 241
Blake, William A., 118
Bland, Benjamin, 119
Blany, Ambrose, 230

Blevin, Edward, 6
Blevin, James, 6
Blevin, Robert C./P., 6, 114

Bliss, N. P., 218

Blivens, Edward, 82
Blivens, Robert, 82

Blodget, Lewis, 25, 95, 215

Boast, Wm. M., 217

Bodurthee, William, 38

Boice, E., 247
Boice, Elizabeth, 183, 240, 246, 247
Boice, Ephraim, 183, 184, 240, 246, 247
Boice, John (heir), 183
Boice, John J., 183, 184, 240, 246, 247
Boice, John M., 183, 240
Boice, William H., 183, 184, 240, 246, 247

Boies, John S., 246

Bond, Charlotte, 41, 126, 205, 232
Bond, Ira, 41,126, 205, 232
Bond, Isaac V., 258
Bond, Jesse, 41, 126, 205, 232
Bond, John, 126, 232, 233
Bond, Lydia, 232
Bond, William C., 91
Bond, William, 126, 232, 233
Bond, William, Sr., 41
Boner, John, 32
Bonesteel, ____, 221
Bonnside, Andrew, 85

Booth, Edwin, 223
Booth, Samuel, 47
Booth, Sheldon, 55, 149
Boothe, C., 248
Boothe, Edwin, 210
Boothe, Sheldon, 210

Borst, W. M., 249
Borst, William M., 229, 247, 248, 249

Bosley, Richard, 220
Boss, Edward, 210
Bosserman, Caroline, 46, 47, 195
Bosserman, David, 252
Bosserman, George, 46, 47, 119, 195, 196, 252
Bosserman, John W., 252
Bosserman, John, 46, 47
Bosserman, Philip, 93, 252
Bostwick, J. B., 218
Bostwick, W. R., 218

Bowell, B. C., 247
Bowell, John, 193, 231
Bowers, James, 134
Bowman, John, 147

Boyles, Elijah, 67
Boyles, Sally Ann, 67

Bradley C./Cornelius, 203, 249
Bradley, Bart, 95, 215
Bradley, Bartholomew, 25, 95, 96, 99, 164, 165, 215

Bradley, Cornelius/C., 203, 229, 249
Bradley, Erasmus D., 25, 215
Bradley, Erasmus, 165
Bradley, George W., 25, 40, 161, 165, 215
Bradley, James 25, 26, 66, 81, 100, 104, 109, 114, 120, 122, 123, 153, 167, 204, 207, 214, 215, 216, 217, 221, 223, 226, 232, 237, 253
Bradley, John H., 6, 24, 39, 47, 56, 65, 97, 129, 145, 147, 167, 180, 208, 209, 213, 214, 217
Bradley, John W., 98, 99
Bradley, John, 107, 130, 146, 165, 207
Bradley, Joseph, 165
Bradley, Joseph E., 25, 161, 165, 215
Bradley, Joseph L., 166
Bradley, Julia H., 25, 161, 215
Bradley, Lydia H., 161, 165
Bradley, Lydia S., 25, 164, 215
Bradley, Peter, 221, 244
Bradley, Sidney S., 25, 95, 99, 164, 215, 216
Bradley, Taylor, 167, 214
Bradley, William C., 25, 161, 165, 215
Bradley, William Erasmus, 215
Bradley, William H., 24

Brand, Michael, 8
Branson, C. W., 214
Braton, Russell C., 197
Brauded, John, 203
Brawley?, Peter, 244
Brayton, Wm., 229

Brewer, Benjamin, 71, 193
Brewer, John, 230

Briant, Benjamin T., 207, 208, *see also Bryant*
Briant, Benjamin Y., 202
Briant, Benjamin, 208
Briant, Jacob, 217
Briant, Josiah, 207, 208, 221
Bricket, D. C., 233
Brinckerhoff, David, 226
Brinckerhoff, Derrick, 226
Bristol, Solomon W., 202

Broaded, John, 54
Brodded, John, 217
Bronson, C. H., 197
Brooks, Benjamin, 214
Brookville, 239
Brown, Alfred, 69
Brown, America, 54
Brown, Brownell, 234
Brown, C. W., 181, 214, 225, 226, 244
Brown, Catharine (infant heir), 69
Brown, Catharine, 69
Brown, Chapel W., 5, 191, 218
Brown, Daniel, 16, 23, 69, 88, 134, 206
Brown, David, 236, 237
Brown, Dexter, 236
Brown, E. H., 197
Brown, Elisha K., 76
Brown, Elizabeth, 69
Brown, Ezekiel, 199, 207, 213
Brown, Fitch, 155, 204, 214
Brown, Hamilton, 69

Brown, Harry (?), 69
Brown, Henrietta, 237
Brown, Henry, 245, 253
Brown, J., 206
Brown, James, 54
Brown, John (child), 54
Brown, John (father), 55
Brown, John, 7, 14, 69, 71, 84, 87, 92, 102, 194, 198, 204, 217, 241
Brown, Levi, 5
Brown, Manlius, 54
Brown, Mary, 69
Brown, Miles, 54
Brown, Philamena, 144
Brown, Philena, 35, 36
Brown, Philura, 208, 211
Brown, Rush, 69
Brown, Sarah, 69
Brown, Virginia, 54
Brown, W., 5
Brown, William, 35, 36, 69, 125, 134, 145, 156, 178, 208, 209, 210, 211
Brownell, Giles, 171, 225, 229
Brownhelm, Ohio, 223

Brunson, Bush, 236
Brunson, George W., 236
Brunson, Nancy, 236

Bryant, Benjamin G., 39, *see also Briant*
Bryant, Benjamin T., 33, 103, 202
Bryant, Benjamin, 208
Bryant, Jacob, 217
Bryant, Josiah, 33, 39, 103, 208, 217

Buck, Belzar, 244
Buck, Melzah, 214
Buck, Melzai, 221
Buckman, Harding, 222
Bucks(?), Waterman, 157

Buffalo and Mississippi Railroad Co., 30

Bull, William D., 209
Bull, William, 145
Bullock, Moses, 157, 202, 225

Bumstead, William J., 244

Bunce, Clarissa, 7, 82, 83, 193, 197
Bunce, G. L., 250
Bunce, George L., 7, 193
Bunce, Harriet, 7, 193
Bunce, Lafayette, 7, 82
Bunce, Simon G., 6, 82, 193, 197
Bunce, W., 197
Bunce, William, 7, 193
Bunse, Asa, 229
Bunson, Samuel, 81

Bur, David, 201
Burch, Admiral, 223
Burch, Amanda, 18, 24
Burch, DeWitt, 18
Burch, Hetty, 18
Burch, Lucy, 18
Burch, Perry, 18
Burch, Peter, 18, 24
Burch, Washington, 18
Burch, William, 18
Burger, A. G., 227
Burger, Abram G., 238
Burget, Abm. G., 234
Burget, Thos., 250
Burgher, A. G., 238
Burke, Sidney, 192
Burke, Udney, 233, 234
Burleigh, Richard, 30
Burlingame, Abel, 88, 135
Burlingame, Ethel?, 206
Burlingame, James, 218
Burlingame, Simon, 135, 206
Burlingame, Wanton?, 206
Burner, Abraham, 217
Burnside, ____, 150
Burnside, A., 85, 200
Burnside, Andrew, 7, 9,

14, 30, 58, 59, 92, 116, 117, 138, 193, 198, 200, 217
Burr, Ames, 243
Burr, George A., 243
Burr, Horace, 243
Burr, Jonas, 243
Burr, Jonathan, 159, 177, 218
Burson, Samuel, 78, 112, 151, 157, 236, 252

Busch, Admiral, 83
Busch, Amanda, 83
Busch, Hetty, 83
Busch, Lucy, 83
Busch, Perry, 83
Busch, Peter, 83
Busch, Washington, 83
Busch, William, 83
Bush, ____, 247
Bush, John, 120, 123, 244, 250
Bushnell, Newton, 221
Bushnell/Burwell, Anson, 205

Bussey, George, 234
Bussey, Hezekiah, 225
Bussey, John, 234

Butin, Martin, 91
Butler, Benjamin, 114
Butler County, Ohio, 57
Butler, Joel, 27, 80, 87, 103, 114, 130, 141, 168, 200, 204, 212, 232, 224
Butler, W. G., 223
Butt, George, 246
Butterfield and Collins, 44, 131, 210
Butterfield, Justin, 44, 210
Butterworth, Benjamin, 27, 43, 65, 106, 146, 209, 210, 214

C

Cadwallader, Amos, 36, 91, 201, 232
Cadwallader, B., 206, 209, 249
Cadwallader, Byron/Byram/Birum, 115, 171, 209, 214, 226

Cain, James P., 221

California, 251
Calkins, Cornelius, 239
Callison, James Jr., 210
Callison, James, 221, 242
Callison, Wm., 20

Campbell, A. B., 249
Campbell, Alexander, 242
Campbell, Charles, 202, 208
Campbell, Cynthia, 107, 108
Campbell, E. E., 244
Campbell, Isom, 221
Campbell, William, 198

Canada, 237
Canadey, Joshua, 233
Cannon, James, 200, 217

Caplin, B., 141

Carey/Cary Mission School, 9, 185, 186, 187, 188
Carl, John, 39
Carl, Rachel, 39
Carlisle, Daniel, 201, 208
Carmichael, Charles, 139, 244
Carpenter, Danl., 205, 247
Carpenter, David, 250
Carpenter, S.L./A. S., 250
Carr, Mary Jane, 211
Carr, Nancy, 211
Carr, Sarah Ann, 211
Carroll County, 32

Carter & Carter, 229
Carter, John C., 26, 27
Carter, John E., 147, 148

Case, John, 245
Case, John B., 245
Case, Luther, 217, 228
Case, Nathaniel, 217, 236
Case, T., 245
Case, Theopolis, 245
Casida, A., 197
Cass, Lewis, 39
Castle, James S., 98

Cater, Hiram, 234
Caterlin, James, 209, 233
Cathcart, C. H., 217
Cathcart, Charles W., 6,
69, 102, 133, 142, 197,
207, 208, 217
Catlin, Arad S., 59
Catlin, Joseph, 52, 59,
140, 234
Catlin, Theodore, 59, 71,
114, 127
Cator, Calvin, 17
Cator, Julia, 17
Cator, Sally Maria, 17
Cator, William H., 17
Catron, Peter, 221
Catterlin, James, 71, 193,
250
Catterlin, S./L., 207
Catterton, James, 27
Cattlin, Henry, 113
Cattron, Hezekiah, 66,
146, 220, 221, 222
Cattron, James B., 66,
146, 221
Cattron, John A. G., 66,
80, 146, 220, 221
Cattron, Mary, 221
Cattron, Samuel, 66, 79,
146, 147, 221
Cattron, Thomas, 66, 146,
221
Cattron, Valentine, 66,
146, 208, 220, 221
Cattron, Wesley F., 66,

79, 146, 147, 221
Cattron, William, 66, 146,
147, 221

Center Township, 152,
156, 214, 225, 233, 241

Chalmers, John, 75
Chambers, Andrew, 200
Chambers, Obadiah, 237,
246
Chambers, Preston, 246
Chapin, Reuben, 223
Chapman, _____, 158
Chapman, Francis Marion,
240
Chapman, Frederick, 241
Chapman, Henry Clay,
240
Chapman, J. M., 235
Chapman, Jared, 14, 15,
40, 92, 231, 250
Chapman, John, 218,
240
Chapman, Joseph W., 44,
76, 77, 132
Chapman, Joseph, 231,
240
Chapman, Matilda, 208
Chapman, S. E., 214
Charlesworth, John, 236
Chase, William C., 207

Che Kau Ketch, 7
Chenault, Wesley M., 246
Cheney, E. J., 219
Cheney, Harriett, 45
Cheney, Horace, 45
Cheney, John E., 45, 219
Cheney, John, 44, 45
Cheney, Malvina, 45
Cheney, Rachel, 45
Cheney, Rufus, 45

Chicago, Illinois, 140,
210, 215, 239

Cissne, Jane, 245, *see also
Sisny*

Cissne, John, 5, 16, 191,
244, 245
Cissne, Jonathan, 245
Cissne, Joseph, 245
Cissne, Robert, 245
Cissne? /Sisny, Robert G.,
204

Clark, _____, 154
Clark, A., 91, 214, 217,
218, 240, 246, *see also
Clarke*
Clark, Amzi, 28, 35, 136,
138, 145, 202, 213, 218,
219
Clark, C. W., 242
Clark, Charles, 36, 40,
41, 42, 242
Clark, Elam, 79, 131, 184,
206, 217, 240
Clark, Elizabeth, 18, 70,
83, 142, 199, 207
Clark, Ezra C., 242
Clark, Ezra, 242
Clark, G. W., 242
Clark, George W., 41
Clark, George, 242
Clark, Glenn, 196
Clark, James, 142
Clark, Jesse, 142
Clark, John M., 207
Clark, John W., 70, 141
Clark, John, 13, 100, 124,
142, 208
Clark, Jonas, 208
Clark, Lewis P., 40, 242
Clark, Lewis, 242
Clark, Lucy, 36, 40, 41,
242
Clark, M. C.?, 242
Clark, M.? W., 208
Clark, Marsana/Marsena,
50, 107, 202
Clark, Mary Malosh, 142
Clark, Solomon, 199
Clark, Wesley, 242
Clark, William, 10, 11, 19,
24, 56, 73, 142, 166, 180,
181, 194, 206, 212, 213,

214, 222, 232, 242
Clark, Wilson B., 18, 83, 199
Clarkam, John M., 26, 72
Clarke & Howell, 236
Clarke, Elam, 118, *see also Clark*
Clarke, John W., 200
Clarkson, _____, 208
Clarkson, Charles, 249, 254
Clarkson, J. M., 215, 218
Clarkson, John M., 72, 165, 205, 215, 244
Clarkson, N., 153

Cleghorn, William W., 253
Clement, W. S., 240
Clement, William, 168, 240
Clemon, Wm., 240
Clendenen, Samuel, 159
Clettin (?), Seonarse (?), 81

Cline, George, 84
Cline, W., 145
Clinton Township, 94, 202, 227, 238, 239

Closer, John, 217
Clossen, Daniel, 206
Closser, Clark, 130-1
Closser, D. M. F., 221
Closser, David, 37
Closser, Franklin, 229
Closser, Hester Hale, 130
Closser, John, 228, 229, 239, 240
Closser, Nicholas W., 79
Closser, Nicholas, 221
Clough, Alonzo, 135, 206
Clough, Elmina? E., 206
Clough, Moses, 206

Clyburn, H., 220
Clyburn, Henly, 200, 220, 221
Clyburn, Henry, 80, 163

Cobbs, J. P., 223
Cobbs, John P., 71, 204
Cobbs, Robert L., 118

Cole, Avery A., 248
Cole, Barnard, 248
Cole, J. C., 248
Cole, John C., 248
Cole, John W., 19, 29, 54, 216, 248
Cole, Thos. B., 248
Cole, Warren, 10, 62, 89, 210
Coleman, Jesse, 64, 139
Collam, Jesse, 231
Collenbach, Peter, 206
Collins, Aaron M., 50
Collins, Albert, 35, 125, 144, 208, 210, 211
Collins, Amina, 35
Collins, Anna, 144
Collins, Arenna/Areuna, 125, 208, 210, 211
Collins, Charlotte C., 125, 208
Collins, Charlotte E., 35
Collins, Charlotte, 125, 144, 210
Collins, Harriet, 35, 125, 144, 208, 210
Collins, Harvey, 35, 125, 126, 144, 208, 210, 211
Collins, J. L., 220
Collins, James H., 44, 210
Collins, Mrs., 209
Collins, Paulina, 144
Collins, Philena, 35, 36
Collins, Philomena, 144
Collins, Philura, 208, 210
Collins, Zebulin, 230
Colman, Jacob, 197
Colter, James, 221

Comer, Lewis, 84

Conklin, Aaron, 69
Conner, Cader, 211, 212
Conner, Calvin, 211
Conner, Crawford, 211

Conner, George W., 211
Conner, John, 211
Conner, Martin, 211
Conner, Mary, 211
Conner, Nancy, 211
Conner, Rebecca, 211,
Conner, William L., 211
Conner, William, 211, 227

Cook County, Illinois, 239
Cook, Levi, 30
Cooley, Aaron, 217
Cooley, Wesley, 244
Coolspring Township, 171, 217, 218, 225, 229
Cooly, ___, 225
Cooper, Chancy, 217
Cooper, Charles, 27, 148, 217
Cooper, Ephraim, 42, 233
Cooper, Horace, 207
Cooper, John, 43, 209, 233
Cooper, Jon, 227
Cooper, Mary, 233

Copland, Isaac B., 227
Coplin, Isaac B., 56
Coplin, Jesse H. G., 237

Corliss/Corlys, Isaac, 46, 133, 134, 178, 217, 228, 236
Corlys, Jeremiah, 165
Cornwall County, England, 197
Cortes, Isaac, 239

Cote, Thos. B., 248
Cotter, James, 201

Coulter, James, 201
Courier, Albert, 217

Cox, Samuel, 217, 248
Cox, Willis, 231

Crall, Dr. Samuel, 252

Crall, Nancy M., 252
Crammer, Richard, 81
Crandal, Charles C., 203
Crandal, Francis T., 203
Crandal, Nancy, 203
Crandal, Octavia, 203
Crandal, P.J., 129
Crandall, John J., 47, 130, 200, 203, 204, 217
Crandle, H.N., 89
Crane, Daniel, 118
Crane, Sally, 63
Crane, Shadrach, 63
Cranney, Gad, 165
Crawford, George 165

Crome?, Alexr., 229
Crook, James, 44, 250
Crook, Sylvanus, 44
Crook, Wm. H., 178
Cross, Daniel, 231
Cross, Horace, 217
Crown Point, 248

Crumpacker Polly, 51
Crumpacker, Abram/Abraham, 51, 243
Crumpacker, B., 252
Crumpacker, Benjamin, 31, 35, 40, 81, 84, 86, 124, 144, 200, 204, 209, 224, 250, 251
Crumpacker, Jacob, 51, 243
Crumpacker, Joel, 51, 243
Crumpacker, John, 51, 243
Crumpacker, Owen, 51, 220, 243
Crumpacker, Peter, 51, 243
Crumpacker, Polly, 51, 243

Cullen/Cullin, John, 167
Cullen/Cullin, John Jr., 167
Cullen/Cullin, Otelia, 167, 168

Cummins, William C., 254

Cunningham, Hannah, 169, 226
Cunningham, James C., 45, 49
Cunningham, James, 125
Cunningham, Mary Catharine, 49

Currie, Andrew H., 75
Currie, David C., 75
Currie, Ebenezer, 75
Currie, Elizabeth, 75
Currie, George, 75
Currie, James A., 75
Currie, James, 75, 210
Currie, Walter, 75
Curry, James, 67, 236
Curry, Mary Eliza, 67
Curtis, Carter, 241
Curtis, J., 218

Cutler, James, 206
Cutler, L., 247
Cutler, Leonard, 51, 204, 251

D

Dade, Isaac, 226

Dalhousie, Upper Canada, 237

Darling, Thomas W., 243
Darling, Wes, 225
Darling, West, 72, 157, 214, 243
Darlington, _____, 206
Darlington, S., 247
Darlington, Samuel, 240, *see also Durlington*

Davis, _____, 128
Davis, C. B., 209, 233
Davis, Caleb B., 115, 168, 170, 226, 227, 246, 254

Davis, Caleb C., 209
Davis, Candy [Handy??], 112, 113
Davis, Christopher L., 212
Davis, E., 227
Davis, Eliza, 76, 112
Davis, Elizabeth Jane, 21
Davis, Elnathan, 227
Davis, George Washington, 75, 76, 112, 113
Davis, H. C., 233
Davis, Handy, 51, 74, 76, 105, 138, 140, 225
Davis, Harrison C., 155
Davis, Henry, (heir), 76
Davis, Henry, 10, 21, 51, 75, 76, 105, 112, 113, 140, 179, 230
Davis, Henson P., 227
Davis, James, 76, 112
Davis, John C., 21
Davis, John, 21, 76, 112, 197, 201, 234, 245
Davis, Joseph, 26, 27, 30, 86, 134, 152, 153, 199, 200, 203, 208, 217, 236
Davis, Joshua, 75, 76, 112
Davis, Loren, 55, 148
Davis, Margaret, 76, 112
Davis, Nancy, 51, 76, 113
Davis, Nathaniel, 21
Davis, Philip, 238
Davis, Polly, 75, 76, 112, 113
Davis, Priscilla, 76, 112
Davis, William, 253
Davis, Willy, 113

Dawson, Elizabeth, 139
Dawson, George, 34, 64, 130, 138, 139, 204
Dawson, Joseph, 64, 139
Dawson, Lane, 124
Dawson, Mary, 64, 139
Dawson, Matthias, 64, 139
Dawson, Matthew, 139

Dawson, Nancy, 139
Dawson, Pamela, 139
Dawson, Rachel, 139
Dawson, R. H./Richard, 223
Dawson, Saml., 204
Dawson, Saul L., 45
Dawson, Saul/Samuel, 34

Day, Lot, 182
Day, Peter, 198

Dean, Jonathan M., 48
Deardorf/Deardorff, Deardruf, _____, 195, 196
Deardorf, Jesse, 46, 47, 195
Deardorf, Peter, 195
Deardorf, Rebecca, 46, 47, 195

Decatur County, 37
Decker, J. F., 225, 226, 247
Decker, John 157, 234, 242
Decker, John F. Jr., 79, 156, 224
Decker, John F., 79, 224, 225, 234
Decker, Michael, 138

Dees?, Hiram, 244
Dees?, Mixon, 244

Defries, Anthony, 223

Delphi Insurance Co., 30

Denham, John, 27, 114, 204
Denslow, H., 245
Denslow, Henry, 244, 245
Denslow, Sarah, 245

Des Moines, Wisconsin Territory, 199

Devalle (?), Abner, 77

Dewitt, Benjamin, 73, 238
DeWitt, Egbert R., 73, 157, 158

Dillingham, John, 160, 228
Dilley, Mary, 218
Dilly, M., 218

Dingman, Corrintha, 26, 27, 54, 147, 216
Dingman, Corrintha (minor), 54
Dingman, Marin, 148
Dingman, William, 26, 27, 54, 147, 203, 216, 217
Dinwiddie, David Jr., 28, 136, 218
Dinwiddie, David, 5, 13, 17, 27, 136, 197, 217, 218, 238
Dinwiddie, Francis W., 28, 136, 218
Dinwiddie, Henrietta, 136
Dinwiddie, John, 28, 136, 237
Dinwiddie, Margaret Jane, 28, 136
Dinwiddie, Margaret June, 218
Dinwiddie, Marietta, 28, 218
Dinwiddie, Mary, 28, 136, 218
Dinwiddie, Thomas, 218
Dinwiddie, W. H.?, 197
Dinwiddie, Wm., 218

Disbro, Henry V., 30

Dizard?, John, 206

Door Village, 242

Doran, Patrick, 237

Doty, John, 248

Dowling, R., 218
Downing, B. F., 228
Downing, C. H., 228, 249
Downing, C. W., 247
Downing, Caleb H., 248
Downing, Catherine, 9, 178
Downing, Daniel B., 179
Downing, Joseph, 228, 248
Downing, Joshua, 228
Downing, Katharine, 230
Downing, Nathaniel B., 178, 230, 231
Downing, Nathaniel R., 9

Drake, P., 250

Dresden, Samuel, 202

Drollinger, Gabriel, 240, *see also Druliner, Drulinger, Drullinger*
Drom, Jacob, 17, 119, 221, *see also Drum*
Drow---?, Zachariah, 217

Drulesis(?), John, 190
Druliner, Gamailel, 5
Druliner, John, 5, 17, *see also Drollinger*
Drulinger, Daniel, 221
Drullinger, Gabriel, 16
Drullinger, John, 17
Drum, Jacob, 17, 205, 210, 218, *see also Drom*
Drummond, James, 88, 237

Dudley, Catherine, 161
Dudley, John, 55, 121, 125, 161
Dudley, Jonathan, 204

Dukes, Elizabeth, 207
Dukes, Ephraim Jr., 207
Dukes, Ephraim, 23, 133, 142, 207
Dukes, John, 200, 207

Dukes, Rhoda, 207
Dukes, Robert, 207
Dukes, Wm., 207

Duncan, Ivey? H., 223
Dunham, F., 224
Dunham, Angelina, 141
Dunham, Ferdinand, 81,
141, 143, 224
Dunkin, Perry, 233

Durlington, Samuel, 151,
see also Darlington

E

*Eagans/Eagen, see also
Egans*
Eagen, Rebecca, 72
Eager, Elise, 243
Eager, Mary, 243
Eager, Rebecca, 243
Eager, William, 243

Eahart/Eheart, William,
54, 60, 80, 162, 201, 220
Eaheart, Abram, 221
Eaheart, John, 221

Earhart, William, 90
Earl, Aaron, 39
Earl, Charlotte, 39
Early, E. J., 219
Early, J. P., 251
Early, J., 219
Early, Jacob, 224, 241
Easley, J&P, 164
Easton, Charles, 236

Eaton, Charles, 50, 90, 95,
103, 107, 201, 202, 208,
227
Eaton, John, 202, 227

Edinger, Philip, 237

Edwards, J. S., 39

Edwards, William, 240,
241

Egans, James, 19, 93, 231,
231
Egans, Matilda, 231
Egans, Nancy, 231
Egans, S. T., 239
Egans, Samuel, 15, 19,
231
Egans, William, 14, 93,
231

Egbert, Alfred, 181, 182,
238
Egbert, Anna/Anney, 181,
182, 238
Egbert, Charles, 9, 181,
182, 191, 231, 238
Egbert, Clarissa, 181, 182,
256
Egbert, Courtland, 181,
182, 238
Egbert, Elisha, 238
Egbert, Jacob, 238
Egbert, John, 7, 181,
182, 238
Egbert, Mary, 9
Egbert, Noory, 116
Egbert, Paul, 238
Egbert, Wesley, 181, 182,
238
Egbert, William, 238
Egburt, Charles, 218
Egburt, Mary, 218

Elkhart County, 26, 161,
162, 164, 165, 215

Elliot, Elfonzo, 227
Ellithorp, Daniel, 249
Ellithorp, Samael, 249
Ellsworth, Thomas, 176,
230

Elyea, H., 208

Emmons,
Celicia/Cecelia/Celia, 8, 9,

185, 187, 188

England, 197
English, Jno., 224

Enos, A.W., 159, 207, 230
Enos, Alonson W., 22
Enos, H.W., 132
Enos, J. F., 206
Enos, Orvel A., 245

Erie County, Ohio, 248

Ervin, Arthur, 237

Eslinger, ____, 207
Eslinger, Andrew, 40
**Eslinger/Esslinger,
Antoine C.**, 40, 133, 207
**Eslinger/Esslinger,
Ephraim D.**, 40, 133, 207

Etherington, Elizabeth,
230
Etherington, Richard, 230,
244

Etinger, Philip, 237

Evans, Calvin, 151
Evans, C. R., 218
Evans, Calvin R., 122
Evans, David, 5, 86, 191
Evans, Edward, 221
Evans, Joseph, 182

Event?, Elenor, 252
Everetts, G. A., 220
Everhart, C., 247
Everheart, Magdelein, 151
Evers, Calvin R., 207
Everts & Osborn, 133
Everts, G., 224
Everts, G. H., 83, 132
Everts, Gustavus A., 51
Everts, S., 242
Everts, Sylvanus, 51, 207,
215, 221, 223, 227, 235,
236, 241, 248

Everts, Timothy A., 254
Everts, Timothy C., 50, 74, 222, 223, 235

Evins, Isaac S., 237

Ewan, Thorton, 37

Ewing/Ewings, James, 55, 148, 218
Ewing, John, 250
Ewing, Laura, 55, 148, 149
Ewing, W. G. & S. W., 101

F

Fail, Benajah S., 250
Fail, P., 247
Fail, Philip, 86, 190, 250

Fall, Michael W., 29, 90, 199
Fall, Michael, 199

Farewell, Chapen, 217
Farley, Thomas, 220
Farmer, Emerson, 21, 140
Farmer, Henry, 140
Farmer, Nancy Ann, 21, 140
Farmer's Hotel, 89
Farnsworth, ___, 206, 225
Farrand, M.K., 185

Fauts, Eri W., 214

Faye, Wm., 206
Fayette County, 12, 16, 231

Fenley, William, 237
Fenner, John, 246

Ferguson, James A., 249

Ferguson, S. L., 250

Fessonden, C., 244

Field, Joseph, 229
Field, Josephine, 172
Field, Rodney, B., 192
Field, Thomas I., 30

Fifer, Orlando F., 204

Findly, James, 249
Finley, David, 223
Finley, J. H., 250
Finley, John, 206
Finley, Jonas, 212
Finley, W. G., 250
Finley, William G., 251
Finley, William W., 237
Finn, Charles, 138

Fisher & Ames, 159
Fisher, John, 90
Fisher, Saml., 214
Fisher, Thomas, 161, 247
Fisk, Martha M., 44, 131
Fisk, Samuel/Lemuel, 44, 131

Fitch, Lemuel, 130, 185, 234, 241

Flood, Benjamin, 217, 221
Floyd County, 10

Fogle, Benj., 250
Fogle, Jacob, 172
Fogle, Levi, 225
Fogle, Susannah, 172

Ford, Edward, 230
Forester, Michael, 206
Forrester, James, 77, 228
Forrester, Matthew, 229
Fort, Julia, 48

Fosdick, George, 130, 185, 214, *see also Fozdick*
Fosdick, James Arthur, 19
Fosdick, James, 180, 213
Fosdick, John Alfred, 19
Fosdick, John, 180, 213
Fosdick, Martha A., 19, 180, 213
Fosdick, Mary Francis, 19
Fosdick, Mary, 180, 213
Fosdick, Timothy, 10, 19, 180, 212, 213
Foster, Aaron, 220, 226
Foster, Alanzo/Alcanzo L., 23, 36, 87
Foster, Alonzo S., 23, 36, 87
Foster, Amanda H., 23, 36, 87
Foster, Andrew, 245
Foster, Cyphus, 233
Foster, Harriet N., 23, 36
Foster, James, 266
Foster, Laura G./L., 23, 36, 87
Foster, Lucetta, 72
Foster, Melinda/Belinda S., 23, 87
Foster, Narcissa H., 23, 36, 87
Foster, Orlander, 72
Foster, Perlina/Paulina, 23, 87, 96
Foster, Phebe, 220
Foster, Scipha 170, 230
Foster, Seneca/Senicus, 17, 22, 36, 87, 96
Foster, Sophronia H., 23, 36, 87
Foster, Thomas (child), 72
Foster, Thomas J., 70

Fountain County, 66, 147, 199, 222

Fox, Casper, 245
Fox, Truman, 109, 152, 153

Fozdick, William, 213,
see also Fosdick

Frances, C., 233
Frances, John, 210
Francis, Charles, 209, 230,
233, 254
Francis, J. H., 227
Francis, John, 49, 191,
233, 234
Francis, Joseph H., 254
Francis, Thompson W.,
177
Franklin County, 19, 92,
231, 239
Fravel, Abraham, 18, 20,
83, 131, 157, 195, 213
Fravel, Alvin, 157
Fravel, Jacob, 237
Fravel, Jno., 242
Fravel, John B., 208, 217,
221, 231, 241
Frazier, John A., 226, 249,
254
Frazier, John, 227, 230
Frazier, R.T., 147

Frederickson, Henry, 21,
217, 220
Fredrickson, H., 218
Freece/Frees, Simeon, 234
Freehold, Hass, 8
Freeland, Wm., 236
Freeman, David B., 16,
122, 207
Freese, Peter, 202, 203

Frye, Daniel, 178
Frye, William, 178, 206,
235

Fuller, Joseph, 170, 226,
254
Fuller, Prudence J., 9
Fuller, Prudence, 8, 186,
187, 188
Fulton, Robert, 246

G

Galbreath, James, 244
Galena Township, 114,
169, 211, 227, 230, 233
Galloway/Galloway,
Thomas, 248

Gardner, Edmond S., 238
Gardner, Orange, 50
Gardner, William, 210
Gargan, John, 122
Garland, George, 254
Garner, Daniel, 208
Garnsey, D. E., 243
Garrard, John, 91, 129,
200
Garwood, Wm., 221, 229

Gates, Jacob, 204

Gawley, Ichabod, 90

Geer, Frederick, 240

Geist, Henry, 221, 236

Gent, John, 246

Gerry, Caleb, 134, 206
Gerry, Cynthia A., 134,
206

Gilbreath, Benjamin, 115,
241, 242
Gillespie, Litheland, 240
Gillispie, Harriet, 15
Gillispie, Hugh, 15
Gilman, John, 221

Gish, Geo. W., 252
Gish, John A., 250
Gish, John O., 250, 251
Gish, John, 253

Glime, John, 56, 234
Glimpse?, Jonathan, 202
Glinn, John, 234

Goble, Isaac P., 63, 88

Godfrey, H., 218
Godfrey, Miles, 218

Gogan, Wm., 239

Goit, W., 233
Goit, Wightman, 209

Gold, Ingraham, 214, *see
also Gould*
Gold, J., 218
Gold, James M., 219
Gold, Orrin, 218
Goldsmith, Richard, 239

Goodhue & Barker, 252
Goodhue, Charles, S., 177
Goodhue, William, 176,
177
Goodhue, William H., 210
Goodpaster?, Isaac, 228
Goodrich, Jacob, 223,
224, 246
Goodwin, Rolly, 207
Goodwin, William B., 62,
89

Goshen, 26, 161, 165
Goss, W., 206
Gossett, John, 34, 71,
101, 102, 130, 204
Gossett, Joseph, 35, 101,
130, 204
Gossett, Mary, 35, 71,
101, 130, 204
Gossett, William, 101, 224

Gott, Nathaniel W., 10
Gott, William, 248

Gould, Anna C., 191, 233,
234, *see also Gold*
Gould, Anna, 49
Gould, Aphia/Apria, 49,
191
Gould, Helen, 191
Gould, Ingraham, 69, 74,

192, 231, 233, 234
Gould, Jeremiah, 49,
191, 192, 233
Gould, Llewellyn, 49, 191
Gould, Oren, 89, 192, 233,
234
Gould, Theresa Ann, 49,
191
Gould, Wellen, 49

Graham, Benjamin F.,
135, 136
Graham, Hugh, 45, 125
Graham, Robe, 228
Grange [Orange?] County,
32
Grant, David, 190
Gray, John, 235

Green, Ephram, 249
Green, J.W., 91
Greencastle, 208
Greerson, James, 236
Gregg, Anson, 221
Gregory, B. F., 221
Gregory, Elnathan, 65,
219
Gregory, Matilda, 198

Griffin, Alethea/Aletha,
73, 129, 130
Griffin, Angeline, 129
Griffin, Anson, 73, 74,
129
Griffin, Augustus, 73
Griffin, Daniel, 73, 129
Griffin, Edgar, 73
Griffin, Edwin, 226
Griffin, Hiram, 53, 234
Griffin, Homer, 73, 129
Griffin, Levi, 73
Griffin, Martin, 202
Griffin, Patrick, 132, 210
Griffin, Samuel, 53, 69,
181, 226
Griffin, Sarah Ann, 129
Griffin, Seth, 53
Griffin, Sylvester, 53

Griffin, Wellington, 73
Griffith, Hiram, 209, 218
Griffith, J. B. M., 238
Griffith, Jacob, 238
Grigg, Edwd. D., 227
Grill, John, 227

Gross, N., 206
Groves, Josiah, 223

Gurtine, W.B., 177

Gwinn, Andrew, 238

H

Hackley & Chenney, 30
Hackley, Joseph H., 30

Hagenback, William, 112
Hagenbuch & Orton, 247
Hagenbuch, William, 32,
204, 206, 218, 240, 241,
247, 251

Haladay, Wm., 221
Halas, Jacob, 122
Hale, Almira, 130
Hale, Eva, 131
Hale, Hester, 130
Hale, Hester Ann, 131
Hale, John D., 130
Hale, Mariah, 130
Hale, Sarah, 130
Hale, Silas, 130, 131, 204
Hale, Silas F., 131
Hale, William B., 131
Hall, Amos, 74, 76, 105,
13
Hall, Bankes/Banks, 218,
236, 246
Hall, Edward, 227
Hall, Eliza, 76, 112, 113
Hall, G. J., 225
Hall, George, 228
Hall, Gustavus, 74, 76,
105, 112, 113
Hall, J. R., 218

Hall, J., 240
Hall, Jacob R., 85, 200,
207
Hall, John, 74, 222
Hall, S. D., 228
Hall, Thomas, 225
Hall, Wesley, 75, 105
Haloday, Sterling, 221
Halsey, D./Daniel, 225,
245

Hamilton County, Ohio,
239
Hamilton, Adam, 221
Hamilton, J., 234
Hamison & Talcott, 239
Hampshire County,
Massachusetts, 243

Hancock County, 16
Hanks, Minor/Monor P.,
221
Hannah, _____, 11
Hannah, W. C., 156, 215,
241
Hannah, William C., 8, 10,
32, 61, 69, 71, 84, 112,
117, 126, 127, 186, 211,
239
Hannah, William E., 32
Hannum, James, 205

Harding, Eldridge, 202
Harding, Henry, 48, 134,
203, 220
Harding, Wm. G., 217
Harman, Andrew, 23
Harman/Harmon, David,
72, 151, 205, 232
Harmon, D., 233
Harness, John, 223
Harper, Archibald, 23, 87
Harper, Melinda/Belinda
S., 23, 87
Harree, C., 221
Harris, John, 217, 221
Harris, Richard, 5, 191
Harris, Wm. D., 225
Harrison, Abram/Abraham

W., 6, 10, 13, 15, 20, 32, 95, 100, 112, 194

Harrison, David, 213

Harrison, Eliza, 107, 108

Harrison, Elizabeth, 37, 96

Harrison, Francis P., 13, 107, 108

Harrison, Francis Porterfield, 13

Harrison, John L., 37, 96

Harrison, John, 242

Hart, Philip, 241

Hartford, A. S., 250

Hartswell, Albert, 228

Hartwell, Allerton, 236

Harvey, John, 72, 79, 93, 205, 243, 244

Harvey, Russell, 26, 215, 216

Harvey, Rysel, 165

Has, S. G., 246

Haseltine, John, 69, 226

Hasithin?, John, 214

Haskill, James, 238

Hastings, Alexander, 78, 161, 204, 222, 223

Hastings, John, 223

Hastings, William, 223

Hathaway, G., 205-6

Hathaway, Gilbert, 108, 158, 182, 194, 220, 235

Hauley, Gideon, 35

Havens/Havins, George C., 35, 125, 144, 208, 209, 210

Hawkins, William 9, 119, 218, 235, 236, 256

Hawley, Daniel, 253; see also Holley

Hayward, Joseph, 85

Haywood, Joseph, 178, 217, 241

Head?, Kelogg, 227

Heald, ____, 249

Heald, Arba, 198, 221, 228

Heath, Samuel, 168

Heath, Richd., 205

Heaton, Cyrus, 201

Heaton?, John, 231

Heckman, Jacob, 209, 233

Hefner, Henry, 55, 121

Hefner, John, 14, 19, 55, 77, 78, 92, 120, 125, 161, 231

Hefner, Joseph, 121

Heiser, Peter, 251

Hemenway, Wm. D., 223

Hemlock, Burwell, 121

Hempstead, Queens County, New York, 219

Hemrod, Horace, 248

Henchley, Harrison. F., 126, see also Hinkley

Henderson & Baxley, 222

Henker, Daniel, 208

Henry County, 102, 204, 211

Henry, Charles W., 140

Henson, Charles, 241

Henton, John R., 222

Henton, Peter, 221

Henton?, John K., 221

Hepner, John, 92, 162

Herbert, James, 39, 97, 209, see also Hurbut

Herbert, Mary, 97, 209

Herbert, Richard, 39, 97, 114, 209

Herbert, Samuel, 209, 229, 233

Herbet, Daniel, 249

Herrold, Henry, 248

Heveslin?, Samuel, 209

Hewit, James C., 66

Hews, Eleanor/Elenor, 9, 116, 198, see also Hughs

Hews, John F., 62, 151, 198

Hews, John, 9

Hews, R. B., 217, 218, 225

Hews, Richard B., 21, 26, 140, 216

Hibbard, Annis/Aunis S., 26, 27, 54, 69, 102, 216, 217, 237

Hibbard, C. H., 252

Hibbard, Charles, 217

Hibbard, Corrintha, 26, 54, 216

Hibbard, Daniel W., 26, 54, 69, 147, 216

Hibbard, Geo., 252

Hibbard, H. B., 236

Hibbard, Horace B., 19, 26, 54, 69, 99, 102, 109, 113, 148, 152 153, 217, 237

Hibbard, Horace Bonaparte, 216

Hibbard, Horace, 26, 54, 110, 147, 148, 217, 218, 219, 222, 235

Hibbard, John W., 26, 54, 69, 102, 216

Hibbard, Marian, 26, 54, 69, 216

Hickman, Jacob, 83, 115, 214, 244

Hicks, Benjamin, 212, 253

Higgins, W.W., 99, 159, 180

Higgins, William W., 44, 132, 173, 210

Higgins, Wm., 197

Highley/Highly, James, 5, 141, 191

Hill, Amos B., 246
Hill, D. B., 244
Hill, Edward, 203
Hill, John, 218
Hill, Robert, 214, 215
Hills, R. B., 207
Hills?, Randall, 224
Hilyar, Henry, 233
Hilyar, Mary, 233

Hinckley, H., 154
Hines, Sarah, 251
Hinkley, Harrison F., 178,
see also Henchley
Hinton, Peter, 208

Hiser, Jeremiah, 200, 237

Hitchcock, Jeremiah, 44,
132, 210

Hixon, T. J. S., 238
Hixson, Jeremy Jr., 202

Hoar, J., 207

Hobbs, John, 102
Hobson, John, 31, 47, 86,
87, 120, 200

Hodge, Hiram H., 207
Hodges, H. H., 226

Holbrook & King 171
Holbrook, H. P., 217
Holiday, Stephen, 220
Holland, Granville, 197
Holland, J., 198
Holland, L. J., 225
Holland, Lemuel? J., 224
Holland, Samuel, 157
Holley, Daniel, 55, 207,
234; *see also Hawley*
Holley, Sophronia, 234
Holliday, Sterling, 217
Holliday, William, 220
Holloway, Amos Jr., 222
Holloway, Amos, 67, 167,

218, 222
Holloway, D. P., 214
Holloway, Jason, 60, 155,
156
Holloway, John S., 60,
155, 156
Holloway, Nathan, 167,
241
Holloway, Stephen F., 217
Holloway, Stephen, 24,
61, 67, 126, 155, 156, 167,
178, 198, 205, 206, 213,
214, 222, 232, 241, 251
Holmes, Elisha M., 235
Holmes, Silas W., 249

Hopkins, James V., 252
Hopper, Melinda S., 36

Hornich, Solomon, 214

Hosmer, Austin, 199
Hosmer, George, 199, 200
Hosmer, Jackson, 30, 85,
199, 200
Hosmer, Nancy, 30, 85,
199, 200
Hosmer, Robert, 30, 85,
199
Hosmer, Ursula, 199
Hostetler, Joseph, 247

Hough, Jesse, 41, 232
Hough, Lawson, 71
Houghton, John, 206
Houseman, Martin, 40,
183, 235, 236, 239, 246

Howard, Sparry, 197
Howe, Amos J., 39
Howe, Mary Jane, 39
Howe, T.A., 132
Howel, ____, 210
Howell, J. C., 217, 218
Howell, James C., 26, 28,
70, 99, 138, 218
Howell, Jas. R., 238

Hubbard, Aliza, 128

Hubbard, Alonzo, 38, 128

Hudson Township, 104,
231, 244, 245, 253
Hudson, Bradley, 230
Hudson, David, 227, 254
Hudson, Elijah P., 66,
235
Hudson, Mariah, 254
Hudson, Patty, 235
Hudson, Pliny, 66, 78,
235
Hudson, Richard, 233,
254
Hudson, Saml. E., 235

Huggins, N. P., 223-224
Hughes, John, 213
Hughs, Elenor, 198
Hughs, John F., 198
Hughs, John, 198, 213
Hughs, Thomas, 204

Hulbert, John Wesley, 156,
224
Hulbert, John, 202
Hulbert, Mary E., 202
Hulbert, Mary Elizabeth,
156, 224
Hulbert, Mary, 202
Hulbert, Nancy, 156,
202, 224, 225
Hulbert, Noah, 157, 202,
224, 225
Hull, Charles, 138
Hull, Isaac, 10

Hunt, Charles W., 47, 80,
173, 219, 220
Hunt, Charles, 244
Hunt, David M., 173, 219,
220
Hunt, David, 223
Hunt, Elizabeth, 80
Hunt, F. W., 245
Hunt, Francina/Francine,
173, 219
Hunt, George S., 80
Hunt, George Sr., 47

Hunt, George, 64, 80, 139, 174, 175, 220
Hunt, Isaac E., 245
Hunt, Isaac, 244
Hunt, James A., 219
Hunt, James, 47, 173, 174, 218, 219, 220
Hunt, Jasper S., 47, 161,173, 219, 220, 223
Hunt, Jasper, 174, 175, 241
Hunt, Jeremiah, 228
Hunt, John M., 219, 220
Hunt, John S., 122, 207, 227
Hunt, John, 16, 207
Hunt, Jonathan S., 173, 219, 220, 227, 230
Hunt, Lucy C., 220
Hunt, Nancy, 47, 173, 219, 220
Hunt, Phebe, 173, 174, 219
Hunt, Phineas, 237
Hunt, Polly, 173, 174, 219
Hunt, Stephen G., 42, 80, 89
Hunt, Timothy, 245
Hunt, William H., 80
Huntley, Henry E., 237
Huntsman, Howell, 214

Hupp, A., 206, 218
Hupp, Isaac, 133
Hupp, Jacob B., 116
Hupp, Jacob, 34, 117, 241

Hurbut, James, 39, *see also Herbert*
Hurbut, Richard, 39

Hutchins, Isaac, 224

Huyser/Hyser, Jeremiah, 51, 75, 76
Huyser, Priscilla, 76

Hymon?, Geo. J., 244

I

Illinois, 131, 132, 147, 150, 213, 221, 228, 239

Indiana Tocsin, 163, 229
Indianapolis, 220

Ingram, John, 162
Ingram, Sarah, 247
Ingram, William, 204

Inman, Hiram, 113, 210
Inman, R.C., 123

Ireland, Lewis, 250

Irvin, Thomas, 248
Irving, Thomas, 248

Irwin, Polly, 248
Irwin, Thomas, 247, 248
Irwin, Wm., 245

Ives, Charles, 5, 191
Ives, Miron/Myron, 214

J

Jack, Elijah, 246
Jackson, Abigail, 17, 88
Jackson, Edmund, 17, 88
Jackson, Elizabeth, 100
Jackson, Ezra, 100
Jackson, Jesse, 71, 81, 100, 232
Jackson, Joseph, 248
Jackson, Sally, 81
Jackson, Samuel, 100, 101
Jackson, Sarah Maria, 71, 100, 101
Jackson, Stephen, 236
Jackson, Zeddok, 100
Jacobus, John, 61, 201

James, H. F., 8
James, Joseph, 224

Jeffers, Wm., 244

Jenkins, Edward, 115, 242
Jenkins, Mark, 115, 242
Jenkins, William, 115, 242

Jernegan & Harris, 229
Jernegan, Thomas, 163, 217, 220, 230, 252
Jernigan, A., 249

Jessop, John, 198, 229
Jessup, Abiezer M., 236
Jessup, Ann, 177, 236
Jessup, Daniel, 177, 217, 236
Jessup, Irwin/Erwin S., 171, 177, 228, 236
Jessup, J., 197
Jessup, John S., 228, 236
Jessup, John, 117, 177, 197, 218
Jessup, Simeon, 217
Jessup, Stephen, 220

Johnson & Stewart, 225
Johnson, Almira Hale, 130
Johnson, Christopher C., 201
Johnson, Elizabeth, 27, 114
Johnson, Isaac, 130
Johnson, John, 30
Johnson, Joseph, 27, 114
Johnson, Judge, 11
Johnson, Nathan, 45
Johnson, Samuel, 60, 162, 220

Jones, Ansalem, 209
Jones, Charles, 198
Jones, Eli, 209
Jones, Elihu, 209
Jones, Harry, 217
Jones, Henry, 234
Jones, Hiram, 233
Jones, Ja., 247
Jones, James, 198, 214

Jones, Jesse, 39, 115, 209, 246
Jones, Miciah/Micajah, 39, 97, 114, 209
Jones, Stephen, 133
Jones, Sylvanus, 250
Jones, Theadore/Theodore, 7, 82
Jones, Theodore D., 197
Jones, Theodore, 83
Jones, Wili, 221
Jones, William D., 129

Jordan, Edwin, 193
Jordan, Joshua, 245

Jouin?, Arthur, 236

Judson, E. S., 250
Judson, Joshuway, 249

Justice, Elizabeth, 16
Justice, Hannah, 72, 243, 244
Justice, Henry C., 244
Justice, Joanna, 244
Justice, Lorenzo, 244
Justice, Patrick C., 244
Justice, Sarah Ann, 244
Justice, Sarah, 243
Justice, William, 16, 72, 243
Justine, William B., 160

K

Kankakee (Township), 197, 198, 209, 213, 220, 226, 240, 244

Keeley, Conrad, 225
Keeley, Jacob, 151, 225
Keeley, John Jr., 225
Keeley, John, 225
Keeley, Joseph, 225
Keeley, Levi W., 157, 203, 225
Keeley, Margaret, 225

Keeley, Matthias, 157, 225

Kellips, David C., 105, *see also McKellips*
Kellogg, Charles 159

Kennedy, Edward/Ed, 207, 208
Kennedy, Joseph, 240
Kent, Elijah, 232

Kerby, Jacob, 129

Kewley, Isabella, 59, 149, 150, 200
Kewley, Jeremiah, 58, 149, 150
Kewley, John (son), 200
Kewley, John, 30, 58, 59, 85, 149, 200
Kewley, Philip, 58, 149, 150
Kewley, Thomas, 30, 85, 200
Kewley, William, 58, 59, 150, 200

Kidd, Wm., 221
Kidder, Aaron, 172, 228, 229, 247, 248
Kidel, Thomas, 210

Kimbell/Kimble, Moody, 248
Kimberly, George W., 13, 107, 108
Kimberly, Isabella, 13, 37, 107
Kimberly, Jeremiah Sullivan, 37, 107
Kimberly, Jeremiah, 13, 107, 108
Kimberly, Louisa, 108
Kimberly, Lucian P., 13, 108
Kimberly, Lucian Proctor Busk, 37, 107
Kimberly, Mary Ann

McLaughlin, 13, 107
Kimberly, Zenas, 13, 37, 107
Kimes, Catharine, 226
Kimes, Jas., 226
Kimes, Joseph, 226

King/Ring, Jos. R., 236
King, P., 248
King, Peter, 226
Kingsbury, 113, 219, 241
Kingsbury, Donald B., 89

Kirkville, Missouri, 250, 251
Kirton, Edward, 240

Knellingen?, Daniel, 221

Koontz, John, 241

Krop, Benjamin, 112

Kustardt, James, 250

L

La Porte County Whig, 13, 21, 23, 27, 28, 30, 31, 32, 33, 36, 37, 38, 45, 47, 48, 50, 52, 60, 71, 74, 127, 128, 136, 146, 147, 148, 154, 159, 163, 182, 192, 193, 218, 225

Laber, Wm. D., 220

Ladd, Charles, 240

LaFramboise, Globe, 8, 186
LaFramboise, St. Antoine, 8, 186

Lake County, 147, 203, 221, 248

Laman, Susanna, 251

Lamb, Oren, 250
Lambert, Benjamin, 172

Lane, Shubel F., 250, 251
Langburn, Mr., 240
Langdon, A., 234
Langdon, Abraham, 151

Laramore, 198

Lashbaugh, Thos. H., 248

Lathrop, Abiel, 176, 230

Layman, Susan, 251

Leach, A., 218
Leaming/Leming, D. M., 225, 234, 241, 250
Leaming, Daniel (M.), 56, 185
Leaming, Joseph, 5
Leaming, T., 231

Leery, Daniel, 246

Leland, Elder, 229

Lemon, Jno. M. Jr., 209, 246
Lemon, John M., 11, 14, 58, 83, 117, 197, 198
Lemon, Thomas D., 14, 37, 170, 222, 238

Lenawee County Michigan, 215

Lerwill, William, 229

Lewis, Amos, 245, 246
Lewis, Angeline, 141, 211, 231
Lewis, Ellen Mariah, 245
Lewis, Enoch, 227
Lewis, Isabelle Sutherland, 245
Lewis, Israel, 211
Lewis, J. B., 224

Lewis, Jabez, 56, 141
Lewis, Joel, 245, 246, 249
Lewis, John William, 245
Lewis, John, 214, 245, 246
Lewis, Joseph B., 56, 141
Lewis, Lucy M., 245, 246
Lewis, Moses, 214, 245, 246

Lexington, 100
Lexington, Massachusetts, 202

Ligget, Horace?, 221

Lilly, A., 237
Lilly, Albert, 236

Limig?, Juach, 214

Linard, Joseph, 236
Lindsley, Ab. S., 214
Lindsley, Betsey, 199, 214
Line, Jonathan, 11, 72, 84, 243, 244
Linen/Sineren, Samuel, 30
Linn, Jonathan, 198

Livingston, Catharine, 248
Livingston, Isaac, 223
Livingston, Jacob J., 56, 105
Livingston, Jacob, 203
Livingston, James, 142, 203
Livingston, John, 203, 249
Livingston, Mary, 56, 105, 203
Livingston, Matthew, 48

Lockwood, L. W., 240

Logan, Abraham, 202

Lomax, A., 218
Lomax, Abel, 43
Lomax, Constantine, 175, 205, 229, 230

Lomax, Gregory Abel, 146
Lomax, Joseph, 200, 208, 214, 217, 220
Lomax, L., 218
Lomax, Sarah, 175, 230
Lomax, William, 175, 229, 230

Long, Benjamin, 201, 221
Long, Gideon, 201, 221
Longshore, Richard A., 241

Looker, James, 200
Loomis, Henry, 229
Loomis, Lester, 228, 236
Loomis, Ralph, 87, 200, 201
Looney, Abigail, 159, 228
Looney, James L., 159
Looney, James, 160, 228

Lorain County, Ohio, 223
Lord, Lucricia, 45
Lord, Moses G., 45
Loring/Loving, James C., 250

Loveing, Right, 236
Loving, Silas, 217, 221, 254, 242
Loving, Wright, 242, 246

Low, Daniel, 64, 88, 206
Low, Jesse M., 223, 224
Low, William W., 132, 210
Low?, Joseph, 209
Lowe, Elias, 246
Lowe, John, 238
Lowell, William, 229
Lowell? Jabez, 204

Lucas, Aaron, 5, 118
Lucas, Abigail, 118
Lucas, Albert, 7, 194, 197
Lucas, Belinda, 118
Lucas, Christiana, 118

Lucas, Daniel, 118
Lucas, Debra, 118
Lucas, Elizabeth, 118
Lucas, Francis, 67, 118, 123
Lucas, George, 118
Lucas, Mary, 118
Lucas, Rhoda, 118
Lucas, Samuel, 118
Lucas, Sarah, 118
Luck, Allen, 217

Lumbar, Benjamin J., 229

Lunpas, Levi, 12

Lush, Henry, 168
Lusk, Henry, 240
Lusk, Harvey, 112

Luther, Edmon, 245

Lykins, Joseph W., 16, 18, 61, 122, 129, 207, 245, 253

Lynn, Wm., 221

M

Mabee, John P., 138, 225

Macado/Macadoo, James, 176
Macadoo, John, 176
Macadoo, Mary Jane, 176
Macadoo, Nancy C., 176
Macadoo, widow, 177
Macentaffee, Eli, 234

Maguire, D., 163

Mahony, Daniel, 202, 221

Maine/Maines, Daniel, 146, 147, 221, 240
Maine/Maines, Mary, 146, 221, 240

Maine, Samuel, 221
Mains, Daniel, 66
Mains, Mary, 66

Malbera, George, 88
Malosh, James, 142
Malosh, Mary, 142
Malks, John, 7
Malone, Wilson, 5

Mann, Jacob H., 240
Manville, D./Dewitt, 225

Maple, Wm. M., 224, 231
Maple, Wm., 204
Maples, William M., 117

Markham, A., 244
Markham, Hiram, 224
Markham, Israel, 5, 191
Marks, Iver, 209
Marsh, Catherine, 39
Marsh, Harry, 39, 217
Marsh, Henry, 200
Marshal, A. F., 202
Marshall County, 32, 33, 70, 111, 112, 119, 127, 182, 204, 238, 246
Marshall, Aaron Foster, 237
Marshall, Amelia, 237
Marshall, F., 229
Marshall, Henry, 237
Marshall, Maria, 237
Marston, John, 227
Marston, Olive, 226
Marston, Oliver, 253, 254
Martin, Charles, 67, 123
Martin, Isaac A., 223
Martin, Isaac D., 161
Martin, Isaac, 223, 244
Martin, Joel, 249
Martin, Josiah, 223
Martin, Mary, 66, 123
Martin, T. Tyrell, 192
Martin, William A., 64, 139, 223

Mason, A., 249

Mason, Alice, 24, 166
Mason, Allice Anna, 194, 214
Mason, Alva, 56, 200
Mason, Alvah, 217, 248
Mason, Edward, 166
Mason, Elizabeth, 24, 166, 194, 214
Mason, Elwood, 24, 194, 214
Mason, Horatio, 12
Mason, Howard, (heir), 24, 166, 194
Mason, Howard, 24, 166, 194, 214, 215
Mason, John, 172
Mason, Sidney/Sydney, 24, 166, 194, 214
Mason, Wm., 208
Massachusetts, 202, 243
Massey, Levi, 221
Maston, John, 227

Mathews, A. H., 228
Mathews, Edwin G., 160, 228
Mathis Jesse, 247, 248, 250
Matthews, Abner T., 45
Matthews, Lucretia, 45

Maxon, see Maxson
Maxson, George/Lee H. T., 44, 131, 210, 230
Maxson, Martha (M.), 44, 131, 132, 210, 230
Maxson, Paul (H.), 44, 76, 131, 210, 230
Maxwell, Arthur, 227
Maxwell, Elizabeth, 227
Maxwell, John, 227
Maxwell, William, 206, 221, 227, 249

Mayes, Matthew, 233
Mayhew, E., 145
Mayhew, Elijah, 58, 85, 98, 200
Mays, Matthew, 209, 233

Mayze, Mary D., 209
Mayze, Mathew, 209

Maze, Alex, 238

McAntush, John?, 227

McCallum, F., 237
McCarty & Howell?, 207
McCarty, Benjamin, 5
McCarty, Nicholas, 26, 99
McCaskey, Catharine W., 252
McCaskey, Jacob, 47, 252
McClain, Andrew, 73 *(see also McClane, McLain)*
(McClanahan = McClanihan)
McClanahan, Belinda B., 31, 40, 86, 123, 124, 200
McClanahan, Emily, 31, 40, 86, 200
McClanahan, Everett E., 86
McClanahan, Harriet H., 31, 40, 123, 124, 200
McClanahan, Herbert [Harriet??] H., 86
McClanahan, James E., 31, 40, 86, 123, 200
McClanahan, James, 31, 40, 84, 86, 123, 200
McClanahan, Joseph, 31, 86, 123, 200
McClanahan, Josephus, 40
McClane, Washington, 242 *(see also McClain, McLain)*
McClintock, Joseph A., 56
McClure, Arthur, 5, 58, 59, 62, 98, 100, 116, 122, 152, 191, 204, 207, 232, 242
McClure, Charles, 18, 19, 34, 36, 58, 83, 86, 87, 95, 98, 100, 112, 152, 204,

218, 242
(McCollum = McCollom = McCollam)
McCollum, Frederick, 224
McCollum, George, 162, 207, 208
McCollum, George G., 56
McCollum, George S., 130, 141, 204, 224
McCollum, James, 143, 245
McCollum, Pikeland, 81, 143, 224
McCollum, S., 130
McCollum, William A., 81, 143, 224
McCord, George, 66, 220, 221
McCord, James, 60, 163, 220, 221
McCord, Jesse, 201, 221
McCormick, Henry, 249
McCormick, John, 180
McCormick, Robert, 249
McCormick, S. S., 240
McCoy, Wm., 208
McCreery, Alexander, 247, 248, 249
McCrera, Alexander, 248
McCrera, Sarah, 248

McDaniel, J. S., 247
McDonald/McDonel, John B., 121, 162
McDowell, J., 212
McDowell, J. S., 185
McDowell, Joshua S., 212

McEntafee, John, 249
McEntaffee, Augusta, 249
McEntaffee, Birt, 249
McEntaffee, Lydia, 249
McEntaffee, Ruth, 249
McEntaffee, Stephen W., 249

McGogey, James F., 253
McGogey, Mary T., 253

McIntosh, John, 227

McKay, James, 271
McKee?, Thomas H., 213
McKelips, David, 249, *see also Kellips*
McKelleps, D.C., 123
McKellip, David, 236
McKellips, David C., 142
McKellops, David C., 70
McKellups, David, 178
McKillips, D. C., 249
McKillips, David C., 249
McKinney, A., 248

McLane, Jesse, 244 *(see also McClane, McClain)*
McLane, Wm., 231
McLaughlin, Mary Ann, 13
McLean, Andrew, 218
McLean, Daniel 157
McLean, Jesse, 5
McLellan, Joseph, 43, 201
McLone, Wm., 236

McPatterson, William, 71
McPherson, Joseph, 223, 246

Mead, Lewis, 233

Meeker & Bradley, 159
Meeker, Anna, 248, 249
Meeker, Clark, 228, 236, 249
Meeker, Daniel, 200, 206, 207, 243
Meeker, Henry, 118, 248, 249
Meeker, John, 249
Meeker, Robert, 206
Meereanz, Alexander, 236

Melville, Andrew, 23, 96, 118, 228
Melville, Andrew Jr., 96
Melville, John Jr., 23

Merriam, Abner W., 202
Merriam, Charles, 202
Merryfield, R., 209, 232
Merryfield, Robert, 7, 10,
13, 19, 41, 92, 97, 148,
194, 198, 242

Messen?, Chester Jr., 236
Messenger, Charles, 205

Metzker, Jacob, 210, see
also Mitzker

Meyers, Benjamin W.,
171, see also Myers

Micasky, Jacob, 209
Michigan City, 10, 53, 55,
57, 89, 118, 131,132, 158,
159, 173, 176, 179, 191,
202, 205, 206, 210, 213,
214, 224, 228, 229, 233,
243, 252
Michigan City Gazette,
17, 44, 45, 132, 192
Michigan City Gazette
and Comercial Advertizer,
53
Michigan Road (lands),
28, 32, 111, 137, 217
Michigan, 127, 215, 216,
220, 230, 238

Middlebury, 95, 215
Middlesex County,
Massachusetts, 202
Middleton, Geo. H., 235
Middleton, John, 204
Middletown, Jonathan,
178
Middleton, Jonathan D., 9,
230
Middleton, Margaret, 76,
112

Milan, Ohio, 248
Milford, Robert, 66, 146,
147, 221, 222
Millard/Willard, Almira,

38, 127
Millard/Willard, Eleazer,
38, 127
Miller, Alex, 234
Miller, Almasa P., 206
Miller, Daniel, 49
Miller, Delila, 49
Miller, Denton, 206
Miller, Dudley, 135, 206
Miller, Elijah, 49
Miller, Elizabeth Ann, 49
Miller, Elizabeth, 48, 49
Miller, Emily, 107, 108
Miller, Eve, 49
Miller, Francis, 206
Miller, George W., 13
Miller, Henry, 204
Miller, Jacob, 5, 22, 38,
49, 86, 98, 127, 128, 181,
209, 226, 235, 246, 247
Miller, James, 206
Miller, Jeremiah, 49
Miller, Jesse F., 82
Miller, Jesse, 197
Miller, John, 34, 162, 245
Miller, Noah, 226
Miller, Peter, 34, 49, 205
Miller, Polly, 49
Miller, Robert, 247
Miller, Roswell, 236
Miller, Samuel, 13, 15,
57, 90, 107, 108
Miller, Tobias, 120, 123,
204, 247
Millikan, J., 215
Millikan, John, 226, 228,
229, 230
Millikan, W. & J., 239,
247, 248, 251
Millikan, W. T., 239
Mills, J. P., 202, 237
Mills, John, 129, 207
Mills, Mason, 248
Mills, Sidney, 248
Mills, William P., 248
Mills, Wm. G., 248
Milspaugh, S. S., 247

Min Nah Che Ques Mo

Qua, 9
Minor, O. J., 201
Minor, Orrin J., 210

Mirren, A. M., 18

Mise, Stephen, 172
Miser, Henry, 84
Mishewah/Niswhewak,
8, 185, 186
Missouri, 233, 251, 253

Mitchell, David, 75
Mitzker, Jacob, 132, see
also Metzker

Mix Na Che Quas Mo
Qua Wa, 187
Mix, ___, 225
Mix, Charlotte, 138, 225
Mix, Eben, 209
Mix, Jay, 5
Mix, John, 138, 225
Mix, Orange/George?,
225, 229
Mix, Stephen, 225, 229

Monday, Reuben, 121,
168
Monroe, Angeline, 73, 129
Monroe, Henry, 73, 129
Montgomery County, 251
Montgomery, William,
131, 210

Moody, R. G., 220
Moody, Saml., 249
Moore, Eliza, 91, 201, see
also Morre
Moore, John Jr., 76, 113
Moore, John, 218
Moorhed, W. W., 240
Moorman, Archibald, 50,
95
Moorman, Charles, 83
Moothe, Edwin, 210
Moothe, Sheldon, 210

Morgan Isaac, 7, 82, 197

Morgan, J. G., 224
Morgan, Jacob G., 160, 228, 248
Morgan, Jonathan, 197
Morgan, Wesley/Westley, 210, 223, 236
Morgan, William, 197
Morison, E., 198
Morley, Richard, 34
Morman, Jess, 227
Morre, John, 199, *see also Moore*
Morris, A., 229
Morrison, E., 227
Morrison, Ezekiel, 14, 31, 42, 55, 71, 78, 79, 81, 90, 91, 93, 95, 100, 110, 127, 138, 152, 198, 203, 205, 218
Morrison, R. S., 82, 213
Morrison, Robert S./L., 9, 10, 11, 14, 83, 84, 92, 117, 180, 212, 213
Morrow, Charles, 18, 199
Morse, Delia, 41
Morse, Frederick, 48
Morse, James, 40, 48, 61
Morse, Mary, 61
Morton, A., 238

Moser, Aaron, 224
Mossman, ?, 106
Mossman, John S., 45
Mossman, Rachel, 45

Mott, James, 239
Motter, Andrew, 229
Motter, Patience, 230

Moulton, Jonathan D., 84
Moulton, Lydia, 239
Moulton, Moses, 183, 236, 239
Mounts, John C., 53

Mowery?, Nancy, 231
Mowlan(?), Charles, 5
Mowlan, Charlotte E., 222

Moyes?, Matthew, 227

Mudge, Enoch, 10

Muir?, Hervey, 239

Mukes?, Daniel, 224

Mulks, Daniel, 6, 188, 189
Mulks, John, 82, 197

Mun, Harry, 236
Mun, Harvey, 240
Munday, H., 250
Munday, R., 241
Munger, Gaius W., 19

Mupuch, 7

Murray, Daniel, 190

Mussuch, 7

Myers, B. W., 228, *see also Meyers*
Myers, Henry, 251

N

Napier, Calvin, 220

Nathan, E. L., 164
Nathan, E., 146

Neal, Ashel, 84

Neff, Abraham, 46, 47, 195
Neff, Allen, 46, 47, 195
Neff, Francis, 46, 47, 195
Neff, Jesse, 46, 195

Negoncone, 8, 185

Nelson, Wm. C., 236

Nesbit, Minor, 237

Neville, N., 138
Nevins, Samuel, 240

New Durham Township, 142, 200, 215, 216, 217, 218, 221, 228, 236
New York City, 176, 239
New York, 39, 78, 111, 127, 181, 188, 219, 230, 235, 251, 252
Newburg, New York, 39
Newell, Elbridge G., 48
Newell, Elisha, 165
Newell, James C., 136
Newell, Noah, 25, 26, 32, 46, 48, 112, 134, 152, 165, 194, 215, 216, 235
Newell, North, 165
Newhall, Elisha, 82, 197
Newkirk, Benoni M., 7, 83, 235
Newport, Pennsylvania, 252
Newton, John, 135, 136

Nicholas/Nichols, N. B., 214, 244
Nichols, Nathan B., 5, 20, 41, 47, 154, 190, 213, 214, 220, 226, 244
Nicholson, Catherine, 38
Nicholson, James, 38
Nickel, Andrew, 200
Nickerson, Alexander, 217
Nickerson, Allen, 225
Nickerson, Chansey, 227
Nickerson, Marquis, 203
Nickles?, Henderson, 202

Nile & Osborn, 136, 182
Niles, John B., 16, 19, 23, 26, 28, 36, 47, 49, 66, 70, 84, 88, 92, 97, 103, 108, 112, 116, 118, 122, 127, 131, 138, 148, 150, 152, 155, 163, 165, 184, 187, 196, 215, 216, 217, 218, 219, 231, 239, 240

Niles, John, 130
Niles, Michigan, 198
Niles, Nathaniel, 198
Niles, Orrin, 85
Niles, Rodney B., 234
Niles, Samuel, 164
Niles, William W., 239
Niles, William, 227

Niswhewak/Mishewah, 8

No-a-quet, 253

Noble Township, 222,
223, 224, 235, 240, 242

Nofsinger, Samuel H., 250

Noland, Barbara, 236
Noland, Silas, 237
Noland, Stephen, 237

Norris, Harvey, 145, 209
Norris, Thomas, 91, 127
Northam, Asa, 244
Norton, Daniel, 134, 206
Norton, David, 53, 104
Norton, Isaac, 247
Norton, Stephen, 52, 80,
103, 104

Nowland, Stephen, 217

Nye, Ira C., 230

O

Oaks, David J., 168

Odell, Hannah, 251
Odell, John, 251

Ogden, William B., 239

Ohannan, Patrick, 238
O'Hara, Edward, 239, 241
O'Hara, Edwin, 224
O'Hara, Michael, 236

O'Hara, Samuel, 246
O'Hara, William, 239

Ohio Life Insurance &
Trust Company, 257
Ohio, 57, 118, 213, 223,
239, 248, 251

Olive Township, St.
Joseph County, 244
Oliver, E., 218

Ontario County, New
York, 235

Organ, E. S., 178, 200,
208, 209

Orr, Henry, 23, 87
Orr, Joseph, 23, 87, 96

Orton, Doctor, 197
Orton, M. C., 225
Orton, M. H., 102, 184,
207, 263, 246, 247
Orton, Myron H., 104, 130
Orton, W. H., 148

Orum, Hiram, 214

Orvis?, Harris, 217

Osborn, A. L., 196, 210
Osborn, A. S., 170
Osborn, Andrew L./D., 53,
95, 131, 132, 133, 237,
239
Osborn(e), Andrew S., 76,
77
Osborn, Andy L., 244
Osborn/Osbourn/Osburn,
Jonathan, 90, 201, 221
Osborn, Joseph, 69, 217
Osborn, Samuel, 176, 177

Oswego County, New
York, 252

Otis, Clarissa, 170, 171,

228
Otis, Mrs., 229
Otis, William M., 170,
228, 229

Overmeyer, Solomon, 12
Overmire, Solomon, 210
Overmyer, Daniel, 225

Owens, Asa, 71, 127
Owens, Owen A., 24, 71

P

Paddock, James, 72, 212
Paddock, Matthew, 209

Pagan, David, 184, 241
Pagan, Joseph, 241
Pagan, Lewis, 244
Pagan, Mary Elizabeth,
184, 241
Pagan, Rebecca, 184, 241
Pagin, Erastus, 203

Pallion, Jacob, 231
Palmer, C., 206, *see also
Parmer*
Palmer Charles, Jr., 159,
206
Palmer, Charles, 135, 159,
206, 228
Palmer, E., 85, 207, 234
Palmer, Ebenezer, 53, 55,
56, 234
Palmer, J. D., 251
Palmer, Milton, 247, 248,
249
Palmer, Nathan, 251
Palmer, Solomon L., 230
Palmer, Wm., 227

Pangburn, Daniel, 240

Parker, Branson, 228, 229
Parker, W. D., 135
Parker, Wm. D., 206, 217,
221, 228, 229

Parker, Wm. J., 206
Parkinson, Samuel, 221
Parmer(?), Ziba, 173, *see
also Palmer*
Parmer, M., 249
Parmer, Milton, 249
Parnell, Wm., 245
Parrott, E., 204
Parrott, John, 204
Parsons, Lydia, 8
Parsons, Solomon, 8
Partridge, Eliza, 230

Patre, Jeremiah, 74
Pattee, Elenore, 247
Pattee, Eliphalet, 229
Pattee, Elizabeth, 247
Pattee, Elmore, 229, 247,
248
Pattee, John, 221
Pattee, Levi, 247, 248
Pattee, Lewis, 247, 248
Pattee, Luis, 248
Pattee, Orson, 221, 247,
248
Pattee, Polly, 248
Pattee, Sarah, 248
Patten, Davison, 168, 195,
196, *see also Patton*
Patten, M. W., 222
Patten/Potter, Davison,
238
Patter, Levi, 221
Patterson, Darwin, 227
Patterson, M. A., 238
Patterson, W. M., 178
Patterson, Wm., 236
Patton, Wilson, 119, *see
also Patten*
Pattrick, Robard, 221

Payne, Alonso D., 229
Payne, E. H., 229
Payne, Erastus H., 171,
225, 229
Payne, Erastus, 46, 234,
249
Payne, Henry C., 229

Peace, L., 207
Peak, Frances, 204
Pearce, Henry, 57
Pearce, Michael, 57
Pearce, Phebe, 57
Pearce, Thomas, 57
Pearsall, J. H., 228
Pease, Alvin R./B., 20, 54,
213
Pease, Artemisia R., 20,
154, 213
Pease, Asa C., 20, 41, 154,
155, 213, 214
Pease, Buenos A., 20,154,
213, 214
Pease, David H., 20, 41,
154, 213
Pease, Enos A., 20, 213
Pease, Enos, 20, 41, 153,
154, 213, 214
Pease, Isabel, 20, 154,
213, 214
Pease, Lucinda Ann, 20,
41, 154, 213
Pease, Nancy A., 20, 154,
213
Pease, Susan W., 20, 154,
213
Peattelum?, D. D., 227

Peck, Jacob, 248
Peck, W., 221
Peck, Willis/Willys, 53,
64, 98, 132, 192, 210, 233,
234, 243

Peek, Frances, 204
Peer, Jacob, 51, 248

Pence, Ball H., 241
Pendile, James P., 30
Pennsylvania, 189, 198,
251, 252
Penwell, E. S., 240

Perkins, Bailey M., 236
Perkins, J., 240, 242, 244
Perkins, Jacob, 237
Perkins, Jeremiah, 207,

217, 239, 241-42, 246
Perry County,
Pennsylvania, 252
Perry, Aaron F., 239
Perry, Betsey, 39
Perry, Elizabeth W., 239
Perry, Hugh, 39
Perry, Joseph, 249
Perry, Lucy, 249
Perry, Martin, 223
Perry, Titus, 223
Perry, Willard, 223
Perry, William S., 158
Person, Alexander, 217
Persons, Wm., 204

Peters, George, 221
Peters, Joseph, 232
Petre, Daniel J. Jr., 45
Petre, Daniel, 45
Petre, John, 45
Petro, George, 67, 201,
208
Petro, Wm., 221
Petry, Daniel, 124
Petry, Daniel J., 124, 125
Petry, Eve, 124
Petry, John, 124, 125
Pettee, Orson, 208
Petton?, M. W., 225
Petty, George, 201
Petty, Levi, 201

Philadelphia,
Pennsylvania, 111, 204
Phillips, Nimrod, 210,
221, 223, 235
Phillips, Thomas H., 21
Phillips, W. H., 223
Phillips?, David C., 203

Pickle, Andrew, 231
Pickle, Jacob, 231

Pierce, Ferris, 240
Pierce, Thomas, 234

Pigget, John, 201

Pinney, Daniel, 90
Pinney, Horace (admr.), 221
Pinney, Horace Jr., 54, 68, 221
Pinney, Horace Sr., 54, 68
Pinney, Horace, 68, 90, 143, 201, 238
Pinney, Lois, 68, 143
Pinney, Mary, 68, 142, 143
Pinney, Nancy, 54, 143, 201
Pinney, William, 68, 222

Pittsburgh, Pennsylvania, 198

Place, W. A., 225, 235, 238, 240, 243
Place, Willard A., 91, 184, 235
Plank, Abraham, 63
Plank, Asa Rilburn, 63
Platt, Eldred, 219
Platt, Jeremiah, 33, 173, 219
Platt, Richard, 219
Platt, Watts, 219

Pleasant Township, 106, 128, 130, 144, 201, 203, 205, 209, 210, 224, 234, 252

Plymouth, 111, 246

Polk, A.G., 88
Polk, Adam G., 85, 116, 117, 121, 138
Polk, H.G., 86
Polk, William, 138
Polke, A. G., 197, 200, 206, 207, 218
Polke, A. J., 198
Polke, Adam G., 5, 7, 9, 12, 14, 15, 19, 30, 36, 43, 58, 59, 85, 92, 149, 150,

167, 168, 190, 194, 200, 201, 207
Polke, Adam, 92, 198
Polke, Otelia Cullen, 167

Porter County, 11, 45, 84, 102, 131, 133, 137, 198, 204, 211, 218, 219, 239, 244
Porter, Nathan, 38, 127, 128, 129
Porter, Oliver, 15
Porterfield, Francis, 13

Potter, C., 229
Potter, D., 238
Potter/Pottle, B. C., 252
Pottinger, Samuel, 138, 252

Pound, David, 116
Pound, J., 244

Powell, C. G., 237
Powell, Thomas, 231
Powers, David, 218, 242

Prator, Wm., 223
Pratt, J., 244
Pratt, John, 218, 221, 242, 244
Pratt, Laura Ewing, 149
Pratt, William, 242
Pratton, George, 228
Pray, William S., 228

Preston, Albert G., 213
Preston, E., 250
Preston, Erbin, 244
Preston, Zenas, 6, 188, 189
Prett?, Samuel, 240

Price, John, 218

Provolt, E., 214
Provolt, Delilah, 117
Provolt, Eliza Ann, 78, 117

Provolt/Provalt/Provault /Prevolt, Ezekiel, 5, 78, 117, 190, 191, 204, 231
Provolt, John, 117
Provolt, Mary Catherine, 117
Provolt, Maryann, 117
Provolt/Provalt, William, 117

Pulaski County, 81, 100, 101
Pulaski, New York, 252
Pulford, ____, 210
Pulver, David, 202

Putnam County, 133, 208

Q

Queens County, New York, 219

R

Rambo, Absalom, 50
Rambo, Adonijah, 50, 222
Rambo, Charlotte, 50, 74, 222
Rambo, Isaac Nuton, 222
Rambo, J. P., 241
Rambo, Rueben, 8
Rambo, Smith, 74, 222

Randolph County, 211

Rathbone, Daniel, 233
Rathborne, Daniel F., 197
Rathbone, E., 83
Rathbun, ____, 243
Ratliff, Cornelius, 234

Rawley, John, 207

Ray, James, 221
Ray, James M., 103, 208

Reamer, George, 209, 218

Redding, Aaron V., 172
Redding, Alfred, 172
Redding, David, 172
Redding, John, 172
Redding, Josiah, 172, 199
Redding, Louis/Lewis,
172, 199
Redding, Nancy, 172
Redding, Sarah, 172
Redding, Susannah, 172

Reed, B., 221
Reed, David, 221
Reed, George, 221
Reed, Hugh, 12
Reed, J. C., 218
Reed, Joseph B., 217
Reed, Joseph K., 220, 221
Reed, Joseph, 197, 217
Reed, King, 208
Reed, William, 51, 236,
243
Reester/Keester, John, 213
Reeve, C., 224
Reeve, Inez?, 202
Reeve, J., 224
Reeve, James, 60, 202
Reeves, Catherine, 5, 190,
191
Reeves, James Madison,
5, 190, 191
Reeves, Josiah, 5, 190,
191

Regersfree, Aquilla W.,
128, *see also Rogers*

Reighard, J. D., 202
Reighard, John, 203
Reighard, Mary, 203
Reighard, Mrs. M. E., 202

Remes, George, 68

Reymer/Reamer, George,
218

Reynolds, A. A., 241
Reynolds, Allen W., 175,
230
Reynolds, Ann, 212
Reynolds, Clarissa, 181,
238
Reynolds, F., 250
Reynolds, G. W., 245
Reynolds, George W., 50,
62
Reynolds, George, 212
Reynolds, Harriet Maria,
176, 230
Reynolds, J., 245
Reynolds, John, 181, 238
Reynolds, Lewis, 225
Reynolds, Nancy Matilda,
212
Reynolds, Nathan, 212

Rhineheart, John, 112

Rhodes, B., 212
Rhodes, Benjamin, 212

Rice, Ann S., 253
Rice, George W., 236
Rice, Henry, 209, 224
Rice, Luther, 253
Rice, William M., 253
Richards, John R., 204,
208, 217
Richardson, Andrew, 202
Richey, Joseph, 231
Richley, Peter, 238
Richmond, 215
Richmond, New York, 252
Rickinson, Likins, 202

Ridgley, Westell, 218
Ridgway, A. J., 246, 250
Ridgway, James, 85, 200

Ring, Joshua, 247

Ritter, John, 179, 219
Ritter, Pemelia/Pamela,
46, 73, 179
Ritter, Peter, 46, 179

Ritter, Simon, 46, 179
Ritter, Susan, 179

Rizer, Blake, 236

Robb, David, 101
Roberts, C. S., 159
Roberts, Charles F., 159
Roberts, F., 240
Roberts, Ferdinand, 246
Robertson, Daniel, 103,
207, 208
Robertson, Hezekiah, 207
Robinson, A. H., 228, 229,
241
Robinson, A. W., 229
Robinson, Alexander H.,
229
Robinson, Alexander, 172
Robinson, E., 229
Robinson, Joseph, 25,
207
Robinson, Lemuel, 23, 86,
133, 207, 208
Robinson,
Lemuel/Samuel, 20, 23,
25
Robinson, Samuel, 107,
202
Robinson, Thomas, 20, 25,
202
Robinson, Wyllis A., 223
Robison, Joseph, 227

Rock County, Wisconsin,
130, 131

Rodifer, Harrison, 51

Rogers, Aquila W., 71,
140, 237, *see also
Regersfree*
Rogers, G. C., 239

Rolling Prairie, 245

Rood, James, 56, 105,
160, 203, 228, 229
Root, Josiah, 204

Rose, D. G., 236
Rose, G. A., 201, 204, 236
Rose, G., 200
Ross, Catharine, 237
Ross, Elizabeth A., 237
Ross, Martha Ellen, 211
Ross, Solomon, 237, 241
Ross, Walker, 220
Ross, William Wesley
Conner, 211
Ross, William, 145, 240, 241
Ross, William O., 117, 194

Roundy, John, 77
Rouse, Mary, 35, 71, 101, 130, 204

Rulen, Martin, 213

Rupel, John, 6

Rush, Hiram, 5
Rush, Israel, 5
Rush, Israel H., 190
Russell, C., 197

Ruthbrin, Daniel D., 18
Ruton, Martin W., 232

Ryckman, David S., 41

Rythes/Ryther?, E., 209

S

Sabin, S. S., 215

Sailor, Benjamin, 197
Sailsbury, M., 5

Sale, John F., 40
Sale, Thomas W., 40
Sales, Francis, 208
Sallevison (?), Robert, 12
Salor, B., 197
Salsbery, Bejmin, 245

Sams, Henry F., 9

Sanford, George, 221

Sareen, Annis S., 216, *see also Sovereign and similar*
Sarreen, Abram, 216

Satterlee, Artemisia R., 20, 213
Satterlee, Milton, 20
Satterlee, Orson, 20
Satterlee, Susan W., 20

Saulsbery, Benjamin, 245

Sawin, George, 21
Sawley, C. S., 217

Sayborn, Newlove, 121
Sayles, Thomas, 221

Scarce, Elizabeth, 79, 93, 205, 225
Scarce, John N./V., 93, 205
Scarce, Nancy Ellen, 93, 205
Scarce, Samuel, 72, 79, 93, 151, 205, 231
Scarce, William, 93, 205

Schofield, see Scofield
Schultz, Jacob, 12
Schultz, John, 12
Schultz, Philip, 12

Scipio Township, 219, 229, 248

Scofield, Seeley, 52, 104
Scott, Horace, 45
Scott, James M., 33, 46, 57, 173, 219
Scott, James, 180
Scott, Lyman, 248
Scott, Martha Jane, 57
Scott, Mary, 248

Scott, Patty M., 45
Scott, Samuel Jr., 57
Scott, Samuel, 173, 219

Scudder, Isaac, 38, 127
Scudder, Julian/Julia, 38, 127

Self, Joseph B., 74, 76, 105, 113, 168
Selkregg, G. R., 89
Selkregg, George R., 62, 89
Selkregg, Martin H., 159

Seymour, Geo., 252

Shaft, Moses, 247
Sharp, Angeline, 61
Sharp, Benjamin, 61
Sharp, Caroline, 61
Sharp, Elizabeth (child), 61
Sharp, Elizabeth, 43, 61, 201
Sharp, John, 61
Sharp, Martha Ann, 61
Sharp, Nelson, 61
Sharp, Robert, 117
Sharp, Thomas, 43, 85, 201
Sharp, William, 117
Shaw, Andrew, 204
Shaw, B., 240, 244
Shaw, Benjamin, 74, 183, 235, 236, 246
Shaw, D., 138, 140, 241
Shaw, Daniel, 75
Shaw, Henry M., 250, 251
Shaw, R., 176, 225, 230
Shaw, Rensselaer, 62, 76, 102, 113, 138, 176, 225, 230

Shead, Kellogg, 254
Shed, Kellog, 233
Shed, Urasmus, 233
Shepard, John E., 219

Shepheard, P., 219
Sheridan, William, 204
Sherman, Mary, 130, 204
Sherwood, John, 152, 153, 202
Shesko, 18
Shetleff, Oliver, 122, *see also Shurtleff*

Shick Kog Wish She Qua, 9
Shimerin, William, 59
Shimmin, William, 30, 85, 200, 234
Shippee, George H., 198

Shoffler?, Reuben, 245
Shop & Boice, 247
Shop, Ann Eliza, 183, 184, 240
Shop, Peter, 183, 184, 240, 246, 247, 250
Shop, P., 247
Shotwell, A. B., 85
Shotwell, Eden, 85

Shults, Jacob, 238
Shultz, ____, 247
Shumway, Pailey D., 165
Shumway, William D., 203, 235
Shurtleff, Oliver, 207, *see also Shetleff*

Sickell, Henderson, 236

Simmons, E. J., 2221
Simon, John M., 8
Sims, Calista, 246
Sineren/Linen, Samuel, 30
Singer, Michael, 46
Singuy, Francis, 206

Small, John, 90, 201
Small, Mary, 143
Small, Phineas/Phenias, 45, 54, 68, 90, 142, 143, 201
Small, William, 30

Smallwood, Burnet, 70
Smallwood, Elizabeth Bennet, 126
Smallwood, Elizabeth Jr., 70, 80, 103, 126
Smallwood, Elizabeth (adult), 70, 80, 103
Smallwood, Samuel (Jr.), 70, 80, 103, 126
Smallwood, Samuel, 70, 80, 103, 126
Smallwood, Sarah Jane, 70, 80, 103, 126

Smedley, Adam, 61, 150, 151

Smith ___, 207
Smith & Chapman & Bixby, 158
Smith James F., 89
Smith, Betsey, 39
Smith, C., 206
Smith, Catherine, 39
Smith, Chadwick, 207
Smith, Charles, 81, 104
Smith, Charlotte, 39
Smith, Cornelius, 88
Smith, Daniel, 212
Smith, Eber, 206
Smith, Edwina, 16
Smith, Elmira, 207
Smith, Frances/Francis C., 81, 104
Smith, H., 206
Smith, Hezekiah, 29, 39, 140, 207
Smith, James F. Jr., 81, 104
Smith, James F., 16, 73, 81, 88, 104, 157, 158
Smith, James J., 221
Smith, Jas., 210
Smith, John, 15, 121, 155, 206, 207
Smith, Johnathan, 218
Smith, Jonathan, 214
Smith, Lester, 16, 121, 207

Smith, Mary Jane, 39, 81, 104,
Smith, Miron, 202
Smith, Obadiah, 29, 39, 140, 141, 207, 217, 228, 248
Smith, Olive, 81, 104, 121, 207
Smith, Oliver, 207
Smith, Olivia M., 73, 80, 104
Smith, Olson, 16
Smith, Orion, 16
Smith, Purdy, 220
Smith, Rachel, 39
Smith, Rhoda, 16, 121, 207
Smith, Richard, 236
Smith, Robert B., 170
Smith, Robert H., 254
Smith, Robert K., 170, 226, 227
Smith, S. J., 252
Smith, Samuel, 16, 207
Smith, Sanford, 81, 104
Smith, Sylvester, 81, 104
Smith, Thomas N., 20, 155, 214

Snedecor, Phebe, 219
Sneed, Isaac, 117

Snodgrass, Abiram, 217
Snow, Thomas, 202

Snyder, Isaac, 198

Soman, Abel, 65
Sommers, Amos, 76
Sommers, Isaac, 76

Soswa, 18

South Bend, 32, 224, 235
Southan, George, 90

Sovereign, A., 249

Sovereign, Abraham, 216, 229, 249
Sovereign, Annis S., 216, 217
Sovine, Abram/Abraham, 26, 27
Sovine, Annis/Aunis S., 26, 27
Sovreen/Soveen, Abram, 26

Sparbuck, Burcholl, 16, *see also Spurlock*
Spaulding, Sylvia, 49, 163
Spaulding, Timothy, 49, 163, 219

Spear, Charles, 248
Speirs, Abigail, 228
Speirs, William R., 228
Spencer, Charles, 207
Sperry, Henry, 233

Sprague, David, 22, 29, 53, 97
Sprague, Edward, 29, 97
Sprague, Henry B., 29
Sprague, James W., 29, 30, 97
Sprague, John, 29, 97
Sprague, Polly, 29, 53, 97
Sprague, Sarah, 29
Sprague, Sudan/Susan, 29, 97
Sprague, Thomas, 29, 97
Sprague, William, 29, 97
Springer, Henry, 247
Springfield Township, 198, 212, 225, 233, 241

Spurlock, B., 212, 217, 221, 233, *see also Sparbuck*
Spurlock, Burwell, 134, 168, 206, 212

St. Clair, Dr., 197

St. Joseph County, 5, 12,
32, 110, 122, 128, 182, 190, 191, 204, 207, 223, 225, 244, 245

Standiford, A. G., 248, 249
Standiford, Abraham G., 85, 201
Standiford, H.G., 85
Stanfield, Robert, 231
Stanton & Pears, 167
Stanton, Aaron T., 30
Stanton, Aaron, 11, 19, 180, 213, 214, 218, 232
Stanton, Alfred 151, 225, 229
Stanton, Benajah/Benj., 206, 250
Stanton, Charlotte, 232
Stanton, E., 206
Stanton, Edward, 233
Stanton, Elijah, 37, 41, 67, 96, 126, 167, 198, 205, 222, 232, 233
Stanton, John, 61, 156, 167, 178, 198, 213, 222, 232
Stanton, Joseph, 233, 249
Stanton, Lydia Ann, 120
Stanton, Melissa, 178
Stanton, Moses, 250
Stanton, Thomas E., 28, 90, 199, 241
Stanton, Thomas, 213
Stanton, William F., 250, 251
Starket?, Alexander, 217
Starkweather, Leonard, 199, 200
Starrett, A., 242
Starret(t), Alexander, 74, 183, 235
Starret(t), Joseph, 74, 183, 231, 235, 236, 242
Starrett, Samuel, 235
Starret(t), Theresa, 74, 183, 235

Stebbins, Joseph S., 235

Stephens, Alfred, 79
Stephens, D. A., 217
Stephens, George, 79
Stephens, H., 220
Stephens, Sophia, 79
Stephens, Walter, 79
Stephens/Steven, Samuel, 79
Stephenson, Thomas, 240, 244
Stephenson, William, 246
Sterns, H. C., 214
Steven/Stephens, Samuel, 79
Stevens, E. C., 220
Stevens, James B., 16
Stevens, Myron, 203, 221
Stevens. H., 220
Stevenson, L., 239
Stevenson, Lewis, 223
Stewart, Daniel, 129, 145, 209, *see also Stuart*
Stewart, John D., 244, 245
Stewart, L. A., 208
Stewart, Robert, 15, 30, 53, 89, 98
Stewart, Samuel, 35, 46, 47, 93, 119, 120, 125, 127, 129, 144, 151, 196, 208-9, 209, 210, 227
Stewart, T. A., 205, 206, 207, 214, 215, 221
Stewart, T. L., 164
Stewart, Thomas A., 118, 138, 223
Stewart, Thomas, 107, 167, 193

Stiteler, John, 226

Stoller, G., 220
Stoner, Barbary, 251
Stoner, Catharine, 251
Stoner, Daniel, 251
Stoner, David, 35, 251, 252
Stoner, Hannah, 251
Stoner, Jacob, 251
Stoner, Joel, 251

Stoner, Lydia, 251
Stoner, Magdaline, 251
Stoner, Rebecca, 251
Stoner, Sarah, 251
Stoner, Susanna, 251
Stoner, William, 35, 84
Stoon(?), John, 194
Stover, George S., 22
Stow, Dennis, 20
Stowe, Nancy (A.), 20, 154, 213
Stown, John, 7

Street?, John D., 207
Strickland, Joseph, 181, 226
Strong, D., 210
Strong, Dewitt, 77
Strong. E. B., 178
Strong, Harvey, 206, 218
Strong, Stephen, 90

Stuart, J. M., 208, 214, *see also Stewart*
Stuart, James M., 200
Stuart?, Saml., 205

Summers, Lucian, 68
Summers, ____, 68

Sutherland, Isabella, 245
Sutherland, John, 244
Sutherland, Wm., 214

Swaney, F. W., 238

Sweney, T. C., 218
Sweny, Thos. C., 218

Swope, Asbury, 11, 84, 198
Swope, George (J.), 37, 86, 96, 117, 208
Swope, Ira, 88
Swope, Matilda, 11, 84, 198
Swope, Michael, 11, 84, 198
Swope, Wilson, 11, 84,

198

Sykes, William N., 134

T

Taber, Jonathan Jr., 221
Taber, Wm. D., 221

Tailor, ____, 197

Talbot, W. L. F., 244
Talbot, William, 178

Taney, Jesse, 119

Tawan?, John, 240

Taylor, J. W., 224
Taylor, John B., 197
Taylor, John, 201
Taylor, L. H., 5
Taylor, L.M., 190
Taylor, P.?, 234
Taylor, William W., 73
Taylor, William, 67, 236, 248

Teagarden, Abram, 63
Teall, William, 132

Teegarden, ____, 249
Teegarden, A., 225, 228, 232, 233, 247, 250, 251
Teegarden, Samuel, 151
Teeple, Clarissa, 7, 83, 193, 197
Teeple, J. P., 205, 250
Teeple, James W., 181, 226
Teeple, James, 193, 233
Teeple, John P., 57, 167
Teeter, Henry, 67, 71, 101, 192, *see also Teter*
Teeter, Jacob, 75, 242
Teeter, Lucy, 242
Teeter, Ralph, 227

Terrell, Joseph (F.), 64, 243
Terricoupie, 225

Teter, Ralph, 226, *see also Teeter*

Thom, Grace, 230
Thom, John, 230
Thomas, Charles, 116
Thomas, Eleanor, 9, 116, 198
Thomas, Elizabeth, 9, 14, 116, 198
Thomas, George, 5, 9, 14, 116, 145, 185, 186, 188, 189, 190, 198
Thomas, Jane, 116
Thomas, Joel, 9, 13, 116, 198
Thomas, Margaret, 252
Thomas, Mary, 9, 218
Thomas, Nancy, 9, 116, 218
Thomas, Noory, 116
Thomas, Perlina, 9, 13
Thomas, Portia, 116
Thomas, Raymond, 198
Thomas, Regina, 116
Thomas, Reynear, 9, 13
Thomas, Ruth Jane, 9, 13, 116, 198
Thompson, Francis, 132
Thompson, Henry A., 158, 228
Thompson, James, 241, 242
Thompson, John Jr., 247
Thompson, John, 247
Thompson, Lemon, 219
Thompson, Mary Ann, 158
Thompson, Olive Jane, 158
Thompson, Polly, 51, 243
Thompson, William Henry, 158
Thomson, John, 206
Thordon, Ralph, 248

Thoring (?), Franklin, 47
Thornburgh, Absalom, 246
Thornton, Amanda, 20, *see also Thorton*
Thornton, Elizabeth (child), 20
Thornton, Elizabeth, 20, 208
Thornton, Louisa, 20
Thornton, Sarah Jane, 20
Thornton, Wesley C., 20
Thornton, William C., 20
Thorp, Amos, 79
Thorp, Horace L., 218
Thorp, Isaac, 79
Thorton, Austin, 20, *see also Thornton*

Thurber, Amos, 249
Thurber, H., 249

Thwing, T., 200-1
Thwing/Strong, Harvey, 206

Tibbits, Wm., 227

Titus, James, 217

Todd, Hiram, 6
Todhunter, Gury, 208
Todhunter, Ivry?, 217
Todhunter, Lewis, 90, 163, 217, 220

Toine, Francis, 246

Tomlinson, John, 214
Tompkins County, New York, 39

Tone, James, 231
Toney, Aaron, 46, 195
Toney, Allen, 46, 195
Toney, Frances, 195
Toney, Jesse, 46, 195, 196

Toney, Mary Jane, 195
Toney, Sebert, 46, 47, 195
Toney, Stephen, 46, 195, 196
Toney, Susan, 195

Tooly, Peter, 201

Travis, Curtis, 57, 90, 129
Travis, Wm. W., 250, 251

Treadway, B. F., 228
Treadway, Griffin, 28, 31, 38, 40, 86, 87, 124, 138, 200, 218
Treadway, John, 40, 124
Treat, A. R., 241
Treat, Alonzo D., 68, 106
Treat, Mary, 106
Treat, Reuben, 66, 235
Treat(s), Samuel, 66, 68, 71, 106, 129, 138, 184, 218, 232, 235
Treat, Sarah, 68
Treat(s), Theodore, 68, 106

Trinkle, Wm., 221

Trobridge, Wm., 245

Tubbs, Hiram, 15, 223
Tubbs, Lemuel/Samuel, 15

Tucker, Aulden/Alden, 25, 165
Tucker, Charles, 73, 157, 225
Tucker, Silas, 74

Tuley, Elizabeth, 94
Tuley, George Milton, 94
Tuley, James, 50, 94
Tuley, John, 94
Tuley, Josephine, 94
Tuley, Julianna, 94
Tuley, Margaret, 94

Tuley Martha, 94
Tuley, Simon Peter, 94
Tuley, Sim(e)on Robinson, 94
Tul(e)y, William, 94, 202
Tuly, Peter, 202
Tuly, Simon P., 202

Turner, David, 218, 233
Turner, Samuel, 214, 217, 221

Tuttle, ____, 245
Tuttle, B. W., 243
Tuttle, F., 132
Tuttle, Robert E., 228

Tyler, Ezra, 26, 27, 54, 86, 99, 109, 113, 114, 147, 148, 152, 153, 163, 200, 216, 217, 220
Tyler, John, 125

Tyner, William, 231

Tyrrell, T., 210

U

Underwood, Barclay, 236, 242
Underwood, Benjamin, 45, 48, 133, 134
Underwood, Elbridge Wright, 46, 48
Underwood, Israel, 242
Underwood, John, 242
Underwood, Lucy Ann, 46, 48
Underwood, Mary Ann, 46, 47, 134

Union County, 32, 110, 122, 124, 207
Union Mills, 227
Union Township, 234, 240

Utley, Almira, 127
Utley, Catherine, 38, 127, 128
Utley, George, 38, 127
Utley, James, 38, 127
Utley, Julia Ann, 127
Utley, Pelig, 38
Utley, Peter, 127
Utley, Sanford, 37, 98, 127, 128
Utley, Uriah, 38, 98, 127, 129

V

Vail, Henry P., 197
Vail, Henry, 140
Vail, Miss Susan, 250
Vail, Thomas D., 88
Vaile, Charles, 230

Van Dolson, Samuel, 125
Van Matre, John, 201
Van Metre, John, 234
Van Nocker, Betsey, 17
Van Nocker, Jerimiah, 17
Van Orde, Harvey, 242
Van Order, Harvey, 36
Van Osdal, Wm., 197
Van Pelt, S., 241
Van Pelt, Sutton, 25, 30, 32, 49, 53, 78, 88, 98, 112, 161, 164, 165, 204, 215, 219
Van Valkenburgh, J., 247
Van Valkinburgh, James, 47

Vance, W., 197
Vandalsem, Eunice, 12, 199
Vandalsem, Henry, 12, 199
Vandalsem, Nasha, 199
Vandalsem, Samuel, 199, 231
Vandemarker, John, 224

Vandevanter, Isaac, 175, 230
Vandevanter, John, 175
Vandevanter, John F., 175
Vandevanter, John T., 230
Vandevanter, Lydia, 175, 229
Vandevanter, Patience/Paterace, 175, 230
Vandevanter, Peter M., 175, 230
Vandevanter, Sarah, 175, 230
Vandoson, ____, 225
Vantasel, C., 206
VanTassel,Cornelius, 69
Vantry, John, 85

Vermillion County, 178, 231
Vermont, 237

Vicory, Elizabeth, 231, 250
Vic(k)ory, John, 55, 121, 162, 253

Viele, S. D., 210
Viele, Samuel D., 44, 132, 210

Viney, Wm. A., 202

Virginia, 231

W

Wa Was Mo Qua, 9, 187

Waddell, A. M., 219

Wagenner, Jane, 247, *see also Wagner, Wegenner*
Wagenner, Marget, 247
Wagner, B. F., 220
Wagner, Jacob, 9, 117
Wagner, Polly Hunt, 174

Wagner, Solomon, 247

Wair, A. J., 212
Wair, Andrew J., 212

Wakefield, Christiana, 60, 107, 202
Wakefield, Jesse, 60, 106, 202
Wakefield, Widow, 202
Wakeman, George, 225

Walbridge, John, 59, 210
Waldo, J. H., 202
Waldo, Jesse H., 64, 243
Waldriff, Hetty, 209
Waldriff, William, 6, 43, 65, 145, 209
Waldruff, Mahetibel, 233
Waldruff, William, 83, 170, 226, 227, 230, 233
Waldrupp, William, 209
Walker, Benj. F., 223
Walker, Eleanor H., 28, 136, 218
Walker, James, 6, 82, 218
Walker, Jn., 205
Walker, Martha L., 136
Walker, Mathew S., 218
Walker, Matthew L., 28
Walker, W. G., 201
Walker, W. J., 206
Walker, Winston, 209

Ward, Henry, 203
Ward, Seth Edmund, 7, 8
Ward, Seth, 8
Ward, Willis P., 132, 210
Warne, J. B., 245
Warner, Aaron, 227
Warner, Anson B., 72
Warner, J. W., 227
Warner, James, 209
Warnick, John, 221
Warnock, James, 23, 123, 207, 208, 216, 220, 221
Warnock, Samuel, 133
Warren, Asa M., 61, 81

Warren, Bennet, 218
Warren County, Ohio, 118
Warren, Mary, 118
Warriner, O., 247

Wasson, Anselm, 91, 201
Wasson, Archibald, 36, 91, 201
Wasson, Calvin, 91, 221, 232
Wasson, Eliza, 91
Wasson, Jehiel, 36, 41, 91, 126, 201, 205, 206, 213, 214, 222, 230, 232, 240, 241
Wasson, Jesse, 36, 91, 201, 206, 222, 229, 230, 232
Wasson, Lydia, 232
Wasson, Macamy, 91, 201
Wasson, Marah, 232

Watkins, Isaac, 234
Watson, James, 200
Watson, Jesse, 41
Watson, John, 234

Waxham, Zechariah, 240, 241

Way, Isaac, 223
Way, Seth, 218, 238
Wayne County, 11, 155, 198, 211, 215
Wayne County, New York, 235
Wayson, _____, 178
Wayson, Jehiel, 167, 178
Wayson, Jesse, 175

Wead, David, 203

Webster, A. G., 217
Webster, Amos G., 202
Webster, Asaph, 60, 107, 202
Webster, Harlow, 217
Webster, James, 35, 71, 84, 87, 102, 125, 130, 200,

204, 224
Webster, John, 236
Webster, Joseph, 203
Webster, Reuben, 224
Webster, Samuel W., 244
Webster, Samuel, 72, 204, 243
Webster, W. A., 223

Weed, Henry, 123
Weed, Lewis, 227
Weed, Samuel M., 223
Weed, Samuel, 80, 223

Wegenner, Marget, 247
see also Wagner,
Wagenner

Welch, Sarah Ann, 14
Welch/Welsh, William A., (son) 14, 58
Welch/Welsh, William A., 11, 14, 58, 65
Wells & Enos, 98
Wells, A. P., 248
Wells, Abby W., 223
Wells, Alice H., 223
Wells, Charles F., 223
Wells, Daniel S., 249
Wells, Harriet, 223
Wells, Henrietta, 223
Wells, I.R., 138
Wells, J.R., 89
Wells, Jabez R., 15, 29, 44
Wells, James, 18
Wells, Jane A., 80, 223, 224
Wells, John, 88
Wells, Lewis P., 223
Wells, Louisa A., 223
Wells, Margaret C., 223
Wells, Mary J., 223
Wells, Theodore H. Jr., 223
Wells, Theodore H., 80, 223, 224

Werner, J. W., 226-7

Wesaw We, 9, 187, 188
West, Edwin A., 221
West, Jesse, 236
West, John, 221
West, Juliann, 231
West, Lucy, 231
West, Nancy, 211, 231
West, Nimrod/Nymrod, 236, 246
West, William, 12, 231
Westcott, Zeri C., 238
Westervelt, Abraham, 73, 119, 205
Westervelt, C., 119
Westervelt, Catherine, 73, 205
Westervelt, Edmon, 205
Westervelt, Edmund, 119
Westervelt, James, 73, 119, 205, 224
Westervelt, John L., 205
Weston, Isaac, 208, 220, 228
Weston, Massachusetts, 202
Weston, Samuel 225, 229, 236
Weston, William S., 230

Whallon, Alfred, 162

Wheaton, Allida F. J., 246
Wheaton, Clinton, 264
Wheaton, Jackson, 246
Wheaton, Joseph B., 264
Wheaton, Joseph, 243, 244, 246
Wheeler, A. S., 32
Wheeler, Anzie L., 112
Wheeler, H. & Co., 157
Wheeler, Hiram, 32, 78, 91, 164, 198, 204
Wheeler, Leander, 90
Wheeler, P., 225
Wheeler, Preserved, 53, 104, 176, 230

White, Asher 17, 88, 118
White, Henry, 199, 225

White, John, 199, 234
White, Peter, 75
Whitehead, Hampton B., 78, 160, 222, 223
Whitehead, Isaac N., 223
Whitehead, J. N., 250
Whitehead, John, 64, 139, 241, 223, 231
Whitehead, Lazarus, 204, 223, 227
Whitehead, Margaret, 78, 160, 223
Whitehead, Thomas, 223
Whitehead, William H. H., 77, 78, 160, 222, 223
Whitehed, Naton, 245
Whitmore, J., 225
Whitney, Samuel, 202, 220
Whitten, James, 11, 164, 180, 198, 212, 213, 244
Whitten, John, 181
Whittenbrock, Adam, 248

Wickens, Wm., 210
Wickham, Eliza/Elisa Ann, 250
Wickham, John R., 250
Wickham, Marvin S., 250

Wilcox, Hiram B., 170, 226, 227
Wilcox, Vi., 249
Wilcox, Virgil, 203, 217, 248, 249
Wilkerson, John W., 217
Wilkinson, D./A., 207
Wilkinson, Henry, 201
Wilkinson, J., 240
Wilkinson, J. A., 217
Wilkinson, J. N., 201
Wilkinson, J.W., 198
Wilkinson, James A., 113, 114, 217
Wilkinson, John W., 117, 142, 200
Wilkinson, Lewis, 159, 228

Wilkinson, Richard H., 200, 217
Wilkinson, Wesley, 221

Will County, Illinois, 228
Willard, John, 89
Willard/Millard, Almira, 38
Willard/Millard, Eleazer, 38
Willcox, Hiram (B.), 168, 169, 170, 226
Willets, Henry, 247
Willett, Thomas, 237
William, Jane E., 238
Williams, _____, 168
Williams, A., 232
Williams, Alfred H., 239
Williams, Azariah, 42, 89, 90, 112, 127
Williams, Charles H., 239
Williams, David, 62, 102
Williams, Elisha, 201
Williams, Elizabeth, 239
Williams, George F., 239
Williams, Granville L., 239
Williams, Hannah J., 239
Williams, Herbert, 202, 227, 237
Williams, J. C., 204
Williams, James E., 241, 247
Williams, James, 249, 250, 254
Williams, John E., 239
Williams, Micajah T., 239
Williams, S. E., 159, 206, 214, 221, 225
Williams, S., 123
Williams, Samuel B., 118
Williams, Samuel E., 120, 130, 157, 172, 194, 223, 224, 251
Williams, Sarah A., 239
Williams, Saul E., 162
Williams, Sidney, 217
Williams, T.E., 126

Williamson, J. W., 27
Williamson, Robt., 249
Willis, Esqr., 242 *see Wyllis*
Willis, Jackson, 241
Willis, Joseph, 241
Willis, Orrin, 69, 79, 217
Willis, Rebecca, 184, 241
Wills Township, 244, 245
Wills, James, 16
Wills, John, 5, 16, 17, 18, 122, 133, 190, 204, 231, 236
Wills, Polly, 245
Willson, Jeremiah, 236
Willson, John, 245
Willys, see Willis
Wilson, _____, 135
Wilson, James, 233
Wilson, John, 80, 103, 131
Wilson, Mathe, 198
Wilson, Sherman, 197
Wilson, William M., 202
Wilson, William, 57
Wilson, Wm. C., 206
Wilson, Wm. L., 200, 240

Wincese (?), Nathaniel, 48
Winch, Joseph, 33, 173, 219, 227, 254

Winchell, David, 24, 52, 76, 113, 176, 179, 230, 234
Winchell, James G., 176, 230
Winchell, James, 24, 179
Winchell, John, 24, 52, 179
Winchell, Sarah "Sally", 52, 234
Winchell, Stephen, 249
Winchell, William B., 52, 234
Winchester, Miles, 204, 231
Winchil, D., 234
Winchill, Amo., 234
Winchill, B., 234

Winchill, Sarah, 234
Winchill, Steven, 234
Winchill, Widow, 234
Wincill, Wm. B., 234
Windle, Wm., 218
Wing, Josiah W., 131, 196, 209
Winship, C. S., 252
Winship, G. C., 252
Winters, Catharine, 251
Winters, George, 237
Winters, Magdaline, 251

Wisconsin Territory, 199

Witenbeck, Adam, 217, 248
Witten, James, 88
Witter, _____, 247
Witter, John, 120, 123, 226, 246, 247

Wood, Bartlet, 73
Wood, Lovina, 77
Wood, Sally Ann, 73
Wood, Sarah Hale, 130
Wood, Silas, 130
Woodard, Alex, 238
Woodard, Benjamin, 13
Woodard, James, 17
Woodard, Margaret, 17
Wooden, Edmund, 87
Woodord, Israel, 222
Woods, Bartlett, 129
Woods, C. L., 236
Woods, G., 202
Woods, L., 207, 208, 217, 221, 227
Woods, Leonard, 220
Woodsen, E.B., 128
Woodson, E. B., 106, 109, 112, 127, 207, 208, 217, 228
Woodson, Edmund B., 40, 61, 124, 153, 171, 200
Woodson, G. B., 180
Woodson, Joseph, 61
Woodson, William Thomas, 61

Woodward, Israel, 167, 214
Woodworth, Ansel, 214
Wooley, Daniel, 171, 221
Wooley, Sarah, 118
Woolverton, Charles, 213

Worly, Robert, 221
Worrell, Richard, 241
Worthington, Massachusetts, 243

Wright, Alexander H., 22, 132
Wright, Edward, 217, 221
Wright, John F., 227
Wright, Joseph Y., 238
Wright, Joseph, 201
Wright, Newell, 22
Wright, William, 26, 216, 217
Wright, Willis G., 209
Wright, Willis, 214, 233

Wyatt, Isaac, 32, 42, 89, 203
Wyatt, James, 32, 42, 203
Wyatt, Joseph, 31, 32, 42, 89, 95, 96, 100, 109, 112, 121, 152, 203, 204
Wyatt, Thomas, 32, 42, 203, 204

Wyllis & Robinson, 235, *see Willis*
Wyllis, Omer?, 217
Wyllis, Orrin, 79, 80, 102, 223

Y

Young, C./Christian T., 228
Young, Christian F., 171
Young, Eliza, 244
Young, Henry, 59
Young, R. B., 244